Contents

Christian Thought in the Modern World

DEAN CLOSE SCHOOL

LIBRARY

This book must be returned by the latest date stamped below.

A LION PAPERBACK

Oxford · Batavia · Sydney

TO MY AUNT

Copyright © 1984 Tony Lane

Published by
Lion Publishing plc
Sandy Lane West, Oxford, England
ISBN 0 7459 2082 9
Lion Publishing Corporation
1705 Hubbard Avenue, Batavia, Illinois 60510, USA
ISBN 0 7459 2082 9
Albatross Books Pty Ltd
PO Box 320, Sutherland, NSW 2232, Australia
ISBN 0 7324 0575 0

First published in 1984 as *The Lion Concise Book of Christian Thought*
This edition 1992

A catalogue record of this book is available
from the British Library

Library of Congress CIP data applied for

Printed and bound in Great Britain

Introduction

Why on earth read about a hundred or so figures from the past? Why not confine our reading to the present? Why read people with whom we might not agree?

We need to read about the past in order to *understand the present*. People without a grasp of history are like a man without a memory. Many of the current beliefs in our society are properly grasped only when we see how they have emerged. A knowledge of history will help us to understand better both ourselves and those with whom we might disagree.

We also need to read about the past in order to *escape the present*. Every generation has its blind spots and its hobby horses and ours is certainly no exception. By studying the thought of past generations we can be challenged where our views are defective and helped to see our own pet ideas in a proper perspective. We do not need an excessive degree of humility to recognize that our own grasp of truth might be less than perfect and that it is possible to learn from those with a different perspective.

How should we view the past? There are two ways to approach history. Some people treat history as a mirror, in which they admire their own faces. By studying only selected periods and people they recreate the past in their own image in order to glorify themselves. But we see our own ugly mugs in the past only by turning history into a distorting mirror. The proper approach is to treat history like a window. A window is there to look outside, to see something different. We can learn from history, because like foreign travel it shows us that ours is not the only way to do things. If we are humble we will not claim, as Job's friends did, that 'we are the people and wisdom will die with us.'

Karl Barth observed that the correct attitude to our theological forebears is summarized in the fifth commandment: honour your father and mother. This command remains binding on children even when they have left home. But for an adult to honour his parents is not always to obey them. There are times when we should say, 'we must obey God rather than men'. We should listen with respect to the voice of the past, but we are not bound by it. The teaching of the past must be tested: not by our prejudices; not by its applicability to our situation today (for which it was not written); but by the word of God, the Scriptures.

The primary purpose of this book is to introduce leading thinkers from the past (and present) and to whet the appetite by giving extracts from their writings. With the modern period especially, I have also introduced an element of evaluation as a guide to the reader—though the primary aim remains to allow the thinkers to speak for themselves and readers to judge for themselves.

How on earth select a particular number of figures for study? Whom should one include? Even harder, whom should one exclude? Anyone who has ever tried such an exercise will be forgiving and will realize that no selection is perfect. Mine is a personal selection, attempting to cover a wide and representative range of Christian thought over the ages, with the aim of selecting those who are most influential and worthwhile. To the reader whose favourite author has been excluded, I apologize.

Who on earth could know all about all these different figures? Certainly not the present author! I have sought to be as fair and as accurate as possible, but 'we all make many mistakes' (James 3:2). My sincere thanks are due to David Wright and Richard Bauckham whose reading of the text has helped to reduce the number of errors from what it might have been. I am also grateful to them both for their friendship, help and encouragement over many years.

When referring to works written in another language I have, except in rare cases, given the title in English, but the other details (such as the date and the number of volumes) refer to the original and *not* to the English translation.

Tony Lane

Note: Names marked by an asterisk in the text (e.g. *Cyprian) indicate that there is a separate article on that person.

PART 1

The Church of the Fathers

TO AD 500

Between the years AD 100 and AD 500 the Christian church changed almost beyond recognition. In AD 100 the church was a small minority, spasmodically persecuted. While the Gospels and epistles were in circulation, they had not yet been gathered together to form a 'New Testament'. While there were brief affirmations of faith like 'Jesus is Lord', there was no formal creed to be recited. The organization of the church was still fluid and varied from region to region, as in New Testament times. Finally, there were no set forms of worship, although particular prayers, like the Lord's Prayer, might be used.

By the year 500 a very different picture had emerged. The great majority of people within the Roman Empire called themselves Christians and Christianity had become the official religion of the state. There were also substantial churches outside the bounds of the empire, as in Ethiopia or in India. The Scriptures consisted of an Old and a New Testament—the latter being identical to ours today, with a few lingering local variations. There were two major creeds which were widely used. There was also a clear understanding of 'orthodoxy' as opposed to heresy, especially regarding the doctrines of the Trinity and the person of Christ. The ministry of the church everywhere took the threefold form of bishops, presbyters and deacons, though lesser regional differences remained. The worship of the church was entirely liturgical, with fixed set forms of prayer.

Most of these changes came gradually over the four hundred years. On the whole they were for the good and reflected healthy growth on the part of the church. But not all of the changes were necessarily for the better. Many today would consider the alliance with the state and the transformation of Christianity into an official religion to be at best a mixed blessing, if not an actual curse. Many would be less than enthusiastic about the pattern of ministry that emerged and about the suppression of free forms of worship.

There were two major turning points in the life of the early church. The first came in AD 70. Until then the disciples of Jesus were predominantly Jewish and would generally have been seen as a 'deviant' group within Judaism. The 'Nazarenes' could be seen as a Jewish sect, alongside the Pharisees, the Sadducees and the Essenes (Acts 24:5). The mother church was at Jerusalem. The apostle Paul had to struggle for the recognition of his mission to the Gentiles. He fought hard to establish the point that Gentile converts did not need to become Jews by being circumcised. But in AD 70 Jerusalem was sacked by the Romans, as Jesus has prophesied, and there was no more Jerusalem church. From this time on it was the Gentile church which was dominant. The leading church soon became the one at Rome, the capital of the Gentile world. While for the New Testament church the burning issue was 'must Gentiles be circumcised (become Jews)?', for the second-century church the question was 'may Jewish believers continue to keep the Jewish laws (remain Jews)?' Christianity had been transformed from a Jewish sect into a potentially universal faith.

The second major turning point came with the conversion of the Emperor Constantine to Christianity, in 312. Until this time, the church was a dissenting minority, persecuted from time to time. This changed rapidly. Constantine ended persecution and offered the church support and official favour. Of the emperors who followed him, only one was a pagan. Christianity became the official state religion.

The link between the church and the state was greeted enthusiastically by some at the time (e.g. *Eusebius of Caesarea) and is still defended by many today. But some had doubts from the beginning, and it is increasingly fashionable today to regard the link as a horrible mistake. A number of issues are involved. First, the adoption of Christianity as the state religion led to a massive influx of superficial converts from paganism. This resulted in declining moral standards and the adoption of some pagan and idolatrous practices. Second, the persecuted church of the martyrs became before long the persecuting state church. Legal coercion was used at first against Christian groups deviating from the mainstream 'Catholic Church' and later against pagan worship. The suffering servant church was in danger of becoming the oppressing church. Third, as Europe became Christian, Christianity was in danger of becoming the tribal religion of the Europeans. The link with the state brought problems with it. But it should be remembered that the mainstream of Christian history has been in Christian Europe. It is there that the church has repeatedly undergone renewal, and from there that the gospel has spread round the world.

The early church, like the Roman Empire, was divided into the Greek-speaking East and the Latin-speaking West. Behind the linguistic difference lay the cultural differences between the Greek and Roman worlds. The earliest Gentile Christianity was Greek and the New Testament was, of course, written in Greek. Even in the West the earliest churches were Greek-speaking—the church at Rome remained predominantly Greek-speaking into the third century. The first traces of Latin Christianity are found in North Africa, and the African *Tertullian (at the end of the second century) was the first important Latin Christian writer. In the early centuries the Greek-speaking and Latin-speaking churches coexisted happily, although there were tensions from time to time. Later on, after the collapse of the Roman Empire in the West in the fifth century, the two churches drifted apart, later to become the Eastern Orthodox and the Roman Catholic churches, respectively.

Platonism and Greek Philosophy

The early Christian Fathers were Gentile Greeks and Romans. As they came to grips with their Christian faith and presented it to their contemporaries they were forced to relate it to the thought patterns of their society: Greek philosophy.

There were three major schools of philosophy which influenced the early Christian writers: Platonism, founded by Plato (died 347 BC) who had been a pupil of Socrates (died 399 BC); Aristotelianism, founded by Plato's pupil Aristotle (died 322 BC); Stoicism, founded by Zeno (died 263 BC). These remained distinct schools of thought, but by the early Christian era they had greatly influenced one another. A typical second-century Platonist would hold to an amalgam of Platonism, Aristotelianism and Stoicism, with the Platonist element being dominant.

In the third century a revised form of Platonism, known as Neo-Platonism, was set forth by Ammonius Saccas and Plotinus. Neo-Platonism stressed the ultimate transcendence of God. It became for a time a pagan alternative to the rapidly growing Christian faith. It was also deeply influential on many Christian thinkers from the fourth century on.

Fundamental to both Plato and Aristotle is the distinction between *being* and *becoming*. In this world, everything is subject to change and decay. Nothing is unchanging—it is always *becoming* something else rather than simply *being* what it is. As an earlier philosopher had noted, you cannot jump into the same river twice—it has changed in the meantime. In contrast to this world of change which is always *becoming* something else, there is, maintained Plato, a realm of *being* which is eternal and unchanging. The contrast between the two realms is seen clearly in Plato's doctrine of Ideas. For Plato there is an eternal unchanging Idea or Form of, for example, 'man'. Individual human beings are merely pale reflections of this eternal Idea. It is the latter that is real. Thus the relation between the Idea 'man' and us men can be compared to that between a gold seal on a ring and the impressions that it makes on a number of different lumps of wax. It is the seal that is the *real* image, not the wax impressions. Reality is the realm of eternal unchanging being—this changing world of becoming is but a pale reflection of reality.

By the Christian era much of Greek philosophy had built on Plato and Aristotle in such a way as to teach clearly that there is one supreme transcendent God. This philosophical monotheism was an obvious point of contact for the Christian apologist. But there was a problem. The Greek God belongs to the realm of being. He is thus unchanging or immutable. This means that he cannot have any direct contact with this world of becoming and change. It also means that he is impassible: not subject to any emotions or feelings. The early Fathers had to grapple with the inherent contradictions between the Greek and the biblical concepts of God.

Because the Greek God is immutable and belongs to the realm of being he can have no direct contact with this world. He therefore needs a mediator between himself and the world. One common title used by Greek thought for this mediating power or principle was Logos, which means both Reason and Word. The concept of one true God with the Word as his mediator has obvious parallels with John 1, for instance, and was another point of contact for the Christian apologist. But there were problems. The Word was needed not because of sin, but simply because God cannot deal directly with a changing world. In addition, the Greek Word was clearly separate from God and inferior to him. These ideas led naturally to a denial of the true deity of the Word, a problem faced by fourth-century Christian theology.

Greek thought was predominantly negative about this world. It is temporal and changing. It was made by an inferior deity, from pre-existent matter. It was not the creation of the supreme God. The philosophical approach to this world was usually ascetic—the philosopher sought to rise above the things of the world. This had obvious affinities with New Testament thought, but the motivation was fundamentally different. The Greek despised the material world because it was material and changing. A concept like the resurrection of the body was radically opposed to Greek thought, as Paul discovered at Athens (Acts 17:32).

The Greek philosophers saw man as essentially twofold: body and soul. The body belongs to this world of becoming and change. The soul is a 'divine spark' from the world of being, and it is rational. Just as the divine Word or Logos indwells and controls the universe, so the body is indwelt and controlled by a miniature logos (or word or reason), the soul. The *real* person is the soul. The body is like a house or a set of clothes in which the person lives. In fact, the body is often seen as the tomb or the prison of the soul. The ultimate destiny of the soul, which is immortal, is to be released from the body. Man's destiny is deification, becoming like God. This includes the goal of impassibility—total absence of all feeling and emotion.

Greek thought drew close to biblical Christianity at many points, while remaining different. The Greeks had arrived at belief in monotheism, but their picture of an immutable, impassible God was contrary to the God of the Bible who suffers and becomes man. Greek thought spoke about a mediating Word, but this concept fell short of the biblical picture of Christ. The Greeks knew that all was not well with the world but saw the problem as change rather than disobedience towards a personal God. Greek thought recognized man's need for 'salvation' but saw this in different terms from the Christian gospel.

The task of the early Christian Fathers was to express the Christian faith in relation to their Greek heritage. This meant expressing it in Greek terms, yet without distorting it. To a large extent, they succeeded in doing this. In due course Greek thought *became* Christian thought. During this process of transformation most of the elements in Greek thought contrary to biblical Christianity were rooted out. But the process was not all one-way. It was not only Greek thought that was transformed. Christianity also came to be seen in a Greek way. Elements of the Greek approach which are opposed to biblical Christianity remained and affected the outcome. God was still seen as impassible, and asceticism was still based on the same ideal of impassibility. But to say that the outcome was not perfect is only to say that the early Fathers were human. It is not to belittle their considerable achievement or to claim that we could have done better.

Apostolic Fathers
AFTER THE APOSTLES

The Apostolic Fathers are the earliest Christian writers outside of the New Testament, belonging to what is called the 'subapostolic age'. Their writings form a bridge between the New Testament and the Apologists who wrote later in the second century, the most noteworthy being *Justin Martyr. They help us to understand the transition from the apostolic church of the first century to the Catholic Church of the end of the second century, as described by *Irenaeus.

I Clement is a letter written from the church at Rome in about AD 96 to the church at Corinth. It is traditionally ascribed to Clement, a leading figure in the Roman Church at that time, though his name does not appear in the text. The Corinthian Church had sacked all its leaders and Clement wrote in response to the ensuing division. There is a great emphasis on the importance of due order in the church, reflecting traditional Roman values as well as biblical influence. Clement also stresses the need for orderly succession in the Christian ministry. God sent Christ, who sent the apostles. They in turn appointed bishops and deacons. These then appointed their successors and those who have duly succeeded them are not to be removed without cause. The Corinthians should therefore restore their deposed leaders to office. While Clement taught the importance of ministerial succession, it is important to note that he was unaware of the later threefold pattern of ministry: bishop, presbyters and deacons. In *I Clement*, as in the New Testament, the words 'bishop' and 'presbyter' refer to the same person.

Ignatius was bishop of Antioch at the beginning of the second century and was taken to Rome to be martyred. On the way he wrote seven letters, to five churches in Asia Minor, to the Roman Church and to Polycarp, bishop of Smyrna. Ignatius is the first writer clearly to present the threefold pattern of ministry: one bishop in a church with his presbyters and deacons. He argues vigorously in defence of this pattern, an indication that it was not yet fully established. His letter to Rome is conspicuously silent about a single (monarchical) bishop there, showing that the threefold pattern had not yet reached the West. Ignatius' main concern is with the unity of the church. The bishop is seen as the focus of unity against both schism and heresy. Finally, his own impending martyrdom preyed heavily on his mind and he welcomed it as the seal upon his discipleship.

Shun divisions, as the beginning of evil. Follow your bishop, as Jesus Christ followed the Father; and the presbyters as the apostles; and to the deacons pay respect, as to God's commandment. Let no one do anything pertaining to the church apart from the bishop. A valid eucharist is one that is under the bishop or someone to whom he has committed it. Wherever the bishop appears, let the people be, even as where Jesus may be, there is the universal [catholic] church.
SMYRNEANS 8

I want all men to know that I die for God of my own freewill ... Let me be given to the wild beasts, for through them I can attain to God. I am God's wheat and I am ground by the teeth of *wild beasts that I may be found pure bread. Entice the wild beasts, that they may become my sepulchre and may leave no part of my body behind, so that I may not, when I am fallen asleep, be burdensome to anyone. Then shall I truly be a disciple of Jesus Christ, when the world shall not so much as see my body.*
ROMANS 4

Polycarp was bishop of Smyrna for many years. As a young man he sat at the feet of the apostle John and he also met Irenaeus, the most important Christian figure of the late second century. He received a letter from Ignatius, while still a young bishop, and later himself wrote a letter to the church at Philippi. Polycarp was martyred, probably in 155 (possibly 166 or 177), as an old man. A stirring account of his martyrdom survives in *The Letter of the Smyrneans on the Martyrdom of Polycarp.* The Roman governor tried to persuade Polycarp to revile Christ in order to gain his freedom, but he replied, '86 years I have been his servant and he has done me no wrong. How can I then blaspheme my king who saved me?'

The *Didache* or *Teaching of the Lord to the Gentiles through the Twelve Apostles* is the oldest surviving manual of church discipline. It was discovered in the 1870s but its origin is uncertain. It probably originates from Syria, late in the first century. It reflects the transition from a mobile ministry of apostles and prophets to a settled ministry of bishops [presbyters] and deacons. It contains instructions for the practice of baptism and the eucharist.

You should baptize in this way. Having recited all these things, baptize in the name of the Father and of the Son and of the Holy Spirit in running water. But if you have no running water, use other water and if you cannot use cold water, use warm. If you have neither, then pour water on the head three times in the name of the Father and of the Son and of the Holy Spirit.
DIDACHE 7

Justin Martyr
DEFENDER OF THE FAITH

Justin was born of Greek parents in Palestine, early in the second century. He looked for the truth in *Greek philosophy. First he attached himself to a Stoic philosopher. But after some time he was disappointed that he had not progressed in the knowledge of God, and that the philosopher did not seem even to consider this necessary. Then he followed an Aristotelian who was 'as *he* fancied, shrewd'. After a few days he pressed Justin for his fee, so Justin left him 'believing him to be no philosopher at all'. He next tried a follower of Pythagoras, but he expected Justin to study music, astronomy and geometry before coming to him for philosophy. Justin was impatient, and instead went to a well-known Platonist. He 'made the greatest improvements daily'. But he proudly overestimated his progress, expecting 'forthwith to look upon God'. At this point he met an old man by the sea, who pointed him to the Old Testament Scriptures and to Christ. (Justin also refers to the impression that had been made upon him, by the fearless way in which Christians faced martyrdom.) Justin then became a Christian, seeing 'this philosophy alone to be safe and profitable'. He concludes his account of his conversion with the statement that 'thus and for this reason I am a philosopher'. From then on Justin wore the philosopher's cloak. He was not just a Christian seeking to relate Christianity to Greek philosophy. He was a Greek who had come to see Christianity as the fulfilment of all that was best in philosophy, especially in Platonism.

Only three works of Justin survive:

● Dialogue with Trypho, the record of a long and courteous debate which he had with a Jew called Trypho. This took place at Ephesus, the probable site of Justin's conversion.

● I Apology, a defence of the Christian faith, addressed to the emperor.

● II Apology, a shorter supplement to the above, addressed to the Roman senate.

Justin spent his last years at Rome, where he taught. In the 160s he was arrested, with others, and put on trial for being a Christian. He refused to renounce his faith by offering sacrifice to the gods and went to his death confident of his salvation in Christ.

Justin's *I & II Apology* is on a considerably higher plane than the writings of the *Apostolic Fathers. It is a masterly presentation of the Christian faith. Justin was resolutely opposed to paganism and had no time for syncretism. He gave his life rather than offer sacrifice to the gods. He was also very critical of Greek philosophy in places. But, at the same time, he portrayed Christ not as a complete outsider but as the fulfilment of the best in Greek thought. He did this by exploiting the Greek concept of the Logos or Word in which all men participate. He also held that Plato and other philosophers had borrowed some of their ideas from the Old Testament.

We have been taught that Christ is the first-born of God, and we have declared above that he is the Word [or reason] of whom all mankind partakes. Those who lived reasonably [with the Word] are Christians, even though they have been called atheists. For example: among the Greeks, Socrates, Heraclitus and men like them; among the barbarians [non-Greeks], Abraham . . . and many others whose actions and names we now decline to recount, because we know it would be tedious.
I APOLOGY 46

I both boast and strive with all my strength to be found a Christian. Not because the teachings of Plato are different from those of Christ, but because they are not totally identical. The same applies to the Stoics, poets and historians. For each man spoke well, in proportion to the share that he had of the seminal Word, seeing what was related to it . . . Whatever things were rightly said by any man, belong to us Christians. For next to God we worship and love the Word, who is from the unbegotten and ineffable God, since he also became man for our sakes, that by sharing in our sufferings he might also bring us healing. For all those writers were able to see reality darkly, through the seed of the implanted Word within them.

II APOLOGY 13

In this way Justin anchored his Christian faith in his Greek heritage. When he became a Christian he did not renounce philosophy, he became a better philosopher, a true philosopher. He said that the relationship between the philosophers and Christ is that between the incomplete and the complete, between the imperfect and the perfect. So while Justin was positive towards his Greek past, he was not bound by it. The Word gave understanding to the philosophers, it is true, but now the Word himself has appeared in Christ. The imperfect must be tested and corrected and completed by the perfect. Justin could be highly critical of Greek thought. 'Reason directs those who are truly pious and philosophical to honour and love only the truth, declining to follow traditional opinions if these be worthless'. Justin repeatedly aligned himself with Socrates, who like the early Christians was called an atheist because he rejected the pagan gods and suffered for his belief. But he said that Christ is vastly superior to Socrates. 'For no one trusted in Socrates, so as to die for this doctrine. But in Christ... not only have philosophers and scholars believed, but also artisans and entirely uneducated people have despised glory, fear and death'. In due course Justin himself demonstrated the Christian's willingness to die for his faith.

Justin's approach of seeing continuity between his Greek past and his Christian faith was continued by *Clement and *Origen at Alexandria. *Tertullian at Carthage was to oppose it vehemently.

Irenaeus
AGAINST THE HERETICS

Irenaeus was a Greek, born in Asia Minor into a Christian family. As a boy he listened to Polycarp, bishop of Smyrna (one of the *Apostolic Fathers), who had known the apostle John. As a young man he moved to Lyons in Gaul (France) where he first became a presbyter. Then, in 177, he succeeded to the martyred bishop. He is traditionally thought to have died at the beginning of the third century.

Irenaeus was influenced by *Justin. He is a bridge between early Greek theology and Western Latin theology, which began with his younger contemporary, *Tertullian. While Justin was primarily an apologist, Irenaeus' main contribution lay in the refutation of heresy and the exposition of apostolic Christianity. His major work was his *Refutation and Overthrow of Knowledge Falsely So-called,* generally known by the shorter title of *Against Heresies.* This was written primarily in opposition to Gnosticism.

Gnosticism is a modern term which covers a variety of second-century sects with certain common elements. They believed in a supreme God who is totally remote from this world. He had no part in its creation—that was the bungling work of a lesser deity, often identified with the God of the Old Testament. Between this evil world and the supreme God there is a hierarchy of divine beings. While our bodies, being physical, are part of this world, our souls are a divine spark, trapped in the body. Salvation is the escape of the soul from the body to the heavenly realms above. In order to reach the supreme God the soul needs to pass through the realms above this world, which are controlled by the stars and planets, potentially hostile divine beings. Salvation is by knowledge (Greek *gnosis).* This could be understood either in a crudely magical way as the knowledge of the passwords needed to pass by the divine beings on the way to the supreme God, or else in a more philosophical way as existential self-knowledge. Gnosticism was a radically different religion from orthodox Christianity. The different Gnostic groups had their own scriptures. They also appealed to secret traditions, which they claimed to have received from one or another *apostle*.

Irenaeus employed a number of arguments against Gnosticism, of which three can be mentioned:

● He described the different Gnostic systems in detail. He sought to expose the ludicrous nature of many of their beliefs. As he himself put it, 'merely to describe such doctrines is to refute them'.

● He challenged the Gnostic claims to secret apostolic traditions. He argues that if the apostles had had special teaching to pass on, they would have entrusted it to the churches which they had founded. He points to the different churches founded by the apostles and shows how there has been a continuous succession of open public teaching in these churches since that time. In support of this, he lists the leaders of these churches, beginning with those appointed by the apostles themselves. Furthermore, these churches, scattered throughout the empire, all teach the same doctrine.

All who wish to see the truth can clearly contemplate, in every church, the tradition of the apostles manifested throughout the whole world. We can list those who were by the apostles appointed bishops in the churches and their successors down to our own time. They neither taught nor knew anything like what these heretics rave about. Suppose the apostles had known hidden mysteries which they were in the habit of imparting to 'the perfect' privately and in secret. Surely they would have handed them down especially to those to whom they were also entrusting the churches themselves. For they wanted their successors to be perfect and blameless in everything.

AGAINST HERESIES 3:3:1

In assessing Irenaeus' case, it is important not to confuse it with modern ideas of 'apostolic succession'. Irenaeus was writing close to the time of the apostles: he himself knew Polycarp who had known the apostle John. The points in dispute between orthodox Christianity and Gnosticism were not minor points of doctrine—these were two radically different religious systems. The question which Irenaeus poses is this: Is one more likely to find apostolic Christianity in the apostolic churches whose teaching has been open and continuous since their foundation and who agree with one another *or* among the Gnostics, whose claims to apostolic tradition are unverifiable and mutually contradictory and who disagree with one another?

Irenaeus' argument is very powerful. This writer discovered that for himself once when debating with two self-confessed 'Gnostics' who had given him a lift. He first tried to answer them from the New Testament but this did not work. They, like their second-century forebears, did not accept what they called '*your* Scriptures'. As Irenaeus himself put it, 'when they are refuted from the Scriptures, they turn round and accuse these same Scriptures, as if they were not correct or authoritative'. Orthodox Christianity and Gnosticism are two religions, with two different sets of Scriptures. The question is: which religion and which set of Scriptures goes back to Christ and the apostles? It is this question which is answered by Irenaeus' argument— and it is hard to see how it could be answered otherwise.

● Irenaeus was one of the first to talk of *New* Testament Scripture alongside the *Old* Testament. Initially 'Scripture' for Christians meant the Old Testament. The apostolic writings were accorded authority, but it was only gradually that they were all gathered together into a *New* Testament. By the time of Irenaeus the New Testament was close to ours: four Gospels, Acts, Paul's letters and other writings. Disagreements about the last category (Hebrews to Revelation in our Bibles) continued for some time, though the writings accepted in any one place at any one time would be not too far removed from our New Testament.

Irenaeus appealed to apostolic Scripture

(New Testament) and to the apostolic teaching handed down (tradition) in the apostolic churches. The latter was not intended to *add* to the message of the New Testament. It was especially because the Gnostics did not accept the New Testament that Irenaeus had to appeal to tradition.Tradition supplied a basic summary of apostolic Christianity (as found later in the *Apostles' Creed, for example), in opposition to the radically different Gnostic beliefs. Irenaeus' appeal to tradition was correct in that it serves to prove his case against Gnosticism. It does not mean that he was infallible in all the details of his understanding of the Christian faith.

The church, though scattered throughout the whole world to the ends of the earth, has received from the apostles and their disciples this faith: in one God, the Father almighty, maker of heaven and earth and the sea and all things in them; and in one Christ Jesus, the Son of God, who was made flesh for our salvation; and in the Holy Spirit, who through the prophets proclaimed God's saving dealings with man and the coming, virgin birth, passion, resurrection from the dead and bodily ascension into heaven of our beloved Lord Jesus Christ and his second coming from heaven in the glory of the Father to sum up all things and to raise up all human flesh so that... he should execute just judgement upon all men.
AGAINST HERESIES 1:10:1

Irenaeus remains of considerable importance as a source of information about the various Gnostic systems. His defence against Gnosticism was largely successful. It was thanks to him and to those who followed in his footsteps that orthodox Christianity triumphed over Gnosticism.

Tertullian
FATHER OF LATIN THEOLOGY

Quintus Septimius Florens Tertullianus was born around the year 160 at Carthage (modern Tunis) into a pagan Roman family. He was educated in rhetoric and law. It is possible that he lived for a time at Rome and practised there as a lawyer. Sometime before the year 197, he became a Christian. For the remainder of his life he wrote extensively as an advocate for the Christian faith. At first he supported the mainstream Catholic Church but sometime before 207 he became disillusioned with the church authorities and began to speak in favour of Montanism.

Montanism, or the 'New Prophecy' as its supporters called it, began in the 170s when Montanus and two women began to prophesy in Phrygia (in modern Turkey). They taught the imminent end of the world and the need for greater austerity in the light of this: no more marriage, longer fasting, and no flight from martyrdom (contrary to Matthew 10:23). At first the leaders of the Catholic Church were not sure how to handle this new movement. *Irenaeus urged the Roman church not to condemn it without due consideration. But eventually there was a parting of the ways and the 'Phrygian heresy', as it came to be called, was rejected.

There is no evidence, until a much later tradition, that Tertullian ever left the Catholic Church and founded or joined any other group. But he did become a critic of the Catholic Church and a defender of Montanism. He died an old man sometime after 220.

Tertullian was the first important Christian to write in Latin. He is the father of Latin, Western theology. Together with *Origen, he is one of the two greatest Christian writers of the second and third centuries. Indeed, he was one of the greatest Latin writers ever and it is said that pagans used to read his works simply to enjoy the style. As a fifth-century writer put it, 'almost every word he uttered was an epigram and every sentence was a victory'. Or as a modern author said, Tertullian 'possessed an ability rare among theologians: he is incapable of being dull'!

Tertullian wrote always as an advocate—defending his own position and attacking all rivals. This he did with the full range of rhetorical skills at his disposal. He has been described as 'an apologist who never apologized'! His aim was the total annihilation of his opponents. They had to be shown to be totally wrong—and morally suspect to boot. Tertullian was not being vindictive or dishonest. He was completely convinced about the rightness of his cause and sincerely sought to argue it as best he could.

He wrote more than thirty works, which fail into three main groups:

● *Apologetic works.* The most famous of these is simply called *Apology.* Tertullian continued the work of the second-century apologists such as *Justin, but with far greater brilliance. He argued with all his legal skills against the injustice of condemning believers to death simply for being Christians.

We are but of yesterday and we have filled all your places—cities, islands, forts, towns, market places, the very camp, tribes, companies, palace, senate, forum. We have left nowhere to you except the temples of your gods.
APOLOGY 37

The name of faction is deserved [not by Christians but] by those who conspire to slander good and virtuous men, who cry out against innocent blood. They justify their enmity by the groundless plea that Christians are the cause of every public disaster, of every affliction visited upon the people. If the Tiber rises to the city walls or the Nile does not rise to the fields, if the heavens stay still or the earth moves, if there is famine or plague, the cry is at once: 'The Christians to the lion'. What! So many of them to one lion?
APOLOGY 40

Your cruelty [against us] does not profit you, however exquisite. Instead, it tempts people to our sect. As often as
you mow us down, the more we grow in number. The blood of the Christians is the seed [of the church]... The very obstinacy you criticize teaches for us. For who on seeing it is not excited to enquire what lies behind it? Who, having enquired, does not embrace our faith?
APOLOGY 50

● *Dogmatic/anti-heretical works.*
Tertullian was, with *Irenaeus, the major opponent of Gnosticism. He wrote a number of treatises against it, the best-known being his *Prescription of Heretics.* He used the same arguments as Irenaeus but, characteristically, took them further. This is seen, for example, in his denial that the heretic has any right even to use the church's Scriptures. But this argument did not prevent him from himself becoming sharply critical of the Catholic Church in his later years. Tertullian's longest work was his five books *Against Marcion.* Marcion was the greatest of the second-century heretics. He had his own distinctive blend of Gnosticism and Pauline Christianity.

Tertullian was strongly critical of *Greek philosophy, viewing it as the parent of heresy. He emphasized the paradoxical nature of faith and the contrast between Christianity and philosophy. Here the accent is very different from Justin and the earlier apologists. But Tertullian's rhetoric should not be misunderstood. He could appeal to elements in Greek philosophy congenial to Christianity, as did the other apologists. His own debt to philosophy, and to Stoicism in particular, was greater than he ever realized. His talk of the 'absurdity' of belief is not to be taken too literally. Tertullian devoted his life to showing the coherence of his beliefs and the inconsistency of his opponents.

As they are heretics they cannot be true Christians ... Thus, not being Christians, they have no right to the Christian Scriptures. We can fairly ask them: 'Who are you? When and whence did you come? As you are none of mine, what are you doing with my property? Indeed, Marcion, what right have you to hew my wood? By whose permission,

Valentinus, are you diverting the streams of my fountain? By what power, Apelles, are you removing my landmarks? This is my property ... I am the heir of the apostles.

PRESCRIPTION OF HERETICS 37

He [Paul] had been at Athens and had in his interviews with its philosophers become acquainted with that human wisdom which pretends to know the truth. In fact it only corrupts it and is itself divided into its own multiple heresies by the variety of its mutually hostile sects. What indeed has Athens to do with Jerusalem? What concord is there between the Academy and the Church? What have heretics to do with Christians? Our instruction comes from the porch of Solomon, who himself taught that the Lord should be sought in simplicity of heart. Away with all attempts to produce a Stoic, Platonic and dialectic Christianity. We want no curious disputation after possessing Christ Jesus, no speculation after enjoying the gospel. With our faith we desire no further belief. For this is our prime belief: that there is nothing more that we should believe besides.

PRESCRIPTION OF HERETICS 7

The Son of God was crucified. I am not ashamed, because it is shameful. The Son of God died. It is credible because it is absurd. He was buried and rose again. It is certain because it is impossible.

THE FLESH OF CHRIST 5

Tertullian also wrote against Monarchianism. The Monarchians stressed the 'monarchy' or sole rule of God—they were strict monotheists. They circumvented the doctrine of the Trinity by the ingenious idea that the Father *is* the Son *is* the Holy Spirit—much as I function as a father, as a husband and as an author. Father, Son and Holy Spirit are three different names for the same being performing three different roles—not names for three distinct beings.

Tertullian answered them in a major work, *Against Praxeas*. Praxeas was an otherwise unknown Monarchian who also opposed Montanism. As Tertullian put it, 'Praxeas managed two pieces of the devil's business at Rome: he drove out prophecy and brought in heresy. He put to flight the Paraclete [by rejecting the prophesies of Montanism] and crucified the Father [by saying that the Son was the Father].' Tertullian, in answering Praxeas, stated that God is one substance in three persons. He coined the terms to be used in the later definitions of the doctrines of the Trinity and the Incarnation. His work was a major step forward in the understanding of these doctrines, though it is not flawless by the standards of a later orthodoxy.

● *Practical Works.* Tertullian wrote many works on practical ethical matters, especially to do with church discipline. These works fall into two groups: the earlier Catholic works and the later Montanist works. But there is an essential continuity between the two stages. Throughout, Tertullian remains a 'rigorist', a moral hardliner. What appealed to him about Montanism was not prophetic gifts nor the heightened expectation of the end but the stricter moral code. In his earlier work, *Repentance,* he had left room for a 'second repentance' for serious sins committed after baptism. But in his Montanist work, *Modesty,* he took a stricter line, in opposition to a recent pronouncement by the bishop of Carthage. For Tertullian discipline took precedence over forgiveness. Indeed, one recent interpreter has charged that, 'judged theologically, he is almost a Jew'.

Christian modesty is being shaken to its foundations ... I hear that there has even been an edict set forth, and a peremptory one too. The 'high priest', the 'bishop of bishops' [probably the bishop of Carthage] issues an edict: 'I remit to all who have discharged the requirements of repentance, the sins both of adultery and of fornication'. O edict, on which cannot be inscribed 'Good deed'! And where will this liberality be posted up? On the very spot,

I suppose, on the very gates of lust, under the very titles of lust. That is the place to publish such a repentance— where the sin itself happens. That is the place to announce such a pardon— where people will enter in the hope of it.
MODESTY I

Clement of Alexandria
INTELLIGENT ORTHODOXY

Titus Flavius Clemens was born in a pagan Greek family in the middle of the second century. After his conversion he travelled widely and sat at the feet of a number of Christian teachers. He was best pleased with the sixth and last: Pantaenus, who ran a Christian philosophical school at Alexandria. Clement stayed with him and eventually (about 190) succeeded him. He left Alexandria at the outbreak of persecution in 202/203 and never returned. He died in Asia Minor before 216.

Second-century Egypt was a hotbed of Gnosticism. Many of the Gnostic leaders originated from or taught in Egypt. By contrast, Pantaenus is the first representative of orthodox Christianity in Egypt of whom we know today. In the face of the overwhelming Gnostic threat, the orthodox in Egypt seem to have opted for obscurantist obscurity—simply believing without facing up to awkward questions. Pantaenus, and Clement after him, sought to present an orthodoxy that was intellectually viable. They sought to show that one can investigate philosophical and intellectual questions without being a heretic. Clement's work was continued by his far greater successor *Origen.

Three major works of Clement survive, corresponding to three stages of Christian instruction.

● *Exhortation to the Greeks* is an apology. It follows the pattern of the earlier second-century apologists, such as *Justin, but on a higher plane.

● *Tutor* is a manual of instruction for the new convert. It is a guide to outward conduct and is seen as a preparation for the reception of spiritual doctrine. It advocates a path of austerity or simple living as a mean between the extremes of luxury and asceticism or renunciation.

● *Carpet Bags* (or *Miscellanies*) is a complex and strange work. Here Clement's spiritual teaching is presented. While for *Tertullian faith is all that we need, for Clement it is only the first stage. It is the foundation on which knowledge is built. Clement presents the ideal of the Christian 'Gnostic', the spiritual man who has progressed beyond faith to knowledge. This is not a mere academic knowledge. It is a spiritual perception, requiring ethical purity and having the contemplation of God as its goal.

Clement's aim was to present an educated and intellectually viable form of orthodoxy. Like Justin, he saw truth in *Greek philosophy. Philosophy prepared the Greeks for Jesus Christ—just as the Old Testament prepared the Jews. Paul's warnings against philosophy (e.g. Colossians 2:8) were directed against *bad* philosophy. Clement embraced much of the Greek world-view, while drawing back from Gnostic heresy. But his teaching shows that where the avoidance of heresy is concerned, one cannot simply accept the will for the deed. In opposition to docetism (the idea that Jesus Christ only *appeared* to be human), Clement affirmed that he had a real body and that he ate and drank. But he could not believe that Jesus *needed* food or drink. In opposition to Gnostic denials of the goodness of marriage, Clement affirmed that it is a gift of God. But he could not believe that the ideal Christian couple would have sexual relations—except strictly for the purpose of procreation, and without any desire.

Before the coming of the Lord, the Greeks needed philosophy for righteousness. And now it leads to piety. It is a kind of preparatory training for those who reach faith through demonstration ... For God is the cause of all good things: of some directly, as with the Old and New Testaments; of others indirectly, as with philosophy. Maybe philosophy was even given to the Greeks directly, until the Lord

*should call them. For it was a schoolmaster
to bring the Greek mind to Christ, as the
[Old Testament] Law did for the Jews.
Thus philosophy was a preparation,
paving the way for those who are brought
to perfection in Christ.*

CARPET BAGS 1:5

*In the case of the Saviour, it is ludicrous to
suppose that his body needed the necessary
aids [of hunger, thirst, etc.] for its
survival. For he ate not for the sake of the
body, which was kept together by a holy
power, but so that it might not enter the
minds of his companions to hold a false
view of him [docetism] ... The apostles,
having through the Lord's teaching most
gnostically mastered anger, fear and lust,
were not liable even to those feelings which
appear good—such as courage, zeal, joy.
Their desire did not change at all, because
of the steady condition of their minds.
They continued unvarying in a state of
training after the resurrection of the Lord.*

CARPET BAGS 6:9

Clement sought an orthodox alternative to
Gnosticism, but was not entirely innocent of
letting in Gnostic ideas through the back door.
It is true that faith leads on to knowledge. But
there was with Clement the tendency for 'faith'
to mean orthodox Christianity and
'knowledge' to mean Greek thought.
Fundamental to his theology is the idea of
impassibility. Greek thought held God to be
impassible: beyond all emotion or feeling. This
state was also seen as the goal for the
philosopher and Clement believed that the
Christian Gnostic could attain to it. While the
pagan philosopher fights against his desires,
the spiritual Christian has none. This ideal of
impassibility, which was to have a very
profound influence on Christian ideals for a
long time, is foreign to the Bible. But Clement's
mistakes should not obscure his achievement
in linking the desire for intellectual and
spiritual progress to the church and to
orthodox Christianity. It was in part through
the labours of Clement and others like him that
Egyptian Christianity had become staunchly
orthodox by the fourth century.

Origen
PLATONISM FOR THE MASSES?

Origen was born around 185 of Christian
parents in Alexandria. In 202 his father,
Leonides, was martyred. Origen wrote to
him urging him to remain firm and it is said
that Origen was himself restrained from
seeking martyrdom only by his mother
hiding his clothes! He devoted himself
totally to a life of austerity and scholarship.
According to tradition, his dedication was so
thorough that he took Matthew 19:12
literally—although he later disapproved of
such a course of action. He was loyal to the
Catholic Church throughout his life and was
appointed by Demetrius, bishop of
Alexandria, as head of the catechetical
school (where those seeking baptism were
instructed). But in due course he fell out with
Demetrius, who was seeking to extend his
authority as bishop. Origen moved to
Caesarea in Palestine, where he continued
his work and was highly respected. In the
Decian persecution (249–51) he was
imprisoned and severely tortured, in the
hope that he would renounce his faith. But he
remained faithful and was eventually
released. He died a few years later as a result
of his injuries.

Origen was a prolific writer, but much of
his work has been lost. Much of it survives
only in translation, sometimes 'doctored' to
improve its orthodoxy. His major writings
can be divided into four groups:

● *Biblical*. Origen produced a massive
edition of the Old Testament with, in parallel
columns, the Hebrew text, the Hebrew text in
Greek characters and four or more Greek
translations. He also wrote many
commentaries (scholarly expositions),
homilies (practical and edificatory) and
'scholia' (notes on particular passages).

● *First Principles* was the first attempt
in the early church to produce a systematic
theology. It is divided into four books: on
God, the world, freedom and the Scriptures.

● *Against Celsus* is Origen's reply to
Celsus' *True Word,* a vehemently anti-
Christian work written in the late 170s.

● *Practical works*. He wrote *Prayer* and *Exhortation to Martyrdom*.

Origen was thoroughly familiar with *Greek philosophy. He studied under leading pagan philosophers. Some think that he studied under Ammonius Saccas, founder of Neo-Platonism, but this is doubtful. It is paradoxical that as one moves from *Justin to *Clement to Origen one encounters increasing hostility towards philosophy together with a steadily increasing absorption of philosophical ideas. The philosophical element was especially acute in Origen and his orthodoxy has been debated from his day to ours. In the fourth century there was a powerful anti-Origenist movement. In the sixth century he was formally condemned as a heretic. And yet he remains the single most influential father of Greek theology.

Origen's aim was nothing other than to be a loyal orthodox Christian. The bulk of his writings were devoted to the explanation of the Bible. And yet even here there are basic problems. Origen felt that the Bible could not be properly understood without the use of allegory. Parts of the Old Testament are offensive if taken literally. These were put there to show us the need to seek a deeper, hidden meaning. This is given by allegory. Origen did not invent the allegorical method. It was first used by Greeks in the attempt to derive some edification from the unsavoury legends of the exploits of the gods. It was applied to the Old Testament by the Jew Philo in the first century AD. His primary aim was to bring the Old Testament into line with Greek thought. Origen's approach was similar. Allegory enabled him to evade the literal meaning of the text when this was deemed unacceptable and to interpret the Bible in harmony with Greek thought. That was not Origen's *conscious* aim—he believed that he was simply drawing out the true and reasonable meaning of the text. To the extent that he was not aware of what he was doing, there is truth in the fourth-century charge that he was 'blinded by Greek culture'. A pagan opponent accused him of

'introducing Platonic ideas into foreign myths'—i.e. reading Platonism into the Bible.

Origen set out the apostolic tradition which he took as the test of orthodoxy. The apostles delivered certain doctrines in plain terms to all believers. Origen lists them. These are to be accepted as the foundation for theology. But the wise, spiritual Christian can move beyond these doctrines, as long as he does not contradict them. This openness to speculation follows Clement, though it contrasts sharply with both *Irenaeus and *Tertullian. As with Clement, the foundation is Christian while the further development tends to be thoroughly Greek. This is seen clearly in his doctrine of salvation. He can explain how Jesus Christ died for our sins on the cross and ransomed us from the devil. But this is teaching for the common herd, for those who can understand no more. Origen's real interest lies elsewhere. For him the essence of salvation is becoming like God, being 'deified' through contemplating him. The soul needs to rise from the world of becoming to the realm of being. The Word appeared to enable this. The knowledgeable Christian will penetrate beyond the earthly Jesus to the eternal Word and achieve salvation through contemplating him. This concept of salvation is thoroughly Greek and has more in common with Gnosticism than with biblical Christianity.

It seems necessary first of all to lay down an unmistakable rule regarding [fundamental questions] and then move on to investigate other points ... The teaching of the church has been transmitted in orderly succession from the apostles and remains in the churches to the present day. That alone is to be accepted as true which in no way conflicts with the tradition of the church and the apostles. The holy apostles, when preaching the faith of Christ, took certain points which they believed to be necessary for everyone and delivered them in the clearest way. These they taught even to those who appeared rather dull in the investigation of divine knowledge. They left those who would deserve the higher gifts of the Spirit to examine the grounds of their statements... The kind of doctrines which are clearly delivered in the teaching of the apostles are as follows: First, that there is one God... Secondly, that Jesus Christ himself... was born of the Father before all creatures... Thirdly, that the Holy Spirit was associated in honour and dignity with the Father and the Son... After these points the apostolic teaching is that the soul... shall after its departure from the world be rewarded according to its deserts... Regarding the devil and his angels and the opposing spiritual powers, the teaching of the church lays down that these beings indeed exist... It is also part of the church's teaching that the world was made and began at a certain time and that it is to be destroyed on account of its wickedness... Then, finally, that the Scriptures were written by the Spirit of God and that they have not only an obvious meaning but also another meaning which escapes the notice of most people.

FIRST PRINCIPLES, BOOK I, PREFACE 2–8

As the Law contains a shadow of good things to come... so the gospel, which is thought to be capable of being understood by anyone, teaches a shadow of the mysteries of Christ... Paul could not benefit the Jews without circumcising Timothy... So also, he who is responsible for the good of the many cannot operate only according to the secret Christianity. That will never enable him to help those who are following the external Christianity or to lead them on to higher and better things. We must be both carnal and spiritual Christians: where a carnal gospel is necessary, in which with those who are carnal we know nothing but Jesus Christ and him crucified, that we must preach. But it is different with

those who are perfect in spirit, bearing fruit and loving the heavenly wisdom. These must be made to partake of the Word who, after he was made flesh, rose again to the position which he held in the beginning with God.

COMMENTARY ON JOHN 1:9

The tension between orthodoxy and heresy in Origen is seen clearly in his doctrine of the Trinity. He was vehemently opposed to Monarchianism (the Father is the Son) and to any other theory which minimized the eternal threeness of God. He insisted that Father, Son and Holy Spirit are eternally three 'hypostases' or (loosely) beings. This threefold character of God, his 'trinity', is part of his eternal nature, not a later afterthought. But to call the second person 'Son' might seem to suggest that he was 'born' or 'begotten' or 'generated' at one particular moment. Origen maintained, to the contrary, that the Son is *eternally* generated or begotten by the Father. This is an eternal process or relationship. It is not a one-off event, not even something which happened once an eternity ago—it is something which is always, eternally happening.

Thus far the orthodox Origen. But there is another side. Origen taught the threeness of God, but his was a *graded* Trinity—the Father is greater than the Son who is greater than the Holy Spirit. It is the Father alone who is 'true God'. The Son is the same as the Father, but at a lower level. If the Father is God, one might say that the Son is god. Thus Origen's Trinity is a three-tier Trinity, God at three different levels. In the following century Arius was to take this further, concluding that only the Father is really God and that the Son and the Holy Spirit are creatures.

Origen taught the doctrine of eternal generation, which came to be seen as orthodox. He argued this philosophically: if the generation of the Son was not eternal it would mean that previously the Father was either unable or unwilling to generate the Son. Either suggestion is unworthy of God, so the Son's generation must be eternal. But

Origen also used this same argument to prove that creation is eternal. He believed that not just the Word or Reason (*logos*), but all rational beings (*logikoi*) have existed eternally. At a certain moment they fell away from contemplating God and became angels, human beings or demons, according to how far they fell. The physical universe was created to accommodate these fallen beings. (Genesis 1–3 needs a stiff dose of allegory to coax it into teaching that the universe was created *after* the fall.) The process of salvation is the reversal of the fall, ending with all rational beings again contemplating God.

Origen's doctrine of the Trinity is not fully understood if the rational beings are left out. There are four levels of being, occupied by Father, Son, Holy Spirit and the rational beings. Each level participates in the being of the level above. Thus the Son participates in the deity of the Father and we in turn are 'deified' through participation in the Son. (The Holy Spirit was often ignored in practice.) There is at no stage a radical discontinuity between God and his creation. Instead there is the permeation of deity from the top to the bottom. This system owed a great deal to Gnosticism—indeed the Gnostics beat Origen to the idea of the eternal generation of the Son.

Was Origen a heretic? Was his theology simply 'Platonism for the masses'? These questions will always continue to be debated. Two points can be clearly stated. There is no doubting Origen's fervent *desire* to be orthodox and his belief that he actually *was* or the sincerity of his devotion to Jesus Christ and dedication to his service. Equally, his actual theology was totally permeated by Platonism. The Platonist element is not like the icing on a cake or the currants in it, which can be removed, but like the sherry flavouring which is inseparable from the cake itself.

Cyprian
THE MARTYR-BISHOP

Thascius Caecilius Cyprianus was born early in the third century into an upper-class pagan family. He taught rhetoric at Carthage and was probably destined for high public office, such as a provincial governorship. But in 245/46 he turned his back on his career prospects by becoming a Christian. He tells us himself how he was attracted to Christianity by his search for moral renewal:

I was myself so entangled and constrained by the very many errors of my former life that I could not believe it possible for me to escape from them... But when the stain of my earlier life had been washed away by the help of the water of birth [baptism]... and the second birth had restored me so as to make me a new man... what before had seemed difficult was now easy.
TO DONATUS 4

Soon after, Cyprian was appointed a presbyter or elder and in 248/49, while still a relatively recent convert, he became bishop of Carthage, the most important church office in the Roman province of Africa.

Cyprian served as bishop for some ten years until his martyrdom in 258. These years happened to be years of immense turmoil for the church. Cyprian found his qualities of leadership tested more than if he had become a Roman provincial governor. His thought and writings were in response to the problems that he faced—he was first and foremost a man of action, not an intellectual. With Cyprian, life and thought cannot be separated and it is not possible to describe the one without the other. He was greatly influenced by *Tertullian, whom he is said to have read daily and called 'the master'. But while Tertullian was a radical non-conformist, a born outsider, Cyprian was above all a practical man of affairs, a born leader. With Cyprian, Tertullian's extreme ideals of moral discipline are tempered and made realistic in the form of ecclesiastical discipline.

Cyprian faced problems as soon as he was appointed bishop. Some of the senior clergy at Carthage were jealous of this high-class upstart who had been appointed bishop over their heads. These tensions might not have proved too serious, but very soon the church had to face the most thorough persecution so far—the Decian persecution of 249–51. This was the first coordinated empire-wide persecution of the church. The emperor Decius planned a two-pronged attack on the church. First, the leading bishops were to be liquidated. The bishops of Rome, Antioch, Jerusalem and Caesarea were all martyred. Cyprian was warned in advance and fled into hiding in the country near Carthage. From there he directed the church during the persecution, by letter. But he faced harsh criticism for his flight, especially from the jealous clergy. The second phase of the persecution was an attempt to force all Christians to sacrifice to the gods. All were required, on pain of death, to obtain a certificate stating that they had done this. The church, which had known some years of relative peace and calm, was not prepared for this onslaught. Large numbers of Christians offered sacrifice to the gods—one bishop even led his entire congregation to sacrifice. Many others evaded the order by bribing the officials to give them the necessary certificate, without actually offering sacrifice.

Traditionally, those who had apostatized (renounced their faith) were not readmitted into the church. But what was to be done with the large numbers now seeking readmission? There were two separate issues. First, should the lapsed be readmitted at once, *or* only after a time of penance (public confession followed by a period of austere penitence), *or* never? Second, *who* was to decide this question? Those who were imprisoned for their faith and ready to die for it (the 'confessors') were taking it upon themselves to reconcile the lapsed to the church. There was some traditional warrant for their action, but some were acting irresponsibly, lavishing 'pardons' on all and sundry. Did this authority lie with the confessors or the

bishops? Cyprian insisted that the right lay with the bishops, though they were to heed the recommendations of the confessors. Cyprian wrote an important work, *The Lapsed,* addressing this question. After the persecution, a council at Carthage in 251 decided that reconciliation was possible for the lapsed, after a period of penance. The following year, in the face of possible renewed persecution, another council decided that all who had at once begun penance would be readmitted forthwith. Cyprian took a leading role at these councils.

These difficult decisions did not meet with universal approval. Some at Carthage thought Cyprian was being too strict. Some of the clergy separated from him and formed a rival congregation, with laxer discipline. In Rome, on the other hand, there was a split or schism in the other direction. A new bishop, Cornelius, was appointed in 251. He favoured reconciliation of the penitent. Novatian, a gifted presbyter who may have been angry at not having been chosen as bishop, set himself up as a rival bishop. His church would not admit those who had lapsed, unlike 'the church of the apostates'.

Cyprian regarded the question of schism or division with the utmost seriousness. His most important treatise, *The Unity of the Church,* is devoted to it. The unity of the church is a given fact. There is no room for a variety of denominations in one place. The only true church is the Catholic Church. It is not possible to *divide* the church, only to *leave* it, as Novatian had done. The schismatic, who leaves the Catholic Church, commits spiritual suicide.

If a branch is broken from a tree, it cannot bud; if a stream is cut off from its source, it dries up ... Nor can he who forsakes the church of Christ attain to the rewards of Christ. He is a stranger, he is an enemy. Without the church for your mother, you cannot have God for your Father. If it was possible to escape outside the ark of Noah, then it may be possible to escape outside of the church ... There is only one baptism, but they [these schismatics] think that

*they can baptize. Although they forsake
the fountain of life, they promise the
grace of living and saving water. Men
are not washed there, they are made
foul; sins are not purged, they are piled
up. That birth makes sons not for God
but for the devil ... Do they fancy that
they have Christ with them, when they
gather together outside of his church?
Suppose these men were to be killed for
confessing Christ's name. The stain [of
schism] is not even washed away by
blood [of martyrdom]; the unforgivable
grievous sin of discord is not even
purged by their suffering. You cannot be
a martyr outside the church.*

THE UNITY OF THE CHURCH 5, 6, 11, 13, 14

The unity of the church is focussed on the
bishops. 'You ought to know that the bishop
is in the church and the church in the bishop.
If anyone is not with the bishop, he is not in
the church'. Bishops are the successors of the
apostles, i.e. they take over the functions of
the apostles. The bishop is supreme in his
own church, though he remains a bishop
only in solidarity with the other bishops of
the Catholic Church. The bishops are like
shareholders in a company (the
episcopate)—the shareholder has a share in
the company only in conjunction with all the
other shareholders.

The bishops must remain in solidarity
with one another and yet each is
independent in his own church. There is a
tension here in Cyprian's thought which was
to be exposed in a further controversy. If
someone is converted to Christianity
through the Novatianists and later wishes to
join the Catholic Church, need he be
rebaptized? Rome said no. Cyprian,
following traditional African practice, said
yes. Stephen, bishop of Rome, sought to
impose his view on others, which led to
controversy. Cyprian maintained that each
bishop could decide for himself. There was
to be no 'bishop of bishops', whether at Rome
or at Carthage. For a time there was
effectively a breach of communion between
Rome and Africa. A number of Eastern
bishops sided with Cyprian and rebuked

Stephen for his arrogance in forcing his view
on others. The situation was overtaken by a
further wave of persecution, in 257 and by
Stephen's death that year. The common
threat led to a closing of the ranks. Africa
and Rome tacitly agreed to go their own
ways over rebaptism, a victory for Cyprian's
position. The following year, in September
258, Cyprian was beheaded. He had fought
hard for the authority of the bishop—for the
'church of the bishops' against the 'church of
the martyrs'. It was fitting that he should
seal his labours by dying as a *martyr* bishop.

Cyprian's influence was immense,
especially on the Western Church. He helped
to make the Catholic Church the
authoritarian 'church of the bishops' rather
than a charismatic 'church of the martyrs'.
His views on rebaptism were rejected by the
fourth-century Catholic Church in Africa.
But there was a breakaway Donatist Church
which saw itself as the 'church of the
martyrs' and which maintained Cyprian's
position on rebaptism. While Cyprian
succeeded in his attempt to magnify the
office of the bishop over the laity and lower
clergy, he was less successful with the
independence of bishops. In due course
Cyprian's view of a college of equal bishops
was overtaken by the Roman Catholic idea of
the pope as the 'bishop of bishops', at least in
the West. It is on the nature and the unity of
the church that Cyprian's influence has been
greatest. His doctrine remained normative
for more than a thousand years and it is only
very recently that it has been relaxed in the
Roman Catholic Church—as in *Karl
Rahner's theory of 'anonymous Christianity',
for example.

Eusebius of Caesarea
FATHER OF CHURCH HISTORY

Eusebius was born in the early 260s in
Palestine. He studied and worked with
Pamphilus, who was in charge of *Origen's
library at Caesarea and who was martyred in
309/10. In gratitude to Pamphilus, Eusebius
took his name, becoming Eusebius Pamphili,
as if he had been his son or slave. Like

Pamphilus, Eusebius was an ardent admirer of Origen and they jointly wrote a defence of him. Eusebius was first and foremost a scholar but in 313/14 he became bishop of Caesarea. He died there in 339/40.

Eusebius is remembered above all as a historian, as *the* father of church history. He wrote a *Chronicle* of the history of the world and also a history of *The Martyrs of Palestine* in the Great Persecution (303–13). But his greatest work is his *History of the Church*, which traces the progress of the church from the earliest times to 324, when Constantine became sole emperor of East as well as West. His work is of immense value in that he preserves many documents which are otherwise unknown. Writing the history of the early church without Eusebius has been compared with attempting to write the history of the apostolic church without the Acts of the Apostles. Eusebius saw the hand of providence in the life of the church—in the deaths of those who persecuted Christians and in the triumph of Christianity.

Eusebius also wrote a *Life of Constantine* as well as two lesser works on him. He was an ardent admirer of the emperor. For Eusebius, the conversion of Constantine and the establishment of a Christian empire was the natural and desirable outworking of the Christian faith. He had no qualms about the linking of Christianity with the empire. He believed strongly in monarchy and had a particularly exalted view of Constantine as a Christian emperor, seeing him as God's representative on earth. Eusebius has been accused of 'baptizing' the Eastern concept of the absolute 'divine' monarch. The Eastern Byzantine Christian emperors were happy to accept this understanding of their status.

[The Word], the preserver of the universe, rules heaven and earth and the heavenly kingdom according to his Father's will. Likewise, our emperor, whom he loves, brings his earthly subjects to the only-begotten Word and Saviour and makes them fit subjects of his kingdom ... The pre-existent Word, the preserver of all things, gives the seeds of true wisdom and salvation to his disciples. He enlightens them and gives them understanding in the knowledge of his Father's kingdom. Our emperor, his friend, acts as interpreter to the Word of God and aims to recall the whole human race to the knowledge of God. He proclaims the laws of truth and godliness clearly to all and declares them with a powerful voice to all who dwell on earth ... His reason he derives from the great source of all reason. He is wise, good and just through his fellowship with perfect Wisdom, Goodness and Righteousness. He is virtuous, through following the pattern of perfect virtue, valiant through partaking of heavenly strength.

ORATION IN PRAISE OF THE EMPEROR CONSTANTINE 2:2,4; 5:1

Eusebius also wrote a number of apologetic, biblical and dogmatic works. He was not as acute a theologian as a historian. He supported the heretic Arius and was provisionally excommunicated at the Council of Antioch, early in 325. At the great *Council of Nicea, later that year, he had the opportunity to rehabilitate himself, which he did. But this was at the price of signing the Creed of Nicea, which he was able to do only with great anguish and not a little duplicity. His letter to his church at Caesarea survives, in which he hastily explains his actions, lest rumours should precede him. He justifies his signature of the creed with an interpretation of it which blatantly empties it of its intended meaning. But Eusebius' theological shortcomings should not be allowed to obscure his achievement as a historian. His *History of the Church* was not particularly well written, but it laid a foundation for the history of the early church on which others built. In the following century Socrates, Sozomen and *Theodoret wrote sequels to Eusebius' *History*.

Council of Nicea (325)

The Council of Nicea met in response to the teaching of Arius. Arius was a presbyter at Alexandria. Like *Origen, he believed that the Father is greater than the Son, who in turn is greater than the Holy Spirit. But unlike Origen, Arius did not believe that it was possible to have a hierarchy of divine beings. He brought a radical monotheism to Origen's system and concluded that the Father alone is God. The Son is the one through whom the Father created the universe, but nonetheless he is only a creature made out of nothing, not God. As a creature he is not eternal but had a beginning. 'There was once when he was not'. Arius himself accurately identified these two points as the crux of the debate: 'We are persecuted because we say that the Son had a beginning ... and likewise because we say that he is made out of nothing'. Arius' teaching is found today in the Jehovah's Witnesses.

Arius was opposed by his bishop Alexander. He appealed to other bishops in the East and was supported by a number of Origenists, such as *Eusebius of Caesarea. When, in 324, Constantine became emperor of the East as well as the West, he was forced to intervene. He called the Council of Nicea, which met in June 325, under his chairmanship. About 220 bishops were present, mostly from the East. (Later tradition gave the number as 318, probably derived from Genesis 14:14!) The council condemned Arius and produced an anti-Arian creed, the Creed of Nicea—not to be confused with the so-called 'Nicene Creed', which originated at the *Council of Constantinople in 381.

We believe in one God, the Father almighty, maker of all things visible and invisible;

And in one Lord Jesus Christ, the Son of God, begotten of the Father, that is from the substance of the Father. He is God from God, light from light, true God from true God, begotten not made, of one substance [homoousios] with the Father.

By him all things were made, things in heaven and on earth. For us men and for our salvation he came down, was made flesh and became man. He suffered, rose again on the third day and ascended into the heavens. He will come again to judge the living and the dead.

And in the Holy Spirit.

But the holy catholic and apostolic church anathematizes [curses] those who say: 'There was once when he was not' and 'He was not, before he was begotten' and 'He was made out of nothing' and those who assert that he is from some being or substance other than the Father or that he is mutable or liable to change.

At this stage there was a basic pattern for creeds in the Eastern Church, though the precise wording varied from church to church. The Creed of Nicea seems to be one of these creeds, with a number of anti-Arian phrases added:

● Arius interpreted the traditional phrase 'begotten of the Father' to mean that Jesus Christ was created by the Father *out of nothing*. Nicea excludes this interpretation by the explanatory clause 'that is, from the substance of the Father'.

● Arius held, with Origen, that only the Father is 'true God'. Nicea responds by calling Jesus Christ 'true God from true God'.

● Jesus Christ is 'begotten, not made'— he is the Son of God, not a creature. The distinction between a child or offspring (from the being of the Father) and a creature (made out of nothing) is at the heart of the controversy. It may be compared to the distinction between having a child of one's own and making a robot.

● Jesus Christ is 'of one substance with the Father'. The Greek word *homoousios* (of one substance) was the most controversial word in the creed. There were qualms about the use of a non-scriptural term, but it was necessary because the Arians could twist all scriptural phrases. For example, Jesus is 'begotten' by God—but so are the dewdrops

(Job 38: 28)! The word *homoousios* had the added advantage that the Arians had already declared it to be unacceptable. The non-scriptural term was used to safeguard the scriptural truth of the deity of Christ.

● At the end of the creed a number of Arian statements are anathematized or condemned. These amount chiefly to the Arian claim that the Son had a beginning and was created out of nothing.

The Council of Nicea later came to be seen as the first of the general or ecumenical councils. But it did not meet with such favour in its own time. Far from ending the debate about the deity of Jesus Christ, Nicea inaugurated it. Why should this be so, since Arius was so forthrightly condemned?

At Nicea, Arius was condemned by the use of the word *homoousios* in particular. The emperor himself advocated the word, probably at the instigation of his western ecclesiastical advisor, the Spaniard Hosius. It was a word which was congenial to the West, which since *Tertullian had thought of the Trinity as three persons in one substance. It was also congenial to the Antiochenes—the minority school in the East who stressed the unity of the Godhead, but were less clear about the distinctness of Father, Son and Holy Spirit. But it was not a congenial word to the Origenists (such as *Eusebius of Caesarea), the majority in the East and at the council. They feared that it would lead to either of two extremes. It could imply a materialist division of God's substance into three. It could open the door to Monarchianism—the blurring together of Father, Son and Holy Spirit. These fears were not without foundation where the Antiochenes were concerned. The Origenists accepted the term and signed the creed, in deference to the emperor, but they were not won over. As a recent writer put it, 'theologically the victory of the *homoousios* was a surprise attack, not a solid conquest'.

Nicea split the church into two major groups. On the one hand, the 'Nicene party' (the West, the school of Antioch and others in the East like *Athanasius) were clear on the full deity of Jesus Christ, but less clear on the eternal threeness of the Godhead. On the other hand, the Origenists were strong on the threeness of the Godhead, but less clear on the deity of Jesus Christ. The Nicene party did not *deny* the distinction between Father, Son and Holy Spirit (i.e. they were not Monarchians)—but they did not state it as forcefully as the Origenists wanted and so appeared to them to be Monarchian. The Origenists were not Arians (i.e. they did not see Jesus Christ as a creature made out of nothing)—but they held him to be *inferior* to the Father and so appeared Arian to the Nicene party. This was a classic instance of two half truths confronting one another— the full deity of Jesus Christ (Nicea) and his eternal distinctness from the Father(Origen).

Because of misunderstanding and polarisation, these two parties confronted one another for nearly half a century. This is traditionally called the 'Arian Controversy' but inaccurately. The major controversy was between the Nicenes and the Origenists, the Arians serving as catalysts in the debate, rather than major participants. In the 350s an extreme Arian party arose, maintaining that the Son is *totally unlike* the Father, and this shocked the Origenists into seeing the need for greater clarity on the status of Jesus Christ. Athanasius and others on the Nicene side responded with conciliatory gestures and the door was opened for a compromise formula, incorporating the insights of both sides. The three hypostases of Father, Son and Holy Spirit (Origen) are of one substance *(homoousios)* with each other (Nicea). This mediating position was adopted by the *Cappodocian fathers, who brought about its acceptance at the Council of Constantinople in 381.

The fourth-century debate about the person of Jesus Christ can seem remote to us today, especially because of the unfamiliar terms used. At times it can appear like an obscure philosophical argument. But the point at issue is fundamental and central to the Christian faith. Is Jesus Christ merely a (super-) creature sent by God, or is he the revelation of God himself? Does 'God loved the world so much that he gave his only son' (John 3:16) in fact only mean that he sent one of his creatures? The deity of Jesus Christ is the foundation of all true Christian faith. Without it, there is no true revelation of God in Jesus. Without it, the Christian doctrine of salvation is undermined. Arius raised one of the most important issues in the history of theology and the early Fathers were right to state the full deity of Jesus Christ clearly in opposition to him.

Athanasius
THE DEITY OF CHRIST

Athanasius was born at the end of the third century. He entered the household of Alexander, bishop of Alexandria, and in due course became a deacon. He accompanied the bishop to the *Council of Nicea. When Alexander died in 328, Athanasius succeeded him as bishop of Alexandria. He was bishop for forty-five years, dying in 373.

The chief preoccupation of Athanasius' life was the struggle against Arianism. Arius had been condemned at Nicea, but the Creed of Nicea was not acceptable to the Origenist majority in the East. The emperor wanted unity above all else, so favoured a more tolerant approach to orthodoxy which could embrace a suitably chastened Arius. Athanasius would have none of this. He saw the deity of Jesus Christ as the foundation of the Christian faith. Arianism meant the end of Christianity. Athanasius fought Arianism with every weapon at his disposal, including that of ecclesiastical politics. His uncompromising stand made him unpopular with bishops and rulers alike. Seventeen of his forty-five years as bishop were spent in five different exiles. Most important of his years in exile were those spent in Rome from 340 to 346. This was a time of considerable mutual influence between Athanasius and his hosts. After this exile he spent the 'Golden Decade' of 346–56 at Alexandria, his longest uninterrupted time as bishop.

Athanasius remained firm even when all around him appeared to be weakening. But at the same time he knew when to be flexible. The anti-Arian party (the West, the Antiochene school, Athanasius) held that God was one hypostasis or heir while the Origenist majority in the East held that God is three hypostases. At the Council of Alexandria in 362 (held in a brief respite between two exiles), it was recognized that either formula could be understood in an orthodox way. It is what is believed that is primary—the wording is less important. This recognition paved the way for a combination of the Nicene *homoousios* (the Son is of one substance with the Father) and *Origen's statement that God is three hypostases. This combination was popularized by the *Cappadocian fathers and became the established orthodoxy at the *Council of Constantinople in 381.

Athanasius was a prolific writer, on a variety of themes:

● *Anti-Arian works.* Most of Athanasius' works were dedicated to the struggle against Arianism. He made good use of the leisure given him by his exiles. Best known is his longest work, the *Orations against the Arians.*

● *Apologetic works.* Athanasius wrote an apology in two parts: *Against the Greeks* and *The Incarnation of the Word.* Traditionally these were thought to have been written in about 318, before the Arian controversy. But the evidence seems to favour a date during his first exile, 335–37.

● *Easter Letters.* Each year Athanasius wrote a letter to the Egyptian churches, to be read at Easter. His 367 letter is important in that it sets out for the first time the New Testament canon (list of books) exactly as we have it today. This was one of the fruits from Athanasius' stay at Rome and the mutual influence that followed.

● *Life of Antony,* whom Athanasius portrays as the first monk. In the second and third centuries there were those who lived an especially ascetic life—remaining single, embracing poverty and devoting themselves to prayer and fasting. Such people remained within the normal congregations and are called 'domestic ascetics' because they practised their asceticism at home, within society. But in the fourth century, as the moral standards of the church became diluted by the increasing number of superficial pagan converts, the ascetics began to withdraw from society, especially into the deserts of Egypt and Syria. As Athanasius put it: 'Cells arose even in the mountains and the desert was colonized by monks—who came forth from their own people and enrolled themselves for a heavenly citizenship.' Some of these monks (like Antony) lived a solitary life in remote places while others lived in community together. Still others opted for some combination of these two approaches. Athanasius' book helped to spread the monastic ideal, especially to the West. It played an important part in the conversion of *Augustine.

Athanasius fought so hard for the deity of Jesus Christ because he saw that our salvation depends on it. Only a divine Christ could save us. This theme is expounded in *The Incarnation of the Word*. Athanasius faced Jewish and pagan charges that the incarnation and crucifixion of God's Son is unfitting and degrading. In response to this, Athanasius argues that the incarnation and cross are indeed suitable, fitting and eminently reasonable. This is because only the one through whom the world was created could restore it. This restoration could not take place in any way other than by the cross.

We were the cause of his becoming flesh. For our salvation he loved us so much as to appear and be born in a human body... No one else but the Saviour himself, who in the beginning made everything out of nothing, could bring the corrupted to incorruption; no one else but the Image of the Father could recreate men in God's image; no one else but our Lord Jesus Christ, who is Life itself, could make the mortal immortal; no one else but the Word, who orders everything and is alone the true and only-begotten Son of the Father, could teach men about the Father and destroy idolatry. Since the debt owed by all men had to be paid (for all men had to die), he came among us. After he had demonstrated his deity by his works, he offered his sacrifice on behalf of all and surrendered his temple (body) to death in the place of all men. He did this to free men from the guilt of the first sin and to prove himself more powerful than death, showing his own body incorruptible, as a first-fruit of the resurrection of all ... Two miracles happened at once: the death of all men was accomplished in the Lord's body, and death and corruption were destroyed because of the Word who was united with it. By death immortality has reached all and by the Word becoming man the universal providence and its creator and leader, the very Word of God, has been made known. For he became human that we might become divine; he revealed himself in a body that we might understand the unseen Father; he endured men's insults that we might inherit immortality.
THE INCARNATION OF THE WORD 4,20,54

The idea of 'deification' (becoming divine) is an indication of the Greek influence on Athanasius' thought. This influence is strongest in his two-part apology. Adam before the fall is portrayed as a Greek philosopher—contemplating the Word, the image of the Father. His mind had nothing to do with his body. It transcended all bodily desires and senses and contemplated 'intellectual reality'. But Adam turned from intellectual reality and began to consider his body and its senses, thus falling into fleshy desires. This view of the fall owes more to *Greek philosophy and to Origen than to the Bible.

Athanasius used a variety of arguments against Arianism. Primarily he argued from Scripture. He presented the biblical case for the deity of Jesus Christ. He also answered the biblical arguments put forward by the Arians. They cited passages to prove the Son's inferiority to the Father. Athanasius referred these to his status as a man, not to his eternal status as God. Secondly, Athanasius appealed to Christian worship of Jesus Christ, both in the New Testament and in his own time. This would be idolatry if Jesus were merely a creature. Thirdly, Athanasius argued that only God is capable of saving us—the argument of his *The Incarnation of the Word*. Finally, he used philosophical arguments—e.g. that God could never have been irrational, without his Reason or Word.

Were he [the Word] a mere creature he would not have been worshipped nor spoken of [as in the Bible]. But he is in fact the real offspring of the substance of the God who is worshipped, his Son by nature, not a creature. Therefore he is worshipped and believed to be God... The sun's rays belong really to it and yet the sun's substance is not divided or lessened. The sun's substance is whole and its rays are perfect and whole. These rays do not lessen the substance of the light but are a true offspring from it. Likewise we understand that the Son is begotten not from outside the Father but from the Father himself. The Father remains whole while 'the stamp of his substance' [Hebrews 1:3] is eternal and preserves the Father's likeness and unchanging image.
ORATIONS AGAINST THE ARIANS 2: 24,33

Athanasius was also the first to devote serious attention to the status of the Holy Spirit. Until the middle of the fourth century attention was devoted to the relation between the Father and the Son. The Creed of Nicea's bare 'And in the Holy Spirit' is an indication of how little attention had been given to the Holy Spirit. But in 359/60 Athanasius was forced to address himself to this question. An obscure Egyptian group, called the Tropici, taught the deity of the Son but held that the Holy Spirit was created out of nothing—they were Nicene towards the Son, Arian towards the Holy Spirit. They clashed with their bishop, Serapion, who wrote to Athanasius for advice. He replied in a number of *Letters to Serapion*, in which he spells out for the first time a fully *Trinitarian* theology, considering in detail the status of the Holy Spirit as well as the Son. He argues for the deity of the Holy Spirit, who is not a Son of God but 'proceeds from the Father' (John 15:26).

Ephrem the Syrian
THE LYRE OF THE HOLY SPIRIT

Not all the early Christian Fathers were Greek or Latin speaking. In the second century, the Christian faith reached the Syriac-speaking kingdom of Osrhoene, whose capital was at Edessa. The leading figure in the second-century Syriac church was an outstanding man called Bardesanes. He was an opponent of Gnosticism, but his own views were dubious enough for him to be suspected of heresy. The king, Abgar IX, who died in 212, himself became a Christian. In the third century the kingdom came within the Roman Empire and links between Syriac Christianity at Edessa and Greek Christianity at Antioch were strengthened.

Ephrem was born at Nisibis, near the border with Persia, at the beginning of the fourth century. He was baptized and instructed by James, bishop of Nisibis, until the latter's death in 338. James was a leading ascetic (renouncing the world and accepting poverty and celibacy) and Ephrem himself became a monk. He taught at Nisibis. The Persians attacked the city several times and finally, in 363, it was ceded to them. Ephrem, with many other Christians, then moved to Edessa, where he taught until his death in 373.

Ephrem is the leading writer of the Syriac church. He wrote biblical commentaries, sermons, dogmatic works against heresy, and hymns. He was greatly revered as a poet and came to be known as 'the lyre of the Holy Spirit'. His works were widely translated into Greek and Armenian.

[Jesus], the son of a carpenter, cleverly made his cross a bridge over Sheol [the abode of the dead], that swallows everyone, and brought mankind over it into the dwelling of life. Because it was through the tree [in the Garden of Eden] that mankind had fallen into Sheol, so it was on the tree [the cross] that they passed over into the dwelling of life. Thus the tree brought not only bitterness but also sweetness—that we might learn that none of God's creatures can resist him. Glory be to you who laid your cross as a

*bridge over death, that souls might pass
over it from the dwelling of the dead to
the dwelling of life!*
HOMILY ON OUR LORD 4

The Cappadocian
Fathers
DEFINING THE TRINITY

The Cappadocian Fathers were Basil of
Caesarea, his friend Gregory of Nazianzus
and his younger brother Gregory of Nyssa.
They came from the Roman province of
Cappadocia, in modern Turkey. They shared
a common ambition to integrate Christianity
with all that was good in classical culture.

Basil was born into a wealthy Christian
family, in about 330. He had a good
education in both Christianity and the
classics and philosophy. His education came
to a climax at Athens, where he studied from
351 and met Gregory of Nazianzus. On his
return home he taught rhetoric for a while,
but then was baptized and pursued the
monastic life. He toured the leading
monastic sites in the East and then set up a
small community of his own on the family
estates. But his leisure was short-lived. In
364 he was appointed presbyter at Caesarea
and in 370 he succeeded the bishop. He
devoted himself to social schemes for the
poor and to the struggle against Arianism.
He died in 379.

Gregory of Nazianzus also came from the
Cappadocian nobility. His father was bishop
of Nazianzus. He studied at Athens where he
met Basil. Eventually he became Basil's
follower and joined him in his monastic
retreat. Gregory's ecclesiastical career was a
succession of frustrations. His father
appointed him presbyter at Nazianzus, but
that was not a success. Then Basil pushed
him into becoming bishop of a small town, in
the interests of ecclesiastical politics and the
struggle against Arianism. Gregory never
took up his duties there. Finally, be became
bishop of the Nicene party at
Constantinople, the Eastern capital. This
was a crucial position and Gregory devoted

himself wholeheartedly to it. In 380 he
preached five famous *Theological Orations*
there, in defence of Nicene orthodoxy. In 381
he played a leading role at the *Council of
Constantinople. But he fell foul of
ecclesiastical rivalries and resigned his
bishopric at the council. He died in 389/90.

Gregory of Nyssa, who was born in about
335, was Basil's brother and disciple. He was
the most intellectual of the trio and for a time
became a rhetorician. He also married,
though this did not prevent him from later
embracing the monastic life. In 371 Basil
bullied him into becoming bishop of Nyssa.
For a few years he was deposed and replaced
by an Arian, but otherwise he remained
bishop there for the rest of his life. All three
Cappadocians were Origenists, but Gregory
of Nyssa was the most ardent disciple of
*Origen. He was more interested than the
others in philosophy and theological
speculation, though he also distinguished
himself as a defender of orthodoxy. He died
in 394 or soon after.

The Cappadocians are remembered
especially for their opposition to Arianism
and their trinitarian teaching. They fused
together the Nicene belief that Father and
Son are *homoousios* (of one substance) and
the Origenist belief that Father, Son and
Holy Spirit are three hypostases or beings.
The one substance of the Godhead exists
simultaneously in three different hypostases
or modes of being. But what does it actually
mean to say that God is one substance in
three hypostases? Basil saw the difference
between substance and hypostasis as that
between the universal and the particular—
e.g. the difference between 'humanity' and
an individual person, such as Fred Smith.
Each individual person is comprised of the
common substance of humanity (the
universal) together with their own
distinguishing features or individual
characteristics, which make them a
particular person. In the same way, each of
the three divine hypostases is the common
substance of deity together with his own
distinctive features. In other words, Fred
Smith = human nature stamped with the
distinctive characteristics of 'Fred

Smithness': God the Father = divine nature, deity, with the distinctive characteristics of 'Fatherhood'. Thus, Father, Son and Holy Spirit are, as it were, three different ways of being God.

Substance relates to hypostasis as universal relates to particular. Each of us shares in existence through the common substance and yet is a specific individual because of his own characteristics. So also with God, substance refers to that which is common, like goodness, deity or other attributes, while hypostasis is seen in the special characteristics of fatherhood, sonship or sanctifying power.

BASIL, LETTER 214:4

When I speak of God, you must be enlightened at the same time by one flash of light and by three. There are three individualities or hypostases or, if you prefer, persons. (Why argue about names when the words amount to the same meaning?) There is one substance—i.e. deity. For God is divided without division, if I may put it like that, and united in division. The Godhead is one in three and the three are one. The Godhead has its being in the three or, to be more precise, the Godhead is the three ... We must neither heretically fuse God together into one [Monarchianism] nor chop him up into inequality [Arianism].

GREGORY OF NAZIANZUS, ORATION 39:11

The Cappadocians offered a clear explanation of how the unity and the threeness of God are to be related. But their explanation lays them open to the charge of tritheism (belief in three Gods). If the relation between the common substance of the Godhead and the individual hypostases is like that between humanity and individual people, then surely there must be three Gods? The problem is compounded by the fact that the comparison with three people is no mere passing analogy. Basil offers it as part of his *definition* of the terms substance and hypostasis.

Of course the Cappadocians had no desire to be tritheists. They were aware of the problem and sought to answer the charge. Gregory of Nyssa wrote a treatise called *That There are Not Three Gods*. But whatever their intentions, the suspicion persists that their theology in fact points to tritheism. The question is: did they offer a satisfactory explanation of *why* the persons are not three Gods? They tried hard, invoking concepts such as the perfect harmony and common action of the three. But a football team playing 'as one man' remains eleven men. The Cappadocians greatly advanced the understanding of the Trinity in their time, but their conception of the unity of the Godhead needed to be strengthened.

Since with men we can distinguish each one's action while they are pursuing the same task, they are rightly called many men. Each of them is separated from the others by his particular environment and way of working. It is not so with God. We do not learn that the Father does anything on his own without the co-operation of the Son. Nor does the Son act on his own without the Holy Spirit. But every act which extends from God to the creation ... originates with the Father, proceeds through the Son and is completed by the Holy Spirit ... The holy Trinity effects every act, not by separate action according to the number of the persons, but so that there is one motion and disposition of the goodwill which proceeds from the Father, through the Son to the Spirit. So we cannot call those who jointly, inseparably and mutually exercise divine and superintending power and activity to us and all creation, three Gods.

GREGORY OF NYSSA,
THAT THERE ARE NOT THREE GODS

In addition to Arianism, the Cappadocians also had to face the Macedonians. These were a group under bishop Macedonius who, like the Egyptian Tropici, affirmed the deity of the Son but held the Holy Spirit to be a creature. Basil answered them in his *The Holy Spirit*. He affirmed the deity of the Spirit, though without explicitly calling him God. Gregory of Nazianzus, who outlived Basil, was more explicit and openly called the Holy Spirit God.

Another heresy faced by the Gregories was Apollinarianism. Apollinaris denied that Jesus had a human soul or mind. If I am a soul dwelling in a body, Jesus was the Word dwelling in a body. Thus the Word took the place of a human soul in Jesus. This had been acceptable Alexandrian teaching for some time and *Athanasius held something similar. But Apollinaris took it to an extreme and by his time the deficiencies of such a view were widely recognized. The Gregories argued that Jesus Christ had to be fully human in order to save us fully.

Anyone who has trusted Christ as a man without a human mind is himself mindless and unworthy of complete salvation. For what [Christ] has not assumed, he has not healed. It is what he has united to his Godhead that is saved. If only half of Adam fell, then it would suffice for Christ to assume and save only half of man. But if it is the whole of human nature that fell, it must be united to the whole nature of [Christ] and thus be saved wholly.
GREGORY OF NAZIANZUS, LETTER 101

Council of Constantinople (381)

In 379 the Westerner Theodosius became emperor in the East. He was staunchly Nicene in his beliefs and resolved to deal with Arianism once and for all. To this end he called a council, which met at Constantinople from May to July 381. This was very much the *Cappadocian Fathers' council. The Gregories were both present at the council. Gregory of Nazianzus played a leading role, although it ended his career as a bishop. The heresies which the Cappadocians had fought

were rejected at the council, in accordance with their teaching.

It is all but certain that this council produced what is today known as the 'Nicene Creed'. As with the creed of the *Council of Nicea, it appears to be a local Eastern creed with polemical additions:

We believe in one God, the Father almighty, maker of heaven and earth and of all things visible and invisible;

And in one Lord Jesus Christ, the only-begotten Son of God, begotten from the Father before all ages, light from light, true God from true God. begotten not made, of one substance [homoousios] with the Father. By him all things were made. For us men and for our salvation he came down from heaven, was made flesh from the Holy Spirit and Mary the virgin and became man. He was crucified for us under Pontius Pilate, suffered and was buried. He rose again on the third day, according to the Scriptures, and ascended into the heavens. He sits on the right hand of the Father and will come again with glory to judge the living and the dead. His kingdom will not end;

And in the Holy Spirit, the Lord and life-giver, who proceeds from the Father. Together with the Father and the Son he is worshipped and glorified. He spoke through the prophets; And in one holy catholic and apostolic church. We confess one baptism for the remission of sins. We look forward to the resurrection of the dead and the life of the age to come. Amen.

Three heresies were condemned at Constantinople.

● *Arianism.* The creed contains three of the four anti-Arian phrases from Nicea. The following year, another gathering of bishops at Constantinople wrote to Rome. They summarized the faith of the 381 council as belief in 'one Godhead, power and substance of the Father, the Son and the

Holy Spirit, whose dignity is equal and majesty co-eternal, who are in three perfect hypostases or three perfect persons'. This was an apt summary of the Cappadocian doctrine of the Trinity.

● *Macedonianism.* Thirty-six of the bishops who came to the council were Macedonians—they believed in the deity of the Son but held the Holy Spirit to be a creature. An attempt was made to win them over for the truth. The creed states the deity of the Holy Spirit, but only by implication. It keeps to biblical phrases, except for the statement that he is worshipped and glorified together with the Father and the Son. He is not directly called 'God'. Despite this diplomatic approach, the Macedonian bishops walked out of the council.

● *Apollinarianism.* Apollinaris, who denied that Jesus had a human soul, was condemned at Rome in 377. He was also condemned at this council.

The Council of Constantinople came to be seen as the second of the ecumenical councils. Its creed may not have persuaded the Macedonians at that time, but it has become the most ecumenical of the creeds of Christendom. It is the one creed that is used widely in both Eastern and Western Churches—but with one important difference.

In the East the belief was and is that the Holy Spirit proceeds from the Father *through* the Son. In the West, however, the belief grew that the Holy Spirit proceeds from the Father *and* the Son. (This minor verbal difference reflects an underlying difference in approach to the doctrine of the Trinity.) In the West it became customary to add the words 'and the Son' (*filioque* in Latin) into the creed. Rome was always cautious and conservative, but finally she followed suit in the eleventh century and also added the word *filioque*. This helped to precipitate the breach between Rome and Constantinople in 1054.

The Council of Constantinople, in its third canon (law or edict), created a major source of future strife: 'The bishop of Constantinople is to be honoured next after the bishop of Rome, because Constantinople

is the New Rome.' This canon was unpopular at Rome because it implied that Rome's primacy was based on its position as the secular capital. At this time the Roman bishops were beginning to claim a special position as the heirs of Peter. The canon was even more unpopular at Alexandria, which had previously been the number two see or bishopric, after Rome. The bishops of Alexandria, who were ambitious and immensely powerful, did not miss opportunities to humiliate the bishops of Constantinople, who had little power, despite their theoretical status. This can be seen in the affair of *John Chrysostom, *Cyril of Alexandria's attack on Nestorius, and the struggle preceding the *Council of Chalcedon in 451.

The Council of Constantinople affirmed that Jesus Christ was both fully God (against Arius) and fully man (against Apollinaris). But how can he be *both* fully God and fully man? Two wrong answers came to be given to this question. From the Antiochene school came Nestorius, who divided Jesus Christ into God the Word and Jesus the man. He was opposed by Cyril and condemned at the *Council of Ephesus in 431. After Nestorius came Eutyches, from the Alexandrian school, who sought to maintain the unity of Jesus Christ by blurring his humanity into his deity. He was opposed by *Leo and condemned at the *Council of Chalcedon in 451.

Should we not recognize that the person of Jesus Christ is and must remain a mystery? Were the early Fathers not guilty of trying to comprehend the incomprehensible and unscrew the inscrutable? No. Their aim was not to *explain* the incarnation or to remove all mystery, but to *define* it. As these four major heresies undermined central elements of the doctrine of the incarnation, the church was forced to clarify each of them in turn. The aim was to *protect* the doctrine from denial, not to explain it in such a way as to eliminate the mystery. If any of the four heresies had won the day it would have been a distorted picture of Jesus Christ that would have been handed down to us.

Ambrose
THE CHURCH ABOVE THE EMPEROR

Ambrose was born at Trier in 339. His father
was prefect of Gaul (France) and both his
parents were Christians. Ambrose followed
in his father's footsteps and became a
provincial governor in Italy. But in 374 there
was strife over the appointment of a new
bishop of Milan and Ambrose was chosen, as
an outsider. At the time he was still only a
catechumen, preparing for baptism. It was
normal in the fourth-century church for
those in public office, and therefore liable to
have to put people to death, to delay
baptism. Since baptism was seen as a one-off
washing away of all sins, this was best
deferred until the moral dangers of public
office were past.

Ambrose devoted himself
wholeheartedly to his new task and became
the greatest Western Church leader of the
fourth century. He fought hard and
successfully for the establishment of Nicene
orthodoxy. In the previous twenty years the
emperors had favoured a less dogmatic
Christianity, more open to Arian ideas.
Ambrose led the struggle for a church based
firmly on the truth of the deity of Jesus
Christ. He was a gifted and popular
preacher. He introduced from the East the
method of allegory. This approach to the
Bible, which turned the Old Testament into a
'spiritual' book pleasing to Platonists, paved
the way for the conversion of *Augustine at
Milan. Ambrose also introduced from the
East the newly-developed emphasis on the
change or conversion of the bread and the
wine in the communion service. This led, in
due course, to the doctrine of
transubstantiation, defined at the *Fourth
Lateran Council in 1215. Ambrose also
prepared the ground for Augustine's
teaching on the fall and original sin: 'In
Adam I fell, in Adam I was cast out of
Paradise, in Adam I died ... guilty as I was
in Adam, now I am justified in Christ' *(The
Death of Satyrus 2:6).*

*If the word of Elijah had such power as
to bring down fire from heaven [1*
*Kings 18], shall not the word of Christ
have power to change the nature of the
elements? The Lord Jesus himself
proclaims: 'This is my body'. Before the
blessing of the heavenly words, another
nature is spoken of [bread], after the
consecration the body is signified ...
And you say 'Amen'. i.e. 'It is true'.
What the mouth utters, let the heart
confess; what the voice speaks, let the
soul feel.*
THE MYSTERIES 9:52, 54

*We show forth the Lord's death as often
as we receive the sacramental elements,
which are transformed into the flesh
and the blood by the mysterious efficacy
of holy prayer.*
THE CHRISTIAN FAITH 4:125

Ambrose's most important contribution lay
in his dealings with the imperial court. He
established important principles of the
independence of the church and the duties of
the Christian ruler, which were to be
developed in the Middle Ages. Three major
conflicts with the court illustrate these
principles. First, a pagan altar and statue of
Victory had been removed from the Senate
house at Rome. Two years later, in 384, a
leading Neo-Platonist rhetorician by the
name of Symmachus (distantly related to
Ambrose as it happened) wrote a petition to
the newly-appointed emperor Valentinian.
He urged toleration of paganism and the
restoration of the statue of Victory. The
emperor was inclined to give way, but
Ambrose wrote to him in no uncertain terms,
stressing that a Christian cannot support
paganism.

Valentinian gave way. But his mother,
Justina, who supported the 'Arian' (i.e. non-
Nicene) party, was determined to take
revenge on Ambrose. In 385 and 386 there
were attempts by the imperial court to force
Ambrose to hand over a church building for
the use of non-Nicenes. Ambrose refused.
The things of God are to be rendered to God,
not Caesar, and this includes church
buildings. Ambrose brazened it out with the
empress, arranging a sit-in at the disputed

church and announcing his readiness to accept martyrdom. It was at this time that he introduced to the West the practice of congregational hymn-singing—to keep up the spirits of the congregation occupying the church. The empress gave way.

Finally, in 390, the emperor Theodosius, who had called the *Council of Constantinople in 381, ordered a particularly brutal massacre of thousands of citizens at Thessalonica, following a riot there. Theodosius belonged to Ambrose's congregation, and Ambrose saw it as a pastoral matter. He wrote the emperor a discreet letter requiring him to do penance or be excommunicated. Theodosius, who had tried to cancel the order and who regretted his deed, gave way and appeared in church as a penitent. He accepted Ambrose's rebuke and future relations between them were cordial. Ambrose died in 397.

You, most Christian emperor, owe God both faith and zeal, care and devotion for the faith. How then do some hope that you will feel it your duty to command the restoration of altars to the heathen gods and to pay for profane sacrifices? ... If anything other [than we wish] is decreed, we bishops cannot contentedly suffer it and take no notice. You may cone to church but you will find either no priest there or one who will resist you.

LETTER 17:3,13 [TO VALENTINIAN]

The church belongs to God, therefore it ought not to be assigned to Caesar. The temple of God cannot be Caesar's by right. No one can deny that I say this with respectful feeling for the emperor. For what is more respectful than to call the emperor the son of the church? ... For the emperor is within the church, not above it.

SERMON AGAINST AUXENTIUS 35, 36

John Chrysostom
PREACHING THE BIBLE

John Chrysostom was born at Antioch in the middle of the fourth century. He was brought up by his Christian mother, who had been widowed when only twenty. When he grew up he was baptized and after a while devoted himself to the monastic life. He lived for several years in a cave outside Antioch and damaged his health by his austerities. Ill-health forced him to return to Antioch where he became deacon and then presbyter (or priest, as it was now called). He studied there under Diodore of Tarsus, who introduced him to the world of biblical scholarship. The school of Antioch was noted for its opposition to allegory. The Antiochenes insisted that the Bible should be interpreted according to its natural meaning, the 'literal' sense as it was called. There was scope for typology (drawing parallels between God's dealings with man at different times), but not for fanciful interpretations which evaded the plain historical meaning of the text. Chrysostom adopted this Antiochene approach.

The name Chrysostom or 'golden-mouthed' was first given to him in the sixth century. It was a tribute to his excellence as a preacher. He preached regularly, normally working his way through an entire book of the Bible. These sermons were then published as commentaries. He also preached sermons on specific subjects and wrote a number of treatises. Best-known of these is his *The Priesthood,* a classic work on pastoral care. Chrysostom was not especially gifted in theological matters—his sermons are above all practical and devotional.

As a presbyter at Antioch and a preacher Chrysostom was in his natural element and excelled. He was an extremely able orator and his sermons were very popular. But he was not allowed to remain there. In 397 there was fierce competition to fill the vacant bishopric at Constantinople, the capital. Imperial officials sought to resolve the matter by appointing an outsider and Chrysostom was chosen and forced to accept the post. The bishops of Alexandria were especially jealous of Constantinople because it had, at the *Council of Constantinople in 381, replaced Alexandria as the second see or bishopric of Christendom. Theophilus, bishop of Alexandria, who had hoped to have his own man elected bishop of Constantinople, was forced to consecrate Chrysostom bishop with his own hands.

Chrysostom had been landed in a position which was fraught with danger for even the most skilful politician. He, by contrast, was quite without guile. He preached fearlessly and set about correcting abuses. His relations with the court deteriorated, thanks to Theophilus' intrigues and slanders, and eventually he was exiled on trumped-up charges—in 403 and, after a brief return, in 404. In 407 he was forcibly marched to another distant site of exile and died as a result. At first there was controversy between East and West over his case, but eventually all came to recognize his sanctity and greatness. As a modern writer put it, 'he whose life was embittered and destroyed by his enemies now has no enemies at all'.

It is not wine that is bad, but drunkenness. A covetous man is not the same as a rich man. The covetous man is not rich. He wants many things and while he lacks them he can never be rich. The covetous man is a keeper, not a master of wealth, a slave not a lord. For he would sooner give away a portion of his flesh than his buried gold... Since he has not the ability to give his riches to others or to distribute them to the needy... how can he possibly call them his own? In what way does he possess them when he has neither the free use nor the enjoyment of them?... To be rich is not to possess much but to give much... Let us decorate our souls rather than our houses. Is it not a disgrace to clothe our walls with marble, vainly and for no purpose, and to neglect Christ who is going about unclothed [in the poor]? What will your house profit you? Will you take it with

you when you leave [this world]? You cannot take your house with you but you will surely take your soul with you... We build houses to live in, not for ambitious display. What is beyond your needs is superfluous and useless. Try putting on a shoe that is too large! You will not be able to endure it because it will hinder your step. So also, a house larger than your needs is a hindrance to your progress towards heaven... You are an alien and a pilgrim with regard to the things of this world. You have a native country—in the heavens. Transfer your wealth there... Do you want to be rich? Have God as your friend and you will be richer than all men!... It is clear that the only people who own property are those who despise its use and deride its enjoyment. For the man who has cast his wealth away and bestowed it on the poor has used it rightly. He takes the ownership of it with him when he departs, not being stripped of possession even in death, but then receiving it all back again.

HOMILIES ON THE STATUES 2:14–18

Jerome
THE BIBLE INTO LATIN

Sophronius Eusebius Hieronymus (Jerome) was born in the 340s near the border of Italy and Dalmatia (modern Yugoslavia). He studied at Rome and while there began to build up an extensive personal library of the classics. He was baptized when about nineteen years of age. Soon after he renounced a secular career and dedicated himself to an ascetic and scholarly life.

In some ways he was a reluctant ascetic. In 373/74 he went East on pilgrimage, but did not get beyond Antioch due to ill-health. He was beguiled by the intellectual stimulus of the city and made no further progress in the direction of the monastic centres. Then he tells us that he had a remarkable dream:

Many years ago I had, for the sake of the kingdom of heaven, cut myself off

*from home, parents, sister, relations
and (hardest of all) from the dainty food
to which I had become accustomed. I
was on my way to Jerusalem to wage my
warfare, but I still could not bring
myself to part with the library which I
had collected with such care and toil at
Rome. And so, miserable man that I
was, I would fast only that I might
afterwards read Cicero ... And when at
times I returned to my right mind and
began ... to read the prophets, their style
seemed rude and repulsive. I failed to
see the light with my blinded eyes, but I
attributed the fault, not to them but to
the sun ... Suddenly I was caught up in
the spirit and dragged before the
judgement seat of the Judge ... Asked
who and what I was, I replied 'I am a
Christian'. 'You lie,' said he who
presided, 'You are a Ciceronian, not a
Christian. For where your treasure is,
there will your heart be also.' Instantly I
became dumb and amid the strokes of
the lash—for he had ordered me to be
whipped—I was tortured even more
severely by the fire of conscience ... I
made an oath and called upon his name,
saying: 'Lord, if I ever again possess
worldly books or read them, I have
denied you' ... From then on I read the
books of God with a zeal greater than I
had previously given to the books of
men.*

LETTER 22:30

After this Jerome went into the desert and
set himself up as a hermit in a cave. But he
managed to take his entire library with him!
He received occasional visitors and
corresponded extensively. The solitary life
was not for Jerome. 'How often, when I was
living in the desert, in the vast solitude
which gives the hermits a savage dwelling-
place, parched by the blazing sun, how often
did I fancy myself among the pleasures of
Rome!' (*Letter 22:7*). After about two and a
half years in the desert Jerome returned to
civilization. But while he drew back from
solitude, he never doubted the superiority of
celibacy and virginity:

*Virginity is natural while marriage only
follows guilt [the fall] ... I praise
marriage—because it gives me virgins. I
gather the rose from the thorns ... Why,
mother, do you grudge your daughter
her virginity? ... Are you angry with her
because she has chosen to be married to
a king [Christ] rather than to a soldier?
She has conferred on you a high
privilege: you are now the mother-in-law
of God!*

LETTER 22:19,20

Jerome was most at home in the world of
scholarship. He never gave up the pagan
classics, despite the dream, but he did
subordinate them to his theological
concerns. He became a leading Greek and
Hebrew scholar. In 382 he went to Rome and
became private secretary and librarian to
Damascus, the bishop. But Damascus died at
the end of 384 and Jerome found himself
without a job. He loved the company of
wealthy female ascetics, among whom he
had many disciples. But this had not made
him popular at Rome and Jerome decided to
leave. In 385 he headed East and went with
Paula and Eustochium, two of his lady
friends, on pilgrimage to Palestine. In 386
they founded a monastery and a convent at
Bethlehem and Jerome stayed there until his
death in 420.

One of Jerome's greatest achievements
was his Latin translation of the Bible—the
Vulgate or commonly used version, as it later
came to be known. While it was not flawless,
it was a vast improvement on earlier
translations. At this time there was
considerable confusion regarding the Old
Testament. The early Christians, who were
Greek-speaking and largely ignorant of
Hebrew, used the Greek Septuagint
translation (which is often quoted in the New
Testament). The trouble was that this
translation contained not only the Hebrew
books of the Old Testament (which comprise
the Protestant Old Testament and are the
only books now accepted by Jews) but also
other works (overlapping what is today
called the Apocrypha). There was
uncertainty in the early church about which

books were to be accepted in the Old Testament. Jerome insisted that it is only the Hebrew books which are canonical or scriptural. He also made a point of translating the Vulgate from the Hebrew original, not from the Septuagint. He had grasped the important principle that the Old Testament Scriptures are entrusted to the Jews (Romans 3:2; 9:4) and that the Christian church has no right to add any books not recognized by them.

Jerome became entangled in an unseemly controversy over *Origen. In his early years he was an ardent admirer of Origen. Then in 393 he suddenly turned around and became a bitter opponent of Origenist heresy. This led to an unpleasant row with his old friend Rufinus, who remained an apologist for Origen. Polemic brought out the worst in Jerome. He could be coarse, vulgar and malicious. His polemics were regularly conducted at the level of the petty and the personal. Furthermore, his character was such that he was constantly falling out with people and engaging them in controversy. A modern writer said, 'apart from a small circle of friendly woman ascetics and blindly devoted adherents, hardly anyone succeeded in living continuously at peace with Jerome'. Perhaps it was just as well that he was opposed to marriage! But Jerome's reputation is merited—not by personal sanctity nor by theological profundity but by his scholarship. He could be careless and arrogant as a scholar, but his achievements were great and it is for these that he is justly remembered.

Augustine
BLUEPRINT FOR THE FAITH

Augustine is the greatest Christian theologian since the apostle Paul. He is *the* Father of the Western Church. His thought dominated the Middle Ages—the good and the bad alike. In the sixteenth century the Reformation and the Catholic Counter-Reformation were both rediscoveries of Augustine. *B. B. Warfield called the Reformation 'the ultimate triumph of

Augustine's doctrine of grace over Augustine's doctrine of the church'.

Aurelius Augustine was born in 354 at Thagaste, in modern Algeria, of a pagan father and a Catholic Christian mother, Monica. In his student days at Carthage he resolved to devote himself to a life of philosophy. As a Catholic catechumen (candidate for baptism) he naturally turned to the Old Testament. But a rude shock awaited him there. To the mind attuned to *Greek philosophy, the Old Testament appears crude and unspiritual. Augustine reacted against it and allied himself with the Manichees. Manicheism was a Persian religion with two ultimate principles or gods: Light and Darkness. These are in constant conflict. The physical universe originates from the Darkness, while the human soul is the product of the Light. This theory explained the origin of evil. It also served to deny our responsibility for our evil deeds (which originate with the dark element). But Augustine came eventually to see that Manicheism raises as many problems as it solves, and he began to search for the truth elsewhere.

At this time, in 384, he was appointed professor of rhetoric at Milan. This was an important post which could naturally lead to high government office. Augustine began to read some Neo-Platonist works and found there a more satisfactory answer to the problem of evil. Evil is not a positive principle, independent of God. It is not something which exists in its own right, but is rather the absence or lack of the good. In more modern terms, we might say that evil is parasitic on goodness or that it is something good which has been spoiled. Lust, for instance, is misdirected love. Augustine also began to attend the sermons of *Ambrose. He was impressed by the way in which Ambrose, through allegory, reconciled the Old Testament with Platonist spirituality. This prepared the way for his return to the Christian faith.

Augustine was challenged by the accounts of the conversions of the prominent Neo-Platonist philosopher Victorinus and the simple monk Antony. He was intellectually convinced about the truth of Christianity but baulked at the prospect of celibacy. (He assumed, as was normal at this time, that a wholly dedicated Christian life involved celibacy.) Torn two ways, he one day rushed out into the garden. There he heard a child's voice crying, 'Take up and read'. Augustine opened his copy of Paul's letters at Romans 13:13–14. He got no further than 'Clothe yourselves with the Lord Jesus Christ and do not think about how to gratify the desires of the sinful nature.' Augustine later wrote, 'I did not want nor need to read any further. Instantly, as I finished the sentence, the light of confidence flooded into my heart and all the darkness of doubt vanished.' This was in August 386 and Augustine was baptized by Ambrose the following Easter.

After his conversion Augustine, with a number of like-minded companions, devoted himself to an ascetic life of study. In the next few years he wrote a number of philosophical works. He also wrote thirteen works against the Manichees, between 387 and 400. He felt a particular responsibility to do this because of his own first-hand experience of Manicheism and also because he had himself led people into the heresy. In these works he argued for human free-will (denied by the Manichees). Sin is not created by God, nor co-eternal with him, but arises from the misuse of free-will. The will is free, not coerced, and we are therefore responsible for our deeds. These points are argued in detail in Augustine's *Free Choice of the Will*.

In 388 Augustine returned to Africa. There he took care to avoid towns without a bishop, since he was aware of the danger of being forced into the office. But in 391, while visiting Hippo, he was spotted and 'forcibly' ordained as presbyter or priest. When the bishop died, in 396, Augustine succeeded him. He remained bishop of Hippo until his death in 430.

As a cleric he was brought face to face with the Donatist schism, which was ruining the church in Africa. The schism began in 312 over the disputed validity of the consecration of the Catholic bishop of Carthage. Essentially it was a struggle between the older African 'church of the martyrs', which looked back to *Cyprian, and the newer international Catholic Church. As always, it proved easier to start a division than to heal one. When Augustine came on the scene, the Donatists were in the ascendency and the Catholic Church in Africa was in a precarious condition. But by 412 he had managed to reverse the relationship and to force Donatism into a permanent downward spiral. This he did by a variety of means. He researched the Donatists' history and publicized their inconsistencies and excesses. He indulged in popular propaganda by preaching and even by composing pop songs!

He also used state power and coercion against the Donatists. At first he had been opposed to the use of force, but eventually he came to accept it—as a necessary response to the considerable Donatist violence and as a valid educational tool, comparable to the role of the cane in education. Augustine found sanction for the use of force in the Old Testament and, more dubiously, in Luke 14:23: *'Compel* them to come in'. His often quoted words, 'Love and do what you will' *(Homilies on I John, 7:8)* served as a defence of coercion on the grounds that it is for the ultimate benefit of the recipient, and therefore 'loving'. Augustine opposed the death penalty for heresy, but he had already provided the theoretical justification for the medieval inquisition.

Augustine's primary attack on Donatism was theological and centred on the doctrine of the church. He said that the church is catholic (or worldwide), while the Donatists were confined to Africa. They were 'frogs in the marshes croaking, "We are the only Christians"'. They were guilty of the sin of schism, cutting themselves off from the church of Jesus Christ. This was the opposite of love and was evidence that they did not have the Holy Spirit. The Donatist case was based on the alleged unholiness of certain leaders in the Catholic Church (though in fact many of their own leaders were far from blameless). But Augustine answered this by saying that the church is holy because it is the church of *Christ*. The sacraments remain valid even when administered by an unholy minister because it is *Christ* who gives the sacrament. This principle enabled Augustine, unlike Cyprian, to recognize sacraments administered outside the Catholic Church (e.g. by Donatists) as *valid*, though not *efficacious* until the recipient joined the Catholic Church.

Augustine was the first to develop the doctrine of the 'invisible church'. Not all within the church are genuine Christians—many are Christians in name alone. We cannot distinguish the true from the false. It is God alone who can read the hearts of men and who knows who are his. Thus the boundaries of the true church are invisible, known to God alone. Augustine distinguishes between the visible church (the outward organization) and the invisible church (the body of true Christians), seen only by God. For Augustine, the invisible church lies entirely within the Catholic Church—there are no true Christians outside it. His contemporary, the Donatist Tyconius whose ideas influenced him, held that the invisible church is the true people of God within either the Donatist or the Catholic churches. This attitude, which today is commonplace, is all but unparalleled in the early church.

In the unspeakable foreknowledge of God, many who seem to be outside [the church] are really inside [because they will be converted] and many who seem to be inside are really outside [because they are only nominal Christians] ... It is clear that when we talk of inside and outside in relation to the church, we must consider the position of the heart, not the body ... It was the same water that saved those who were inside [Noah's] ark and destroyed those who were left outside. So it is by one and the same baptism that good catholics are saved and bad catholics and heretics perish.
BAPTISM, AGAINST THE DONATISTS 5: 38–39

In 411, just as the Donatists were being put to rout, Augustine was made aware of

Pelagianism. Pelagius was a Scots or Irish monk. (*Jerome said that Pelagius had been befuddled by too much porridge!) He believed that a Christian could lead a life without sin, with no more help from God than his teaching and the example of Jesus Christ. He did not believe that Adam's fall had done more than introduce death and the example of sin—it did not make sin inevitable. Augustine was vehemently opposed to these ideas and fought them with all his energy until his death.

In his earliest days as a Christian, Augustine believed that we need God's grace, the inner help of the Holy Spirit, to live the Christian life. But he also believed that the unbeliever can, of his own unaided free-will, make the first move and turn to God. In other words, God gives his grace (or the Holy Spirit) to those who respond to the gospel in faith. But after a few years, Augustine came to a deeper understanding of grace. He came to see that even faith is a gift of God, the work of his grace. 'What do you have that you did not receive?' (1 Corinthians 4:7). Salvation is *all* of God's grace—the beginning as well as the continuance. This grace is not given to all—not all believe. It is given to those whom God has chosen, his elect. 'It does not ... depend on man's desire or effort, but on God's mercy (Romans 9:16). Augustine reached these views by 397. They arose from his deeper experience of human nature and his deeper study of the apostle Paul. He then wrote his *Confessions,* in which he recounts the story of his life until the death of his mother, shortly after his conversion, interpreting it in the light of his new beliefs about God's grace.

You move us to delight in praising you—for you have made us for yourself and our hearts are restless till they find their rest in you ... I will now call to mind my past foulness and the sins of my flesh, not because I love them, but because I love you, O my God ... In [the books of the Platonists] I read ... that in the beginning was the Word and the Word was with God and the Word was God ... but I did not read there that the

Word became flesh and dwelt among us ... I longed [to serve God alone] but was bound, not with the iron fetters of another, but by my own iron will. The enemy controlled my will and with it had made a chain for me and bound me. Lust had grown from a perverse will, habit had come from indulgence in lust, and necessity was the result of not resisting habit ... Give [the grace to do] what you command and command what you will.

CONFESSIONS 1:1; 2:1; 7:9; 8:5; 10:29

While Augustine's mature views were essentially complete by 397, it was the controversy with Pelagius that led to their detailed outworking. For nearly twenty years Augustine campaigned furiously against the Pelagians—by ecclesiastical and secular politics and above all by writing. He believed that all men sinned 'in Adam' and that as a result all (including infants) are guilty and biassed towards sin. This bias takes the form of 'concupiscence' (or lust), which rules mankind (of which sexual lust is merely the supreme example). Fallen man is in the sad position of sinning inevitably, yet 'freely' or willingly. He retains free-will and responsibility in that he is free to will what he *wants*—but he is not free to will what he *ought*.

God, in his mercy, has chosen to save some, but not all. This he does by his grace. First comes *operating grace*. This is prevenient—that is, it precedes any good will in man. 'Grace does not find a man willing [the good], but makes him willing.' It is also efficacious—it infallibly achieves its end, the conversion of the will. This it does not by destroying free-will but by wooing it. God is the infallible seducer—he wins the soul, but in such a way that the soul responds gladly and freely. Once the will is converted it can co-operate with grace. *Co-operating grace* is necessary because our converted wills are still weak, and without God's help we would soon lapse. If we are to last to the end and be saved, a further grace is necessary: the *gift of perseverance*. This is given not to all who begin the Christian life but only to the elect.

[God] extends his mercy to [men] not because they already know him but in order that they may know him. He extends to [men] his righteousness, by which he justifies the ungodly, not because they already are but in order that they might become upright in heart ... If a commandment is kept through fear of punishment and not for love of righteousness, it is kept slavishly, not freely, and therefore is not [truly] kept at all. For fruit is good only if it grows from the root of love ... That man has progressed a long way ... in righteousness ... who has discovered by that very progress how far he is from the perfection of righteousness.

THE SPIRIT AND THE LETTER 11, 26, 64

Two other major works of Augustine must be mentioned. Between 399 and 419 he wrote his greatest dogmatic work, *The Trinity*. In it he draws together the achievements of the early Fathers before his time and presents a systematic account of the doctrine of the Trinity. But he does not content himself with stating the doctrine.

Let us believe in ... a trinity of persons mutually interrelated and a unity of equal essence. And let us seek to understand this, praying for help from him whom we seek to understand ... Faith seeks, understanding finds. This is why the prophet says, 'Unless you believe, you will not understand' [Isaiah 7:9].

THE TRINITY 9:1; 15:2

On the basis of authority (Scripture as expounded by the church) we believe the doctrine of the Trinity: that God is three persons in one substance. But what does this *mean*? Reason seeks to understand what faith believes. Augustine attempts to do this by using analogies. He seeks these analogies in the human soul, made in the image of God. He examines a range of possible analogies, mostly based on the trio of being, knowing and willing. His final and best analogy is the mind remembering, understanding and loving God. By examining the relationship between the mind's memory, understanding and love of God, Augustine sought insights into the relationships of the persons of the Trinity. But at the end of the day he recognizes that even the best analogy is imperfect, for now we see only 'in a glass darkly' (1 Corinthians 13:12).

Between 413 and 427 Augustine wrote his longest work, *The City of God*. In 410 Rome had fallen to barbarian invaders. This unprecedented disaster was blamed on Christianity—the gods were angry because they were no longer being worshipped. Augustine responded to this crisis with the greatest apologetic work of the early church. In the first part he argues that the pagan gods had not in fact provided either earthly or heavenly fortune. For Augustine, Christianity does not offer temporal worldly success (contrary to the high hopes of, for example, *Eusebius of Caesarea, following Constantine's conversion). The gospel offers *inner* peace and an *eternal* destiny. In the second part, Augustine traces the course, from creation to eternity, of two different cities or societies: the city of God and the city of Satan; the heavenly and the earthly city; Jerusalem and Babylon. These are not two rival nations, nor two organizations (such as the church and the state) but two groups of people. They are marked by two different loves: the love of God versus the love of self; the love of the eternal versus the love of temporal things.

Two cities have been formed by two loves: the earthly city by the love of self, leading to contempt of God and the heavenly city by the love of God, leading to contempt of self. The former glories in itself, the latter in the Lord ... In the one city, the rulers and the nations that it subdues are ruled by the love of ruling; in the other city, rulers and subjects serve one another in love—the subjects by obeying, the rulers by caring for all ... These two cities are two communities of men. One is predestined to reign eternally with God, the other to suffer eternal punishment with the
devil ... Citizens are born into the earthly city by a nature spoiled by sin, but they are born into the heavenly city by grace freeing nature from sin.
THE CITY OF GOD 14:28–15:2

Augustine died in 430, as an invading barbarian army was about to take the city of Hippo. Western Roman civilization was crumbling. But in his *City of God* he had taken classical culture and transposed it into a new Christian culture. This, one of the greatest works of the early church, was in many ways a blueprint for the Middle Ages.

Cyril of Alexandria
JESUS THE INCARNATE WORD

Cyril became bishop of Alexandria in 412, in succession to his uncle Theophilus. His main claim to fame lies in his controversy with Nestorius, bishop of Constantinople. Since the *Council of Constantinople in 381, which promoted Constantinople to second see in the place of Alexandria, there had been bitter rivalry between the two sees. Cyril's uncle Theophilus had secured the exile of *John Chrysostom and Cyril was to follow suit with Nestorius. After his death, Cyril's own nephew and successor, Dioscorus, was to follow in the family tradition. But it would be wrong to see this purely as an ecclesiastical political struggle. Cyril opposed Nestorius because of fundamental differences concerning the person of Jesus Christ.

Nestorius was a popular preacher who in 428 became bishop of Constantinople. He belonged to the Antiochene school of thought on the person of Jesus Christ. That meant that he followed the 'Word–man' approach—he saw Christ as Jesus the man indwelt by God the Word. There is the closest possible conjunction between Jesus the man and God the Word—they are united in purpose and will. But when all is said and done, despite Nestorius' attempts to unite them, they remain two individuals. Nestorius has been accused of teaching a 'pantomime horse' theory of the incarnation.

In 1910 a long-lost work of Nestorius, *The Bazaar of Heracleides,* was discovered. This confirms Nestorius' *desire* to be orthodox and to affirm the unity of Jesus Christ, but not his success in this aim.

Nestorius, in his preaching at Constantinople, denied that the virgin Mary was *theotokos* ('God-bearer'). It was Jesus the man who was born of Mary, not God the Word. Cyril heard of this and reacted. First he wrote Nestorius a polite but firm letter, explaining his own position and urging Nestorius to accept *theotokos* and be at peace with him. Nestorius remained adamant and, in the meantime, Cyril obtained the support of Rome. He then wrote Nestorius an uncompromising letter, demanding submission within ten days. Cyril required Nestorius to sign twelve 'anathemas'—that is, to condemn twelve statements setting out what Cyril considered to be his heresies. Nestorius refused and the emperor called the *Council of Ephesus, at which he was deposed.

The essence of Cyril's position is very simple. Jesus Christ is not a man indwelt by or conjoined to God the Word—he *is* God the Word, made flesh. The doctrine for which Cyril fought against Nestorius was simply the doctrine of the incarnation. God the Word, who is eternally begotten or born of God the Father, was in time born of the virgin Mary as man. Therefore Mary is *theotokos*—because the man Jesus born of her was God. Christ is not a conjunction of Jesus the man and God the Word. Instead, 'the Word became flesh' (John 1:14)—i.e. God the Word united to himself complete human nature (including a soul) and became a man. This union makes of Jesus Christ one hypostasis, one being. The union between the Word and his humanity was therefore called a 'hypostatic union'.

Cyril also used a formula which he believed to come from *Athanasius but which in fact originated with Apollinaris. He affirmed the 'one incarnate nature of God the Word'. This was to cause trouble later when orthodoxy came to be defined as belief in the *two* natures of Christ. But Cyril was happy to see Jesus Christ as a unity 'out of two natures'. That is, the two natures of humanity and deity are indivisibly united in Jesus Christ to form a single reality—just as body and soul came together to form one human person. Furthermore, 'the difference of the natures is not taken away by the union' *(Letter 4).*

The difference between Cyril and Nestorius can be summarized as follows: Nestorius spoke of Jesus *and* God the Word, while Cyril believed that Jesus *was* the Word. Again, *who* was the man Jesus? Nestorius believed him to be a man united with the Word in a unique and perfect way. Cyril insisted that he was the Word, incarnate. Nestorius very revealingly stated: 'I could not call a baby two or three months old God' (Socrates, *Church History* 7:34).

Cyril's opposition to Nestorius, like that of Athanasius to Arius, was motivated by a concern for the doctrine of salvation. He believed that in the communion service we receive life from Jesus' lifegiving flesh (John 6:48–58). His flesh gives life because it is the flesh not of a mere man but of the incarnate Word.

We do not say that the nature of the Word was changed and became flesh, nor that it was converted into a whole man, consisting of body and soul. But this we say: that the Word, in a way beyond words or understanding, hypostatically united to himself flesh animated by a rational soul and became man ... So then, he who had an existence before all ages and was born of the Father, is said to have been born after the flesh, from a woman. It is not that his divine nature took its beginning from the holy virgin ... but because for us and for our salvation he hypostatically united to himself a human body and came forth from a woman, he is said to be born after the flesh ... We must not divide the one Lord Jesus Christ into two sons [Son of God and son of man]. Nor is it sufficient for sound doctrine merely to hold a union of [two] persons, as do some [Nestorius]. For Scripture says not that the Word united himself to the person of a man, but that he was made flesh. That means nothing else than that he partook of flesh and blood like us. He made our body his own, not ceasing to be God.

LETTER 4

If anyone will not confess that Emmanuel is truly God and that the holy virgin is therefore theotokos, in that in the flesh she bore the Word of God made flesh, let him be anathema.

ANATHEMA I

If anyone will not confess that the Lord's flesh is lifegiving and that it is the own flesh of the Word of God the Father—but pretends that it belongs to some other person who is united with him only in honour and in whom the deity dwells—if anyone will not confess that his flesh gives life because it is the flesh of the Word who gives life to all, let him be anathema.

ANATHEMA II

Cyril died in 444. He remains today, as he was in his own time, a source of contention. For the Egyptian church and for many others he has always been the great father of orthodoxy who defended the doctrine of the incarnation. Others would prefer the judgement attributed to *Theodoret:

At last and with difficulty the villain has gone. The good and gentle pass away all too soon; the bad prolong their life for years... Knowing that the fellow's malice has been growing daily and doing harm to the body of the church, the Lord has lopped him off like a plague and taken away the reproach from Israel. His survivors are indeed delighted at his departure. The dead, maybe, are sorry. There is some ground for alarm lest they should be so much annoyed at his company as to send him back to us... Great care must then be taken. It is especially your holiness' business to undertake this duty: to tell the guild of undertakers to lay a very big and heavy stone upon his grave, for fear that he

should come back again and show his fickle mind once more. Let him take his new doctrines to the shades below and preach to them all day and all night... I really am sorry for the poor fellow!

LETTER 180 (TO BISHOP DOMNUS OF ANTIOCH)

It is not necessary to portray Cyril as pure light or pure darkness. One can recognize his great achievement in maintaining the doctrine of the incarnation, while recognizing that it was not a totally unpleasant duty for him to unseat the bishop of Constantinople.

Council of Ephesus (431)

The emperor Theodosius II called the Council of Ephesus, which met in June 431, to resolve the controversy between *Cyril and Nestorius. The Antiochene party of bishops, who supported Nestorius, were late in arriving. Cyril, who already had the support of Rome, waited fifteen days and then started the council. Nestorius was deposed.

Four days later the Antiochenes arrived. They refused to acknowledge Cyril's council and set up their own, which condemned Cyril. There were only about thirty Antiochene bishops, compared with over two hundred at Cyril's council. Two weeks later the Western delegates arrived and confirmed Cyril's council. It came to be seen as the third of the ecumenical councils.

The outcome was confusion and division in the East. Alexandria was split from Antioch. Eventually there was a settlement, in 433. Cyril accepted a moderate Antiochene document called the Formula of Reunion, while the Antiochenes agreed to accept the deposition of Nestorius. Despite accusations to the contrary, Cyril did not go against his earlier teaching in accepting the Formula of Reunion. It did not say all that he might have said and its wording was not identical to his, but the primary point for which he had fought against Nestorius, the incarnation, was clearly stated. Alleged points of contradiction between the Formula and

Cyril's teaching elsewhere are illusory.

We confess therefore our Lord Jesus Christ, the only-begotten Son of God, to be perfect God and perfect man, consisting of a rational soul and a body. He was begotten before the ages from the Father, as God, and in the last days, for us and for our salvation, the same one was begotten of Mary the virgin, as man. He is of one substance (homoousios) with the Father, as God, and of one substance (homoousios) with us, as man. For there is a union of two natures and therefore we confess one Christ, one Son, one Lord.

According to this understanding of the unconfused union, we confess the holy virgin to be theotokos, *because God the Word was incarnate and became man and from his conception itself united to himself the temple that he took from her.*

As regards the expressions in the Gospels and the Epistles concerning the Lord, we know that theologians understand some of these to be common (relating to the one person), while others they distinguish (as relating to the two natures)—the worthy ones they attribute to the deity of Christ; the lowly ones they attribute to his humanity.
FORMULA OF REUNION

Theodoret of Cyrus
JESUS: GOD AND MAN

Theodoret was born towards the end of the fourth century, at Antioch. He became a monk and in 423 was pressed into becoming bishop of Cyrus, some fifty miles from Antioch. He was the last of the major Antiochene theologians of the fourth and fifth centuries. He was outstanding as a pastor at Cyrus and also as an exegete, interpreting the Bible 'literally', in the Antiochene manner. He wrote extensively, including apologetic works. He also composed a *Church History,* covering the period from 325 (where *Eusebius of Caesarea left off) to 428. It is generally reckoned to be inferior to the church histories of Socrates and Sozomen, which cover similar periods.

Theodoret's major contribution to theology lies in his teaching on the person of Jesus Christ. He supported Nestorius in his controversy with *Cyril and wrote against the latter, including a *Refutation of Cyril's Twelve Anathemas.* He misunderstood Cyril, believing him to teach that the Word suffered as God, in his deity. But Cyril clearly distinguished between that which is true of the Word as God, in his own divine nature, and that which is true of him as man, 'after the flesh', by virtue of his union with human nature. Thus Cyril believed that the Word is impassible or incapable of suffering as God, while as man, in the flesh, he suffered for us. Theodoret's early, anti-Cyrilline writings were to be condemned at the *Council of Constantinople in 553.

As time went by, Theodoret's understanding matured. Earlier he had held that Jesus Christ had two natures and two hypostases. But later he moved towards a distinction between his one hypostasis or person and his two natures or substances (i.e. deity and humanity). He sought to steer a middle course between dividing Jesus Christ into two persons or sons (son of God and son of man) and blurring the two natures into one. This was the position taken at the *Council of Chalcedon.

In 449 he was deposed at the Council of Ephesus, the so-called 'Robber Synod', and sent into exile. He was reinstated two years later at the Council of Chalcedon, at which he anathematized Nestorius, albeit reluctantly.

I have been taught to believe in one only-begotten, our Lord Jesus Christ, God the Word made man. But I know the distinction between flesh and Godhead and regard as profane all who divide our one Lord Jesus Christ into two sons—as well as those who, going the other way, call the deity and humanity of the master Christ one nature. These extremes are opposed to one another while between them lies the way of the doctrines of the gospel.

LETTER 109

God the Word was made man, not to render the impassible [divine] nature passible, but in order to bestow on the passible nature [our humanity], by means of the Passion, the boon of impassibility.

LETTER 145

Leo the Great
'UNWORTHY HEIR'

Leo was bishop of Rome from 440 to 461 and was one of the greatest of the popes—he is often called 'Leo the Great'. He was a formidable person. In 452 he personally persuaded Attila the Hun to turn back from attacking Rome. Three years later, when the Vandals did take Rome, he managed to check the destruction and killing. Leo is famous especially for his teaching on the person of Jesus Christ and the Roman papacy. His teaching on Jesus Christ is found especially in his *Tome,* written in refutation of the heretic Eutyches.

Eutychianism is the fourth and last of the ancient heresies concerning the person of Jesus Christ. Arius denied his true deity, Apollinaris denied his full humanity, Nestorius was accused of dividing him into two people—God the Word and Jesus the man. Eutyches was accused of blurring his two natures (deity and humanity) into one and creating a mixture. If yellow paint is mixed with blue, the outcome is green paint, which is neither yellow nor blue; if a horse is crossed with a donkey, the outcome is a mule, which is neither a horse nor a donkey. Likewise, Eutyches was accused of making of Jesus Christ a mixture of deity and humanity, a *tertium quid* or 'third something', which is neither God nor man but a sort of mongrel.

Eutyches was an elderly and highly respected monk at Constantinople. In 448 he was accused of heresy and the bishop,

Flavian, was forced to put him on trial. The outcome was his condemnation for confusing the two natures of Jesus Christ—though it has been argued that it was Eutyches himself who was confused or muddled, rather than wilfully heretical. The condemnation played into the hands of Dioscorus, bishop of Alexandria since 444. He was eager to enter the fray on Eutyches' side, and thus to follow in the footsteps of his uncle *Cyril. Eutyches appealed to Dioscorus, who persuaded the emperor to call a council. This met at Ephesus in 449. It was meant to be a replay of the 431 *Council of Ephesus, with Flavian playing Nestorius to Dioscorus' Cyril. But there was one vital difference—this time the West, in the person of Leo, supported Constantinople instead of Alexandria. But the council was effectively controlled by Dioscorus, through the imperial officials. Leo's *Tome* was not allowed to be read. Eutyches was restored and the leading Antiochene bishops (including *Theodoret) were deposed. Flavian of Constantinople died a few days later of the rough treatment that he had received.

The deposed Antiochene bishops appealed to Leo, who was himself totally opposed to the outcome of the council. He gave it its historic name, the 'Robber Synod'. Leo protested, but in the East he was effectively powerless. Dioscorus had the ear of the emperor and the new bishop of Constantinople was his man. So things might have remained, but in July 450 the emperor fell off his horse and died. The new emperor, Marcian, leaned more to the Antiochene school and called the *Council of Chalcedon.

Leo's *Tome* draws together the Western teaching on Christology up to his time. His understanding of the person of Jesus Christ is based on his understanding of salvation. In order to save us, Jesus Christ needed to be both God and man. His humanity needed to be 'complete in what belongs to us', though without sin. It follows therefore that he has two natures: deity and humanity. Against Eutyches, Leo stressed that 'each nature retains its own properties without loss'.

Jesus hungered and yet fed the five thousand—the former was human, the latter divine. As man he wept for his friend Lazarus, as God he raised him from the dead. He is one person, but this must not be misunderstood in such a way as to blur the distinction between the natures—there must be no *tertium quid*. Leo placed less stress than Cyril on the unity of Jesus Christ, but it was not absent from his teaching. It was the Son of God, the second person of the Trinity, who was born of Mary. 'The impassible God did not disdain to become passible man.'

At the Council of Chalcedon, Leo's *Tome* was read and the bishops shouted, 'Peter has spoken through Leo. Thus Cyril taught. Leo and Cyril teach the same.' That statement has been contested ever since. One thing is for sure: Leo and Cyril did not teach the same in the sense that there is no difference between them. Whether or not they taught the same in the sense that it is possible to accept both without contradicting oneself is a matter for debate.

The only-begotten and eternal Son of the eternal Father was born of the Holy Spirit and the virgin Mary. This birth in time in no way detracts from, in no way adds to his divine and eternal birth [from the Father]. It is wholly concerned with the work of restoring man, who had been deceived [by the devil]—in order to overcome death and by its own power destroy the devil who had the power of death. For we could not have overcome the author of sin and death had not he, who could neither be contaminated by sin nor be detained by death, taken our nature and made it his own.
TOME 2

Leo is also famous for his teaching on the Roman papacy. The claims of Rome began to be heightened in the second half of the fourth century. Leo drew together the teaching of his predecessors and made of it a coherent whole—falling not far short of present-day papal claims. He saw the Pope as the 'unworthy heir' of Peter. In Roman law, the heir takes the place of the deceased. This means that the pope has, as heir of Peter, inherited all the authority given to Peter by Jesus Christ (Matthew 16:18–19). In a sense it is Peter himself who acts and speaks through the pope. This puts the pope on a different plane from all other bishops. He is far more than merely the first or chief bishop. They all derive their authority from the pope and he can remove them at will. The pope has the responsibility of governing the whole world-wide church.

Leo's claims were never accepted in the East. In the West they received a varying measure of acceptance throughout the Middle Ages. Leo saw the pope as the *unworthy* heir of Peter. The qualification is important. The pope's status is legal and does not depend on his personal holiness or merit. During the Middle Ages and later this distinction has often had to be invoked since the morality of many of the popes has been infamous rather than famous.

The blessed Peter, persevering in the strength of the rock which he has received, has not abandoned the helm of the church which he undertook ... Still today he more fully and effectually performs what has been entrusted to him and carries out every part of his duty and charge ... And so if anything is rightly done and rightly decreed by us ... it is of his work and merits whose power lives and whose authority prevails in his see ... [Peter] may be recognized and honoured in my humble person ... and his dignity is not lessened even in so unworthy an heir ... When therefore we utter our exhortations in your ears, holy brethren, believe that he is speaking whose representative we are.
SERMON 3: 3–4

Council of Chalcedon (451)

The Council of Chalcedon was called by the emperor Marcian to resolve the affair of

Eutyches, who had already been condemned by *Leo. The council met at Chalcedon (across the Bosphorus from Constantinople) in October 451. It came to be seen as the fourth of the general or ecumenical councils.

The council reinstated those Antiochenes condemned at the 'Robber Synod' of Ephesus in 449. Eutyches and Dioscorus of Alexandria were deposed. The creeds of the *Councils of Nicea and Constantinople, two of *Cyril's letters (one of which included the *Formula of Reunion)* and Leo's *Tome* were all read and approved. The bishops wished to stop there, but the emperor was determined to have a confession of faith to unite the empire. And so the Chalcedonian Definition was born.

The Definition quotes the Creeds of Nicea and Constantinople. These ought to have sufficed for the establishment of orthodoxy, but unfortunately the teaching of Nestorius and Eutyches meant that more was required. Two of Cyril's letters were received as a refutation of Nestorianism, and Leo's Tome was received as an antidote for Eutychianism. Then comes the key section:

[The Synod] opposes those who would rend the mystery of the incarnation into a duality of Sons [of which Nestorius was accused]; it expels from the priesthood those who dare to say that the Godhead of the Only-begotten is passible/capable of suffering [Arius or Eutyches?]; it resists those who imagine a mixture or confusion of the two natures of Christ [Eutyches]; it drives away those who fancy that the 'form of a servant' [i.e. humanity] which he took from us was of a heavenly or some other [non-human] substance [of which Apollinaris was falsely accused]; and it anathematizes those who imagine that the Lord had two natures before their union, but only one afterwards [Eutyches].

Following the holy fathers, we confess with one voice that the one and only Son, our Lord Jesus Christ, is perfect in Godhead and perfect in manhood, truly God and truly man, that
he has a rational soul and a body. He is of one substance [homoousios] with the Father as God, he is also of one substance [homoousios] with us as man. He is like us in all things except sin. He was begotten of his Father before the ages as God, but in these last days and for our salvation he was born of Mary the virgin, the theotokos, as man. This one and the same Christ, Son, Lord, Only-begotten is made known in two natures [which exist] without confusion, without change, without division, without separation. The distinction of the natures is in no way taken away by their union, but rather the distinctive properties of each nature are preserved. [Both natures] unite into one person and one hypostasis. They are not separated or divided into two persons but [they form] one and the same Son, Only-begotten, God, Word, Lord Jesus Christ, just as the prophets of old [have spoken] concerning him and as the Lord Jesus Christ himself has taught us and as the creed of the fathers has delivered to us.

A case can be made for seeing the Definition as primarily positive, as an exposition of the Creeds of Nicea and Constantinople. But the purpose of this exposition was the exclusion of heresy and it is more helpful to think of it primarily in these negative terms—as the safeguard against the four ancient heresies. Chalcedon does not lay down one normative Christology—it sets out the limits within which an orthodox Christology must remain. It is to be seen as a boundary fence rather than a straitjacket.

The Definition makes four points in opposition to the four ancient heresies: In Jesus Christ, true deity (against Arius) and full humanity (against Apollinaris) are indivisibly united in the one person (against Nestorius), without being confused (against Eutyches). Its teaching can be summarized in the phrase 'one person in two natures'. But what does this *mean?* What is the difference between 'person' and 'nature'? The two terms can best be thought of as the answers to two different questions: *Who* was Jesus Christ? The one person of God the Word, made flesh. *What* was he? Truly divine and truly human—two natures. To put it differently, there was in Jesus Christ only one 'I', only one 'subject' of all that he experienced. This one subject or person is God the Word—there is not someone else (another 'person') who was the human Jesus. The Word remained God, with no lessening of his deity or divine nature, and yet he also took everything that belongs to humanity or human nature.

The Definition draws together material from different traditions: Alexandrian (Cyril), Antiochene *(Formula of Reunion)*, Constantinopolitan (Flavian) and Western (*Tertullian and Leo). But the dominant hand was Western. It was at Roman insistence that the final text read *'in* two natures' rather than 'out of two natures' as the majority of Eastern bishops preferred. In the West the Definition was accepted at once. It is only recently, since *Schleiermacher, that it has been seriously questioned. In the East the story was totally different. The emperor intended this document to cement unity with the Eastern church. Its effect was more like dynamite than cement. Egypt and other areas have never accepted Chalcedon to this day.

A substantial portion of the Alexandrian party refused to accept Chalcedon. Attempts were made to conciliate them, culminating in the *Council of Constantinople in 553, which gave an Alexandrian interpretation of Chalcedon. But this did not satisfy the rebels. A further attempt was made to conciliate them by the introduction of the doctrine that Jesus Christ had only one will. This was opposed by *Maximus the Confessor and rejected at the *Council of Constantinople in 680/81. The teaching of the councils was drawn together by *John of Damascus. While the early debates, up to Chalcedon, are about vital issues substantially affecting the person of Jesus Christ, the later debates often give the impression of being merely disputes about words. Increasingly they become arguments about the interpretation of tradition and the use of formulas rather than the living Jesus Christ of the Gospels.

Apostles' Creed

There is an ancient legend, from the fourth century, that the Apostles' Creed was composed by the twelve apostles, each of whom wrote one clause. Not least of the objections to this theory is the fact that the creed does not naturally divide into twelve clauses! The legend was not questioned until the fifteenth century. In the sixteenth century it was generally abandoned.

The Apostles' Creed is the end-product of the gradual development of Western creeds. These all appear to have a common ancestor—the 'Old Roman Creed', which probably dates back to the end of the second century. Over the years new clauses were added and there were minor changes in wording. Today's version dates from the sixth or seventh century. Gradually it became *the* accepted version, being adopted at Rome sometime between 800 and 1100.

I believe in God the Father almighty, creator of heaven and earth;

And in Jesus Christ, his only Son, our Lord. He was conceived by the Holy Spirit, born from Mary the virgin, suffered under Pontius Pilate, was crucified, died, was buried and descended to the underworld. On the third day he rose again from the dead, ascended to heaven and sits on the right hand of God the Father almighty. From there he will come to judge the living and the dead.

I believe in the Holy Spirit, the holy catholic church, the communion of saints, the forgiveness of sins, the resurrection of the flesh and eternal life. Amen.

Most of the Apostles' Creed is ancient, though some of the clauses originate from the fourth or fifth centuries:

● 'He descended to the underworld' (*inferna* or 'lower regions'). This phrase did not enter Western creeds until late in the fourth century, but it has an earlier history in the East. It was linked with ideas of the 'harrowing of hell': Jesus Christ descended into hell to release his people and to triumph over the devil. This became a very popular theme in art.

● 'the communion of saints'. The first evidence for this clause in a Western creed is from the fifth century. It probably means 'fellowship with saints/holy persons'. In the fifth century it was used to defend the growing cult of the saints—the practice of venerating them and their relics (remains).

The Apostles' Creed has always enjoyed wide acceptance in the West—among most Protestant groups as well as among Roman Catholics. It has never been in general use in the Eastern Church, though it is treated with respect.

PART 2

The Eastern Tradition
FROM AD 500

After AD 70, the centre of gravity of Christianity lay in the Greek world. By the time of *Augustine the Latin West had come a long way, but had still not caught up with the East. The barbarian invasions, which led to the collapse of the Western empire in the fifth century, set the West back and it was not until the twelfth century that the West again began seriously to challenge the East for prominence.

Westerners think of the Middle Ages as coming between the early church and later recovery. It was not so in the East. The age of the Fathers was followed not by collapse but by the Byzantine Christian Empire, whose capital was at Byzantium (Constantinople). Empire and church alike were subject to the emperor. The greatest of these emperors was Justinian, who ruled from 527 to 565. In many ways his reign marks the high point of the Byzantine empire. Its decline was to begin in the following century, with the Muslim invasions. By the middle of the century, within a few years of the death of Muhammad in 632, Muslim armies had taken all of the Empire south and east of modern Turkey. Thereafter further advance was slow, but in 1453 Constantinople finally fell and became Istanbul. These conquests did not mean the end of the church in the occupied territories. Muslim rulers tolerated Christians, though as second-class citizens. The price for such toleration was the tacit agreement not to seek to convert Muslims. The Coptic Church in Egypt still numbers more than 10% of the population and is a significant force in Egyptian society. These losses were to some extent compensated for by the conversion of Russia to Orthodox Christianity in the tenth century.

The Eastern Church was preoccupied with controversy over the person of Jesus Christ for centuries after the *Council of Chalcedon. The council was never accepted in Egypt and in other areas in the East. This placed the emperors in a dilemma. They could seek reconciliation with the non-Chalcedonians by dropping Chalcedon—but the price was breach with Rome. Alternatively, they could maintain unity with the West by upholding Chalcedon—but at the price of a bitterly fragmented East. Both ways were tried, but neither was satisfactory. In the end, the Muslim invasions removed the dissenting areas from the empire and the problem was 'solved'. Eastern Orthodoxy held to Chalcedon, in union with the West, and the non-Chalcedonian churches went their own way—as they do to this day.

The Eastern Church became fiercely traditional. After the age of the Fathers, the overwhelming concern became the preservation of the orthodox tradition without the slightest variation. This applied both to dogma or belief and to liturgy or worship. This process began in the fifth century with the amassing of quotations from the Fathers in support of rival views of the person of Jesus Christ. The period of the Fathers was brought to a final conclusion by *John of Damascus, who drew together the patristic teaching into a systematic work.

By the beginning of the Middle Ages, the final authority in the Western Church had become the pope. Rome was the only 'apostolic see' in the West—i.e. the only church which could claim to have been founded by an apostle. In the East there were many such, preventing the domination of any one bishop. The leading bishops (of Constantinople, Alexandria, Antioch and Jerusalem) came to be known as 'patriarchs'. Also, because of the political stability of the East and its more absolutist traditions of rulership, the emperors always remained firmly in control of the Eastern Church. The Scriptures were to be understood according to the tradition of the Fathers and the consensus of the Fathers was found especially in the councils. For the Eastern Orthodox Church, the supreme authority in the church lies with the general or ecumenical (world-wide) councils, which can only be called by an emperor. The Orthodox Church recognizes only seven such councils, the councils of the 'undivided' church. (That means undivided from Rome, not undivided from Egypt and the other non-Chalcedonian areas.) These are *Nicea (325), *Constantinople (381), *Ephesus (431), *Chalcedon (451), *Constantinople (553), *Constantinople (680/81), *Nicea (787).

East and West were divided by language from the third century, when the Western Church became Latin-speaking. In the fourth century there was serious division during the controversies over the doctrine of the Trinity, but this was largely healed by the Eastern settlement at the Council of Constantinople in 381. But in the fifth century, with the collapse of the Western Empire, the political unity between East and West was destroyed and the two churches began to drift apart. This was only gradual—the Eastern emperors continued to have an interest in Rome and the popes were concerned for union with the Eastern Church, with civilization.

But in the eleventh century things changed at Rome. There was a new 'reform papacy' whose interests lay more with Northern and Western Europe than with the East. This new approach led to a hardening of attitudes towards the East—the introduction of the word *filioque* ('and the Son') into the Nicene Creed, for example. The result was mutual excommunications, in 1054. But this was not the end of the story. There were attempts at reconciliation, especially in the fourteenth and fifteenth centuries as Constantinople faced final capitulation to the Muslims. But no lasting reconciliation was possible as Rome was adamant about papal authority, which the East would never accept.

Dionysius the Areopagite

WHAT GOD IS NOT

Dionysius the Areopagite was one of Paul's converts at Athens (Acts 17:34). From the sixth century, a number of major writings circulated under his name. Their author appears to have been a Syrian monk, writing in about 500. His works were immensely influential, in part because of their own value, in part because of their supposed author. Their authenticity was not seriously questioned until the fifteenth century.

Four major works of 'Dionysius' survive:

● *Divine Names* discusses the biblical names for God and his nature.

● *Mystical Theology* is about the mystical union of the soul with God.

● *Heavenly Hierarchy* discusses the nature of angels, who are divided into a hierarchy of nine choirs: Seraphim, Cherubim and Thrones; Dominations, Virtues and Powers; Principalities, Archangels and Angels.

● *Ecclesiastical Hierarchy* portrays the church as the image of the heavenly world and, like it, as a hierarchy. There are three orders of ministry (bishop, priest, deacon) and three lower levels (monk, layman, catechumen). There are also three sacraments (baptism, eucharist, confirmation) and three stages to God, or three 'ways' of the spiritual life (purification, enlightenment, union).

Dionysius is not easy to read and a recent translator has stated that he 'tortured language to express the truth'. His thought is thoroughly permeated by Neo-Platonism. (He drew heavily on the Neo-Platonist philosopher Proclus, who died in 485.) Some have thought that he taught Neo-Platonism with a thin Christian veneer; others that he successfully taught Christian truth in a Neo-Platonist setting, and yet others that his teaching is an unsuccessful juxtaposition of Christian and Neo-Platonist elements. He emphasizes, with Neo-Platonism, God's utter transcendence and unity. God is beyond anything that we can understand—beyond existence, essence or personality. God is 'the Universal Cause of existence while Itself not existing, for It is beyond all Being' (*Divine Names 1.1*). This utter transcendence of God implies the *via negativa* (negative way) or 'apophatic' approach to theology. We talk about God not by saying what he *is* (the positive or 'cathaphatic' way) but by saying what he is *not*.

[God] is greater than all reason and all knowledge and has Its firm abode altogether beyond Mind and Being ... and cannot be reached by any perception, imagination, conjecture, name, discourse, apprehension or understanding ... It is impossible to describe or to conceive in Its ultimate nature ... [Mystics] being deified and united, through the ceasing of their natural activities, unto the Light which surpasses Deity, can find no more fitting method to celebrate Its praises than to deny It every manner of attribute.

DIVINE NAMES 1:5

There is some truth in this approach. Normally we talk of God in positive terms (e.g. as Father or as Judge) but we need to recognize that all such terms are analogies. When we call God Father or Judge, we are comparing him with human fathers or judges. But to say this is at once to recognize that all such statements need to be qualified. God is Father, but he transcends human fatherhood. There is room for the negative way, in balance with the positive way. The trouble with Dionysius is that the pendulum has swung too far in one direction.

The negative way is not just a way of 'doing theology'. It is, for Dionysius, a way of drawing near to God and entering into union with him. Dionysius 'baptized' Neo-Platonist mysticism—that is the Neo-Platonist way of rising to communion and union with 'the One' through the way of negation. The mystic attains union with God and is 'deified' by rising above all perception of the senses and reasoning of the mind:

I counsel that, in the earnest exercise of mystic contemplation, you leave the senses and the activities of the intellect and all that the senses or the intellect can perceive, and all in this world of nothingness or in that world of being. Having laid your understanding to rest, strain as far as you can towards a union with Him whom neither being nor understanding can contain. For, by the ceaseless and absolute renunciation of yourself and all things, you shall in purity cast all things aside and be released from them all. So you shall be led upwards to the Ray of that divine Darkness which surpasses all existence.

MYSTICAL THEOLOGY I

*Maximus the Confessor wrote commentaries on Dionysius' works, doctoring up his orthodoxy and ensuring his influence in the East. His influence in the West was also considerable. *John Scotus Erigena wrote a Latin translation of his works in about 850. Through this, Dionysius influenced *Thomas Aquinas and much medieval mysticism (e.g. *The Cloud of Unknowing*).

Council of Constantinople (553)

The *Council of Chalcedon led to bitter division in the East. The Antiochene school, who were in the minority, supported Chalcedon. A large number of Alexandrians opposed Chalcedon and held to *Cyril's formula 'the one incarnate nature of the Word'. They were therefore called Monophysites (from the Greek for 'sole nature'). They rejected Chalcedon with its doctrine of 'two natures'. In between these two groups was another, sometimes called the 'neo-Alexandrians'. These were enthusiastic Alexandrian supporters of Cyril's teaching who were happy to accept Chalcedon. They saw it as a protection against possible misinterpretation of Cyril. They argued that Chalcedon should be accepted in the same way that Cyril himself accepted the *Formula of Reunion*. They held to Chalcedon, but interpreted it in a strongly Cyrilline way.

The Monophysites controlled Egypt and other areas of the East. They were too powerful to be ignored or suppressed. Their objections to Chalcedon fell into two classes. *First*, they complained that certain Alexandrian/Cyrilline teaching was missing from Chalcedon: the 'one incarnate nature' formula, the term 'hypostatic union' and the idea that Christ was 'one *out* of two natures'. All of these terms were found in Cyril. *Secondly*, they objected to passages in Chalcedon which, they believed, divided Jesus Christ into two: the phrase '*in* two natures' and several passages in *Leo's Tome*.

The Eastern emperors struggled to resolve the controversy. At first Chalcedon was upheld. Then in 482 the emperor Zeno issued a *Henotikon*, which proclaimed the only criteria for orthodoxy to be the Nicene Creed and Cyril's *Twelve Anathemas*. Those who had taught otherwise, 'whether at Chalcedon or in any other synod whatever', were anathematized. This united the East— but at the price of schism from the West. Zeno's successor, Anastasius, went further and openly rejected Chalcedon. But when he died, his successors, Justin and Justinian, opted for Chalcedon and peace with Rome.

In 553 Justinian called the Council of Constantinople, the fifth of the ecumenical councils. It sought to appease the Monophysites by presenting a Cyrilline interpretation of Chalcedon. There are three main parts to the council's work:

● There had been a controversy from the 530s over certain aspects of *Origen's teaching. In 543 Justinian issued an edict against the Origenists. In 553 the council ratified this condemnation by issuing fifteen anathemas against the teaching of Origen and Evagrius, one of his more extreme disciples.

● In 544, at Alexandrian insistence, the emperor had also issued an edict against the 'Three Chapters': that is against the Antiochene theologian Theodore of Mopsuestia (died 428, probably a teacher of

Nestorius) and against the early anti-Cyrilline writings of two other Antiochene theologians, *Theodoret and Ibas. It was only the early works of Theodoret and Ibas which were condemned—they themselves had been restored to office at Chalcedon. The last three of the fourteen anathemas of the 553 council reaffirmed the condemnation of the 'Three Chapters'.

● Most importantly, the council showed that Chalcedon was to be understood in an Alexandrian way. The bishops confess 'that we receive the four holy synods, that is the Nicene, the Constantinopolitan, the first of Ephesus and that of Chalcedon, and we have taught and do teach all that they defined respecting the one faith'. They also issued fourteen anathemas. These reject a Nestorian interpretation of Chalcedon. The aim was to placate Monophysite fears that Chalcedon had opened the door to Nestorianism. The anathemas also show that the Cyrilline terms missing from Chalcedon (such as 'hypostatic union') were acceptable as long as they were not understood to imply a mixture or confusion of the two natures. Finally, an Alexandrian formula popular with the Monophysites was approved: one of the Trinity was crucified in the flesh.

If anyone using the expression 'in two natures' ... shall make use of the number [two] to divide the natures or to make of them persons properly so called, let him be anathema.
ANATHEMA 7

If anyone uses the expression 'out of two natures' ... or the expression 'the one incarnate nature of God the Word' and shall not understand these expressions as the holy fathers have taught ... but shall try to introduce one nature or substance of the Godhead and manhood of Christ, let him be anathema. For in teaching that the only-begotten Word was united hypostatically [to humanity] we do not mean to say that there was a mutual confusion of natures.
ANATHEMA 8

If anyone does not confess that our Lord Jesus Christ who was crucified in the flesh is true God and the Lord of Glory and one of the Holy Trinity, let him be anathema.
ANATHEMA 10

Despite these concessions, the Monophysites were not reconciled to Chalcedon. The tragedy is that the moderates on each side recognized that the others were orthodox. The division was not so much about the substance of the faith as about the acceptability of certain terms, and about the orthodoxy of Chalcedon.

Maximus the Confessor
FATHER OF BYZANTINE THEOLOGY

Maximus was born in about 580. He became chief secretary to the emperor at Constantinople. But in about 614 he renounced his secular career and became a monk. In 626 he fled from a Persian invasion to North Africa. At this time, Eastern policy was to teach that Jesus Christ had only one will, in the hope of conciliating the Monophysites. Maximus opposed this, being a firm believer in the two wills, human and divine, of Jesus Christ. In 645, at Carthage, he engaged the exiled patriarch of Constantinople, Pyrrhus, in a debate over this question. Maximus was deemed to have won the debate and successfully upheld the two wills of Jesus Christ. He helped to focus attention in the West upon this issue.

He went to Rome in 649 where he took a leading part in a synod which proclaimed the doctrine of two wills. When Pope Martin was exiled as a result of this synod, Maximus was also captured and brought back to Constantinople in 653. Pressure was brought on him to accept the doctrine of one will, but he refused and was exiled. He was again brought back to Constantinople in 661 and more pressure was brought to bear upon him. It is said that his tongue and right hand were cut off. He was again sent into exile where he died in 662. He is called 'the Confessor' because he suffered for the truth.

His beliefs triumphed at the *Council of Constantinople in 680–81.

Maximus was the most significant Orthodox theologian of the seventh century. Indeed, he has been called 'the real father of Byzantine theology'. He wrote some ninety works on a wide range of topics, including influential commentaries on *Dionysius the Areopagite. He was the major theological opponent of the doctrine of one will. He argued that unless Jesus Christ had a human will he was not truly human. He also argued that as the persons of the Trinity have a common will because they share a common nature, so Jesus Christ has two wills because he has two natures.

Christ was God by nature and made use of a will which was naturally divine and paternal, for he had but one will with his Father. He was also man by nature and made use of a naturally human will, which was in no way opposed to the Father's will.

THEOLOGICAL AND POLEMICAL WORKS: SHORT NOTE

If anyone does not confess, in accordance with the holy fathers, that exactly and truthfully the two wills of the one and same Christ our God, divine and human, are continuously united and that it follows that he is [the author] of our salvation through each of his natures, voluntarily and naturally, let him be condemned.

CANON 10 OF LATERAN COUNCIL OF 649, AT WHICH MAXIMUS PLAYED A LEADING ROLE

Maximus is also renowned as a mystical teacher. He drew together the earlier teaching of Evagrius (a fourth-century disciple of *Origen) and *Dionysius the Areopagite, thus curbing some of the imbalance of each of them. The goal of the life of prayer is the vision of God. Here Maximus anticipates the distinction, later made by *Gregory Palamas, between God's essence and his energies.

We know God not in his essence but by the magnificence of his creation and the action of his providence, which present to us, as in a mirror, the reflection of his goodness, his wisdom and his infinite powers.

CENTURIES ON CHARITY 1:96

God, and so also the divine, is comprehensible from a certain point of view, incomprehensible from others. Comprehensible in the contemplation of his attributes, incomprehensible in the contemplation of his essence.

CENTURIES ON CHARITY 4:7

The goal for the Christian is deification. 'While remaining in his soul and body entirely man by nature, he becomes in his soul and body entirely god by grace.'

AMBIGUITIES

Council of Constantinople (680–81)

The Monophysites were not appeased by the *Council of Constantinople in 553. Further attempts were made to conciliate them. Sergius, patriarch of Constantinople, proposed the formula, taken from the moderate Monophysite Severus of Antioch, that Christ had one 'theandric' (divine/human) energy, by which he performed both divine and human acts. On the basis of this formula, Constantinople was reunited with Egypt, but objections came from the patriarch of Jerusalem. Sergius then proposed another formula: that Jesus Christ had only one will. Pope Honorius of Rome agreed and in 638 he and Sergius jointly published an *Exposition of the Faith*. This outlawed debate about one energy or two. Instead it proclaimed 'the one will of our Lord Jesus Christ', and maintained that not even Nestorius would have dared to say that Jesus Christ had two wills. But within a few years another pope, John IV, was to condemn the view that Jesus Christ had only one will (called Monotheletism, from the Greek for 'sole will'). It was also opposed by *Maximus the Confessor. In 649 Pope Martin called a synod at Rome which proclaimed that Jesus Christ had two wills, but he was exiled for his pains. Thereafter Roman opposition to Monotheletism was more muted, until the time of Pope Agatho (678–81). He managed to persuade the Eastern Emperor to call another council at Constantinople, the sixth ecumenical council.

The council met from 680 to 681. Pope Agatho had written a letter to the council, intended to parallel *Leo's *Tome*. This was read and approved by the council. Agatho claimed in his letter that the Roman Church 'has never erred from the path of the apostolic tradition', but this claim was not to be unopposed. Rome had to accept the condemnation of Pope Honorius as a heretic by the council. 'We define that there shall be expelled from the holy church of God and anathematized Honorius, who was once pope of Old Rome.' This only goes to prove that if you want to be infallible you cannot be too careful about what you say.

The council also produced a *Definition of Faith*. This stated that the council 'has piously given its full assent to the five holy and ecumenical synods'. After quoting the *Chalcedonian Definition in full, it proceeds:

We likewise declare that in [Jesus Christ] are two natural wills and two natural operations, without division, without change, without separation, without confusion, according to the teaching of the holy fathers. These two natural wills are not contrary to one another (God forbid!) as the impious heretics assert, but his human will follows his divine and omnipotent will— not resisting or reluctant but subject to it ... We believe our Lord Jesus Christ to be one of the Trinity and our true God, even after the incarnation. We say that his two natures shine forth in his one hypostasis, in which he both performed miracles and endured sufferings through the whole course of the incarnation. This was not merely in appearance but in reality, because of the difference of nature which must be recognized in the same one hypostasis. Though joined together, yet each nature wills and does the things proper to it, and that without division and without confusion. Therefore we confess two wills and two operations, combining with each other for the salvation of the human race.

Three main arguments were put forward in support of the doctrine of two wills:

● Pope Agatho appealed to a number of passages of Scripture. But these all contrasted the will of Jesus with the will of his Father—e.g. 'I seek not my own will but the will of him who sent me' (John 5:30). These passages do not strictly support the idea of two wills in Jesus Christ.

● Agatho also argued that the doctrine of two natures must imply two wills. Those who hold that Christ had one will 'must needs say that this will is either human or divine or else composite from both, mixed and confused, or ... that Christ has one will and one operation, proceeding from his one composite nature'. Any of these options would be contrary to the teaching of Chalcedon that the distinctive properties of each nature are preserved. There can be little doubt that the doctrine of two wills is the inevitable consequence of Chalcedon's two natures.

● It was argued that without a human will Jesus would have had an incomplete human nature and would not have been truly man. Without a human will there would be no human obedience or virtue. Jesus would then cease to be our pattern and example. If he had no human will, we could not say that he 'has been tempted in every way, just as we are' (Hebrews 4:15). This argument, which echoes the argument used by the *Cappadocian Fathers against Apollinaris' denial of Jesus' human soul, is the most powerful.

The third Council of Constantinople marks the end of the early development of teaching on the person of Jesus Christ and the outworking of the implications of the Chalcedonian Definition. It was the end of the attempt to conciliate the Monophysites in the East—which was no longer a pressing need now that they had been removed from the Byzantine Empire by the Muslim invasions.

John of Damascus
LAST OF THE GREEK FATHERS

John Mansour was born in the third quarter of the seventh century, at Damascus. Syria was by then under Muslim rule and John followed his father in working for the caliph. He later left this work and became a monk. He died in the middle of the eighth century.

John is often called the last of the Greek Fathers. His main achievement was to gather together the earlier teaching of the Fathers into a systematic manual. He himself saw his aim in these terms:

Like a bee I shall gather all that conforms to the truth, even deriving help from the writings of our enemies ... I am not offering you my own conclusions, but those which were laboriously arrived at by the most eminent theologians, while I have merely collected them and summarized them, as far as was possible, into one treatise.
DIALECTIC, PROLOGUE

This comes at the beginning of his most famous work, his *Fount of Knowledge*, which is divided into three parts:

● *Dialectic:* a discussion of philosophical terms and concepts, especially those used in formulating the doctrines of the Trinity and the person of Jesus Christ.

● *Heresies in Epitome:* a brief summary of 103 heresies, drawing heavily on the earlier works of Epiphanius (died 403) and *Theodoret.

● *Exact Exposition of the Orthodox Faith:* a systematic summary of the teaching of the Greek Fathers in 100 chapters (later divided into four books). This concentrates especially on the doctrines of the Trinity and the person of Jesus Christ. On the Trinity, he expounds the teaching of the *Cappadocian

Fathers, supplemented by an important seventh-century work, *The Holy Trinity*, falsely attributed to *Cyril. On the person of Jesus Christ he expounds the teaching of the *Council of Chalcedon, supplemented by *Maximus the Confessor.

Since Christ has two natures, we hold that he also has two natural wills and two natural energies. But since his two natures have one hypostasis, we hold that it is one and the same person who wills and energizes naturally in both natures ... and moreover that he wills and energizes without separation but a united whole. For he wills and energizes in either form [nature] in close communion with the other. For things that have the same essence also have the same will and energy, while things that are different in essence are different in will and energy.
EXACT EXPOSITION OF THE ORTHODOX FAITH 3:14

Such arguments have some value in clarifying our understanding of Jesus Christ and eliminating wrong ideas about him. But there is a danger that this sort of discussion will be done in isolation from the figure of Jesus presented to us in the Gospels and become abstract and irrelevant. Indeed the charge has been made that 'practically the whole of Byzantine religion could have been built without the historical Christ of the Gospels'. While this is doubtless an exaggeration, it does point to the danger inherent in such intricate enquiry.

John was also involved in the controversy over icons or images. He opposed the iconoclasts (destroyers of images), writing three *Orations in Defence of Sacred Images*. He was anathematized at the iconoclast Council of Hieria in 754, but his views prevailed at the *Council of Nicea in 787.

Concerning this business of images, we must search for the intention of those who make them. If it is really and truly for the glory of God and of his saints, to promote virtue, the avoidance of evil,

*and the salvation of souls, then accept
them with due honour as images,
remembrances, likenesses and books for
the illiterate. Embrace them with the
eyes, the lips, the heart; bow down
before them; love them, for they are
likenesses of God incarnate, of his
mother and of the communion of saints.*
ORATIONS IN DEFENCE OF THE SACRED IMAGES 3:10

Council of Nicea (787)

After the conclusion of the debates over the
person of Jesus Christ, the Eastern Church
was torn for more than a hundred years by
controversy over icons. Icons are pictures of
Jesus Christ and the saints. These had
become widespread in the Orthodox Church
and they were venerated: that is, people
would bow down before them, kiss them and
pray to them. In the eighth century there was
a reaction against the icons by the
iconoclasts (destroyers of icons). These were
opposed by the iconodules (worshippers of
icons). The first steps against the icons were
taken in 719/20 by a Muslim ruler, Islam
being completely opposed to such images. A
few years later the cause was taken up by
the Byzantine emperor Leo III, who ordered
the destruction of all icons. This provoked
fierce opposition. The battle raged for many
years, with changes of fortune according to
the views of successive emperors or
empresses. In 754 a council was held at
Hieria which upheld the iconoclast position.
Some years later an iconodule Council of
Nicea was held, in 787. This came to be seen
as the seventh ecumenical council. There
were still more changes of direction to come,
but finally in 843 the iconodules triumphed.
Their final victory is still celebrated on the
first Sunday in Lent as the 'triumph of
Orthodoxy'.

A variety of arguments were used in
this debate:

● Is the worship of icons idolatry? To
the iconoclasts it was. They invoked the
second commandment: 'You shall not make
for yourself an idol in the form of anything
in heaven above or on the earth beneath or in
the waters below. You shall not bow down to
them or worship them' (Exodus 20: 4–5). The
iconodules maintained that the worship of
icons was not idolatry because, unlike pagan
worship, it was not the worship of *false* gods.
(This and other iconodule arguments were
put forward by *John of Damascus, among
others.) This raises an important question:
does the Bible prohibit the worship of idols
only because they represent *false* gods, or is
it also illegitimate to worship the true God
this way? The iconodules invoked the
principle that 'honour paid to the image
passes on to the original'. But this was one of
the arguments used by pagan idolaters and
rejected by the early Fathers, such as
*Augustine: '[Those pagans] seem to
themselves to have a purer religion who say,
"I worship neither an idol nor a devil, but in
the bodily image I behold an emblem of that
which I am bound to worship." ... They
presume to reply that they worship not the
bodies themselves but the deities who
preside over the government of them'
(*Expositions on Psalm 113*).

● What was the earliest Christian
practice? There is little doubt that until the
fourth century the Christian church was
predominantly opposed to any direct
representation of God or Jesus Christ. In the
fourth and fifth centuries a change took
place. As paganism declined as a rival
religion, so Christians began to adopt pagan
practices and arguments concerning images.
The Neo-Platonist theory of images was
adopted—they are the bottom rung of an
ascending ladder which leads at the top to
the direct contemplation of God himself. If
there is any danger in images it is not that
they lead to idolatry (as in the Old
Testament) but that they might distract one
from ascending higher up the ladder. The
iconodules made up for the lack of early
tradition on their side by appealing to the
idea of unwritten tradition, and by using (in
good faith) later forgeries, such as
*'Dionysius the Areopagite'.

● What is best for simple folk? The
iconodules saw icons as the books of the
unlearned, as the way to bring spiritual
realities home to them. The iconoclasts

retorted that the simple could not distinguish between worship offered to an icon and worship offered to God himself, or between the veneration due to a saint and the adoration due to God alone. Icons would therefore lead the simple astray into idolatry.

● Both sides sought to accuse the other of heresy concerning the person of Jesus Christ, although neither side questioned the truth of the first six councils. (After more than two hundred years of intense controversy on this doctrine it was natural that any other debate should be referred to it and seen in terms of the doctrine of Jesus Christ.) The iconodules claimed that the incarnation is the warrant for visible representations of God—in Jesus Christ the invisible God became visible man. They accused the iconoclasts of docetism— of not taking seriously the humanity of Jesus Christ. They also accused them of Manicheism (the denial of the goodness of physical creation), since they would not allow material representations of Jesus Christ. The debate was polarized in that neither side allowed the possibility that there could be representations of Jesus Christ without these being worshipped (as with a modern visual aid).

● Other beliefs became involved in the controversy. The iconoclasts allowed a greater role to the emperor in the church, though this was only a difference in degree. The attack on icons was linked in some cases to an attack on the cult of the saints—the veneration of the saints and of their relics. These practices grew in the church at the same time as the icons, in the fourth and fifth centuries, when there was a large influx of pagans into the church. Relics, like icons, were seen as manifestations of God's presence through which he worked in a special way.

The only permissible figure of the humanity of Christ is bread and wine in the holy Supper. This and no other form, this and no other type, has he chosen to represent his incarnation. Bread he ordered to be brought, but not

a representation of the human form, so that idolatry might not arise ... Christianity has rejected the whole of paganism: not merely pagan sacrifices but also the pagan worship of images. Supported by the holy Scriptures and the Fathers, we declare unanimously in the name of the holy Trinity that every likeness which is made out of any material and colour whatever by the evil art of painters shall be rejected and removed and cursed out of the Christian church.

DEFINITION OF THE COUNCIL OF HIERIA, 754

Following the royal pathway and the divinely inspired authority of our holy fathers and the traditions of the Catholic Church, we define with all certitude and accuracy that, just like the figure of the precious and life-giving cross, the venerable and holy images (in painting, mosaic and of other fit materials) are to be set up in the holy churches of God, on the sacred vessels, on the vestments, on walls and in pictures, in houses and by the roadside. This means images of our Lord, God and Saviour, Jesus Christ, of our undefiled Lady, the Theotokos, of the honourable angels and of all saints and holy men. For the more men see them in artistic representation, the more readily they will be aroused to remember the originals and to long after them. Images should receive due salutation and honourable reverence, but not the true worship of faith which is due to the divine nature alone. In accordance with ancient pious custom, incense and lights may be offered to images, as they are to the figure of the precious and life-giving cross, to the book of the Gospels and to other holy objects. For the honour paid to the image passes on to its original and he who reveres the image reveres in it the person represented.

DEFINITION OF THE COUNCIL OF NICEA, 787

The seventh general council falls into a different category to the first six. These were serious attempts to come to terms with the central biblical doctrines about God and Jesus Christ. The seventh, by contrast, is an attempt to justify a relatively late practice which at best has no biblical warrant and at worst is blatantly unbiblical. Protestantism in general has tended to approve the first four councils (*Nicea to *Chalcedon) and, to a lesser extent, the next two (both at *Constantinople), but to reject the seventh.

Simeon the New Theologian
PERSONAL SPIRITUAL EXPERIENCE

Simeon was born of noble parents in Asia Minor, in 949. At the age of fourteen he became a disciple of Simeon the Studite, a leading spiritual teacher. After a period in secular employment on Simeon's advice, he joined him in the Studion monastery at Constantinople. Soon after he left there to join the St Mamos monastery, remaining Simeon's disciple. He was abbot of St Mamos from 980 to his retirement in 1005. During this time he was involved in controversy—with his own monks, who found his regime too strict, and later with bishop Stephen of Nicomedia, the official court theologian. The controversy with Stephen resulted in a period of exile, from 1009. Simeon died, restored to favour, in 1022.

Simeon has been called 'the most outstanding of Byzantine medieval mystics'. He has been given the title 'New Theologian'. Previously John the apostle and Gregory of Nazianzus (one of the *Cappadocian Fathers) were called 'theologian' for their teaching on God. Simeon's teaching was considered worthy of comparison with theirs. He was the first systematic exponent of the technique of inner prayer. He was also unique among medieval Orthodox mystics in speaking freely of his own personal spiritual experiences.

So I entered the place where I usually prayed and, mindful of the words of the holy man [Simeon the Studite] I began to say 'Holy God'. At once I was so greatly moved to tears and loving desire for God that I would be unable to describe in words the joy and delight I then felt. I fell prostrate on the ground, and at once I saw, and behold, a great light was immaterially shining on me and seized hold of my whole mind and soul, so that I was struck with amazement at the unexpected marvel and I was, as it were, in ecstasy. 'Whether I was in the body or outside the body' [2 Corinthians 12:2], I conversed with this light. The light itself knows it; it scattered whatever mist there was in my soul and cast out every earthly care. It expelled from me all material denseness and bodily heaviness that made my members sluggish and numb ... There was poured into my soul in unutterable fashion a great spiritual joy and perception and a sweetness surpassing every taste of visible objects, together with a freedom and forgetfulness of all thoughts pertaining to this life. In a marvellous way there was granted to me and revealed to me the manner of the departure from this present life. Thus all the perceptions of my mind and my soul were wholly concentrated on the ineffable joy of that light.

CATECHETICAL DISCOURSES 16:3

His controversy with Stephen involved the conflict between two different approaches. Stephen's approach to theology was philosophical and abstract—similar to the approach of Western Scholastic theology. Simeon's approach was monastic and spiritual—he placed a great stress on the need to experience that about which one talks. The conflict between Simeon and Stephen has been compared to that between *Bernard and *Abelard in the West—with the important difference that in the East it was the mystic, Simeon, who won the ultimate victory.

The controversy with Stephen was also a conflict between the 'institutional' and the 'charismatic' approaches. Simeon was not opposed to the institutional authorities of the church and did not deny the importance of the sacraments. But at the same time he maintained that sins could be confessed to unordained monks, and he taught that baptism is of no value unless we go on to bear fruit in the form of a holy life. Simeon was opposed to formalism, to a merely nominal Christianity which did not involve a changed life. He taught the need for a 'baptism in the Holy Spirit' to follow water baptism. This involves repentance and conversion to Jesus Christ, awareness of him as Lord and Saviour. It means a personal experience of God for oneself, understood in terms of deification. It means a life of obedience.

Is not Christ's name spoken everywhere—in cities, in villages, in monasteries, on the mountains? Search, if you will, and examine carefully whether men keep his commandments. Truly, among thousands and tens of thousands you will find scarcely one who is a Christian in word and deed.
CATECHETICAL DISCOURSES 22:8

In his mystical teaching Simeon follows the tradition of *Dionysius the Areopagite and *Maximus the Confessor. He portrayed the vision of God as the vision of the divine light, uncreated and invisible. This experience is not just for an elite, it is not even confined to monks who can devote all their time to it—it is for *all* Christians.

God is light and those whom he makes worthy to see him, see him as light; those who receive him, receive him as light. For the light of his glory goes before his face and it is impossible that he should appear otherwise than as light. Those who have not seen this light have not seen God: for God is light. Those who have not received this light have not yet received grace, for in receiving grace one receives the divine light and God himself.
SERMON 79:2

Gregory Palamas
GOD KNOWN IN SILENCE

Gregory was born at the end of the thirteenth century. In 1318 he went to Mt Athos, the centre of Orthodox monasticism, to become a monk. He made rapid progress in the life of prayer, being taught by the Hesychasts. He left Mt Athos for a time because of Turkish raids, but returned. In the 1330s he became embroiled in controversy with Barlaam, an Orthodox monk from southern Italy who had attacked Hesychasm.

Gregory is remembered as the chief theological exponent of Hesychasm. The word derives from the Greek *hesychia* (quiet, silence, rest). Hesychasm was a tradition of spirituality going back to the early church, but attaining precise form only shortly before the time of Gregory. The aim was to attain victory over the passions, and thus inner tranquillity (*hesychia*), from which one could proceed to the contemplation of God. There was a stress on silent meditation and a particular physical posture was recommended as an aid to the concentration: the chin rested on the chest and the eyes were fixed on the navel, the place of the heart. Breathing was carefully regulated and a simple prayer was recited, the Jesus Prayer: 'Lord Jesus Christ, Son of God, have mercy on me'. It does not show that the Hesychasts saw prayer purely as a mechanical technique. This method was recommended only as an aid, as a preparation for further progress. The goal was the vision of the divine light and union with God. Barlaam attacked Gregory on a number of grounds. He ridiculed the Hesychast method of prayer, especially the physical posture. He also took the negative way of *Dionysius the Areopagite to mean that God cannot be known *directly*, but only indirectly, through created means. Barlaam's relation to Gregory was similar to that of Stephen to *Simeon the New Theologian, in that Barlaam wanted to allow philosophy a significant and independent role in theology, while Gregory would not allow this. Barlaam's attitude here had affinities with some Western approaches, and at the end of the controversy he became a Roman Catholic.

Gregory responded to Barlaam in his *Triads in Defence of the Holy Hesychasts*. He argued that God can be known directly. But how is this possible since 'apophatic' theology, the negative way, says that God surpasses all knowledge? Gregory acknowledged a paradox here. The divine nature is in one sense communicable, in another sense incommunicable. We participate in God's nature, yet he remains inaccessible. Gregory was not prepared to let negative theology have the last word.

The mark made on the mind by the divine and mysterious signs of the Spirit is very different from apophatic theology ... theology is as far from the vision of God in light, and as distinct from intimate conversation with God, as knowledge is different from possession.
TRIADS 1: 3: 42

While the mind cannot penetrate to God, he can be known in experience—which for Gregory, as for Simeon the New Theologian, is an integral part of theology. This experience is not just for the mystic. Again following Simeon, Gregory states that *all* Christians participate in God's life—through the sacraments and through prayer. This participation is a true knowledge of God.

But how is this knowledge of God possible if God is unknowable? Gregory resolves this dilemma by use of a traditional distinction, which goes back to the *Cappadocian Fathers. God is inaccessible in his essence, but not in his *energies*. We cannot know or participate in his essence, his innermost being, but we can participate in his energies, his activity towards us, his grace.

Since one can participate in God and since the super-essential essence of God is absolutely above participation, there exists something between the essence (which cannot be participated in) and those who participate, to make it possible for them to participate in God ... He makes himself present to be all things by his manifestations and by his creative and providential energies. In one word, we must seek a God in whom we can participate in one way or another, so that by participating each of us, in the manner proper to each and by the analogy of participation, may receive being, life and deification.
TRIADS 3: 2: 24

We know God in particular through the vision of the divine, uncreated light. It is this light that was seen by the apostles at the transfiguration of Jesus (Mark 9:2–8). The mystic sees this divine light—not a created light but the uncreated light of God himself. Thus he sees not the essence but the energies of God.

Gregory was accused of postulating two Gods by his distinction between God's essence and his energies. In fact he saw them as two different modes of God's existence—inside and outside his nature. He was called a heretic by Barlaam and others. He responded by winning the support of a synod of monks on Mount Athos. Several synods at Constantinople in 1341 rejected Barlaam's accusations, but later that year there was a coup which changed the political situation. For some years Gregory was out of favour. He was condemned at further synods and even excommunicated in 1344. But in 1347 there was a new emperor who favoured Gregory. He was appointed bishop of Thessalonica. In 1351 a council was called at Constantinople which first cleared Gregory of all charges against him then produced a Tome, expounding Gregory's leading ideas. This was not an ecumenical council, but its decisions were, in the course of the fourteenth century, accepted by all the Eastern Orthodox churches. Gregory died in 1359 and in 1368 he was canonized.

It has been said that Gregory gave a theological rigour to the mystical experiences of Simeon the New Theologian. He integrated Hesychasm into Orthodox Theology as a whole. But the Western Church did not accept Gregory's teaching and it has become a further source of division between East and West.

Confession of Dositheus (1672)

Cyril Lucaris (1572–1638) was a Greek Orthodox theologian who became patriarch of Alexandria in 1602 and of Constantinople in 1620/21. His views moved towards Protestantism and, in particular, Calvinism. In 1629 he produced an *Eastern Confession of the Christian Faith* in eighteen chapters, in which he blended Eastern Orthodoxy with a mild Calvinism. On the doctrines of the Trinity and the person of Jesus Christ he kept to the Orthodox dogmas. But he took advantage of the silence of official Orthodox pronouncements to introduce leading Protestant doctrines.

● The Bible is the infallible Word of God. 'We believe the authority of the Holy Scripture to be above the authority of the church' (Chapter 2).

● Predestination is before the beginning of the world and is not based on God's foreknowledge of any good in us. The elect are chosen only by 'the good will and mercy of God' (Chapter 3).

● The church is taught by the Holy Spirit, but 'it is true and certain that the church on earth may err, choosing falsehood instead of truth' (Chapter 12).

● Justification is by faith and not by works. 'When we say faith, we understand ... the object of faith, which is the righteousness of Christ. Faith, as if by a hand, apprehends it and applies it to us for our salvation.' This is not to deny the need for good works, but they cannot merit salvation. 'It is only the righteousness of Christ applied to the penitent that justifies and saves the faithful' (Chapter 13).

● Free-will in the unconverted is free only to sin. That is, unless God's grace comes first, we can do no good (Chapter 14).

● Jesus Christ is present in the eucharist, to the believer. It is by faith and not by our bodily teeth, that we eat and partake of his body and blood. The Roman doctrine of transubstantiation [defined at the *Fourth Lateran Council] is false (Chapter 17).

Cyril sought to introduce Protestant beliefs to the Eastern Orthodox Church. But he met with considerable opposition, not least from Jesuits active at Constantinople. In 1638 the Turkish government was induced to have him put to death. After his death there was a strong reaction against his views in the Orthodox Church and they were repeatedly condemned. Most important of the reactions was the Confession of Dositheus, drawn up mainly by Dositheus (1641–1707), patriarch of Jerusalem, and approved at the Synod of Jerusalem in 1672. It contained eighteen decrees, in response to the eighteen chapters of Cyril's *Confession*.

● The Bible is indeed inspired by God. But, 'the witness of the Catholic Church is, we believe, not of inferior authority to that of the divine Scriptures. As one and the same Holy Spirit is the author of both, it is quite the same to be taught by the Scriptures and by the Catholic Church' (Decree 2).

● Predestination is based on God's foreknowledge. 'Since he foreknew that the one would make a right use of his free-will and the other a wrong use, he predestined the one or condemned the other' (Decree 3).

● The Catholic Church is taught by the Holy Spirit, through the medium of the Fathers, doctors and councils of the church. It follows that 'it is impossible for the Catholic Church to err or at all be deceived or ever to choose falsehood instead of truth. For the all-holy Spirit, continually working through the faithful ministry of the holy fathers and leaders, delivers the church from error of every kind' (Decree 12).

● Justification is not simply through faith alone, but through faith working through love—i.e. through faith and works. '[The notion] that faith fulfils the function of a hand and lays hold on the righteousness which is in Christ and applies it to us for our salvation, we know to be far from all Orthodoxy'. Good works merit reward (Decree 13).

● The unconverted can by nature, without God's grace, do moral good. But without grace such good works do not contribute to salvation (Decree 14).

● Jesus Christ is present in the

eucharist 'truly and really, so that after the consecration of the bread ... the bread is transmuted, transubstantiated, converted and transformed into the true body itself of the Lord'. Furthermore, after the consecration, 'there no longer remains the substance of the bread and of the wine, but the body itself and the blood of the Lord, under the appearance and form of bread and wine—that is under the accidents of the bread' (Decree 17).

PART 3

The Medieval West

500–1500

For Western Europe, the first part of the Middle Ages, until about 1000, can aptly be called the Dark Ages. The western half of the Roman Empire began to crumble before barbarian invasions at the end of the fourth century, and in 410 the unthinkable happened—the city of Rome itself was taken. In 476 the last Western Emperor was deposed by a barbarian Gothic king and the Western Empire had effectively ceased to exist. The West continued to be subject to waves of invasions—from Islam through Spain and from the Scandinavians in the north. This was a time of turmoil and anarchy, with the near collapse of civilization. The heritage of the past was in danger of being lost. The knowledge of philosophy, for example, was limited largely to the works of *Boethius. The church provided what little learning there was, especially through the monasteries, which were often oases of stability. There was a brief respite through the achievements of Charlemagne, who was crowned emperor in 800. He built a united and stable empire, in which civilization and learning were again possible. There was a brief flowering of scholarship during this 'Carolingian Renaissance'. It produced the one truly original thinker of the Dark Ages, the philosopher–theologian *John Scotus Erigena. But before long Charlemagne's empire fragmented and Viking raids brought further setbacks.

Theology during this period was largely confined to the monasteries and is therefore called monastic theology. It was produced in an atmosphere of commitment and devotion, within the framework of a life lived according to the *Rule* of *Benedict, for example. The goal was not the pursuit of knowledge for its own sake, but edification and worship. The approach was one of contemplation and adoration. The theologian was not a detached academic observer studying his material from outside, but a committed, involved participant.

On new year's eve, 1000, a crowd gathered at Rome, awaiting the end of the world. Midnight came, nothing happened and the pope, Sylvester II, blessed the crowd and sent them home. But Sylvester, formerly the scholar Gerbert of Aurillac, was himself one of the first-fruits of a new age. Greater stability was leading to the rebirth of Western civilization. The barbarian invaders had been 'converted' during the Dark Ages and by now all of Western Europe was nominally Christian—apart from the Jews in their ghettoes and the Muslims in Spain.

The eleventh century was a time of new movements. There was a revival of monasticism, a new 'reform papacy' set about purging the church of corruption and there was a revival of learning. The theologian found himself faced with the question of the relation between faith (theology) and reason (philosophy). One modern writer says, 'The effort to harmonize reason and faith was the motive force of medieval Christian thought.' The impact of philosophy led to a new approach to theology: Scholastic theology or Scholasticism. Theology came to be studied outside of the cloister—in the university, and in other 'secular' (non-monastic) settings. The goal was objective intellectual knowledge. The approach was one of questioning, logic, speculation and disputation. It was more important for the theologian to be a trained philosopher than a godly man. Theology had become a detached objective science. This approach did not eliminate the older monastic approach, but it displaced it from the front line of theology.

The impact of philosophy on theology began in the eleventh century with the emergence of reason (philosophy) as a method to be used in theology. *Anselm used it to demonstrate the rationality of Christian doctrine. Reason had entered theology not (yet) as a means of defining Christian doctrine (which was based on revelation) but as a technique for defending and further understanding this faith. In the following century the role of reason was further expanded. Lawyers had begun to use philosophical methods to decide or arbitrate between conflicting authorities. *Peter Abelard proceeded to apply the same methods to theology. He was not always discreet in his approach and he was condemned for his teaching, due to the intervention of *Bernard of Clairvaux, the last great representative of the older monastic theology. But Abelard's methods were followed (more cautiously) by his disciple *Peter Lombard, who enjoyed Bernard's support.

In the thirteenth century, theology entered a new and more dangerous phase. Philosophy now appeared not just as a tool for use in theology but as a rival system of thought. This arose through the translation into Latin of Aristotle's metaphysical works. These writings presented a new way of looking at reality, a new worldview or philosophy of life as an alternative to Christianity. How was the challenge to be faced? For a time Aristotle's metaphysical writings were banned, but this was only a temporary measure to gain breathing space. Some tried to maintain the older Platonist world-view in opposition to the new Aristotelian outlook. The Franciscan theologian *Bonaventure led the field in doing this. But most influential in the long term was the approach of *Thomas Aquinas, who attempted to make a synthesis between faith (theology) and reason (Aristotle). He set out to show that Aristotle's philosophy (rightly interpreted and corrected where necessary) could be consistently held alongside Christian theology.

The fourteenth and fifteenth centuries brought decline in the church, though some view them as the flowering of the Middle Ages. The papacy suffered its 'Babylonian Captivity', the popes being at Avignon and under French control from 1305 to 1377. The pope's return to Rome resulted almost immediately in the Great Schism (1378–1414), during which time there were always at least two rival popes. The religious orders also suffered decline. The fervour of the earlier centuries became rarer. Numbers fell and corruption increased.

In the fourteenth and fifteenth centuries there was also increasing scepticism about the possibility of harmonizing theology and philosophy. This process was begun by *John Duns Scotus and came to a head in the teaching of *William of Ockham and his followers. Philosophy and theology went their separate ways, with theology retreating out of the 'natural' realm and relying increasingly on naked faith in God's revelation (the rationality of which could not be shown). In addition, Scholastic theology became divorced from practical spirituality, as exemplified by *Thomas à Kempis, to the detriment of both.

The Middle Ages are often neglected, especially by Protestants. This is a mistake. The medieval period spans some thousand years—more than half the time from the birth of Jesus Christ to today. It may not be the most glorious period of church history, but it must be taken seriously as an important part of it. The medieval theologians wrestled with the problem of the relation between faith and reason. This remains a burning issue today and there is much to learn from the medieval experience. Then it was Aristotle, today it may be Darwin or Marx, but the basic issues remain the same.

Athanasian Creed

It is said of the Athanasian Creed that it is neither by *Athanasius nor a creed. It was certainly not written by Athanasius. It was attributed to him from the seventh century, probably because he was seen as the father of the orthodox doctrine of the Trinity. This tradition was questioned in the sixteenth century and demolished in the seventeenth. There is no general consensus concerning its origin, but the evidence seems to indicate that it was written around the year 500 in the south of Gaul (France). It is often known as the *Quicunque Vult*, the opening words in the original Latin.

Strictly speaking, the Athanasian Creed is a definition rather than a creed, but this is perhaps an over-pedantic distinction. In the earliest times it was used as a test of the orthodoxy of the clergy and as a simple compendium of Catholic doctrine for instructing the laity. By the thirteenth century it had come to be seen, in the West, as one of the 'three creeds', together with the *Nicene and *Apostles' Creeds. It was widely accepted by Protestant churches (e.g. in the Anglican *Thirty-nine Articles, the Lutheran *Formula of Concord and at the Reformed *Synod of Dort). The Eastern churches were torn between respecting its Athanasian authorship and rejecting its *filioque* teaching (the Holy Spirit proceeds from the Father *and the Son*). They either denied that Athanasius wrote it or claimed that the *filioque* was a later addition. The Creed was used frequently in Anglican and Roman Catholic worship, but in the present century it has fallen largely out of use. There has been considerable opposition to the Creed, not so much because of the theology it proclaims as because it consigns to eternal damnation those who do not accept it.

The Creed consists of two sections: one on the Trinity and one on the person of Jesus Christ. Each section is preceded and followed by a 'damnatory clause', stating the necessity to believe it if one is to be saved. While the Creed tells us how to think or speak about God, the emphasis is also on rightly worshipping him. The Creed is more than an exercise in speculative theology.

Whoever wants to be saved must first of all hold the Catholic faith. Unless one keeps this faith whole and inviolate, he will without doubt perish eternally.

Now this is the Catholic faith: that we worship one God in trinity and trinity in unity—neither confusing persons, nor dividing the substance. For the Father's person is one, the Son's another and the Holy Spirit's another. But the deity of Father, Son and Holy Spirit is one. Their glory is equal and their majesty coeternal.

Whatever the Father is, such is the Son and such also the Holy Spirit. The Father is uncreated, the Son uncreated and the Holy Spirit uncreated. The Father is infinite, the Son infinite and the Holy Spirit infinite. The Father is eternal, the Son eternal and the Holy Spirit eternal. Yet there are not three eternals but only one eternal—just as there are not three uncreateds nor three infinites but only one uncreated and only one infinite. Likewise, the Father is almighty, the Son almighty and the Holy Spirit almighty—yet there are not three almighties but only one almighty.

Thus the Father is God, the Son is God and the Holy Spirit is God—yet there are not three Gods but only one God. Thus the Father is Lord, the Son Lord and the Holy Spirit Lord—yet there are not three Lords but only one Lord. For just as Christian truth compels us to acknowledge each person by himself to be God and Lord, so the Catholic religion forbids us to speak of three Gods or Lords.

The Father is neither made nor created nor begotten from anything. The Son is from the Father alone—not made nor created but begotten. The Holy Spirit is from the Father and the Son—not made nor created nor begotten but proceeding. So there is one Father, not three Fathers; one Son, not three Sons; one Holy Spirit, not three Holy Spirits. And in this trinity no one is before or after another; no one is greater or less than another, but all three persons are coeternal and coequal with each other. Thus in all things, as has been said, both trinity in unity and unity in trinity are to be worshipped. This is how to think of the Trinity if you want to be saved.

But for eternal salvation it is also necessary to believe faithfully in the Incarnation of our Lord Jesus Christ. For correct faith is believing and confessing that our Lord Jesus Christ, the Son of God, is equally God and man. God he is, begotten from the Father's substance before time; man he is, born from his mother's substance in time. He is both perfect God and perfect man, composed of a rational soul and human flesh. He is equal to the Father, as God; less than the Father, as man.

Although he is both God and man, yet he is not two but one Christ. He is one however, not by the conversion of his deity into flesh, but by the taking up of his humanity into God. He is one indeed, not by confusion of substance, but by unity of person. For just as rational soul and flesh make one man, so also God and man make one Christ.

He suffered for our salvation, descended into hell, rose from the dead, ascended into the heavens and sat at the right hand of the Father. He will come from there to judge the living and the dead. When he comes, all men will rise again with their bodies and will render account for their own deeds. Those who have done good will go to eternal life, those who have done evil to eternal fire.

This is the Catholic faith. Unless one believes it faithfully and firmly, one cannot be saved.

The trinitarian section is a masterly summary of the Western doctrine of the Trinity, drawing heavily upon *Augustine. Indeed, it has been called 'codified and condensed Augustinianism'. It presents the paradox of the unity and the trinity, the oneness and the threeness of God. These are set against the two errors of Monarchianism ('confusing the persons') and Arianism ('dividing the substance'). The Monarchians resolved the paradox of the Trinity by teaching that the Father *is* the Son *is* the Holy Spirit. A contemporary Spanish movement, Priscillianism, tended in the direction of Monarchianism. The 'Arianism' opposed by the Creed is in fact the *Origenism of the barbarian Gothic rulers in the West, who had been converted to Christianity at a time when the official Eastern faith fell short of Nicene faith in the full deity of Jesus Christ. The Creed opposes two errors that they were deemed to hold: it upholds the full deity of Christ against the 'Arian' belief that the Father is greater than the Son; it upholds the unity of the Godhead against the 'Arian' tendency towards three Gods. Thus the Athanasian Creed affirms the three main elements of the doctrine of the Trinity: there is one God; Father, Son and Holy Spirit are God; the Father is not the Son is not the Holy Spirit.

The Christological section presents a doctrine similar to that of the *Council of Chalcedon, but in Western terms. The four heresies condemned at Chalcedon are all clearly excluded. The first paragraph maintains his full deity and full humanity, excluding Arianism and Apollinarianism. The second paragraph affirms that he is one person, but without any confusion of his substances (natures), thus excluding Nestorianism and Eutychianism.

The 'damnatory clauses' stipulate that without correct belief salvation is not possible. This was long held to be so, but today there is a greater readiness on all sides to allow for sincerely-held error. Making a small mistake on the finer details of the doctrine of the Trinity need not result in eternal damnation. If the Athanasian Creed were taken at its face value, all Easterners who reject the Western *filioque* would be lost. It is sad that these damnatory clauses have diverted attention from the rest of the Creed. The trinitarian section, in particular, is a masterly concise summary of a difficult doctrine in simple terms.

Boethius

CONVERSATIONS WITH PHILOSOPHY

Anicius Manlius Severinus Boethius was
born in about 480 into an aristocratic Roman
family. He was related to two former
emperors. His father died when he was young
and he was brought up by Symmachus, who
later became head of the Senate. Symmachus
brought Boethius up as his own son and in
due course became his father-in-law and his
close friend. Boethius had a first-rate
education. He acquired a perfect command of
Greek, then a rarity in the West.

Boethius dedicated himself to a life of
philosophy. He saw himself as 'schoolmaster
of the West'. His great aim was to make the
philosophies of Plato and Aristotle
accessible to Latin Westerners. His plan was
to translate all of Aristotle's writings,
adding his own explanatory commentary.
Then he planned to do the same for all of
Plato's Dialogues. He also wished to
demonstrate that the philosophies of Plato
and Aristotle were in essential harmony and
not, as many (rightly) imagined,
contradictory. Boethius had learnt this idea
of the harmony between the two great
philosophers from Neo-Platonism. It meant
interpreting Aristotle's philosophy in an
essentially Platonist framework.
Unfortunately, Boethius managed to
translate only part of Aristotle (his works on
logic), and none of Plato.

Boethius might have completed his
translation project had he not entered public
life. In 476 the last Western Emperor was
deposed and Rome was ruled by Gothic
barbarian kings. In 510 Boethius was
appointed sole consul for the year, a high
honour since normally two were appointed.
In 522 his two young sons were chosen as
the two consuls, a great honour for their
father and the pinnacle of his worldly
success. He accepted a high office under the
king, Theodoric, as chief of the civil service.
But Boethius became the victim of a
combination of political intrigue and his own
indiscretion. He was convicted of treason
and exiled to Pavia to await execution. This
came in 524/25.

Boethius' last and most famous work,
written during his final imprisonment, is
The Consolation of Philosophy. It is a short
work in five books. It takes the form of a
dialogue between Boethius and the lady
Philosophy.

● In Book 1, Boethius tells Philosophy
of his misfortunes. She points him to the true
nature of his problem—it is not so much that
he has been banished from his home, but
that he has wandered away from *himself*.
What concerns her is not *where* he is, nor
even what will happen to him, but his state:

*And so it is not the sight of this place
which gives me concern but your own
appearance. It is 'not the walls of your
library with their glass and ivory
decoration that I am looking for, but the
seat of your mind. That is the place
where I once stored away—not my
books, but—the thing that makes them
have any value, the philosophy they
contain.*
CONSOLATION 1:5

● In Book 2, Philosophy shows him the
true character of Fortune and outward
prosperity. The essence of Fortune is change
and it is this that Boethius has learned
through his sudden reversal. She seeks to
show him that in Fortune he neither had nor
lost anything of lasting value. 'If the things
whose loss you are bemoaning were really
yours, you could never have lost them' 2:2.
There is nothing more precious to a man
than his own self. That is something that
Fortune can neither give nor take away—all
else is merely transitory. That is why bad
fortune is of more value than good fortune:

*Good fortune always seems to bring
happiness, but deceives you with her
smiles, whereas bad fortune is always
truthful because by changing she shows
her true fickleness. Good fortune
deceives, but bad fortune enlightens.
With her display of specious riches good
fortune enslaves the minds of those who
enjoy her, while bad fortune gives men
release through the recognition of how*

*fragile a thing happiness is ... Good
fortune lures men away from the path
of true good, but adverse fortune
frequently draws men back to their true
good like a shepherdess with her crook.*
CONSOLATION 2:8

● In Book 3, they discuss the nature of
true happiness. They see that only God can
give true happiness. Man's problem is that
'nature is satisfied with little, whereas
nothing satisfies greed' (3:3).

● In Book 4, Philosophy meets an
objection raised by Boethius: how can evil
exist and remain unpunished in a world
ruled by a good God who is omniscient and
omnipotent? Philosophy does not deny God's
omnipotence. Providence, which is divine
reason, is set at the head of all things and
controls them. This happens according to
justice, despite the apparent injustices of
this life. Good men are rewarded by good
fortune or disciplined by bad fortune, as
Providence deems necessary. Evil men are
corrected by bad fortune, while good fortune
does not bring them real happiness. Thus:

*All fortune whether pleasant or adverse
is meant either to reward or discipline
the good or to punish or correct the bad.
We agree, therefore, on the justice or
usefulness of fortune, and so all fortune
is good.*
CONSOLATION 4:7

● In Book 5, Philosophy reconciles
God's foreknowledge with human free-will.
God's knowledge is 'not a kind of
foreknowledge of the future but the
knowledge of a never ending present, 'God
sees all things in his eternal present' (5:6).
Thus God's eternal knowledge of all my
actions does not contradict my freedom of
will.

The Consolation of Philosophy is rightly
seen as one of the great spiritual classics.
Yet it poses an important question. As he
faced death, Boethius found consolation in
philosophy, not theology. His book is a work
of devotional piety towards God, but there is
nothing distinctively Christian in it. There is

no mention of Christianity, Jesus Christ,
revelation, grace, faith, forgiveness of sins or
the church. The message of the book can be
summarized as salvation by Neo-Platonist
philosophy. Why is this?

Some have supposed that Boethius
professed Christianity insincerely, merely in
order to rise to high office. But this theory
does not square with what is known of his
life. Others have suggested that at the end of
his life he renounced Christianity in favour
of Neo-Platonism. But *The Consolation of
Philosophy* contains nothing blatantly
contrary to Christianity and no hint of any
rejection of Christianity. Yet others have
argued that there is no problem here.
Boethius was writing a work on philosophy,
not theology, and one should not expect
overt Christianity here any more than one
would expect to find geology in a book on
music. But the problem cannot be side-
stepped so deftly. *The Consolation of
Philosophy* is a spiritual autobiography, an
account of how Boethius came to face his
end. The fact is that he found his consolation
in *philosophy*.

The 'problem' arises largely through a
tendency to see Christianity and philosophy
(Neo-Platonism) as somehow opposed to one
another. By the time of Boethius the two had
largely come to be blended together. There is
nothing *un*Christian about Boethius' Neo-
Platonism. *Augustine could have written
almost everything that Boethius wrote. But
the difference is that with Augustine there is
no question about the centrality of Jesus
Christ and the Christian revelation in his
thought. There is no reason to question
Boethius' sincere acceptance of the Christian
faith, but for him it appears to be Neo-
Platonism that is central rather than
Christianity. Augustine and Boethius were
both 'Christianized Neo-Platonists', but with
Boethius the Christianization is more
superficial, while with Augustine it is
radical.

Boethius' influence on the Middle Ages
was profound. It was he who mediated
classical philosophy to the succeeding
centuries. Until the thirteenth century, the
knowledge of Aristotle in the West was

limited to the logical works, in Boethius' translation. Boethius has rightly been called the last Roman and the first Scholastic. He marked the end of the classical Roman era and helped to transmit some of its treasures to the Middle Ages. At the same time, he provided the materials for early Scholastic theology and even anticipated some of its methods.

Council of Orange (529)

*Augustine's teaching on grace and predestination met with opposition in the south of Gaul (France). Monks there felt that too much stress on God's grace and man's inability could encourage laziness. They felt it was important to stress what we *can* do, and the need to get on with it. They believed that God's help is necessary in order to live the Christian life, but they also believed that we can make the first move on our own. When it comes to righteousness, the sinner is sick, not dead, and the sick man can take the initiative in asking the doctor for help. If we ask, it will be given to us; if we seek, we will find; if we knock, it will be opened to us. In short, their teaching can be summarized by the slogan, 'God helps those who help themselves'. This position is called Semi-Pelagianism (a term coined around 1600).

The Semi-Pelagians included some of the leading figures of the day, such as John Cassian at Marseilles, one of the greatest leaders of Western monasticism.

Augustine wrote two works against them at the end of his life: *The Predestination of the Saints* and *The Gift of Perseverance*. He treated them with respect as erring brethren, not as heretics. Semi-Pelagian views were common in the church before the time of Augustine and he himself had held them in his early years as a Christian. After Augustine's death, his cause was defended in Gaul by Prosper of Aquitaine. The controversy dragged on for a whole century, with different councils taking different sides. It was brought to a conclusion by the Council of Orange (Arausiacum) in 529, which was led by

Caesarius of Arles, who had the support of the pope, Felix IV.

The council produced twenty-five canons or short doctrinal statements, followed by a conclusion. Above all else, Semi-Pelagianism is rejected. Thirteen of the twenty-five canons deny that man can take the initiative in turning to God and insist that God's grace needs to be 'prevenient' (i.e. that it must precede or come before any move to God on our part). This is necessary because Adam's fall has changed the whole of man (body and soul) for the worse. Prevenient grace is necessary if we are to start on the Christian way and co-operating grace is necessary if we are to keep going.

The canons affirm our need for grace, but this grace is tied to the sacraments. Free-will is healed by the grace of *baptism*. With the grace of baptism and the aid and co-operation of Jesus Christ, we have the power to do all that is necessary for salvation, if we so desire. By this time infant *baptism* was universal, so the teaching on grace is pushed back to a forgotten infancy. The practical emphasis lies in the baptized Christian's present *ability* to do all that is necessary for salvation. The council teaches a form of Augustinianism, but it has been tied to a popular Catholicism in the form of the sacramental system and an emphasis on good works. It was this form of Augustinianism which predominated in the Middle Ages. Finally, the council condemns, not Augustine's doctrine of predestination to *salvation*, but the idea of predestination to *evil*.

If anyone denies that it is the whole man, that is both body and soul, that was 'changed for the worse' through the offence of Adam's sin, but believes that the freedom of the soul remains unimpaired and that only the body is subject to corruption, he is deceived by the error of Pelagius.
CANON 1

If anyone maintains that God awaits our will to be cleansed from sin, but does not confess that even our wish to

be cleansed comes to us through the infusion and working of the Holy Spirit, he resists the Holy Spirit himself who says through Solomon, 'The will is prepared by the Lord' [Proverbs 8:35, in the Septuagint translation].

CANON 4

The regenerate and converted also [i.e. as well as the unconverted] need always to seek God's help in order to be able to come to a good end or persevere in good works.

CANON 10

God loves us for what we shall be by his gift, not what we are by our own merit.

CANON 12

The freedom of will that was destroyed in the first man can be restored only by the grace of baptism.

CANON 13

Good works deserve a reward, if they are performed; but grace, which is not deserved, precedes them, to enable them to be performed.

CANON 18

The sin of the first man has so impaired and weakened free-will that no-one thereafter can either love God as he ought or believe in God or do good for God's sake, unless the grace of divine mercy has preceded him ... According to the Catholic faith we also believe that after grace has been received through baptism, all baptized persons have the ability and the responsibility, if they desire to labour faithfully, to perform with the aid and co-operation of Christ what is of essential importance for the salvation of their soul. We not only do not believe that any are predestined to evil by the power of God, but we even state with utter abhorrence that if there are those who want to believe so evil a thing, they are anathema.

CONCLUSION

Benedict
A RULE FOR THE MONKS

The only original account of the life of Benedict is found in the *Dialogues* of Pope *Gregory I. Benedict was born in about 480 at Nursia in central Italy. As a student he went to Rome, but he was disgusted by its low moral standards. He therefore withdrew from the world in about 500, becoming a hermit in a cave at Subiaco. In due course others came to join him and he founded a number of small monasteries in the area. In about 529 local tensions forced him to leave and he moved with some of his disciples to Monte Cassino, where he founded a monastery. He remained there until his death in the middle of the century.

Benedict is remembered primarily for his *Rule* for the monastic life. For this he drew heavily on the work of his predecessors. Basil the Great (of the *Cappadocian Fathers), John Cassian of Marseilles and, especially, on an earlier *Rule of the Master*, from which he copied extensively. But this is not to deny Benedict's originality. He set his own mark on his sources and created a distinctive work of great genius—one of the most influential documents in European history. Initially it was not widely used, but in the eighth century Benedict of Aniane helped to spread it widely. In 817 a synod at Aachen, the capital of Charlemagne's empire, made Benedict's *Rule* the official rule for all monks. But while it came to be accepted everywhere, it was not the sole rule. Monasticism at this time drew on other sources of inspiration. Cassiodore, who was a disciple of *Boethius and founder of a monastery at Vivarium, was also influential, viewing the monastery as a centre of learning.

Benedict's *Rule* combines brevity with completeness in that it covers a wide range of eventualities in a short space. It is a mixture of clarity and explicitness with a lack of rigidity—it is a very flexible document when it comes to application. Benedict adopted a policy of mildness. This is a rule which can be kept by beginners, not a goal for veterans to aim at. The monastery is seen as a family, with the abbot as father. Asceticism is to be moderate. The monk's life was comparable to that of the contemporary peasant. Provision is made for human weakness and frailty. Benedict was realistic when it came to the standards to be anticipated—a whole chapter is devoted to telling the monks not to strike one another.

Central to the *Rule* is obedience. The monk was not seen as especially poor—in fact provision is made for giving the monks' cast-off clothes to the poor. But the monk is someone who has submitted himself to obedience—to Christ, to the *Rule* and to the abbot, whose commands are to be obeyed as if from God himself. This obedience is the first step to humility. It is to be an obedience from the heart—without delay, coldness, grumbling or reluctance.

There were three main occupations for the monk: manual work (which was often dropped in medieval monasticism); 'divine reading' (reading and meditation on the Bible and other spiritual works); and the 'work of God' (liturgical worship).

The monks were to worship seven times daily, in accordance with Psalm 119:164.

Listen, my son, to the precepts ot the master and incline the ear of your heart. Willingly receive and faithfully fulfil the admonition of your loving father. Thus by the labour of obedience you will return to him from whom you departed through the sloth of disobedience ... If we want to escape the pains oF hell and arrive at eternal life, then ... we must hasten to do now what will profit us in eternity. Our aim therefore is to establish a school of the Lord's service. In setting it up we hope to order nothing harsh or rigorous.
PROLOGUE

The first stage of humility is that a man always keeps the fear of God before his eyes, avoiding all forgetfulness. He should always remember what God has commanded and that those who despise God will burn in hell for their sins while eternal life is prepared for those who fear him ...

The second stage of humility is that a man love not his own will nor delight in fulfilling his own desires ...

The third degree of humility is that a man, for the love of God, submit himself to his superior in all obedience ...

The fourth stage of humility is that if, in the course of this obedience, he meets with hardship, contradiction or even injury, he should embrace them patiently, with a quiet conscience and not grow weary or give in ...

The fifth stage of humility is not to hide from the abbot any of the evil thoughts that beset one's heart nor those sins committed in secret, but humbly to confess them ...

The sixth stage of humility is for a monk to be contented with the meanest and worst of everything and in all that is commanded him to reckon himself a bad and worthless labourer ...

The seventh stage of humility is that he should not only with his tongue call himself lower and viler than all but also believe it in his heart ...

The eighth stage of humility is for a monk to do nothing not authorized by the common rule of the monastery or the example of his seniors.

The ninth stage of humility is that a monk refrain his tongue from speaking, keeping silent until asked a question ...

The tenth stage of humility is that he should not laugh easily or quickly ...

The eleventh stage of humility is that when a monk speaks he do so gently, without laughter, humbly, gravely. His words should be few and reasonable and he should not raise his voice ...

The twelfth degree of humility is that the monk always show his humility to all that see him, not just in his heart but in his outward behaviour.
CHAPTER 7

The vice of private ownership is especially to be eradicated from the monastery. No one is to presume to give or to receive anything without consent of the abbot, nor to keep anything as

their own—neither books, writing tablets, pens, nor anything else at all.
CHAPTER 33

Idleness is the enemy of the soul so at certain times the brothers should occupy themselves in manual labour and at other times in holy reading.
CHAPTER 48

All guests should be received as Christ himself... When they arrive or depart, Christ (who is indeed being received as a guest) should be adored in them, with a bow of the head or even prostration on the ground.
CHAPTER 53

We have written this rule so that, by keeping it in the monasteries, we may show ourselves to have some virtue and a beginning of holiness. Those who wish to press on to a perfect life should read the teaching of the holy fathers... Whoever you are, then, that hastens to the heavenly country, keep, with the help of Christ, this little rule for beginners. Eventually, with God's protection, you will arrive at the lofty heights of doctrine and virtue which we have described above.
CHAPTER 73

A striking tribute to the *Rule* came from the modern Evangelical leader David Watson, who noted that many of the problems faced by communities in the church today 'could have been avoided if the remarkably wise sixth-century *Rule of Benedict* had been known or followed more closely'.

Gregory the Great
'SERVANT OF THE SERVANTS OF GOD'

Gregory was born in 540 at Rome. He came from a godly and aristocratic family—his great-great-grandfather was Pope Felix III. In 572/73 he was appointed Prefect of the City of Rome, a high post for one so young. Soon afterwards, his father died. Gregory

then founded six monasteries on the family estates in Sicily and one at Rome. The last he entered himself, as an ordinary monk. But before long he was appointed one of the seven Roman deacons by the pope, who then sent him for five years (about 578–83) as his representative to Constantinople. This time in the East convinced Gregory that the papacy needed to pursue a policy more independent of the Eastern Emperors, from whom he saw little prospect of practical help for the West. On his return to Rome he became abbot of his monastery. In 590 the pope died and Gregory was elected to succeed him. He accepted only with genuine reluctance, but then threw himself with fervour into the task. He is known as Gregory the Great and he is one of the few popes to be both a great leader and a genuinely saintly figure. He died in 604. He is seen as the last of the four Doctors of the Latin church, after *Ambrose, *Jerome and *Augustine.

Gregory was an able administrator and he extended the power of the papacy in the West. He assumed some of the tasks previously exercised by the Eastern Emperor, a move which in the long term led to the papacy ruling the papal states in central Italy. He is remembered for his concern for the English ('not Angles but angels'). It was Gregory who, in 596, sent Augustine to England to become the first archbishop of Canterbury.

Gregory's writings were widely read in the Middle Ages.

● *Letters.* Some 850 of Gregory's letters survive. They tell us a lot about both Gregory himself and his times.

● *Dialogues.* These contain the life and miracles of *Benedict and other Latin saints. Gregory did not appear to be able to distinguish between fact and legend.

● *Book of Morals* or *Exposition of Job.* This is the longest of Gregory's works. He expounds Job in three different ways, giving the historical meaning, the allegorical meaning (interpreting it in terms of Jesus Christ and his church) and the moral or ethical meaning.

● *Homilies.* He wrote homilies on

Ezekiel and the Gospels.

● *Pastoral Rule*. This was Gregory's greatest work and became the textbook for the medieval bishop:

There are some who investigate spiritual precepts with cunning care, but what they penetrate with their understanding, they trample on in their lives. They teach immediately things which they have learnt by study, but not by putting into practice. That which they preach in words they discredit by their behaviour.
PASTORAL RULE 1:2

The leader should always be pure in thought, inasmuch as no impurity ought to pollute him who has undertaken the office of wiping away the stains of pollution in the hearts of others.
PASTORAL RULE 2:2

The leader should be a near neighbour to everyone in sympathy, and yet exalted above all in contemplation... The same eye of the heart, which in his elevation he lifts to the invisible, he bends in his compassion upon the secrets of those who are subject to infirmity.
PASTORAL RULE 2:5

Supreme rule is properly ordered when he who presides lords it over vices rather than over his brethren... Gentleness is to be mingled with severity and a sort of compound made of both. Subjects should be neither aggravated by too much harshness nor relaxed by too much kindness.
PASTORAL RULE 2:6

The leader should understand how often vices pass themselves off as virtues. Stinginess often excuses itself under the name of frugality while, on the other hand, extravagance hides itself under the name of generosity. Often inordinate laxity is mistaken for loving-kindness, while unbridled wrath is seen as the virtue of spiritual zeal.
PASTORAL RULE 2:9

Every preacher should give forth a sound more by his deeds than by his words. He should, by his good life, imprint footsteps for men to follow rather than, by speaking, merely show them the way to walk in.
PASTORAL RULE 3:40

Gregory taught a blend of Augustinianism and popular Catholicism, which predominated in the early Middle Ages. He furthered the doctrine of purgatory, elevating it from a probable opinion into a dogma. He believed that souls in purgatory could be released by the sacrifice of the mass. He encouraged some of the superstitions of the age—such as the veneration of relics. But on the question of images he took a balanced middle position between those who would destroy them and those who would worship them. In the Eastern Church there was a later conflict between these two extremes, leading to the *Council of Nicea in 787.

It has come to our ears that when you [Serenus of Marseilles] saw people adoring images in the churches you broke the images and threw them down. We commend you for your zeal against the adoration of anything handmade, but you should not have broken these images. The purpose of pictorial representation in the churches is that the illiterate might read, by looking at the walls, what they cannot read in books.
LETTER 9: 105

It is one thing to adore a picture; it is another thing to learn through the story of a picture what to adore. What a book presents to the reader, this a picture presents to the illiterate beholder. In the picture, even the ignorant see what to follow. In it, the illiterate read. Hence pictures take the place of books, especially for the barbarians [who cannot read].
LETTER 11:13

Gregory was engaged in controversy with the bishop of Constantinople, who had claimed for himself the title of 'Ecumenical [Universal] Patriarch'. Gregory fought hard against this 'execrable and profane assumption'. Such a 'proud and foolish title' is a denial of humility, a 'sin of elation'. Gregory claimed (inaccurately) that the *Council of Chalcedon had offered the title 'Universal' to the Roman bishops, but that none of them had ever consented to it. Peter was the first of the apostles and to him were entrusted the keys of the kingdom of heaven. But all of the apostles were under the one head, Jesus Christ, and none of them wished to be called 'Universal'. To claim such a title is the sin of the devil, as described in Isaiah 14:13. The bishop of Constantinople's 'attempt at diabolical usurpation' is evidence that the times of Antichrist are near. 'Now I confidently say that whoever calls himself, or desires to be called Universal Priest, is in his elation the precursor of Antichrist because he proudly puts himself above all others'.

Gregory's objection was not in order to claim the title for himself. When the bishop of Alexandria called him 'Universal Pope' he repudiated the title. 'Away with words that inflate vanity and wound charity' (*Letter 8:30*). Gregory believed that each of the 'patriarchs' (of Rome, Constantinople, Alexandria, Antioch and Jerusalem) ruled in his own area, and that none should attempt to dominate the others. His own preferred title for himself was 'servant of the servants of God'. His successors in the papacy have retained this title, while at the same time claiming the title of universal head of the church.

John Scotus Erigena
THEOLOGIAN OF THE DARK AGES

John Scotus Erigena was an Irishman (*scotus*) who was born in about 810. He was the greatest intellectual of the Carolingian Renaissance and the one truly original thinker of the Dark Ages. He became head of the palace school at Paris under the emperor Charles the Bald. He evidently lacked neither wit nor courage. When the emperor (a

pioneer of the Irish joke) leaned across the table and asked him what separates a Scot from a sot, John's answer was 'this table'! He died in about 877.

John was one of the few Westerners of his time to know Greek. He translated the works of *Dionysius the Areopagite, together with *Maximus the Confessor's commentary on him. This translation was highly influential on a number of later medieval theologians, such as *Thomas Aquinas.

John intervened in the two hot theological debates of the century. The first concerned the doctrine of predestination. A monk called Gottschalk was teaching an extreme form of Augustinianism, including the idea that God predestines evil. While a number of leading theologians supported him, others dissented and he was imprisoned for his views. John was asked to write on the subject, by Bishop Hincmar of Reims, Gottschalk's leading opponent. John's work, *Predestination*, opposed Gottschalk, but it was no more acceptable to Hincmar than were Gottschalk's views. John fell out with Hincmar and wrote him an unflattering epitaph: 'Here lies Hincmar, a thief on avarice fed/His sole achievement this—that he is dead.'

The ninth century also saw controversy concerning the presence of Christ's body and blood in the eucharist. Two monks from the abbey of Corbie, Paschasius Radbertus and Ratramnus, debated whether the bread and the wine become Christ's body and blood in truth or in a figure and whether the body of Christ present in the eucharist is the same body that was born of Mary and crucified for us. John wrote a treatise on this question, which is lost. It appears that he favoured a more spiritual interpretation of Christ's presence. Believers eat Christ 'not dentally but mentally'.

John's chief work was his *Division of Nature* in which he interpreted Christianity in a radically Neo-Platonist framework. He suggested a fourfold division of 'nature' (all reality): nature which is uncreated and creative—God as Creator; nature which is created yet creative—the heavenly Ideas (in Plato's sense) on which all creation is modelled; nature which is created but not creative—the universe (including man); nature which is neither created nor creative—God as the End/Final Cause.

John sought to balance the 'positive way with the 'negative way' of Dionysius the Aeropagite. Thus, for instance, the positive way tells us that God is wise. But the negative way tells us that God is not wise—not in the sense that he is *less* than wise, but in that his wisdom transcends all human wisdom. Thus the statement that he is wise should be seen as a metaphor, in that he transcends all wisdom that we know (Isaiah 55:8–9). The contradiction between the positive and negative ways (God is wise/God is not wise) is resolved by stating that God is super-wisdom—that he transcends human wisdom.

John's Neo-Platonism led him to view creation as an emanation proceeding from God. He maintained, in loyalty to Christian revelation, that God created 'out of nothing', but this does not fit happily into his system. 'When we hear that God makes all things, we should understand nothing else but that God is in all things, that is, he is the essence of all things. For he alone truly is, and everything which is truly said to be in those things which are, is God alone' (*Division* 1:72). John did not wish to be a pantheist (blurring the distinction between God and the universe) and believed himself not to be one, but the logic of his system frequently points that way.

The same problem arises when John considers the End. He taught a doctrine of 'cosmic return' to God. In the end God will be all in all and nothing will exist but God alone. John could appeal to Paul's statement that God will be 'all in all' (1 Corinthians 15:28), and he denied that he taught the total absorption of man into God. But his Christian beliefs did not fit comfortably within his Neo-Platonist framework and he had considerable difficulty in avoiding universalism, the belief that all will be saved. 'Every creature will be cast into the shade, that is, changed into God, as the stars at the rising of the sun' (*Division* 3:23). John's intentions were orthodox. He has

been accused of rationalism, but unfairly. While he was a Neo-Platonist through and through, his aim was not to produce a rational Neo-Platonist system *independent* of Christianity, but rather to expound Christian revelation within a Neo-Platonist framework. He has been accused, with greater plausibility, of pantheism. In the thirteenth century his writings were used to support pantheism and were condemned by the church. John's Neo-Platonism drags him in the direction of pantheism. But he does not go without a struggle, and his loyalty to Christian revelation preserves him from total absorption into pantheism.

And what, O Lord, is that coming of yours but an ascent through the infinite steps of your contemplation?—for you always come to the intellects of those who seek and find you. You are sought by them always, and are found always, and are not found always. You are found indeed in your appearances. in which in many ways . . . you encounter the minds of those who understand you in the way in which you allow yourself to be understood—not what you are, but what you are not, and that you are. But you are not found in your superessence, by which you surpass and excel all intellect . . .
DIVISION OF NATURE, CONCLUSION

Anselm
FAITH SEEKING UNDERSTANDING

Anselm was born in about 1033 at Aosta, in Italy. As a young man of twenty-six he entered the Benedictine monastery at Bec in Normandy. Before long, in 1063, he became prior of the monastery, in succession to Lanfranc, who became abbot elsewhere. Thereafter his life falls into three periods of about fifteen years each—as prior of Bec (1063–78), as abbot of Bec (1078–93) and as archbishop of Canterbury (1093–1109), again in succession to Lanfranc. Anselm clashed with successive kings over the question of the independence of the English Church from the king and the role of the pope in England. As a result, most of his time as archbishop was spent in exile on the Continent.

Anselm was the first truly great theologian of the medieval West and is seen by some as the founder of Scholasticism. He allowed philosophy to play a significant, though limited, role in theology. It is revelation, not philosophy, that gives us the content of the Christian faith. But the theologian who believes can then seek, by the use of reason, to understand more fully that which he believes. Reason can show the rationality and inner coherence of Christian doctrine. Anselm follows *Augustine's method of 'faith seeking understanding'.

Anselm pursued this method in three major writings. In the *Monologion* (1077), originally called *An Example of Meditation on the Grounds of Faith*, he offers a 'proof' for the existence of God. The fact that we can discern degrees of goodness means that there is an absolute Good, by which we measure it:

All other goods [apart from the Good] are good through a being other than themselves, and this being [the Good] alone is good of itself. It is only this being, which is alone good of itself, that is supremely good. This being is supreme in that it surpasses all other beings. It is neither equalled nor excelled. But if it is supremely good, it is also supremely great. There is, therefore, some one being which is both supremely good and supremely great— i.e. the highest of all existing beings.
MONOLOGION 1

This being is God. Anselm's argument is based on the (Platonist) assumption that the 'universal' is more real than particular manifestations of it. Thus the Idea of humanity is more real than an individual man, such as Anselm. The Idea of goodness is seen as more real than particular manifestations of goodness, as in the life of a good person. This was the accepted view in Anselm's time. But today most people would

think of goodness as an abstract ideal rather than as a being that exists.

The argument of the *Monologion* was not original. Augustine had argued similarly. The following year, Anselm broke new ground with the publication of his *Proslogion*, originally called *Faith Seeking Understanding*. Starting as a believer, he seeks to understand what he already believes:

I am not trying, Lord, to penetrate your sublimity, for my understanding is not up to that. But I long in some measure to understand your truth, which my heart believes and loves. For I am not seeking to understand in order to believe, but I believe in order that I may understand. For this too I believe: that unless I believe, I shall not understand.
PROSLOGION 1

In this work Anselm presents his famous 'ontological argument' for the existence of God. God is defined as 'that, than which nothing greater can be conceived' or, to put it more simply, 'the greatest conceivable being'. This being must exist. Were he not to exist, be would be inferior to an identical being that did exist and thus would not be 'the greatest conceivable being'.

Therefore, if 'the greatest conceivable being' exists only in the imagination, it is possible to conceive of a being greater than 'the greatest conceivable being'. But this is clearly an impossibility. There is no doubt then about the existence of a 'greatest conceivable being' and that it exists not merely in the imagination but also in reality. Furthermore, it exists so certainly that it cannot even be conceived not to exist. For the mind can conceive of a being which cannot be conceived not to exist— and such a being is greater than a being which can be conceived not to exist. Hence, if 'the greatest conceivable being' could be conceived not to exist, it would not be 'the greatest conceivable being'. But that is a contradiction in terms. So surely *then, is there a 'greatest conceivable being' that it cannot even be conceived not to exist. And you are this being, O Lord our God.*

PROSLOGION 2–3

Anselm has, with some justice, been accused of attempting to define God into existence. His approach reflects the supreme confidence of the eleventh century in the power of reason. Anselm considered that his argument should suffice to persuade the 'fool', who denies God's existence (Psalm 14:1). But the validity of his argument was immediately questioned by a monk called Gaunilo, who wrote *On Behalf of the Fool.* The debate about the ontological argument has continued to the present day and shows no sign of abating.

Anselm's most ambitious work was his *Cur Deus Homo (Why God Became Man)*, written in the 1090s. Anselm, like *Athanasius in his *The Incarnation of the Word,* faces the charge that it is unfitting and degrading for God to become man and die to save us. Anselm's defence is that it is fitting because there was no other way possible. The work takes the form of a dialogue between Anselm and one of his monks, Boso. Again, Anselm follows the method of 'faith seeking understanding':

The correct order is to believe the deep things of the Christian faith before undertaking to discuss them by reason. But we are negligent if, having come to a firm faith, we do not seek to understand what we believe. By God's prevenient grace, I consider myself to hold the faith of our redemption, so that even were I totally unable to understand it, nothing could shake the constancy of my belief. Please show me what, as you know, many others as well as I seek to know: Why should God, who is omni-potent, have assumed the smallness and frailty of human nature in order to renew it?

CUR DEUS HOMO (BOSO TO ANSELM) 1:2

Anselm replies that it was absolutely necessary for God to become man and die in order to save us. Granted the existence of God and his character, granted the nature of man and his sin against God, God had no choice. He could not abandon mankind, the pinnacle of his creation. Nor could he simply forgive without some 'satisfaction' to restore his lost honour. But while it is mankind that *owes* this satisfaction, it is only God who is great enough to be *able* to pay it. It follows, therefore, that God had to become man in order, as man, to offer this satisfaction by his voluntary death.

The heart of the matter was this: why did God become man, in order to save man by his death, if he could have done it in some other way? You [Anselm] have shown, by many necessary reasons, both that mankind had to be restored and that this could not take place without man paying the debt which he owed to God for his sin. And this debt was so great that, while it was man alone who owed it, none but God was able to pay it. So he who paid had to be both God and man. Thus it was necessary that God should unite humanity with his own person, so that man, who in his own nature owed the debt but could not pay it, might be able to do so in the person of God.

CUR DEUS HOMO (BOSO TO ANSELM) 2:18

Anselms' argument is impressive, but not without its weaknesses. He went beyond the usual Christian claim that the cross was necessary (i.e. that God had to do *something*) to claim that it was *absolutely* necessary (i.e. that God could not have done anything else). There are also weaknesses in Anselm's understanding of the atonement itself—such as his emphasis on God's honour rather than his justice, and the stress on the cross to the exclusion of the life, resurrection and ascension of Jesus Christ. But Anselm's argument is very flexible and it can be modified to take account of these criticisms. His basic case, suitably modified, remains today a powerful argument that the incarnation and the cross are indeed fitting and reasonable.

Anselm's aim in his writings was to show how reasonable faith is, rather than to offer a strict proof of it. The beauty of the inner harmony of the Christian faith gives joy to the believer, who sees the accord of faith and reason. The unbeliever's objections (e.g. that it is degrading and unfitting for God to have become man) are met, and he is pointed to the truth of the Christian message.

Peter Abelard
A QUESTIONING FAITH

Abelard was the most brilliant thinker of the twelfth century. He was also its *enfant terrible*, both in his erotic behaviour and in his erratic theology.

Abelard was born in Brittany in 1079. He studied first under the theologian Roscellin, who was condemned for heresy, then at Paris under William of Champeaux. These two belonged to opposing camps in the major philosophical debate of the day—over the status of 'universals' and how these relate to particular individuals. What is the relationship, for example, between individual dogs and the universal 'dog'? William was a 'Realist', maintaining that the universal is more real than the individuals and exists independently of them. Roscellin was a 'Nominalist' and was accused of regarding universals as mere words, with no reality of their own. Abelard took a mediating position, seeing universals as mental concepts. They have no existence independently of particular individuals, but they are not arbitrary names. A universal, like 'dog', is real (not a mere word), but it is not a thing, not something that exists independently of individual dogs. It precedes individual dogs in the sense that God planned the creation of dogs and so the idea was in his mind, it exists in individual dogs, and it exists in our minds when we have the concept of 'dog'. This view predominated and closed the debate until the time of *William of Ockham.

Abelard, while a student under William of Champeaux and only about twenty years old, set himself up as a rival teacher. He ruthlessly attacked William's position, arguing that it led to heresy and that it was logically incoherent. The result was that students flocked from William to Abelard and William was forced both to leave Paris and to modify his position. This established Abelard's reputation for brilliance, but did not increase his popularity with the established authorities. Some years later he went to study theology under Anselm of Laon. Anselm was respected as a leading theologian, but not by Abelard: 'He had a remarkable command of words, but their meaning was worthless and devoid of all sense. The fire he kindled filled his house with smoke but did not light it up.' As with William, Abelard started giving rival lectures and drew away many of Anselm's students. Having overstayed his welcome at Laon, he returned to Paris.

At Paris Abelard lived with Fulbert, a canon of Notre Dame cathedral, and became tutor to his attractive and very well educated teenage niece, Heloise. Their relationship soon led to a meeting of more than minds and eventually Heloise had a baby boy. Fulbert was furious and Abelard sought to pacify him by marrying Heloise secretly. But this could not be kept secret and marriage meant, in that age, an end to Abelard's academic career. Accordingly he put Heloise in a convent and the enraged Fulbert determined to have his revenge. Abelard was attacked one night and mutilated in such a way as to guarantee that he would not repeat his offence. This prompted him to become a monk. But that was not quite the end of his relationship with Heloise. Years later he wrote a *Story of his Misfortunes*, which fell into Heloise's hands. She wrote to Abelard and there was a brief exchange of letters. Heloise confesses to being bitter and unreconciled to her fate, while Abelard urges her to repent of the past and to see herself as the bride of Christ. In another age they might have been happily married, but this was not possible in the twelfth century. Appropriately, they are now united, lying in the same grave at Paris.

In 1122 Abelard wrote a major work called *Sic et non (Yes and No)*, in which he juxtaposed apparently conflicting passages from the Bible, the early Fathers and other authorities. His aim was not, as used to be believed, to discredit these authorities. He saw reason as the arbiter to reconcile conflicting authorities and, if necessary, to decide between them. He did not invent this method himself. Lawyers had already begun to use philosophical methods to decide or arbitrate between conflicting authorities. Where one law appeared to conflict with another, logic was used to reconcile them and to determine the law. This method was used with great success by the Italian lawyer Gratian in his *Concord of Disconcordant Canons*, which became a standard textbook for canon (church) law. Abelard's novelty lay in the way that he applied this method to theology and to the documents of revelation. It must also be remembered that he did not always show due reverence to authority, as with William and Anselm.

Behind the *Sic et Non* lay *Abelard's basic approach to theology. Anselm of Canterbury, still in this respect within the monastic tradition, followed the method of faith seeking understanding. 'I believe in order that I may understand.' Abelard reversed this, introducing the method of doubt. The way to reach the truth is to doubt, to ask questions and thus to find the answer. In the preface to *Sic et Non* Abelard stated that 'by doubting we come to enquire and by enquiring we reach truth'. Doubt is not so much a sin (the traditional understanding of it) as the necessary beginning of all knowledge. Abelard sought to understand Christian doctrine in order to know what to believe—a reversal of the method of *Augustine and Anselm. Theology had become a science instead of a meditation. This step points forward to the rise of the modern scientific method some centuries later and also anticipates modern educational methods.

Abelard applied this method to the doctrine of the atonement. What does it mean to say that we are redeemed by the death of Jesus Christ? Abelard questioned two traditional answers to the question. He ridiculed the idea, already declining in

popularity, that the devil had any rights over mankind. If anything, the seduction of the human race by Satan gives us the right of redress over him. The death of Jesus Christ was not offered to Satan as a ransom for mankind. The ransom was paid to the one who really has rights over us—God. But Abelard questions the need for a ransom to be paid to God, who could simply forgive sin.

Indeed, how cruel and wicked it seems that anyone should demand the blood of an innocent person as the price for anything, or that it should in any way please him that an innocent man should be slain—still less that God should consider the death of his Son so agreeable that by it he should be reconciled to the whole world! These and like queries appear to us to pose a considerable problem concerning our redemption or justification through the death of our Lord Jesus Christ.
EXPOSITION OF ROMANS (3:19–26), APPENDIX

Abelard sees the significance of the death of Jesus Christ in the effect that it has on us—when we see his love for us, it awakens a response of love in us.

Now it seems to us that we have been justified by the blood of Christ and reconciled to God in this way: through this unique act of grace manifested to us—in that his Son has taken upon himself our nature and persevered therein in teaching us by word and example even unto death—he has more fully bound us to himself by love. The result is that our hearts should be enkindled by such a gift of divine grace, and true love should not now shrink from enduring anything for him.
EXPOSITION OF ROMANS (3:19–26), APPENDIX

This 'moral influence theory', which sees the cross as the supreme example of love, is true as far as it goes. But the passage of Romans which Abelard is expounding clearly teaches a much deeper significance in the cross. Also, it can be argued that the cross is an example of love only if there was some good *reason* for Jesus Christ to die—otherwise it is merely an act of bravado. It is the need for him to die for our sins to put us right with God that gives a reason for his death and makes it an act of love towards us. But did Abelard deny this? Elsewhere he speaks of Jesus Christ bearing the punishment for our sins. Some would hold that such passages cannot be taken seriously in the light of the passage quoted above. Others would see such passages as proof that Abelard did not wish to reduce the cross to merely an example of love. It may be significant that while he denies that a ransom was paid to Satan, he only asks why it is necessary for a ransom to be paid to God.

Such a brilliant and abrasive thinker could not forever stay out of trouble. One of his works was condemned in his absence at the Council of Soissons in 1121 and burnt. This did not permanently affect Abelard's career. But he felt that he was being hounded by the watchdogs of orthodoxy. Prominent among these was a St Bernard. *Bernard of Clairvaux was radically opposed to Abelard's teaching. He accused him of inventing a fifth Gospel. Bernard arranged for him to be condemned at the Council of Sens in 1140. Abelard appealed to Rome but Bernard wrote a treatise on *The Errors of Peter Abelard* to the pope, with whom he was friendly, and the sentence was confirmed. Abelard died the following year, having become a monk at the famous abbey of Cluny, where he was kindly treated.

Bernard of Clairvaux
THE LAST OF THE FATHERS

Bernard was born in 1090 at Fontaines (near Dijon), of noble parentage. In 1112 he entered the recently-founded abbey of Cîteaux, the first abbey of the new Cistercian order. Three years later, Bernard was appointed abbot of a new monastery at Clairvaux. Under Bernard this monastery grew rapidly and also became parent to some seventy new Cistercian monasteries during his lifetime.

Bernard went to Cîteaux to flee the world, but in time he became one of the most widely-travelled and active leaders of the twelfth-century church. During the 1130s he fought hard for Pope Innocent II, against the rival Pope Anacletus. Eventually he helped to secure Innocent's victory. After this, he was engaged in controversy with *Abelard, securing his condemnation at the Council of Sens in 1140 and thereafter by the pope. In 1145 his authority was further enhanced when a former monk of Clairvaux, Bernard Paganelli, became Pope Eugenius III. In the next two years, at Eugenius' request, Bernard preached round Europe, raising support for the Second Crusade. This was launched in 1148, but failed dismally, a severe blow for Bernard. But his reputation was great enough to survive such a setback. He died in 1153 and his popularity has never really waned.

Bernard has been called 'the last of the Fathers'. He was the last great representative of the early medieval tradition of monastic theology. He was a brilliant writer, earning himself the title 'mellifluous' or sweet as honey. He wrote a number of important works on monasticism. He preached regularly and many of his sermons survive—some in an unpolished state, probably much as preached; others in a highly polished literary form designed for reading. More than five hundred of his letters survive, ranging from the personal and devotional to the official and political.

● In his early years Bernard composed a more academic theological work on *Grace and Free-will*. In this he follows a strongly *Augustinian line. He maintains that our good works are at the same time entirely the work of God's grace (leaving no room for boasting) and entirely the work of our own free-will in that it is we who perform them (thus making them worthy of reward). Man's will is always free in the sense that he wills voluntarily and spontaneously. But left to himself, fallen man wills only to sin. He is free in the sense that he sins willingly, without anyone forcing him to sin—but not in the sense that he can do otherwise. Grace so moves the will that it freely and willingly chooses the good. Grace changes the will from evil to good—not by destroying its freedom but by transferring its allegiance.

What was begun by grace alone is completed by grace and free-will together. This happens in such a way that they contribute to each achievement not singly but jointly, not in turns but simultaneously. It is not that grace does part of the work and free-will the rest. But each does the whole work, according to its peculiar contribution. Grace does it all and so does free-will—except that while all is done in free-will, all is done out of [or 'by'] grace.
GRACE AND FREEWILL 14:47

● Bernard opposed a number of the errors that he saw in Abelard's teaching, including the reduction of the atonement to an example of God's love.

I was made a sinner by deriving my being from Adam; I am made just by being washed in the blood of Christ. Shall generation by a sinner be sufficient to condemn me and shall not the blood of Christ be sufficient to justify me?... Such is the justice which man has obtained through the blood of the Redeemer. But this 'son of perdition' [Abelard] disdains and scoffs at it... [Abelard believes that Christ lived and died] for no other purpose than that he might teach men how to live by his words and example and point out to them by his passion and death to what limits their love should go.
THE ERROR OF PETER ABELARD 6:16–7:17

● Bernard is known especially as a spiritual writer. He wrote a book on *Loving God* and another on *The Steps of Humility and Pride*, based on the twelve steps of humility described by *Benedict in his *Rule*. This work contains some very perceptive insights into human nature.

Humility is a virtue by which a man has a low opinion of himself because he knows himself well... You will never have real mercy on the failings of

another until you know and realize that you have the same failing in yourself... [The proud man's] eyes are closed to anything which shows his own vileness or the excellence of others, wide open to what flatters himself... His aim is not to teach you nor to be taught by you, but to show you how much he knows... He wants not so much to be better as to be seen to be better.
HUMILITY AND PRIDE 1:2; 3:6; 12:40; 13:41–42

Bernard's most famous spiritual work is his eighty-six *Sermons on the Song of Solomon*. In them Bernard teaches his monks about the spiritual life and about the steps towards mystical union with God. He also describes his own experience:

I want to tell you of my own experience, as I promised... I admit that the Word has also come to me—I speak as a fool [2 Corinthians 11:21]—and has come many times. But although he has come to me, I have never been conscious of the moment of his coming. I perceived his presence, I remembered afterwards that he had been with me; sometimes I had a presentiment that he would come, but I was never conscious of his coming or his going.
SERMONS ON THE SONG OF SOLOMON 74:5

Finally, Bernard wrote on *Consideration* for his former disciple, Pope Eugenius III. Bernard urges him to find time for reflection or meditation in his busy life. He should consider himself (his person and his office), those placed under him, those around him at Rome and those above him (in the heavenly world). Bernard had a high view of the papacy. The pope is 'the unique vicar of Christ who presides not over a single people but over all', and he has fullness of power. But Bernard is equally emphatic in his opposition to papal tyranny:

We will understand ourselves better if we realize that a ministry has been imposed upon us rather than a dominion bestowed... It seems to me that you have

*been entrusted with stewardship over the
world, not given possession of it...
There is no poison more dangerous for
you, no sword more deadly, than the
passion to rule.*
CONSIDERATION 2:6:9; 3:1:1–2

Peter Lombard
MASTER OF THE SENTENCES

*Peter Abelard was condemned, through the
intervention of *Bernard of Clairvaux. But
his work was continued by another Peter—
Peter Lombard. This Peter was born at
around the end of the eleventh century in
Lombardy (northern Italy). He studied at
Bologna, Reims and Paris (probably under
Abelard). From about 1140 he taught at
Paris and in 1159 he became bishop of that
city. He died the following year.

Peter's chief contribution was his *Four
Books of Sentences*, written between 1147
and 1151. This is a compilation of extracts
('sentences' meaning maxims, opinions)
from the Bible, the Fathers and other
authorities. Lombard's method is similar to
Abelard's—he uses reason, dialectic and
logic to arbitrate between the different
authorities. But he combined Abelard's
methods with a reverence for authority, with
the result that he won the support even of
Bernard. His aim was not to introduce new
ideas of his own but simply to decide the
truth on the basis of the established
authorities. If he thought that he was
improving on the work of his predecessors, it
would only be in the way described by
Bernard of Chartres (died about 1130):

*We are like dwarves sitting on the
shoulders of giants [the ancients]. We
see more than them and things that are
further away—not because our sight is
better than theirs, nor because we are
taller than they were, but because they
raise us up and add to our stature by
their enormous height.*
QUOTED BY JOHN OF SALISBURY, METALOGICON 3:4

It was not Lombard's aim to be original, but
in at least one area he succeeded. He was the
first to give what is now the standard Roman
Catholic list of seven sacraments. In the
early church the word 'sacrament' was used
both in a restricted sense (to refer to baptism
and the eucharist), and in a wider sense, to
refer to many other rites (such as exorcism
or the Lord's Prayer). Up to the time of Peter
Lombard the total number had been
reckoned to be anything from two to twelve.
But once Lombard proposed seven, this
number (being a 'perfect number') was
rapidly accepted, though not all chose the
same seven rites as did Lombard.
Eventually, however, his list prevailed and it
was defined as orthodoxy by the *Council of
Florence in 1439. It is clear that the decision
to have *seven* sacraments precedes the
choice of *these* seven in particular. It is not
possible to produce a convincing definition
of a sacrament which justifies the inclusion
of these seven and no other rites.

*What is a sacrament? 'A sacrament is a
sign of a sacred thing' (Augustine)...
Again, 'A sacrament is the visible form
of an invisible grace' (Augustine)... A
sacrament bears a likeness of that thing
whose sign it is. 'For if sacraments did
not have a likeness of the things whose
sacraments they are, they would not
properly be called sacraments'
(Augustine). For that is properly called a
sacrament which is a sign of the grace
of God and a form of invisible grace, so
that it bears its image and exists as its
cause. Sacraments were instituted,
therefore, for the sake, not only of
signifying [being signs], but also of
sanctifying [conveying grace].*
SENTENCES 4:1:2,4

*Why the sacraments were instituted:
'The sacraments were instituted for a
threefold cause: as a means of
increasing humility, as a means of
instruction and as a spur to activity. As
a means of increasing humility indeed,
so that a man should submit himself
(out of respect for God's command) to
material things which are inferior to*

*him by nature ... They were also
instituted as a means for instruction so
that through the outward visible form
the mind may be taught to understand
the inward invisible virtue ... Similarly,
they were instituted as a means of
spurring into activity. As a man cannot
be unoccupied, the sacraments provide
him with a useful and healthy spur, to
turn him away from empty and harmful
occupations' (Hugh of St Victor) ... God
could give grace to man without the
sacraments and has not tied his power
to them, but for the above reasons he
has instituted sacraments.*

SENTENCES 4:1:5

*On the sacraments of the New Law:
Now let us approach the sacraments of
the New Law [i.e. the New Testament].
These are: baptism, confirmation, the
bread of blessing (i.e. the eucharist),
penance, extreme unction, ordination
and marriage. Some of these provide a
remedy against sin and confer assisting
grace (e.g. baptism); others are only a
remedy (e.g. marriage); others
strengthen us with grace and power
(e.g. the eucharist and ordination).*

SENTENCES 4:2:1

Peter Lombard's theology was questioned
immediately after his death, but he was
vindicated at the *Fourth Lateran Council in
1215. Lombard's *Sentences* became a
standard theological textbook until the time
of the Reformation and beyond. Writing a
commentary on it became a regular part of
the preparation for a doctorate in theology.
Lombard came to be known as the 'Master of
the Sentences'.

Joachim of Fiore
THE THREE AGES

Joachim was born about a third of the way
into the twelfth century. As a young man he
went on pilgrimage to Palestine, where he
was converted to the monastic life. He
became a Cistercian monk, rising to become

abbot of Corazzo in 1177. But after a few
years he left to devote himself to writing.
Even-tually he founded a new monastery at
Fiore (Southern Italy) in 1182. He died in
1202.

Christians normally divide history into
two main periods—before and after Jesus
Christ. Joachim was the first to divide it into
three ages—one for each of the three persons
of the Trinity.

● The Age of the Father. This is the
Old Testament dispensation. It was the age
of the married (celibacy being rare in the Old
Testament) and was lived under the Law.

● The Age of the Son. This is the New
Testament dispensation. It is the age of the
cleric and is lived under grace. Joachim saw
this age as lasting forty-two generations of
thirty years each. It would therefore end in
about 1260, to be replaced by:

● The Age of the Spirit. This is the new
age, proclaimed by Joachim, to begin in
about 1260. It will be the age of the contemplative monk and will be lived in the freedom
of spiritual understanding. There will be a
new religious order which will convert the
whole world. The present corrupt church
and leadership will be replaced by a new
spiritual church with a new leader. Just as
the Old Testament rites (such as
circumcision) have been replaced by the New
Testament sacraments (such as baptism),
these latter will in turn be replaced by new
sacraments.

These ideas were dynamite. Incredibly,
Joachim was encouraged by three different
popes to commit them to writing. This he did
in three main works: *Harmony of Old and
New Testaments, Exposition of the Book of
Revelation* and *Psalterium of Ten Strings*.
But some of his ideas (not including the
above) were condemned in the thirteenth
century. Joachim's ideas were to be taken up
and radicalized by a number of fringe
movements, beginning with the Spiritual
Franciscans. These were the more rigorous
of the followers of *Francis of Assisi, who
were rejected by the main Franciscan order.
They adopted Joachim's ideas in the middle
of the thirteenth century and came to see
themselves as the prophesied new religious

order that would usher in the new age. Joachim's ideas were also influential on some of the fringe Anabaptist groups at the Reformation—and to some extent on mainstream Protestantism.

The first of the three dispensations ... was in the time of the Law, when the people of the Lord served like a little child for a time under the elements of the world ... The second dispensation was under the Gospel and lasts until the present. It is free in comparison with the past, but not in comparison with the future ... The third dispensation will come toward the end of the world, no longer under the veil of the letter, but in the full freedom of the Spirit ... The first dispensation is ascribed to the Father, the second to the Son, the third to the Holy Spirit.

EXPOSITION OF THE BOOK OF REVELATION, INTRODUCTION, CHAPTER 5

Fourth Lateran Council (1215)

The Fourth Lateran Council was called in 1215 by the greatest of the medieval popes, Innocent III (1198–1216). Innocent elevated papal power to its peak. He forced King John to submit to him by placing England under interdict—a sort of general strike by the clergy, who were forbidden to perform all but a bare minimum of rites. He concentrated power in the papacy out of a genuine concern for reform, but before long his successors were to seek to increase the power of the papacy for its own sake.

The Fourth Lateran Council produced seventy canons, covering a wide range of topics, of which the most important are as follows:

● The Albigenses were condemned. They held to Gnostic or Manichee beliefs. They were dualists—there are two Gods, a God of Light (the God of the New Testament) and a God of Darkness (the God of the Old

Testament). The physical world was seen as evil. The Albigenses were strong especially in the South of France, where they had support from some rulers. Innocent launched a crusade against them which led to extremes of barbarity. This largely broke the movement, though vestiges remained until the sixteenth century.

● The Waldenses were condemned. They rejected Roman Catholicism from a position of biblical simplicity rather than Gnostic heresy. They began as a movement of popular preachers—necessary because so many clergy were 'dumb dogs who cannot bark', as Innocent himself put it, echoing Isaiah 56:10. Mishandling by the church authorities pushed them reluctantly into opposition and they became an underground movement. They rejected Catholic practices which were contrary to the Bible and would not accept the ministry of immoral priests. In the sixteenth century they linked up with the Protestant Reformation. They have been bitterly persecuted over the years down to the last century. They survive in Italy to this day.

● Some of the teaching of *Joachim of Fiore was condemned. *Peter Lombard was vindicated against criticisms of his theology by Joachim and others.

● All Catholics were required to confess privately to their priest at least once a year. They should also receive communion at least once a year, each Easter. Priests are warned against breaking the 'seal of the confessional'—revealing sins that have been confessed to them in private. Any priest guilty of this is to be deposed from the priesthood and condemned to do lifelong penance in a strict monastery.

● Most importantly, this council produced the first official definition of the doctrine of transubstantiation:

There is one universal church of the faithful, outside of which there is absolutely no salvation. In this church the priest and the sacrifice are both the same Jesus Christ. His body and blood are truly contained in the sacrament of the altar under the forms of bread and

wine. The bread is transubstantiated
into his body and the wine into his
blood, by God's power. This is so that we
may receive of him what he has received
of us [flesh and blood] in order to realize
the mystery of unity [with him]. No one
can effect this sacrament except a duly
ordained priest.

CANON 1

In the early church it was generally accepted
that the bread and the wine in the eucharist
are the body and blood of Jesus Christ. But
there was little attempt to define what this
meant. In the early period it was customary
to call the bread and wine figures or symbols
or signs of Christ's body and blood—but not
in such a way as to deny that the latter were
present. In the fourth century it became
common to say that the bread and the wine
were 'converted' into Christ's body and
blood. These two ways of speaking were not
seen as contrary to one another and often
coexisted in the same writer. In the West,
*Augustine represents the 'symbolic'
tradition while *Ambrose introduced the
'conversion' approach from the East, where
it originated. The early Middle Ages saw a
growing tension between these two
approaches.

In the ninth century there was a
controversy between two monks, Radbertus
and Ratramnus, who represented the
Ambrosian and Augustinian traditions,
respectively. *John Scotus Erigena
supported Ratramnus. Both views were
acceptable in the ninth century, but by the
eleventh century attitudes had hardened.
Berengar of Tours stressed the 'symbolic'
approach, denying that the bread and the
wine are physically changed. He fought
against a growing tendency to see the
sacrament in crudely material terms, using
logic to attack such views. But his protests
were ineffectual and he was forced to sign
two recantations, in 1059 and in 1079. In the
former, he was forced to affirm that:

After consecration, the bread and the
wine which are placed on the altar are
not merely a sacrament, but even the

true body and blood of our Lord Jesus
Christ. His body and blood are handled
and broken by the hands of the priests
and are crushed by the teeth of the
faithful, not merely in a sacrament but
sensually and in truth.

This was a gross form of expression which
was rejected by many later medieval
theologians. In 1079 Berengar had to affirm,
in a more judiciously-worded recantation,
that the bread and wine are 'substantially
converted' into Christ's body and blood.
This idea of substantial conversion led to the
word 'transubstantiation', which was first
introduced in the middle of the twelfth
century. The meaning of the term was
further developed by *Thomas Aquinas.

Francis of Assisi
MARRIED TO LADY POVERTY

Francis of Assisi is the best-loved of
medieval saints. He was born in 1181/82, the
son of Peter Bernardone, a wealthy cloth
merchant of Assisi. His life was uneventful
until, in his early twenties, he had a number
of encounters with God. These led him to
draw back from his worldly life and to
embrace a life of simplicity and poverty.
While he was praying in a ruined church
outside Assisi, he heard a voice telling him
to rebuild the church. This he began to do.
But in an excess of zeal he sold some of his
father's cloth to raise money. His father was
not amused and took him to the bishop's
court in an attempt to recover the money.
Francis, in a dramatic gesture, stripped
naked and returned all of his clothes to his
father. From now on he would have only one
father—our Father in heaven.

Francis began to live a wandering life of
poverty. One day he heard Matthew 10:7–10
read in church and this came to him as a
personal call—he was to go forth and
minister in poverty, as had the apostles.
Disciples began to gather round him and in
1209/10 Francis wrote a Primitive Rule. This
is now unfortunately lost, but it seems to
have been composed mainly of passages

from the Gospels. In 1212 he went to Rome and presented it to the pope, Innocent III, who after initial misgivings gave his qualified verbal approval. This was a crucial decision since the Waldensians had begun much like the Franciscans but unwise handling had provoked them into dissent. They were condemned at the *Fourth Lateran Council in 1215.

The novelty in Francis' ideal was the central position given to poverty. He saw it as an end in itself, not a mere means to an end. He was married to Lady Poverty, the bride of Jesus Christ who had been a widow since he died. Francis' ideal was not merely a simple lifestyle, it was the total renunciation of all property.

In 1212 Francis was joined by Clare, a young heiress from Assisi, who had come to accept his ideals. With Francis' help, she founded the 'Poor Clares', the female version of the Franciscans. After this Francis made various attempts to convert the Muslims, actually meeting the Sultan in Egypt, but without success. When he returned he found that others had taken control of his followers. On the advice of Cardinal Ugolino, a friend of the Franciscans, Francis resigned as leader in 1220. The following year he wrote the *First Rule*. It was further revised, with help from the cardinal, to make it acceptable to the church authorities. In 1223 this *Second Rule* was confirmed by pope Honorius III.

In 1224, while praying on Mount Alverna, Francis had a vision of the cross and received the 'stigmata', the five wounds of Jesus Christ in the hands, feet and side. (He was the first, but by no means the last, to receive them.) Two years later, in 1266, he died, having written a final *Testament* to the order. His *Canticle of Brother Sun*, written in 1225, is also well-known, but he was not the author of the nineteenth-century prayer which is popular today under the title *Prayer of St Francis*.

Francis lived a free and spontaneous life of total poverty. But was this possible for a medieval religious order? As one writer has put it, 'the vast and unwieldy phalanx was attempting to follow in the footsteps of the most spontaneous and unconventional genius of many ages—and with the natural result'. Already in Francis' lifetime adjustments were being made. The Franciscans were not to own property, but a 'spiritual friend' could own it for them and allow them to make use of it. Before long the Franciscans had churches as large and as lavish as any others. This led to conflict in the order between those who wanted a strict observance of the *Rule* and those who wished to be more practical. To some extent this conflict was resolved by *Bonaventure, the 'Second Founder' of the order, but it lingered for centuries.

The rule and form of life of [the Franciscans] is this: to live in obedience and chastity and without property, thus following the doctrine and example of our Lord Jesus Christ ... Those who have promised obedience may have one tunic with a hood and one without, if necessary, and the cord and drawers. Let all the brethren be clothed with mean garments ... Let them not desire costly garments in this world, that they may be clothed gloriously in the kingdom of heaven ... Let the brethren take care that wherever they may be ... they never appropriate any place to themselves, nor maintain it to be theirs. And whoever comes to them, whether friend or foe, thief or robber, let them receive him courteously ... Therefore let none of the brethren, wherever they may be or wherever they may go, take or receive money in any manner, nor cause it to be received, either for their clothing or for books or as the price of their labours or, in short, for any reason except the urgent needs of the sick brethren. For we ought to have no more esteem of money than of stones. The devil seeks to blind those who desire or value it. Let us therefore take care lest, having renounced all things, we lose the kingdom of heaven for so small a matter. If we should chance to find money in any place, let us no more regard it than the dust we tread under

*our feet, for it is 'vanity of vanities and
all vanity'... Let all the brethren be
Catholics and live and speak in a
catholic manner.*

RULE 1, 2, 7, 8, 19

*This is how the Lord granted me,
brother Francis, to begin to do penance.
While I was in sin, it seemed to me too
bitter a thing to see lepers, but the Lord
led me among them and I showed mercy
to them. And when I left them, what had
appeared to me bitter was changed into
sweetness of body and soul. Not long
after this I forsook the world... When
the Lord had given me the care of the
brethren, no one showed me what I
ought to do—but the Most High himself
revealed to me that I should live
according to the form of the holy gospel.
This I had written down in a few simple
words and our lord the pope confirmed
it for me. Those who came to embrace
this life gave all they had to the poor...
As the Lord gave me to speak and write
the* Rule *and these words, purely and
simply, so you must understand them
simply and purely, without gloss, and
doing good, keep them to the end.*

TESTAMENT

Bonaventure
JOURNEY INTO GOD

John of Fidanza was born in Tuscany
(northern Italy) in 1221. In his late teens or
early twenties he joined the Franciscan order
and was given the name Bonaventure. He
says that he was attracted to *Francis
because he was like the early apostles in his
unlearned simplicity. But Bonaventure felt
that it was right that as the church had gone
on to produce learned doctors, so also the
Franciscans should rise to the highest
academic levels. He himself studied at Paris
and taught there from 1248 to 1255. In 1255
the friars (Franciscans and Dominicans,
founded by the Spaniard Dominic in 1216)
had to leave the university because of
opposition from their enemies. But in 1257

they returned, with Bonaventure as a
professor.

The thirteenth century was an age of
crisis for Christian theology. Previously in
the medieval West Aristotle had been known
only through his works on logic. Now, in the
thirteenth century, translations were made
from the original Greek, and Western
thinkers were faced with the full impact of
his philosophy. This challenged the
Platonist world-view, which had until then
been unquestioned in the medieval West.
*Thomas Aquinas adopted Aristotle's
philosophy and sought to reconcile it with
Christian theology. Bonaventure, on the
other hand, held firm to the traditional Neo-
Platonist philosophy. He read Aristotle and
borrowed ideas from him, but these were
fitted into an essentially Platonist
framework. He used Aristotle, but he did not
call him master.

A striking example of Bonaventure's
Neo-Platonism lies in his theory of
illumination. With *Augustine, he believed
that unchanging concepts, such as justice or
beauty, cannot be learned through the bodily
senses—through observation or through
reading or hearing about them. Instead, they
are learned directly in the soul, through the
eternal Ideas of justice or beauty. How can
we judge one action to be more just than
another unless we see the eternal
unchanging Idea of justice? This truth is
seen in 'the true light that gives light to
every man, (John 1:9). 'In your light, we see
light' (Psalm 36:9).

*Nothing can be understood unless God
himself by his eternal truth immediately
enlightens him who understands... God
is to be called our teacher because our
intellect attains to him as to the light of
our minds and the principle by which we
know every truth.*

DISPUTED QUESTIONS CONCERNING CHRIST'S
KNOWLEDGE 4:1:24, 34

In 1257 Bonaventure was appointed to lead
the Franciscan order as its Minister General.
He inherited conflict within the order over the
practicality of Francis' *Rule* and the need to

modify it. Bonaventure helped to resolve these tensions and is known as the 'Second Founder' of the order. In 1260 he was commissioned to write a new biography of Francis and in 1263 his *Life of St Francis* became the official biography. In 1266 a decree ordered the destruction of all copies of earlier accounts—but mercifully failed to suppress them completely. The aim was to 'sanitize' the historical Francis and to exclude all that might conflict with the newly-established order. For example, one of the earlier lives, by Thomas of Celano, recounts how Francis shortly before his death celebrated the eucharist. As he was not an ordained priest, this had been forbidden by the *Fourth Lateran Council in 1215. Bonaventure refers to the same incident, but eliminates any reference to the eucharist.

Bonaventure was offered the archbishopric of York in 1265, but declined. In 1273 he succumbed to pressure and became the cardinal bishop of Albano. He died the following year, at the important Council of Lyons where East and West were negotiating reunion.

Bonaventure is remembered as much as a spiritual writer as a theologian. His best-known work is his *Journey of the Soul into God*. The inspiration for the work came in 1259 while he was meditating at the spot where Francis had received the 'stigmata' (wounds of Jesus Christ). The journey to God is not easy:

Whoever wishes to ascend to God must first avoid sin, which deforms our nature, then exercise his natural powers mentioned above: by praying, to receive restoring grace; by a good life, to receive purifying justice; by meditating, to receive illuminating knowledge; and by contemplating, to receive perfecting wisdom. Just as no one comes to wisdom except through grace, justice and knowledge, so no one comes to contemplation except by penetrating meditation, a holy life and devout prayer.
JOURNEY 1:8

There are three stages in the journey:

● Meditation on nature. As man expresses himself in language, so God expresses himself through creation. His creatures are signs or symbols of him, his shadows or vestiges. Nature is to be studied not for its own sake but to lead us to God.

● Meditation on the soul. Bonaventure's theory of divine illumination means that God is to be found in the soul. The mind knows unchanging eternal truths through the divine light. God is so present that the soul actually grasps him. One cannot say that one thing is better than another without some knowledge of the highest good by which to judge. 'When therefore the soul considers itself, it rises through itself as through a mirror to behold the blessed Trinity, *Journey* 3:5

● Meditation on God is the final stage:

For transcending yourself and all things, by the immeasurable and absolute ecstasy of a pure mind, leaving behind all things and freed from all things, you will ascend to the superessential ray of the divine darkness. But if you wish to know how these things come about, ask grace not instruction, desire not understanding, the groaning of prayer not diligent reading, the Spouse [Jesus Christ] not the teacher, God not man, darkness not clarity, not light but the fire that totally inflames and carries us into God by ecstatic unctions and burning affections.
JOURNEY 7:5–6

Thomas Aquinas
NATURE AND GRACE

Thomas Aquinas was born in 1225 near Naples as the younger son of the count of Aquina. He went to the university of Naples and while there, in 1244, joined the relatively new Order of Preachers, the Dominican friars. In disgust, his family kidnapped him and held him captive for some months—but to no avail. Thomas continued his studies at Paris and at Cologne under the famous Dominican theologian Albert the Great, who greatly influenced him. In 1252 he returned to Paris to lecture. Thereafter he taught at Paris and in Italy until his death in 1274, on the way to the Council of Lyons.

Thomas faced the burning issue of the thirteenth century—how to react to the philosophy of Aristotle. He did not agree with those who wanted to suppress Aristotle and he did not follow his older contemporary *Bonaventure, who kept to the traditional Platonist world-view. Thomas followed Aristotle's philosophy. But here he also parted company with those who followed Aristotle to the point of contradicting Catholic doctrine (e.g. by teaching that the universe was eternal and had no beginning). Thomas's aim was to construct a synthesis between reason and faith, philosophy and theology, Aristotle and Catholic doctrine. He followed Aristotle's philosophy, but not blindly. Occasionally he felt the need to correct him, as with his opinion concerning the age of the universe. But generally he followed him because he believed him to be right. He maintained that Aristotelian philosophy and Catholic theology could be held together, with no conflict between the two.

Thomas did not see philosophy and theology as merely compatible with one another—like music and geology, say. He believed that correct philosophy can greatly aid theology. The aim of God's grace is not to destroy human nature, nor to act separately from it, but to perfect it. Human reason, by the use of philosophy, can discover much that is true about the world, mankind and even God. The purpose of divine revelation is to perfect human philosophy by adding to it, building on it, completing it. Revelation does not basically oppose human philosophy (though it will oppose *false*, incorrect philosophy), but rather supplements it and brings it to completion and perfection. Thomas's system is like a two-storey house: Aristotelian philosophy provides the foundation and the first storey; Catholic theology perfects and completes it by adding the second storey and the roof (with the assistance of philosophy).

Thomas wrote extensively— commentaries on Scripture, philosophical and theological treatises, commentaries on Aristotle. But two of his works stand out especially:

● The *Manual against the Heathen* was written in the early 1260s, in four books. It was written for the benefit of unbelievers, like the Jews and the Muslims. It exemplifies Thomas's nature/grace approach. In Books 1 to 3 he argues on the basis of reason/ philosophy alone. Scripture and tradition are invoked only to confirm conclusions already reached by reason. On this basis Thomas seeks to establish the existence of God, his attributes (such as love, wisdom, omnipotence), his creation of the world, his providence and predestination. In the final book, Thomas goes on to present those doctrines which cannot be reached without Christian revelation—the Trinity, the incarnation of Jesus Christ, the sacraments, the resurrection of the body. These doctrines are *beyond* the grasp of unaided reason, but they are not *contrary* to reason.

● The *Sum of Theology*, written in the last ten years of Thomas's life, was intended as a textbook to replace *Peter Lombard's *Sentences*, though it did not succeed in this aim for some centuries. It is a massive work of more than two million words—some twenty times longer than this volume. Since it is addressed to Catholics rather than to unbelievers, the distinctive truths of revelation are not kept to the end. But Thomas still distinguishes between that which can be discerned by reason and that which can be known only by revelation. In this, his greatest work, Thomas takes the theology of *Augustine which was presented in Neo-Platonist terms, and restates it in Aristotelian terms. It is one of the greatest systematic presentations of the Christian faith ever produced. Thomas did not live to complete this work, but some of his disciples supplied a supplement drawn from his other works to complete it. Near the end of his life Thomas had a vision while saying mass, which caused him to stop writing. He stated that in comparison with what had then been revealed to him, all that he had written seemed like straw.

The layout of the *Sum of Theology* is

distinctive. It is divided into three parts, the second of which is subdivided into two further parts. The whole work is divided into 512 questions, each of which is normally divided into a number (from one to ten) of points of inquiry. Under each point, Thomas begins by marshalling evidence which appears to contradict his position. This consists of philosophical arguments or quotations from authorities such as the Bible or the Fathers. But he then counters this with a reason or a quotation in favour of his own position. Then in a 'reply' he resolves the question to his satisfaction. Aristotle is the most frequently quoted (as 'the philosopher') and after the Bible Augustine heads the list of theological authorities. For the benefit of those without the leisure to read the whole of the *Sum*, Thomas also wrote a relatively brief *Compendium of Theology*.

Thomas is famous for his teaching about analogy. What do we mean when we speak of God—e.g. 'God is good' or 'the Lord is my rock'? Is such language univocal—i.e. do the words 'good' and 'rock' mean exactly the same as when used of people or boulders in everyday language? If God is transcendent, they cannot. Is such language then equivocal—i.e. do the words mean something completely different from their everyday usage, as a dog's bark is totally different from a tree's bark? If that were so, we would have to say that we know *nothing* about God. This would contradict Romans 1:20, which implies that the creation does tell us something about God.

Thomas distinguishes two different types of statement about God. Some are metaphorical—such as 'the Lord is my rock'. This is a metaphor because the word rock applies primarily to physical rocks and only in a secondary way to God, to draw out certain points of comparison, such as God's reliability. Other words are used properly and strictly of God—as when we say that God is good. Such a statement lies between the univocal and the equivocal. God's goodness can be compared to ours, so there is a ground for using the same word. But the word good does not have *exactly* the same

meaning when applied to God and to man. (Thomas uses the argument that man's goodness is distinct from his being—he can cease to be good—while God's is not.)

If God and man are both called good, but in different senses, which sense is primary? As regards our language, the latter. It is human goodness that we know first. 'We cannot speak of God at all except in the language that we use of creatures.' But Ephesians 3:14–15 implies that human fatherhood is named after God's fatherhood. While the word rock applies primarily to physical rocks, words like good apply primarily to God (and therefore are used of him properly and accurately, not metaphorically). That is, it is God who is the *cause* of all creaturely goodness. Furthermore, God's goodness is *perfect*. Therefore the word good is used most appropriately of God. 'No one is good—except God alone' (Mark 10:18). But *our* understanding of the term is derived from human goodness. Thus Thomas leaves us with a real, but imperfect, knowledge of God. 'God surpasses human understanding and speech. He knows God best who acknowledges that whatever he thinks and says falls short of what God really is.'

Names applied to God and to other beings are not used either entirely univocally or entirely equivocally … They are used according to analogy … For, from the fact that we compare other things with God as their first origin, we attribute to God such names as signify perfections in other things. This clearly brings out the truth that, as regards the giving of the names, such names are used primarily of creatures, inasmuch as the intellect that gives the names ascends from creatures to God. But as regards the thing signified by the name, they are used primarily of God, from whom the perfections descend to other beings.
COMPENDIUM OF THEOLOGY 1:27

Thomas is also famous for his teaching on the eucharist. He expounded the doctrine of transubstantiation, which had been barely stated at the *Fourth Lateran Council in 1215.

If the substance of Christ's body and blood are present in the eucharist, what happens to the substance of bread and wine? There were three theories at this time:

● That the substance of bread and wine remains alongside the substance of Christ's body and blood—'consubstantiation'.

● That the substance of bread and wine is annihilated and replaced by the substance of Christ's body and blood—'annihilation'.

● That the substance of bread and wine is changed into the substance of Christ's body and blood—'conversion'.

When the term transubstantiation was first coined in the twelfth century it could be used of *any* of these theories. Indeed, the first known use of the term refers to the annihilation theory. When the Fourth Lateran Council defined the term, it was not understood to have decided between the three theories. But Thomas argued that consubstantiation was heretical and annihilation was 'clearly false'. By the following century, the term transubstantiation was thought to refer to the conversion theory *alone* and the others were deemed to have been excluded by the Fourth Lateran Council.

Some have held that after the consecration the substance of the bread and wine remains in this sacrament. But this position cannot be sustained. First of all, it would destroy the reality of this sacrament, which demands that the very body of Christ exist in it. Now, his body is not there before the consecration. But a thing cannot be where it was not before, except by being brought in locally or by something already there being changed into it ... Now it is clear that the body of Christ does not begin to exist in this sacrament by being brought in locally. First, because it would thereby cease to be in heaven, since anything that is locally

moved begins to be somewhere only by leaving where it was ... For these reasons it remains that there is no other way in which the body of Christ can begin to be in this sacrament except through the substance of bread being changed into it. Now, what is changed into something else is no longer there after the change. The reality of Christ's body in this sacrament demands, then, that the substance of bread be no longer there after the consecration.

SUM OF THEOLOGY 3: 75: 2

Thomas believed that after consecration (the recital of Jesus' words at the Last Supper over the bread and wine), the bread and the wine cease to exist because they are changed into Christ's body and blood. But the undeniable fact remains that the consecrated 'elements' look, feel, taste and smell like bread and wine. How is this explained? The Fourth Lateran Council declared that Christ's body and blood are present under the figures or appearances of bread and wine. Thomas developed a philosophical theory to explain this. Aristotle had distinguished between 'substance' and 'accidents'. In everyday language we distinguish between John Smith as a person and aspects of him which can change without him ceasing to be John Smith—his weight, his marital status, his honesty, his knowledge, his complexion. Aristotle would see these changing aspects as the 'accidents' of the 'substance' John Smith. Thomas maintained that in transubstantiation the substance of bread and wine is entirely converted into the substance of Christ's body and blood, while the accidents of bread and wine remain. This means that to our senses they appear to be bread and wine— whether we taste them, feel them, weigh them, analyse them chemically, etc. But why should there be this deceptive appearance?

It is obvious to our senses that, after the consecration, all the accidents of the bread and wine remain. Divine providence very wisely arranged for this. First of all, men have not the custom of eating human flesh and drinking human blood; indeed the thought revolts them. And so the flesh and blood of Christ are given to us to be taken under the appearances of things in common human use—namely bread and wine. Secondly, lest this sacrament should be an object of contempt for unbelievers, if we were to eat our Lord under his human appearances. Thirdly, in taking the body and blood of our Lord in their invisible presence, we increase the merit of our faith [by believing against the evidence of our senses].

SUM OF THEOLOGY 3:75:5

Thomas expounded the Catholic doctrine of transubstantiation. He defended the doctrine of the real presence, but at the same time he sought to protect it from a crudely material understanding. Christ's body is not present locally, 'as in a place'. His body remains in heaven and cannot be tied down to the consecrated wafer. It is not even correct to say that the substance of Christ's body fills the space vacated by the substance of the bread. His body is present, but 'it does not follow that the body of Christ is in this sacrament as localized'. This means that his body cannot be moved. If the consecrated wafer is moved, Christ's body, which is stationary in heaven, is not moved:

Now according to this mode of his being under the sacrament, Christ is not moved locally in any strict sense, but only after a fashion. Christ is not in this sacrament as if he were in a place, as we have already said; and what is not in a place is not moved locally, but is only said to be moved when that in which it is is moved.

SUM OF THEOLOGY 3:76:6

Thomas was a large man who moved slowly and always remained calm. His fellow students used to call him the 'dumb ox'. But his teacher, Albert the Great, once prophesied that 'this dumb ox will fill the world with his bellowing'. Thomas's reputation was considerable in his own day,

but his views did not go unopposed. Some of them were condemned shortly after his death. It was not until after his canonization as a saint in 1323 that opposition died down. Even then, his influence in the fourteenth and fifteenth centuries was not very great. It is more recently that he has become pre-eminent. In 1879, Pope Leo XIII instructed all theological students to study Thomas's works. However, since the *Second Vatican Council and the desire for modernization in the Roman Catholic Church, Thomas's influence has again declined.

John Duns Scotus
THE SUBTLE DOCTOR

John Duns Scotus was born in about 1265 in Scotland, not far north of the English border. In his early teens he became a Franciscan friar. After studying at Oxford and Paris, he lectured at both universities on the *Sentences* of *Peter Lombard. In 1307 he moved to Cologne where he died, still relatively young, the following year.

Because he died young, Duns wrote little. His major works were his two *Commentaries on the Sentences*, written at Oxford and Paris. He did not live long enough to write a *Sum of Theology*. His thought is not easy to follow, earning him the title 'Subtle Doctor'. In the sixteenth century the Humanists and the Protestant Reformers were not so polite about his obscure style and coined the word 'dunce' from his name.

As a Franciscan, Duns followed *Bonaventure in many ways, but he rejected his theory of divine illumination. Much of Duns' writing was in conscious opposition to *Thomas Aquinas. Indeed his theology has been called 'a counterblast to Thomism'. Thomas believed in the primacy of reason and knowledge over the will. The will follows what reason presents to it as the highest good. God's will can therefore be explained by the use of reason. Duns, by contrast, stressed the primacy of the will. Reason shows the will what is possible, but the will itself is free to choose whichever of these it will. The freedom of the will means that it does not simply follow whatever reason dictates.

Two major implications follow from this. Duns stressed the freedom of God. Things are the way that they are not because reason requires it but because God freely chose it. (But Duns did not teach that God's will is arbitrary or beyond all constraint—God cannot contradict himself, for instance.) One aspect of God's freedom lies in his predestination. Duns identifies four 'moments' in God's predestination. First, he predestines Peter (representing the elect) to eternal glory. Secondly, he decides to give Peter the means to this end—grace. Thirdly, he permits both Peter and Judas (representing the non-elect) to sin. Finally, Peter is saved by God's grace, while Judas is justly rejected because he perseveres in sin.

Duns' stress on the freedom of God means that the role of reason and philosophy is necessarily limited. *Anselm had claimed that the incarnation and the cross of Jesus Christ are so necessary that God had *no choice* but to act in this way. But Duns held that they happened because God *chose* that they should. This emphasized God's freedom and also limited the possibility of showing such doctrines to be reasonable. In his stress on God's freedom, Duns went so far as to suggest that the Son would have become incarnate even had man not sinned—making the incarnation a free choice on God's part, not a necessity imposed on him by man's sin. Duns believed that reason and philosophy could prove God's existence and some of his attributes, such as his infinity. But much that Thomas believed to be demonstrated by reason (God's goodness, justice and mercy, predestination) Duns held to be known only by revelation. Such doctrines are accepted by faith alone, not proved by reason.

Duns is famous as the first major advocate of the doctrine of Mary's immaculate conception (the idea that she was conceived without any sin—that she was pure and sinless from the moment of her conception). The sinlessness of Mary was widely believed by the beginning of the Middle Ages, but all of the important theologians before Duns (Anselm, *Bernard,

Thomas Aquinas, Bonaventure) had held that she was freed from sin *after* her conception. Duns was the one who began to turn the tide—and in a way that was remarkable for one who had so little confidence in the power of reason to tell us about God. He argued that it is more perfect to preserve someone from original sin than to liberate them from it. Jesus Christ, as the perfect redeemer, must have redeemed someone in the most perfect way possible—and who more fittingly than his mother? By presenting Mary's immaculate conception as the most perfect form of redemption, Duns defused the major objection to the doctrine—that it would mean that Mary did not need redemption. But he himself claimed no more for the immaculate conception than its *probability*. Eventually Duns' theory won and was defined as dogma in 1854 by Pope Pius IX in his bull *Ineffabilis Deus*.

Upon this question I say that God was able to effect it that Mary was never in original sin. He was able also to effect it that she remained in sin for a moment or for a certain time and was cleansed of it in the last instant of that time. Which of the three solutions really took place whose possibility I have shown, God knows. If they are not repugnant to the authority of the church or the authority of Scripture, it seems probable that one is to attribute the most excellent to Mary.

COMMENTARY ON PETER LOMBARD'S SENTENCES, 4:1:3

William of Ockham
THE SIMPLEST EXPLANATION

William was born near the end of the thirteenth century at Ockham, near Woking in Surrey. While still a young student at Oxford, he became a Franciscan friar. He went on to teach at Oxford, but some of his views were deemed to be heretical. In 1324 he was summoned to the papal court at Avignon to answer charges of heresy. While there he met with Spiritual Franciscans, who were seeking to follow the absolute poverty of *Francis' *Rule* to the letter. This position was condemned as a heresy by Pope John XXII, of whom it has been said that he 'possessed in his nature not one single feature in common with St Francis'! Ockham sided with the Spirituals and was imprisoned. In 1328 he escaped with the General of the Franciscans and fled to the court of the emperor, Ludwig of Bavaria, the pope's enemy. William was promptly excommunicated. Before long he moved with the imperial court to Munich, where he stayed until his death. There was an understanding that the emperor would defend William with his sword while William would defend the emperor with his pen. After Ludwig's death in 1347 William sought to be reconciled to the church. He died in 1349/50 of the Black Death, which at that time was devastating Europe.

Ockham was the most influential theologian of the fourteenth and fifteenth centuries. He is best known for the famous 'Ockham's Razor' or Law of Economy. This is the principle of simplicity—'the simplest explanation is the best', or 'it is futile to multiply hypotheses when a few will suffice'. This principle Ockham applied to medieval theories about 'universals', with devastating effect.

Ockham reopened the debate over universals, resolved earlier by *Peter Abelard, but moved the debate on to a different plane. He argued that only the individual is real. Universals are purely mental concepts which have no reality or existence outside of the mind of the person thinking them. In my mind I have a mental concept of 'humanity'. This is a useful logical category, but in fact there is no such entity as 'humanity'. All that exists is individual human beings. Universals like 'humanity' do not exist, save as concepts in our minds. They are not more real than individuals, they are not even realities in which individuals participate. William did not deny the validity of universals as concepts, but he did deny them any other reality. We have here a factor that has

encouraged Western individualism, so often mistakenly seen as a Christian ideal. It makes it hard for the modern Westerner to grasp Christian doctrines like original sin or the atonement, which presuppose a certain solidarity of the human race.

Ockham also held that all true knowledge is acquired empirically—through the senses. The only reality to be known is individuals, and they are known by sense experience. There are no real universals to be contemplated in the mind. This severely limits the power of reason to rise above the things of this world. It is not possible to prove the existence of God—only to give 'probable arguments'. The disengagement of theology and philosophy, begun by *Duns Scotus, is taken further by William. God is apprehended not by reason (*Thomas Aquinas), nor by illumination (*Bonaventure), but by faith alone. The theologian must rely simply on God's revelation—reason can offer no more than supporting probable arguments. This is the end of the synthesis between faith and reason. They may not be divorced, but each is kept firmly in its place—reason confines itself to the study of nature, faith to the things of God.

Ockham's stress on empirical knowledge, together with his stress, inherited from Duns Scotus, on God's freedom, helped to pave the way for the rise of modern science in the seventeenth century. Aristotle argued that the planets must move in circles because the circle is the perfect shape. But the doctrine of God's freedom means that he is not forced to place them in any particular orbit. The stress on empirical knowledge points to the need to *look* to see whether the planets move in circles.

While at Munich Ockham wrote extensively on church–state relations, mainly against the pope. He held that the highest authority in the church is not the pope but a general council (including lay representation). Such a view ('Conciliarism') was widespread in the fourteenth and fifteenth centuries, especially during the time of the Great Schism (1378–1414), when there were a number of rival popes. William taught that the pope has no secular power and that the emperor can depose the pope. He also held that only the Bible and the universal church cannot err and that the pope must submit himself to them.

Ockham's teaching on God's grace and human free-will was also influential in the late Middle Ages. He revived Semi-Pelagianism, which had been condemned at the *Council of Orange in 529 (by this time forgotten). Earlier medieval theologians, such as Thomas Aquinas and Duns Scotus, had taught that God will not refuse his grace to those who do their very best—but they had been thinking of the Christian who by God's grace does his best. William took the same principle and applied it to the person who does not yet have God's grace. The unbeliever, or the Christian who has lost God's grace, can merit grace by doing his very best of his own unaided strength. This teaching was opposed by *Thomas Bradwardine and was further developed in the next century by *Gabriel Biel.

Ockham's position came to be known as the 'modern way', in contrast to the 'old way' of Thomas Aquinas and Duns Scotus. It dominated the thinking of the late Middle Ages. It has a further significance in that *Martin Luther and some of the other Protestant Reformers were brought up on this theology. It left its mark on them, both in what they retained and in what they rejected.

Thomas Bradwardine
GOD'S SOVEREIGNTY

Thomas Bradwardine was born towards the end of the thirteenth century in England—probably at Chichester. He studied and taught at Oxford, at Merton and Balliol colleges. In 1337 he was appointed chancellor of St Paul's Cathedral and retained this post until 1348. In 1349 he became archbishop of Canterbury, but died of the Black Death after a mere thirty-eight days in office.

Bradwardine is known especially for his opposition to the New Pelagians. In his student days he was taught the Semi-Pelagianism of *William of Ockham and his disciples—possibly by William himself. This teaching included the idea that the sinner can of his own natural power, without God's grace or the inspiration of the Holy Spirit, merit the gift of God's grace. This grace is not merited *strictly*, in the way that a worker earns his wages, but it can be merited in the sense that the sinner can please God by his good works.

Bradwardine describes how he was taught this Semi-Pelagianism.

At the faculty of philosophy I rarely used to hear about grace, except in an ambiguous way. But the whole day I would hear that we are masters of our own free acts and that it is in our power to do good or evil, to have virtues or sins, and many things like that.

THE CASE OF GOD AGAINST THE PELAGIANS PREFACE

But one day God spoke to Thomas through Romans 9:16 (salvation does not 'depend on man's desire or effort, but on God's mercy'), and he was converted to *Augustinianism.

However, even before I became a theological student, [Romans 9:16] came to me as a beam of grace and in a mental representation of the truth I thought I saw from afar how the grace of God precedes all good works in time and in nature.

THE CASE OF GOD AGAINST THE PELAGIANS, PREFACE

Thomas had come to see that God's grace is given as a free gift and cannot be earned or merited by our unaided efforts. This conversion caused him to write his greatest work, *The Case of God against the Pelagians*, which he completed in about 1344. In this work he opposed the Semi-Pelagians, arguing for a full-blown Augustinianism. But Bradwardine has been accused of going beyond Augustine in two important areas.

Bradwardine opposed the idea of astral

determinism—that our fate is determined by the stars. But he has been accused of a different form of determinism—of teaching that God determines all our actions in such a way that no room is left for human free-will. Thomas taught that all things happen because God causes and directs them—in that sense all things happen 'necessarily'. God does not merely *permit* evil—he permits it because he already *wills* it. Here Bradwardine goes beyond Augustine, but at the same time he takes care to deny that everything happens by an *absolute* necessity. The type of necessity which he maintains does not exclude human free-will. Not that sinful man has *ethical* freedom—he cannot choose the good unless God's grace moves him. But at all times man has *psychological* freedom—he wills freely and spontaneously, not coerced by any external influence.

While Bradwardine followed Augustine in maintaining man's psychological free-will, he did go beyond Augustine. The reason for this is that Bradwardine's primary concern was to protect God's sovereignty, while Augustine's primary concern was to protect the freeness of salvation. Because Bradwardine is concerned with God's sovereignty, he stresses that man, *as man*, can do no good. Even apart from or before the fall, man can do no good without God's grace. In other words, God's predestination is sovereign and man is totally dependent upon grace because he is a *creature*. Augustine, by contrast, holds that man can do no good *because of the fall*. Man needs God's grace because he is a sinner. The sovereignty of predestination and man's need for grace are the consequences of his *sin*. Augustine's emphasis here is biblical. Bradwardine has shifted the emphasis on to a more philo-sophical and less biblical plane, because he has an inadequate concept of the fall.

Bradwardine was not alone in his opposition to the New Pelagians. His contemporary, Gregory of Rimini, who died in 1358 as the General of the Austin friars, also stood against them. Gregory was more influenced than Bradwardine by the

philosophical approach of Ockham and his followers, though he vigorously opposed their theology. He also kept closer to Augustine than did Bradwardine, avoiding some of his extremes. *John Wyclif considered himself a disciple of Bradwardine, though the extent of the influence is debated.

Does Augustine mean that we receive faith before we receive grace? But we cannot walk in faith without being in grace. How would we ever have received this grace? By our preceding merits? Grace is given to you, it is not a payment. That is why it is called grace—because it is freely given. You cannot buy with preceding merits what you have already received as a gift. Therefore the sinner has received first grace in order that his sins might be forgiven. What has he merited? When he demands justice he will receive punishment and when he asks for mercy he will receive grace.

THE CASE OF GOD AGAINST THE PELAGIANS 1:47

John Tauler
PRACTICAL MYSTIC

The fourteenth and fifteenth centuries saw a flowering of mysticism. Many of the greatest mystical writers of all time lived then—such as *Catherine of Siena, *Walter Hilton, Julian of Norwich, Richard Rolle, Henry Suso. There were two strands in the mystical tradition—the intellectual and speculative approach, influenced by Neo-Platonism, and a more practical approach which stressed the imitation of Jesus Christ. The first approach was found in Meister Eckhart (died 1327/28). He was a popular and respected teacher, but he was incautious in some of his statements—for example, in referring to a 'divine spark' within the human soul. Neo-Platonist mysticism was always in danger of lapsing into pantheism (as with *John Scotus Erigena) and in 1326 Eckhart was accused of heresy. While there is no doubt about his desire to be orthodox, in 1329 twenty-eight of his statements were condemned by the pope—eleven as 'dangerous', seventeen as heretical. Eckhart's influence continued through his disciples, especially Tauler.

John Tauler was born at Strassburg in about 1300. While in his teens he became a Dominican friar there and came under the influence of Eckhart, who was teaching at Strassburg at this time. He also later studied under Eckhart at Cologne. Tauler himself became a leading spiritual teacher and he helped to spread some of Eckhart's ideas. But he learned from Eckhart's condemnation, being more cautious and pastorally sensitive in his teaching. He laid his stress on the practical side of mysticism and aimed his teaching not at a spiritual elite but at all Christians. During the Black Death (1348–49) he devoted himself to caring for the sick, which enhanced his reputation. He died in 1361. He was a preacher rather than a writer. The only genuine works which survive are some sermons. These were preached before nuns and recorded at a later date. It was Tauler's brand of mysticism which became popular in the fourteenth and fifteenth centuries. It was influential in the 'Rhineland school' of mysticism (which produced a work called the *German Theology*, admired by *Luther), in the English mystical tradition and in the Modern Devotion, of which *Thomas à Kempis is the best-known representative.

We shall now consider some tokens of true lowliness, which is never without meekness ... He who sincerely desires to become lowly of heart must not be ashamed of performing any outward office such as the worldly heart thinks mean and humiliating. Just as it is a sure sign of conversion from sin that it becomes hateful to the man, so it is a sign of true repentance when he is ready in all things to take the meanest place ... He must always be ready to acknowledge himself in fault towards whomsoever it may be, and esteem others better than himself. By doing this the loving heart can best soften men's dispositions and
touch their hearts and win them over to meekness ... In the third place, it belongs to a lowly heart to be kindly affected towards all, not with a partial love—that is, not to show more kindness to one rather than another, to friends more than to strangers, but to do good to all for God's sake, as our neighbours ... In the fourth place, it is necessary to lowliness of heart that we divest and disencumber ourselves of all things, that we may cleave only to our merciful God and become one with him. For God will not and cannot unite himself or dwell with a worldly heart ... May God help us to learn thus to be meek and lowly of heart. Amen!

SERMON ON MATTHEW 11:29

As our blessed Lord drew St John to himself in a threefold manner, even so does he now draw all who ever arrive at the deepest truth ... Like St John, each man is first called out of the world. This is when all his lower powers come to be governed by his highest reason, so that he learns to know himself and to exercise his free self-guiding power. He then sets a watch over his words ... over his impulses ... over his thoughts ... over his works ... The first step in the Christian course is to convert the outward into the inward man. Secondly, if you want to rest on the loving heart of our Lord Jesus Christ with St John, you must be transformed into the beauteous image of our Lord by a constant earnest contemplation of it. Consider his holy meekness and humility, the deep fiery love that he bore to his friends and to his foes, and the mighty obedient resignation which he manifested in all the paths which his Father called him to tread. Next call to mind the boundless charity which he showed to all men and also his blessed poverty ... But there are many who having advanced thus far, think in their hearts that they have conquered for their own the ground on which they stand—while they are yet far from the goal ... In the third place, when the Holy Spirit was given to St John, then was the door of heaven opened to him. This happens to some with a convulsion of the mind, to others calmly and gradually ... Children, this is not the work of a day or a year. Don't be discouraged. It takes time and requires simplicity, purity and self-surrender and these virtues are the shortest route to it.

SERMON ON JOHN 20:19

Catherine of Siena

Catherine di Giacomo di Benincasa was born in 1347 to a Sienese wool dyer. She was the twenty-fourth of twenty-five children. When she was seven years old she had a vision of Jesus with Peter, Paul and John. As a result of this she resolved to lead a life of celibacy. It took her family some time to come to terms with this and when she was fifteen Catherine had to cut off her hair in order to avoid marriage.

Her first confessor was Tommaso della Fonte, a Dominican. It was as a result of his influence that she became a Dominican lay sister, which meant that she would live a 'religious' life in the world. For a time she lived a life of solitude at home, during which she learned to read. This period culminated in 1368 with her experience of 'mystical betrothal' to Christ.

From 1368 to 1374 Catherine was active in Siena. She devoted herself to the care of the poor. She also embarked upon a wider pastoral ministry through letter writing. Nearly four hundred of her letters have come down to us. During this period she also underwent an experience of 'mystical death', a four-hour period of union with God during which her body appeared to be totally lifeless.

From 1375 Catherine's ministry widened beyond Siena. She found herself playing a role in wider church politics, including negotiations between the pope and the city of Florence. In 1375 she claimed to have received the 'stigmata', the five wounds of Christ, as had *Francis of Assisi, but in such a way that they were visible only to herself.

In 1377 she had further experiences of God which moved her to write her *Dialogue*, her major work.

Since 1305 the pope had been in Avignon under French control. Catherine repeatedly urged Gregory XI to return to Rome, which he finally did in 1377. But he died the following year and his successor Urban VI behaved in such a totalitarian fashion that he soon prompted the election of a rival pope, Clement VII. Thus began the forty-year Great Schism. Catherine sided with Urban and threw herself into the task of supporting him. She went to Rome, at Urban's request, but her health deteriorated and she died there in 1380.

[God to Catherine:] Listen attentively with your whole mind. To love me perfectly three things are necessary. In the first place, to purify and direct the will in its temporal loves and bodily attachments so that nothing passing and perishable is loved except because of me. The important thing is not to love me for your own sake, or yourself for your own sake, or your neighbour for your own sake, but to love me for myself, yourself for myself, your neighbour for myself. Divine love cannot suffer to share with any earthly love, and you lack in perfection and transgress my love in the measure that you let temporal things detract from it ...

In the second place: When you have reached the first stage, you will be able to go on to the second, which needs a greater perfection. Take my honour and my glory as the sole end of your thoughts, your actions, and all that you do.

In the third place: If you do that which I am going to tell you now, you will have reached a consummate perfection and nothing will be wanting in you. It is the attainment of an ardently desired and perseveringly sought disposition of the soul in which you are so closely united with me and your will so conformed to my perfect will

*that you never wish not only evil, but
even the good that I do not wish.*
DIALOGUE

John Wyclif
MORNING STAR OF THE REFORMATION

John Wyclif was born into a propertied
English family in about 1330. His life falls
into three phases. First, his academic life at
Oxford. He studied there and rose to become
Master of Balliol college for a time. He then
proceeded with his studies, financing them
in a dubious manner which was then
commonplace—he accepted ecclesiastical
office and the income attached to it, but
without fulfilling his duties. This enabled
him to continue his academic career at
Oxford until 1371, by when he had become
its leading philosopher and theologian.
Toward the end of that time he had begun to
develop radical doctrines on church
government. He argued that it is only the
godly who can rightfully exercise lordship.
Ungodly rulers have no legitimate authority.
Since the monastic orders were committed to
poverty, all their considerable wealth was
unjustly held and did not legitimately
belong to them.

The second phase of Wyclif's life began
in 1371. His doctrines about church wealth
were very convenient for the secular
government. At that time the church was
immensely wealthy, owning about a third of
all land in England, and yet it claimed
exemption from taxation. Wyclif's doctrines
were a suitable threat to be used to extort
taxes from the reluctant clergy to finance the
expensive war with France. Wyclif enjoyed
the support and protection of John of Gaunt,
the Duke of Lancaster. But in 1377 King
Edward III died, reducing the power of the
duke. Furthermore, 1378 saw the beginning
of the Great Schism, with two or more rival
popes to be played off against each other.
The English government no longer needed
Wyclif's doctrines in order to be able to
manipulate the church.

In 1378 Wyclif entered the final phase of
his life. He was no longer needed in public

life and so was able to return to his studies.
He began to develop more radical ideas, with
the result that in 1381 he was banished from
Oxford. He withdrew to Lutterworth, near
Rugby, whose absentee rector he had been
for some years. He remained there until his
death from a stroke in 1384, protected from
the wrath of the church by his noble patrons.

Wyclif was just one of many then
attacking the corruption and abuses in the
church. But he was the one major figure at
that time to go behind the practices to attack
the doctrines of contemporary Catholicism.

● Wyclif broke with Catholic tradition
in making Scripture the final authority. In
1378 he wrote *The Truth of Holy Scripture*,
in which he portrayed the Bible as the
ultimate norm, by which the church,
tradition, councils and even the pope must
be tested. Scripture contains all that is
necessary for salvation, without any need
for additional traditions. Furthermore, *all*
Christians ought to read it for themselves,
not just the clergy. For this reason Wyclif
encouraged the translation of the Bible into
the everyday language of the time. He also
sent out 'poor preachers' as evangelists to
take the Bible and preach from it. These
itinerant lay preachers were not a complete
novelty—in many ways they resembled the
early friars, except in their opposition to the
church authorities.

● In exalting the Bible, Wyclif also
demoted the papacy. In his 1379 work, *The
Power of the Pope*, he argued that the papacy
is an office instituted by man, not by God. As
*William of Ockham before him, he argued
that the pope's power does not extend to
secular government. Furthermore, the pope's
authority is not derived directly from his
office but depends on him having the moral
character of Peter. A pope who does not
follow Jesus Christ is the Antichrist (the
counterfeit Christ referred to in the New
Testament, who is the enemy of the truth).
Later Wyclif went further and rejected the
papacy completely, seeing all popes (not just
bad popes) as Antichrist.

● Wyclif also opposed the Roman
doctrine of transubstantiation—in 1379 in
his *Apostasy* and the following year more

fully in his *The Eucharist*. He denounced it on several grounds: it was a recent innovation; it was philosophically incoherent; it was contrary to Scripture. Wyclif believed himself to be following Catholic tradition, as found in *Ambrose, *Augustine and even in the 1079 recantation of Berengar. All of these held, Wyclif claimed, that the bread and the wine remain. It was only with the Fourth Lateran Council in 1215 that this was denied. Wyclif criticized both *Thomas Aquinas, for his belief that the bread and wine are converted into Christ's body and blood, and *Duns Scotus for his belief that they were annihilated.

Wyclif believed that after consecration, the bread and wine remain, having become the sacrament of Christ's body and blood. The bread is a sign, sacramentally figuring the body of Christ. But it is not a mere sign. Christ's body is present in the bread in the same way that a man's soul is present in his body. 'Thus should one believe concerning the body of Christ in the sacrament of the altar. For this is whole, sacramentally, spiritually or virtually in every part of the consecrated host [bread], even as the soul is in the body.' But one must avoid the Roman error of *identifying* the bread with Christ's body.

When we see the host we ought to believe not that it is itself the body of Christ, but that the body of Christ is sacramentally concealed in it ... We Christians are permitted to deny that the bread which we consecrate is identical with the body of Christ, although it is the efficacious sign of it ...
[Those who identify them] fail to distinguish between the figure and the thing figured and to heed the figurative meaning ... The spiritual receiving of the body of Christ consists not in bodily receiving, chewing or touching of the consecrated host, but in the feeding of the soul out of the fruitful faith according to which our spirit is nourished in the Lord ... For nothing is more horrible than the necessity of

eating the flesh carnally and of drinking the blood carnally of a man loved so dearly [Jesus Christ].
THE EUCHARIST 1:2,11; 7:58, 1:15

Wyclif could with justice claim to be returning to the position of Augustine, though his interpretation of Berengar's recantation, one of the rudest ever statements of the real presence, is farfetched in the extreme. Wyclif's own position is not totally clear and he has been claimed by the followers of both *Luther and *Calvin.

Wyclif's disciples in England became known as Lollards. They included a number of gentry until an abortive rebellion in 1414, after which they became an underground lower-class movement. The Lollards helped to prepare the ground for the English Reformation—by spreading the English Bible and by fuelling discontent with the Roman Church.

Wyclif's teaching influenced *Jan Hus, who led a reform movement in Bohemia. Hus was burnt him at the stake in 1415 at the Council of Konstanz (1414–18). The council also took the opportunity to condemn 45 errors of Wyclif. Wyclif's bones were dug up and burnt in 1428.

Wyclif and Hus were both precursors of the Protestant Reformation in that they rejected the authority of pope and general council in the name of Scripture. They also anticipated the Reformers in their attacks on individual Roman Catholic doctrines. But the chief Protestant doctrine, justification by faith alone, was not clearly taught by them.

Jan Hus

In 1360 the king of Bohemia (approximately modern-day Czechoslovakia) invited one Conrad of Waldhausen to come and preach against corruption in the church. From that time on there was a national reform movement in Bohemia. The leading figure of this movement was Jan Hus, who was born in about 1372 of poor parents in Bohemia. In 1390 he went to study at the University of Prague, where in 1402 he was appointed rector and preacher at the Bethlehem chapel. This chapel had been founded in 1391 by a wealthy merchant as a centre for reform preaching. Two sermons were preached each day, in Czech. Thus Hus had been appointed to a key position within the national reform movement.

There had been close links between England and Bohemia since 1382. *Wyclif's philosophical writings were already known in Bohemia in the fourteenth century, but in 1401 Jerome of Prague brought back from England copies of several of his more radical theological works. This led to an ongoing controversy between those who wished to condemn Wyclif and his teaching and those who defended him, though without accepting all of his radical doctrines. Hus confessed himself a disciple of Wyclif and was undoubtedly influenced by him, but only to a limited extent.

Wyclif's attack on transubstantiation met with little favour and Hus represented the majority of the Bohemian reformers in remaining loyal to the doctrine. But he followed Wyclif's attacks on clerical corruption, especially simony or the sale of spiritual privileges. Hus also accepted Wyclif's position at one vital point—his appeal from the institutional, hierarchical church to the invisible church of the elect. This was a crucial step since it laid the foundation for the rejection of the authority of wicked church leaders and for the appeal from the institutional church to the Bible.

It is one thing to be of the church, another thing to be in the church. Clearly it does not follow that all living persons who are in the church are of the church. On the contrary, we know that tares grow among the wheat, the raven eats from the same threshing floor as the dove, and the chaff is harvested along with the grain. Some are in the church in name and in reality - such as predestined catholics obedient to Christ. Some are neither in name nor reality in the church—such as reprobate pagans. Others are in the church in name only— such as, for example, reprobate

hypocrites. Still others are in the church in reality and, although they appear to be in name outside it, are predestined Christians—such as those who are seen to be condemned by the satraps of the Antichrist before the church.

THE CHURCH, CHAPTER 3

The controversy over Wyclif began in 1403 with the condemnation, by the university of Prague, of 45 theses from his writings. This condemnation was achieved by virtue of the fact that the Germans could outvote the Bohemians by three to one, which was resented by the latter. But in 1409 the king eliminated the inbuilt German voting majority in the university, with the result that the Germans left *en bloc* and founded a new university at Leipzig. The Bohemians now controlled Prague university and chose Hus to be its rector.

Hus' promotion was to be short-lived. The archbishop of Prague, Zbynek, had at first supported the reformers. But the king and the reformers were divided from the archbishop and the Germans over the issue of which of the rival popes to support. The result was that from 1408 the archbishop opposed the reforming party. The archbishop obtained from the pope a ban on preaching in chapels, including the Bethlehem Chapel. Hus refused to obey and so in 1410 he was excommunicated by the archbishop. In the same year the archbishop burned two hundred volumes of Wyclif's works. Hus and others responded by defending Wyclif's orthodoxy. Hus was summoned to Rome. He wisely declined to go in person, sending legal representatives instead.

In 1412 matters came to a head. Pope John XXIII had launched a crusade against the king of Naples and was even offering full remission of sins to all who supported him. Hus was outraged at the use of spiritual sanctions to further the pope's own personal ends and attacked the sale of the indulgences. The result was that Hus was excommunicated by Rome and the city of Prague was placed under an interdict while he was there. This meant that no religious services, not even baptisms or funerals, could take place. In the circumstances Hus felt obliged to leave the city. He withdrew to the south of Bohemia, where he wrote two of his most important works: *The Church* and *Simony*.

Hus lived during the Great Schism, when Europe was divided between two or even three rival popes who were bitterly anathematizing one another. In 1414 a council met at Konstanz to heal the schism. Hus was invited by the Emperor Sigismund and promised safe conduct in both directions, whatever might be the outcome of the case against him. With hesitations, he decided to go. But within a month the followers of John XXIII had captured and imprisoned him. Hus was put on trial by the council, despite the safe conduct, and eventually found guilty of heresy. Many of the charges made against him were untrue—such as the claim that he denied transubstantiation or that he considered the ministration of wicked priests invalid. But some of his actual teachings, especially on the church, were also tried and deemed to be heretical. Hus refused to recant so on 6 July 1415 he was condemned for heresy and taken to the outskirts of the city to be burnt. The spot is today marked by a memorial stone.

In burning Hus the council was in fact stoking up the fire of Bohemian dissent. Immediate measures were taken against his followers, but these served only to provoke a civil war. The reform movement survived, but divided into two main groups. The majority sought only minor reforms in the Roman Catholic system. Their chief demand was that the laity should receive the cup as well as the bread in communion. (The Roman Catholics reserved the cup for the clergy.) Others sought a more thorough reform. Over the coming century they were alternately tolerated and persecuted. They entered into friendly relations with the Waldensians, another dissenting group to the west. With the rise of the Reformation they made contact with both *Luther and *Calvin.

Council of Florence (1438–45)

The Council of Florence in fact met in three different places—Ferrara (1438–39), Florence (1439–42) and Rome (1443–45)—though the important business took place at Florence. The major business of the council was the reconciliation of the Eastern orthodox churches to Rome. This was the last of a series of councils at which such an attempt was made. The Easterners were desperate for military help as Turkish pressure on Constantinople increased and this forced them to make theological concessions. There were four disputed points to be discussed. In 1439 the Easterners gave way almost completely on these and a decree was issued:

● The Easterners were forced to accept the Western insertion into the 'Nicene Creed' of the word *filioque* (the Holy Spirit proceeds from the Father *and the Son*).

● It is permissible in the eucharist to use either leavened bread (the Eastern practice) or unleavened bread (the Western practice).

● The Easterners accepted the Roman doctrine of purgatory as a place where those who die penitent but without having made 'satisfaction' for their sins suffer temporary punishment.

● The Easterners were forced to accept the pope as 'the successor of blessed Peter (the prince of the apostles) and the true vicar of Christ, the head of the whole church and father and teacher of Christians.' The pope has 'full authority to feed, rule and govern the universal church'.

This decree was repudiated by the Eastern churches when the delegates returned. There was no significant military aid from the West and in 1453 Constantinople fell. The decree then became a dead letter in the East.

Also in 1439, 'agreement' was reached with the Armenian church. This church had never accepted the *Council of Chalcedon, due to an accident of history. The agreement with the Armenians was no more permanent than that with the Orthodox. But the decree issued has a wider significance in that it is the first definition by a council of the seven sacraments, as first listed by *Peter Lombard.

There are seven sacraments of the New law: baptism, confirmation, the eucharist, penance, extreme unction, orders and marriage. These are quite different from the sacraments of the Old Law, which did not cause grace but only foreshadowed the grace that was to be bestowed solely through the passion of Christ. Our sacraments, however, not only contain grace, but also confer it on those who receive them worthily. The first five have been ordained for the spiritual perfection of every individual in himself, the last two for the government and increase of the whole church. Through baptism we are spiritually reborn: through confirmation we grow to grace and are strengthened in faith. Having been regenerated and strengthened, we are sustained by the divine food of the eucharist. But if we become sick in soul through sin, we are healed spiritually through penance, and healed spiritually as well as physically (in proportion as it benefits the soul) through extreme unction. Through orders the church is governed and grows spiritually, while through marriage it grows physically.

Three elements are involved in the full administration of all these sacraments: things as the matter, words as the form, and the person of the minister performing the sacrament with the intention of doing what the church does. If any one of these is lacking, the sacrament is not effected. Three of the sacraments (baptism, confirmation and orders) imprint an indelible character on the soul—that is a kind of spiritual seal distinct from the others. They are not, therefore, to be received more than once by the same individual. The rest, however, do not imprint a character and may be performed more than once.

DECREE CONCERNING THE ARMENIANS

Thomas à Kempis
THE IMITATION OF CHRIST

Thomas Hemerken was born in 1379/80 at Kempen (near Cologne), from which he has acquired the name Thomas à Kempis. His parents were poor but they sent him to a school at Deventer (in Holland) run by the Brethren of the Common Life. This was a movement pioneered by Geert de Groote (1340–84), a wealthy canon of Utrecht who was converted from his worldly life. He started informal lay communities and his followers became involved in the task of education. In 1387 some of his disciples founded a house of Augustinian canons at Windesheim, near Zwolle in Holland, and this became the mother house of an expanding 'order'. By 1500 there were some one hundred daughter houses. These developments formed a movement known as the Modern Devotion. Despite the name, it was essentially traditional rather than novel—the emphasis lay on conversion, on the importance of practical Christian living and holiness, on meditation (especially on the life and death of Jesus) and on frequent communion. It was based especially on the teaching of *Augustine, *Bernard and *Bonaventure. But the idea of lay communities involved in secular work in towns without living under a rule was new.

In 1399 Thomas entered the house of Augustinian canons at Mt St Agues, near Zwolle, a 1398 offshoot from Windesheim. As his older brother was prior, Thomas was not allowed to become a full member, but when in 1406 his brother was transferred elsewhere, Thomas became a novice. He remained there until his death in 1471, writing, preaching, copying manuscripts and acting as a spiritual adviser. He wrote many works, of which the best known is *The Imitation of Christ*.

The Imitation of Christ is composed of four books. Originally these were four separate treatises, all of which were in circulation by 1427. It was customary to include a number of shorter treatises on one manuscript and as these four were especially popular they are often found together. The first printed version, from 1473, contains these four books as we now have them and this rapidly became the standard form.

The treatises were originally anonymous and this led to speculation as to their authorship. Already by 1460 they were being attributed to the popular writer John Gerson. Since then a wide range of other possible authors have been proposed, with less plausibility. Today it is generally accepted that Thomas was the author.

The Imitation of Christ is one of the most popular classics. It reached its ninety-ninth printed edition by the end of the fifteenth century and it has by now reached well over two thousand printings. In some ways its greatness lies in its lack of originality. It is the best representative of the spirituality of the Modern Devotion. The ideas that it proclaims belong to the mainstream of Christian spirituality and are not peculiar to any one school.

The title of the book is misleading. In fact it is only the title to the first chapter of the first book and it is not an accurate indication of the contents of the work. The keynotes of the work are self-examination and humility; self-denial and discipline: acceptance of one's lot and trust in and love for God. Book I is especially devoted to the beginnings of the spiritual life (in a monastery) while the last book is devoted to the subject of receiving holy communion. The middle books are on the inner life and on spiritual comfort.

What good can it do you to discuss the mystery of God the Trinity in learned terms if you lack humility and so displease that God? Learned arguments do not make a man holy and righteous, whereas a good life makes him dear to God. I would rather feel compunction in my heart than be able to define it. If you knew the whole Bible off by heart and all the expositions of scholars, what good would it do you without the love and grace of God?
IMITATION 1:1

Try to be patient in bearing with the

failings and weaknesses of other people, whatever they may be. You too have many faults, which others have to endure. If you cannot make yourself the kind of person that you wish, how can you expect to have someone else to your liking? We want perfection in other people, and yet we do not put right our own failings. It is clear how rarely we apply to our neighbours the same standards as to ourselves.
IMITATION 1:16

Jesus has in these days many people who love his heavenly kingdom but few who bear his cross. He has many who desire comfort, but few who are ready for trials. He has found many to share his table, but few to share his fast. Everyone longs to rejoice with him, but few are ready to suffer for him ... Surely 'mercenary' is the right name for people who are always looking for spiritual comforts. Those who are always thinking about their own profit and advantage quite clearly love themselves, not Christ.
IMITATION 2:11

Progress in the spiritual life is made not so much when you have the gracious gift of spiritual comfort, but when you can bear its removal with humility, self-denial and patience, not letting yourself grow slack in zeal for prayer, or giving up all the other things which are your normal practice.
IMITATION 3:7

If you give way to undisciplined longing for the things of this present life, you will lose the everlasting blessings of heaven. Make use of temporal gifts, but set your heart on eternal ones.
IMITATION 3:16

I [God] am the one that in a moment can raise the humble mind to more understanding of eternal truth than if he had given ten years to study. In my teaching there is no babble of words, no confusion of opinions, no arrogance of authority, no conflict of argument.

IMITATION 3:43

You must beware of trying to fathom the mysteries of this sacrament [the eucharist] out of useless curiosity, unless you want to be drowned in a flood of doubt... It is the simple approach that is blessed, one which avoids the thorny paths of debate and marches along the firm smooth road of God's commands... It is to those who become like children that he gives understanding, and he enlarges the faculties of minds that are pure. But from those who are arrogant and inquisitive he keeps his grace concealed.

IMITATION 4:18

Gabriel Biel
GOD'S MERCY AND JUSTICE

Gabriel Biel was born in Speier (Germany) in the first quarter of the fifteenth century. From 1432 he studied at Heidelberg, Erfurt and Cologne universities. This brought him into contact with both the 'old way' of *Thomas Aquinas and *Duns Scotus and the 'modern way' of *William of Ockham. Biel himself opted for the latter, though he opposed excessive rivalry between the schools. In the 1460s he joined the Brethren of the Common Life and became a leading figure in the movement. He managed to blend the spirituality of the Modern Devotion with his academic studies, avoiding the anti-intellectualism of *Thomas à Kempis. In 1484 he became the first professor of theology in the newly-founded university of Tübingen in southern Germany. In 1485 and 1489 he was elected rector of the university. On his retirement from the university he became provost of a new Brethren house in Schönbuch, where he died in 1495.

The Semi-Pelagianism of the fourteenth and fifteenth centuries is seen clearly in Biel's theology. He sets out an 'order of salvation' for the sinner—whether that be the unbaptized heathen or the baptized Christian who has fallen from God's grace by a serious (or mortal) sin. The first step must be taken by the sinner himself. He must cease from consenting to sin and must turn to God. He must love God supremely above all else. This involves doing his very best. All of this the sinner is expected to achieve of his own unaided free-will, without the grace of the Holy Spirit. This initiative by man merits God's grace—not as a wage strictly earned but because God has generously ordained that he will reward with his grace those who do their very best. Now that the sinner is in a 'state of grace', having received the grace of God, he can proceed to do good works. These merit the reward of being accepted by God, this time as a debt due to man.

Biel distinguishes between two 'pacts' on the part of God. There is the *pact of generosity* by which he promises to reward with his grace those who do their very best. Then there is his *pact of justice*, by which he ordains that those performing good works in a state of grace deserve to be accepted by him as righteous. Neither pact is forced on God—both, even the pact of justice, flow from the fact that God freely and graciously *chose* to ordain them. This enables Biel to combine doctrines of salvation by works and salvation by grace. Salvation is by works in that grace is merited by doing one's very best and God's acceptance is then merited by good works performed in a state of grace. But salvation is also by grace in that God was not obliged to ordain the pacts that he has. He could justly have imposed conditions which were impossible for sinful man. Thus God's mercy and love are seen in the order that he has established. But *within* this order there is no mercy—only justice.

Biel was largely following the doctrine of William of Ockham and others in the fourteenth century, which had been opposed by *Thomas Bradwardine and *John Wyclif. Biel is especially significant as it was his disciples who taught *Martin Luther. The spiritual problems faced by the young Luther were largely induced by Biel's doctrine of grace.

*God accepts the act of a person who
does his very best as a basis for
bestowing the first grace. This is not
because of any obligation in justice, but
because of his generosity. Now when the
soul removes the obstacle [to God's
grace] (by ceasing from the act of sin, by
ceasing to consent to it and by eliciting a
good movement toward God as its
principal and end) it does its very best.
Therefore God, in his liberality, accepts
this act of the removal of the obstacle
and the good movement toward himself
and infuses grace into the soul.*
COMMENTARY ON THE SENTENCES 2:27:1

PART 4

Reformation and Reaction

1500–1800

In 1500 papal supremacy over Christendom appeared secure. The Eastern churches, for long the centre of Christianity, had suffered a devastating blow in the capture of Constantinople by the Turks (1453). 'Conciliarism', the doctrine that the general council is the final authority in Christendom, over the pope, appeared to have been suppressed by repeated condemnations. But the foundations of papal power were not secure. Before long they were to be shaken by the earthquake of the Protestant Reformation, and some would prophesy that the pope would retain control over no more than Italy and Spain.

A number of factors paved the way for the Reformation. The late medieval papacy amply illustrated the maxim that absolute power corrupts absolutely, and there was considerable anti-papal feeling. *Wyclif shows how attack on abuses could develop into criticism of doctrine. The church was in the vulnerable position of owning fabulous wealth while manifestly lacking the moral quali-fications needed to justify her privileges to the populace. There was a revival of interest in the classical past, called 'Humanism' (not to be confused with today's atheist or agnostic Humanism). In Southern Europe this interest focussed mainly on the pagan Greek and Roman classics, but in the North there was a distinctively Christian Humanism, led by *Erasmus. The keyword was 'back to the sources'—the Hebrew and Greek Bible and the early Christian Fathers. Humanists were bitingly critical of much contemporary church life—the lives of the popes and clergy, the state of the monasteries, the obscurities of medieval Scholastic theology. But when the Reformation came, Erasmus' disciples were divided. Some opted for reform at the cost of breaking with Rome, others reckoned unity to be of greater importance than reform.

The pioneer of the Reformation was *Martin Luther. He was prepared to stand alone against the might of the Roman Church. Before long his teaching had spread widely throughout Germany and then further afield to Eastern Europe and Scandinavia. But Lutheranism was not the only version of Protestantism. In Zurich, *Zwingli began to preach reform at much the same time as Luther. While he was to some extent influenced by Luther, he was an independent thinker and differed from Luther on some matters. Before long Protestantism was split into two streams—Lutheran and Reformed (or Swiss) Protestantism. Zwingli died young and his place as the leading Reformed theologian was taken by the Frenchman *John Calvin, with the result that the Reformed faith is often known as Calvinism.

Luther and Zwingli were *magisterial* Reformers—that is, they introduced reform in co-operation with the magistrates or rulers. They did not wish to break the link between the church and the state. Their aim was not to found a new church but to reform the old one. While there was reform of doctrine, the ideal of the state church, to which all citizens belonged, remained. But there were others for whom this was only half a reformation. The radical Reformers wanted to go further than the magisterial Reformers. This they did in a variety of ways. Some were 'rationalists' who questioned fundamental Christian doctrines like the Trinity. Some were 'spiritualists' who disparaged the Bible and all outward forms. They stressed the importance of the Holy Spirit speaking to the individual soul, the 'inner light'. Some were revolutionaries' who believed that the final struggle described in the Book of Revelation was about to take place and that the godly should establish the kingdom of God by force. But the 'evangelicals' were the largest and most important group. They desired a more thorough reform in the light of the Bible. They rejected the idea of a state church and infant baptism, which inevitably accompanied it. Their opponents seized on their practice of 'rebaptizing' those baptized in infancy and called them 'Anabaptists' or 'Rebaptizers'. This was a convenient label as rebaptism was already a capital offence. The Anabaptists were bitterly persecuted and largely exterminated, but their ideas survived and have become steadily more influential.

The Reformation found the Roman Catholic Church largely unprepared. But this situation did not continue for ever. The *Council of Trent met in the middle of the century to define Roman Catholic doctrine in an anti-Protestant direction and to introduce a programme of Catholic reform. The Jesuits, founded by *Ignatius Loyola, were the shock troops of the Catholic Reformation and spearheaded the counter-attack on Protestantism. The heritage of medieval spirituality was not dead in the Roman Catholic Church, as can be seen from the great Spanish mystics John of the Cross and *Teresa of Avila.

The first fifty years of the Reformation was a period of new ideas. But the living creative movements of the early period were before long codified into detailed dogmatic systems. The three major confessions (Roman Catholicism, Lutheranism, Calvinism) all became increasingly preoccupied with a precise and intricate definition of their beliefs, and their energies were largely expended in controversy *within* the different confessions. These especially concerned questions of the relation between God's grace and human free-will. The rise of these new orthodoxies did not go unchallenged. The pietist movement in the seventeenth century, pioneered by *Spener among others, stressed the importance of practical Christian living rather than argument about minor points of theology. The eighteenth century saw the rise of rationalism as a rival to the Christian faith.

For a few this meant atheism, but for many it meant a new religion based on reason rather than revelation. 'Deism' was seen as a religion of reason in opposition to the superstitions of traditional Christianity. Rationalism, being an attack on Christianity from outside the church, had only a limited effect on Christian doctrine, but it did begin to undermine the Christian consensus in Western Europe. A force in the opposite direction was the Evangelical revival, which began in England with the *Wesleys and others and spread throughout the English-speaking world and beyond.

The English Reformation has its own interesting features. In the short space of twenty-five years there were no less than six different settlements of religion.

☐ Until 1534 England was a Roman Catholic country.

☐ In 1534 Henry VIII made himself pope in England—the 'only supreme head in earth' of the English church. But apart from abolishing the pope, Henry kept most Catholic doctrine, being a sixteenth-century 'Anglo-Catholic'.

☐ In 1549 the first prayer book of Edward's reign was issued. This was Protestant and in the English language, yet carefully phrased so as not to cause unnecessary offence to Roman Catholics.

☐ In 1552 the second prayer book of Edward's reign was issued. This was openly and unambiguously Protestant.

☐ Under Mary (1553–58) there was a return to a dogmatic form of Roman Catholicism.

☐ The 'Elizabethan Settlement' of 1559 returned to a prayer book very similar to that of 1552.

The Elizabethan Settlement was long contested by 'puritans' who wished for a more radical form of Protestantism, but in 1662 it became the definitive norm. This settlement is often described as a *via media* or middle path. This is true, but not in the sense that it is often understood today—as a middle path between Protestantism and Roman Catholicism. The Elizabethan Settlement was a compromise between Elizabeth, who wanted a more conservative form of Protestantism, and those who wished for a more radical reform. It could in some ways be seen as a compromise between Calvinism and Lutheranism. The doctrine of the *Thirty-nine Articles was a moderate Calvinism, but the retention of bishops, liturgy and other forms of Catholic ceremony was in line with Lutheran policy.

In due course, the English Reformation gave birth to Anglicanism, a distinct brand of Protestantism which has proved more hospitable to Catholic teaching than have the Reformed or even Lutheran churches. Scotland, by contrast, became and remains staunchly Reformed and Presbyterian. Attempts by the English to impose bishops and the *Book of Common Prayer* on the Scots served only to reinforce the Presbyterian convictions of the kirk.

Desiderius Erasmus
CHRISTIAN HUMANIST

Desiderius Erasmus was born in the late 1460s, the illegitimate son of a priest. He was educated for some years by the Brethren of the Common Life. The Modern Devotion, as found in *Thomas à Kempis, influenced him, though he rejected some aspects of the Brethren. He reluctantly entered one of their monasteries, but before long obtained permission to leave the monastery. After a period of study at Paris, from 1495 he became a freelance scholar, travelling widely throughout Europe. For a time he was a professor at Cambridge. From 1521 he settled at Basel, but in 1529 the Reformation there progressed beyond his liking and he left for nearby Catholic Freiburg. He returned to Basel in 1535 and died there the following year.

Erasmus was the most famous scholar of his time. He was a convinced Christian Humanist, believing that the best way to reform the church was by good scholarship—by a study of the Bible in Hebrew and Greek and by a return to the early church Fathers. He was a master of satire—one modern writer has stated that 'only when humour illuminated that mind did it become truly profound'. His satire was directed against the abuses of the contemporary church—the scandalous lives of the pope and many of the clergy, the state of the monasteries and the obscurities of medieval Scholastic theology. Erasmus' own desire was for peaceful reform of the church.

In this way Erasmus laid the foundations for the Protestant Reformation. As the adage goes, 'Erasmus laid the egg which Luther hatched'. In the early years of the Reformation, a papal agent in Germany wrote to Rome that the satires of Erasmus were harming the papacy more than the denunciations of *Luther. By making people laugh at the Roman system Erasmus had more effect than the protests of Reformers. But Erasmus was not an unqualified supporter of Luther. He approved of Luther's desire for reform, but could not follow him in his breach with the papacy and his division

of the church. In the early years of the Reformation Erasmus forbore from criticizing Luther and this greatly helped the latter at a critical and dangerous time. But in 1524 Erasmus bowed to pressure from the pope and others and wrote an attack on Luther's doctrine of the bondage of the human will. Luther promptly replied and relations between the two great men were permanently soured, though Erasmus remained on good terms with Luther's colleague *Melanchthon.

Erasmus wrote prolifically and edited many works:

● *The Praise of Folly* was written in 1509 at the home of his friend Thomas More and dedicated to him. It is a brilliant satire on, among others, monks and theologians. Of all of Erasmus' works it is the one most read today.

● In 1516 Erasmus published an edition of the New Testament in Greek, with his own Latin translation. This was the first ever printed edition of the New Testament in Greek. It was a hasty work based on too few manuscripts—partly because Erasmus knew of a team working in Spain on a similar project and wished to publish first. It was revised in several later editions. Erasmus' aim was that the Bible should be made available to all. 'I would to God that the ploughman would sing a text of the Scripture at his plough and that the weaver would hum them' to the tune of his shuttle.' This Greek New Testament influenced many towards Protestantism.

● In 1517 there appeared an anonymous work called *Julius Excluded from Heaven*. In it, the notorious former pope Julius II appears before the gates of heaven demanding entry, which is refused. Erasmus was generally believed to be the author, though he denied it. It seems most likely that he wrote it for private consumption and panicked when it was published without his permission.

● Erasmus supervised the publication of many editions of the early church Fathers. This was part of his programme for church reform—a return to the Scriptures and the early Fathers.

● In 1524 Erasmus wrote *The Freedom of the Will*, an attack on Luther's doctrine that the fallen human will is in bondage and unable to do any good. He objected to Luther's position—both because he thought it wrong and because he felt it improper to be dogmatic on what he saw as an obscure issue.

Erasmus fell out with Luther, whose education had been in Scholastic theology with little Humanist influence. But he remained on friendly terms with other Reformers, such as Melanchthon. His disciples were found among Roman, Lutheran and Reformed theologians. He himself was left high and dry by the progress of the tide of history. His preference was for a liberal Catholic reform, while Protestantism was met by an increasingly dogmatic and illiberal Roman Catholicism. Erasmus enjoyed the support of successive popes, but his teaching was condemned in Paris in 1527. As the Counter-Reformation progressed his ideas were seen as dangerous and all his works were placed on the Index of forbidden books in 1559.

JULIUS: What the devil is going on here? Doors won't open, eh? Looks as if the lock has been changed, or tampered with, anyway.

JULIUS' GENIUS: You'd better check and see that you didn't bring the wrong key. You don't open this door, you know, with the same one that opens your money box ...

JULIUS: I'm getting fed up. I'll pound on the door ...

PETER: Well, it's a good thing we have a gate like iron. Otherwise this fellow, whoever he is, would have broken the doors down. It must be that some giant or satrap, a sacker of cities, has arrived. But, immortal God, what a sewer I smell here! ... Who are you? ...

JULIUS: Unless you're just plain blind, I trust you recognize this key, in case you don't know the golden oak Julius' family crest]. And you do see tie [papal] triple crown, as well as this robe shining all over with jewels and gold.

PETER: I recognize the silver key, more or less—although there is just the one, and that quite unlike the ones that the true shepherd of the church, Christ, once entrusted to me. But that arrogant crown you have, how, pray, would I be able to recognize that? Not even a barbarian tyrant has ever ventured to flaunt such a thing as that—still less anyone who expects to be admitted here. As for the robe, that impresses me not at all, since I have always trampled upon and despised jewels and gold as if they were rubbish ...

JULIUS: Why don't you cut out the nonsense and open the door—unless you would rather have it battered down? In a word—do you see what a retinue I have?

PETER: To be sure, I see thoroughly hardened brigands. But in case you don't know it, these doors you must storm with other weapons.

JULIUS: Enough talk, I say! Unless you obey right away, I shall hurl—even against you—*the thunderbolt of excommunication, with which I once terrified the mightiest of kings, or for that matter whole kingdoms. You see the Bull already prepared for this purpose?*

PETER: What damned thunderbolt, what thunder, what Bulls, what bombast are you talking to me about, pray? We never heard anything about these matters from Christ.

JULIUS: Well you'll feel them if you don't obey.

PETER: Maybe you terrified some people with that hot air before, but it means nothing here. Here you have to operate with the truth. This citadel is won by good deeds, not by evil words.

JULIUS EXCLUDED FROM HEAVEN

Perhaps it would be better to pass silently over the theologians. Dealing with them, since they are hot-tempered, is like ... eating poisonous beans. They may attack me with six hundred arguments and force me to retract what

*I hold, for if I refuse, they will
immediately declare me a heretic ... The
methods that our scholastics follow only
render more subtle the subtlest of
subtleties. For you will more easily
escape from a labyrinth than from the
snares of the Realists, Nominalists,
Thomists, Albertists, Occamists and
Scotists. I have not named them all, only
a few of the major ones. But there is so
much learning and difficulty in all of
these sects that I should think the
apostles themselves must need some
help from some other spirit if they were
to try to argue these topics with our new
generation of theologians ... Peter
received the keys from One who did not
commit them to an unworthy person,
and yet I doubt that he ever
understood—for Peter never did have a
profound knowledge for the subtle—that
a person who did not have knowledge
could have the key to knowledge. [The
apostles] went everywhere baptizing
people, and yet they never taught what
the formal, material, efficient and final
causes of baptism were. Nor did they
mention that it has both a delible and an
indelible character ... Furthermore, the
[theologians] draw exact pictures of
every part of hell, as though they had
spent many years in that region ...
Those who are the closest to them in
happiness are generally called 'the
religious' or 'monks', both of which are
deceiving names, since for the most part
they stay as far away from religion as
possible and frequent every sort of
place ... One of their chief beliefs is that
to be illiterate is to be of a high state of
sanctity, and so they make sure that
they are not able to read ... Members of
[some] orders shrink from the mere
touch of money as if it were poison.
They do not, however, retreat from the
touch of wine or of women.*

THE PRAISE OF FOLLY

THE LUTHERAN
TRADITION

Martin Luther
HERE I STAND

Martin Luther was born in 1483 at Eisleben (in East Germany). He was on his way to becoming a lawyer when a close brush with death frightened him into becoming a monk. He joined the Augustinian friars at Erfurt and studied theology there—being taught the 'modern way' by the disciples of *Gabriel Biel. In due course he rose to become professor of theology at the new university of Wittenberg. But Luther had problems. He was taught that in order to please God and earn his grace he must 'do his very best' which included loving God above all else. But this God was portrayed to Luther as a judge weighing up his merits. Luther was trapped—he could not love the God who was condemning him, but until he loved him he would not be accepted. One verse in particular caused Luther difficulty—Romans 1:17—'In it [the gospel] the righteousness of God is revealed'. Luther hated God for righteously condemning man not only by the law but also by the gospel. Then one day his eyes were opened and he saw the meaning of 'the righteousness of God'. It is not the righteousness by which he *condemns* us but the righteousness by which he *justifies* us by faith. The gospel reveals not God's condemnation and wrath but his salvation and justification. Once Luther saw this he felt as if he had been born again and entered paradise.

When did this happen? This is hotly debated and dates as widely apart as 1508 and 1519 are given. It is important to note *what* Luther was converted to. He was freed from the idea that we need to do our very best before God will help us. Instead he saw God as the one who freely justifies us by faith. Righteousness is a gift given to the believer. Luther was turning from the Semi-Pelagianism of his training to the older view of *Augustine. (He says that he later found the same ideas in Augustine's *The Spirit and the Letter*.) This change can be detected in Luther's writings around 1514/15. It was at this time that Luther was converted to Augustine—but not yet to a truly *Protestant* doctrine of justification.

Luther began to preach and teach his new insights. In 1517 he produced ninety-seven theses for debate in the university (a common procedure) in which he put forward a strongly Augustinian line and rejected late medieval Semi-Pelagianism. To Luther's disappointment, these theses aroused little interest. But later that year Luther produced some more theses which *did* arouse interest. 'Indulgences' were being sold near Wittenberg. The theory was that the purchase of an indulgence could free a departed soul from purgatory, but *not* from hell. 'As soon as the coin in the coffer rings, the soul from purgatory springs.' But ordinary folk believed that their sins could be forgiven simply by the purchase of an indulgence. Luther was outraged. (He would have been even more furious had he known that the proceeds were financing Prince Albert's purchase from the pope of yet another archbishopric.) Luther wrote ninety-five theses against the indulgences, sending a copy each to his bishop and to Prince Albert. But a copy fell into the hands of an enterprising printer who saw its potential and published the theses in German. The theses rapidly became a best-seller and all Germany was aroused. Luther became a hero overnight. The theses were relatively conservative, proposing only minor reforms of the existing system. (For example, Luther did not question the existence of purgatory, the authority of the pope or the limited validity of indulgences.) But they were of the greatest importance as they touched the papacy where it hurt most—in the pocket. They encouraged German unrest over the excessive taxes paid to Rome. For this reason, steps were taken to silence Luther, but he had the support of his ruler, Frederick the Wise.

In 1519 Luther and some colleagues went to Leipzig to debate with John Eck, a leading theologian. The topics were those of the ninety-five theses. But Eck was a clever debater. He pushed Luther into admitting that a general council could err and into approving some of the teaching of Hus and *Wyclif. The controversy had moved from points of doctrine to the very nature of authority. The following year the pope excommunicated Luther, who responded by burning the papal bull. This was open rebellion. The following year he was summoned to the Diet of Worms, where the young emperor, Charles V, ordered him to recant. While Luther probably did not say the famous words, 'Here I stand, I can do no other', they accurately summarize his reply.

The breach with Rome was now complete. In the space of four years, the loyal subject of the pope had been pushed into the position that the papacy was the Antichrist prophesied in the New Testament. Luther's chances of survival would have been slight, but Frederick supported him and the emperor was unable to act against him. The Turks were besieging Vienna and Charles needed a united Germany to provide troops for its defence. He could not afford to divide Germany over the religious issue until it was too late—by then Lutheranism was well established and could not be eradicated by force.

In 1520 Luther wrote three major works in which he set out his programme for reform:

● *Appeal to the German Ruling Class*: Luther calls upon rulers to reform the church. This is necessary because the church will not put its own house in order. Rulers are to fulfil their responsibility to govern by acting against oppression and extortion by the church. Furthermore, as baptized Christians, rulers share in the 'priesthood' common to all believers. Luther rejects the Roman Catholic view of the clergy as a separate priestly caste and the common practice of calling the clergy 'the church'. *All* Christians are 'religious' and have a common status. The 'religious' in the church (clergy and monks) do not have a different status or dignity but merely exercise a different function. If they fail to exercise that function, others can step in and take their place.

To call popes, bishops, priests, monks and nuns the religious class, but princes, lords, artisans and farm workers the secular class is but a specious device invented by certain time-servers. But no one ought to be frightened by it, and for good reason. For all Christians whatsoever really and truly belong to the religious class and there is no difference among them except insofar as they do different work ... For baptism, gospel and faith alone make men religious and create a Christian people ... The fact is that our baptism consecrates us all without exception and makes us all priests (1 Peter 2:9, Revelation 5:9–10).
APPEAL TO THE GERMAN RULING CLASS

● *Babylonian Captivity of the Church*: Luther attacked the seven sacraments of the Roman Catholic Church (as defined at the *Council of Florence). He reduced these to the two which were instituted by Jesus Christ himself—baptism and the eucharist. (Over penance Luther was ambiguous—he calls it a sacrament yet he also limits the sacraments to baptism and the eucharist, seeing penance as 'simply a means of reaffirming our baptism'.) But Luther did not merely reduce the number of sacraments. He radically opposed the Roman Catholic doctrine of the eucharist, rejecting the withholding of the cup from the laity, transubstantiation (defined at the *Fourth Lateran Council) and, especially, the idea that the mass is a sacrifice that we offer to God.

● *The Freedom of a Christian*: Luther distinguishes between the inner and the outer man. As regards the inner man, he stresses that we are justified by faith alone. It is only by faith that we become righteous, not by good works. Faith lays hold of God's promises, unites us to Jesus Christ and indeed even fulfils the law (in that it honours God, as the first of the ten commandments requires). Good works are not the *means* of becoming righteous but only the *fruit* of righteousness, the result in the outer man of righteousness in the inner man. Works are to righteousness as fruit is to a tree. 'Our faith in Christ frees us not from works but from false opinions about works—that is, from the foolish presumption that justification is acquired by works'.

A Christian is a perfectly free lord of all, subject to none. A Christian is a perfectly dutiful servant of all, subject to all ... The entire Scripture of God is divided into two parts: commandments and promises. The promises of God give what the commandments of God demand and fulfil what the law prescribes so that all things may be God's alone, both the commandments and the fulfilling of the commandments. He alone commands, he alone fulfils ... Surely we are named after Christ, not because he is absent from us, but because he dwells in us—that is, because we believe in him and are Christs one to another and do to our neighbours as Christ does to us. But in our day we are taught by the doctrine of men to seek nothing but merits, rewards and the things that are ours. Of Christ we have made only a taskmaster far harsher than Moses.

THE FREEDOM OF A CHRISTIAN

After Worms Luther was in great danger. Some of his supporters arranged for him to be kidnapped on his journey home and kept out of harm's way in a castle called the Wartburg. While there, he began his translation of the Bible into German. The *Luther Bible* is of major culture as well as religious significance. As well as bringing the Bible to the common people, it helped to mould the German language into its present form. Its influence can be compared to that of Shakespeare or the Authorized Version on the English language.

In the early years of the reform Luther had a wide following. But inevitably as his teaching became more specific he became alienated from others. Most serious were his disagreements with *Erasmus and *Zwingli. Erasmus at first approved of Luther's stand against abuses, but he did not approve of the division and strife that followed from the reform—his ideals were concord and consensus. At first he forbore from openly attacking Luther, but in 1524 he finally produced his *The Freedom of the Will*, criticizing Luther's stress on the impotence of the human will.

At first Luther prudently remained silent, but in 1525 he responded with his *The Bondage of the Will*. He himself saw this as one of his best works, but it is marred by an immoderate approach. Luther ruthlessly exposes the weaknesses and inconsistencies in Erasmus' book and affirms the traditional Augustinian belief in man's total dependence upon God's grace and predestination. But here he is not altogether clear. He appears to be saying not just that sinful man can do no good without God's grace but that man has no free-will at all—not even in morally neutral matters such as the choice between tea or coffee for breakfast. Luther is guilty here of taking the doctrine of predestination beyond the biblical and Augustinian teaching (as did *Bradwardine)—or at the very least of appearing to do so. Unlike Augustine, Luther did not see the importance of stressing not just the moral impotence of man's fallen will but also the psychological freedom of the will.

At first there was a common front between the German and the Swiss reformers. But serious disagreement arose over the question of the real presence in the Lord's Supper. In the early years of the reform they were agreed in rejecting the Roman doctrine of transubstantiation, but continued to affirm the real presence of

Christ's body and blood in the Lord's Supper. But in 1524 the Swiss reformers were won over by the arguments of one Cornelius Hoen, a Dutchman who saw the bread and wine as merely symbols of Christ's body and blood. Luther had earlier been tempted to take this position, but he felt bound by the clear words of Scripture: 'This is my body'. Luther and Zwingli began to write against one another and in 1529 Philip of Hesse, one of the German princes, persuaded the two sides to meet together at Marburg to seek to resolve their differences and restore Protestant unity. The Marburg Colloquy, of which detailed informal records survive, gives a fascinating insight into the positions of the two main reformers as they faced each other across the table. But it did not cause them to draw significantly closer to one another and Protestantism was permanently divided into Lutheran and Reformed camps.

What is the sacrament of the altar? It is the true body and blood of our Lord Jesus Christ, under the bread and wine, instituted by Christ himself for us Christians to eat and drink.

What benefit is such eating and drinking? It is shown us by these words: 'Given and shed for you, for the remission of sins'. In the sacrament, forgiveness of sins, life and salvation are given us through these words. For where there is forgiveness of sins, there is also life and salvation.

How can bodily eating and drinking do such great things? It is not the eating and drinking indeed that does it, but the words which stand here: 'Given and shed for you, for the remission of sins'. These words, together with bodily eating and drinking, are the chief thing in the sacrament. He that believes these words, has what they say and mean—the forgiveness of sins.

Who then receives this sacrament worthily? Fasting and bodily preparation are indeed a good outward discipline. But he is truly worthy and well-prepared who has faith in these words: 'Given and

shed for you, for the remission of sins'. But he who does not believe these words or doubts is unworthy and unprepared. For the words 'For you' require only believing hearts.
SMALL CATECHISM

Luther is known especially for his doctrine of justification by faith alone. But this doctrine does not figure in the ninety-five theses and it was not the original cause of the reform. Furthermore, it was not until several years *after* the ninety-five theses that Luther reached a distinctively *Protestant* doctrine of justification. In the early years he still held to a basically Augustinian position. Augustine taught justification by faith, in the following sense. When the sinner recognizes his inability to keep God's law and his need of salvation he turns to God in faith. God then gives him his Holy Spirit, who heals his will and pours love into his heart. This is justification—being made righteous, being changed from a selfish into a loving person. Having been justified or changed, the believer can now proceed to keep God's law from the heart, motivated by love.

In the early years of the reform, Luther returned to this Augustinian teaching, but with a greater stress on the need for faith. He was especially against the medieval idea that the sacraments bestow salvation like medicine or like an injection, no more being required from the recipient than not placing an obstacle in the way. Thus Luther's stress lay on the need for a living, personal faith, against a mechanical view of the sacraments—not on the meaning of the word justification. But in due course, in the early 1520s, Luther came to see that for Paul, 'justify' does not mean 'make righteous', or 'change into a good person', but 'reckon righteous', or 'acquit'. Justification concerns my status rather than my state, how God looks upon me rather than what he does in me, God accepting me rather than changing me. Thus Luther arrived at the Protestant distinction between justification (my standing before God) and sanctification (my growth in holiness).

But if we are justified or accepted by God on the basis of faith alone, without good works, surely the believer can 'live it up' without worrying about the consequences. Luther was accused of teaching just this, but unfairly. While he *distinguished* justification and sanctification, he did not *separate* them. He did not imagine that one could exist without the other. When God accepts someone he also changes him. But if they always go together, what is so wonderful about distinguishing them? Simply this. Justification by faith alone (or, more accurately, by Christ alone, *through* faith alone) means that I can be confident of my acceptance by God, not because I am living a good life, but because Christ has died for me. The point is not whether justification can exist without sanctification (it cannot), but the *basis* of justification. If our acceptance by God is based on our good works, there can be no assurance—except for the morally smug like the Pharisee in Luke 18:9–14. But justification by faith alone means that we *can* have assurance before God—on the basis of the cross of Jesus Christ. This means that we can proceed to do good works not *in order to* win God's approval and acceptance but *because* God has already accepted us. Obedience to God is the free, loving response of his children, not the mercenary accumulation of merits by those striving for approval.

Philip Melanchthon
THE TEACHER OF GERMANY

Philip Melanchthon was born in 1497 in southern Germany. He was the great nephew of John Reuchlin (1455–1522), a leading German Humanist and the foremost Christian Hebrew scholar of his day. Melanchthon studied at Heidelberg and Tübingen universities, completing his studies at an unusually early age. While at Tübingen he came under Humanist influence and became a lifelong admirer of *Erasmus. On Reuchlin's recommendation he was appointed professor of Greek at Wittenberg university in 1518. Here he was influenced by *Luther and

drawn into the Reformation camp. In 1519 he joined the theological faculty, though without ever leaving the arts faculty.

Melanchthon was Luther's closest friend, though their temperaments were strikingly different—Melanchthon was a somewhat timid, moderate and conciliatory Humanist scholar. Furthermore, there were marked differences in their theological approaches, as Luther's disciples later observed. But this did not obstruct their warm friendship, although it did give rise to some theological differences.

Melanchthon was the author of the *Augsburg Confession*, the most important Lutheran confession of faith. His main theological work was his *Commonplaces*. This first appeared in 1521, being the first Protestant attempt at a systematic theology. It went through many editions, those of 1521, 1535 and 1555 being the most important. In the introduction to the 1521 edition Melanchthon sets out his approach:

We do better to adore the mysteries of deity than to investigate them. What is more, these matters cannot be probed without great danger, and even holy men have often experienced this ... Therefore, there is no reason why we should labour so much on those exalted topics, such as 'God', 'the unity and trinity of God', 'the mystery of creation' and 'the manner of the incarnation'. What, I ask you, did the scholastics accomplish during the many ages they were examining only these points? ... But as for one who is ignorant of the other fundamentals—namely 'the power of sin', 'the law' and 'grace', I do not see how I can call him a Christian. For from these things Christ is known, since to know Christ means to know his benefits and not, as they [the scholastics] teach, to reflect upon his natures and the modes of his incarnation. For unless you know why Christ put on flesh and was nailed to the cross, what good will it do you to know merely the history about him? ... Christ was given us as a remedy and, to use the language of Scripture, a saving remedy. It is therefore proper that we know Christ in another way than that which the scholastics have set forth.

COMMONPLACES, INTRODUCTION

At this stage it was Melanchthon's aim to rescue theology from philosophical distortions and to give it a firmly scriptural basis. He considered that Platonism had misled the early Fathers and Artistotle the Scholastics. 'For just as we in these latter times of the church have embraced Aristotle instead of Christ, so immediately after the beginnings of the church Christian doctrine was weakened by Platonic philosophy.' But later Melanchthon revised his opinion of Aristotle and even encouraged the study of him in German universities. Melanchthon also came to a deeper appreciation of the early church Fathers. Scripture remained the sole infallible norm, but the consensus of the early Fathers was worthy of great respect.

When controversy arose between Luther and *Zwingli over the real presence, Melanchthon sided with Luther. Indeed, at the Marburg Colloquy in 1529 it was Melanchthon who, uncharacteristically, remained intransigent and held Luther firm. In a letter written that year to Oecolampadius (the Reformer of Basel, and a friend of Zwingli) he argued for the real presence on the grounds that it was scriptural, that it was taught by the early Fathers and that it was fitting and reasonable. But Oecolampadius managed to persuade him that the early Fathers did not all support Luther's position. This caused Melanchthon to move away from Luther's doctrine of the real presence. In 1540 he published a revised version of the *Augsburg Confession*, which no longer taught the real presence. The 1555 *Commonplaces* also omitted any reference to the real presence. Instead Melanchthon taught that:

With this bread and wine [Jesus Christ] gives his body and blood to us and thereby attests that he accepts us, makes us his members, grants us forgiveness of sins and that he has purified us with his blood and will abide in us ... The living Son of God, Jesus Christ, our Saviour, is truly present and active in this

participation, attesting through it that he will abide in us.

COMMONPLACES 22

This statement was acceptable to *Calvin, for instance. Luther was grieved by Melanchthon's change, but did not oppose him openly. Melanchthon claimed that shortly before his death, Luther admitted that he had gone too far on the issue of the real presence but said that he could not now modify his position, because all of his teaching might be brought into disrepute. It is hard to know how to evaluate such a claim, as Melanchthon could not be said to he impartial in this matter.

In 1546 much of Lutheran German, including Wittenberg, was overrun by the armies of the emperor, Charles V. Charles tried to impose an interim settlement on the Lutheran territories, which involved considerable compromise of Lutheran doctrine. Melanchthon vacillated—he would not accept the Interim but he was prepared to compromise and to make some concessions. The result was that he came under fire from both sides. He had the misfortune of being a moderate in an age which was becoming increasingly intransigent and hard-line. This was the beginning of the attacks on Melanchthon by those who considered that he had betrayed the heritage of Luther. These attacks continued until his death in 1560 and beyond, leading to the condemnation of many of his ideas in the *Formula of Concord*. But Melanchthon was not out of favour with everyone, and he has come to be known as the 'Teacher of Germany' for his considerable achievements in educational reform.

Augsburg Confession (1530)

In 1530 the emperor, Charles V, called an imperial diet to meet at Augsburg. His desire was to negotiate with the Protestants and, if possible, to end the dispute. *Melanchthon drew up a Protestant confession of faith, based partly on some earlier writings of

*Luther. The finished product had the approval of Luther, who was unable to be present at the diet because he had been excommunicated. In June it was read to the emperor at Augsburg—thus becoming known as the *Augsburg Confession*. Its tone and language is deliberately moderate, in the hope that the emperor might recognize Protestantism.

Charles commissioned some Roman Catholic theologians to refute the confession and their work was read in August. Melanchthon then wrote an *Apology [Defence] of the Augsburg Confession*, which was presented to the emperor in September—but he refused to accept it. The following year the *Augsburg Confession* was published in Latin and in German and a revised version of the *Apology* was also published.

The Augsburg Confession is in two parts. The first part consists of twenty-one articles setting out Lutheran beliefs. Some of these follow traditional Catholic doctrine (as on God, original sin, baptism); others are distinctively Lutheran (as on justification, the Lord's Supper, good works). The second part consists of seven articles concerning abuses which have been corrected in the Lutheran churches (such as the withholding of the cup from the laity in the holy communion or forbidding the clergy to marry).

It is also taught among us that we cannot obtain forgiveness of sin and righteousness before God by our own merits, works or satisfactions, but that we receive forgiveness of sin and become righteous before God by grace. for Christ's sake, through faith, when we believe that Christ suffered for us and that for his sake our sin is forgiven and righteousness and eternal life are given to us. For God will regard and reckon this faith as righteousness, as Paul says in Romans 3:21–26 and 4:5.
ARTICLE 4 ON JUSTIFICATION

It is taught among us that the true body and blood of Christ are really present in the Supper of our Lord under the form of bread and wine and are there distributed and received.
ARTICLE 10 ON THE HOLY SUPPER OF OUR LORD

It is also taught among us that good works should and must be done, not that we are to rely on them to earn grace but that we may do God's will and glorify him. It is always faith alone that apprehends grace and forgiveness of sin. When through faith the Holy Spirit is given, the heart is moved to do good works.
ARTICLE 20 ON FAITH AND GOOD WORKS

In 1540 Melanchthon published a revised edition of the confession. The most significant change was in the tenth article which now stated that 'the body and blood of Christ are truly exhibited with the bread and wine to those partaking in the Lord's Supper'. This comes close to the position of *Bucer and *Calvin, who approved of it. Luther was grieved, but said nothing. After his death, Melanchthon came increasingly under fire from the hard-line Lutherans.

The 1531 editions of the *Augsburg Confession* and the *Apology* are among the creeds of the Lutheran church which, together with the *Formula of Concord*, are included in the *Book of Concord*.

Formula of Concord (1577)

After *Luther's death, Lutheranism lacked a single authoritative leader. *Melanchthon was in many ways the natural candidate to succeed Luther, but many deeply distrusted him and saw him as the betrayer of Luther. Lutheranism was divided into several parties which differed violently over key doctrines. At one stage the professors at Königsberg were taking guns into their lectures, so heated was the debate! At the 1557 Colloquy of Worms (with the Roman Catholics) the Lutherans were embarrassed by the public exposure of their divisions. The controversies continued and attempts were made to resolve the disputed points. In the 1570s a number of confessions were produced and in 1577 some of these were drawn together to form the *Formula of Concord*, which won the approval of many of the German Lutheran states. In 1580, fifty years to the day from the reading of the *Augsburg Confession* to the emperor, the *Book of Concord* was published. This contains: the three ancient creeds, the *Augsburg Confession* and Melanchthon's *Apology* [*Defence*] of it, Luther's *Smalcald Articles* (1537), Melanchthon's treatise on *The Power and Primacy of the Pope* (1537), Luther's *Small and Large Catechisms* (both 1529) and the *Formula of Concord*.

In many ways the *Formula of Concord* did for Lutheranism what the *Council of Trent did for Roman Catholicism—it defined the Lutheran position on a wide range of issues, thus creating a precise Lutheran orthodoxy. But the *Book of Concord* did not meet with the approval of all Lutherans. The (Lutheran) king of Denmark was so disgusted that he threw his copy into the fire. It has never been adopted by the Danish church. A number of German Lutheran states also refused to accept it and some of these later joined the Reformed camp.

The *Formula of Concord* is divided into two parts. First, 'A summary epitome of the articles in controversy among the theologians of the *Augsburg Confession* expounded and settled in Christian fashion in conformity with God's Word in the recapitulation here following.' This comprises an introduction and twelve articles, covering the disputed points. Secondly, there is a 'Solid Declaration', some four times as long, which covers the same points in more detail.

The introduction affirms that the Bible is the only rule and norm for doctrine. But while the Bible is the only touchstone by which all doctrine must be judged, the Lutheran confessions of faith, as found in the *Book of Concord*, are also set up as a standard for doctrine. As by no means all of the doctrines of the *Formula of Concord* are

self-evidently scriptural, there is a tension between the theoretical affirmation of the role of Scripture as the sole norm and the practical elevation of the Lutheran confessions to that position—although it is claimed that they are 'not judges like Holy Scripture, but merely witnesses and expositions of the faith'.

Melanchthon had at first followed Luther's belief in the bondage of the human will. But by 1555, Melanchthon had changed his mind and allowed a significant independent role for human free-will in salvation. This is rejected in the first two articles, which affirm a fully *Augustinian position. Conversion is wholly the work of God, who 'changes stubborn and unwilling people into willing people'.

Melanchthon was opposed especially for his retreat from Luther's doctrine of the real presence, as in his 1540 revision of the *Augsburg Confession*. Melanchthon was branded a 'crypto-Calvinist'. The seventh article unequivocally repudiates such a position, affirming a full Lutheran belief in the real presence:

The question is this: In the Holy Communion are the true body and blood of our Lord Jesus Christ truly and essentially present? Are they distributed with the bread and wine? Are they received orally [through the mouth] by all those who use the sacrament, be they worthy or unworthy, godly or godless, believers or unbelievers—the believers for life and salvation, the unbelievers for judgement? The sacramentarians [deniers of the real presence] say no; we say yes.

*In order to explain this controversy it is first necessary to mention that there are two kinds of sacramentarians. Some are crass sacramentarians [e.g. *Zwingli], who set forth in clear German words what they believe in their hearts, namely that in the Holy Supper only bread and wine are present, distributed and received orally. Others, however, are subtle sacramentarians [e.g. Melanchthon and *Calvin], the* *most harmful kind, who in part talk our language very plausibly and claim to believe a true presence of the true essential and living body and blood of Christ in the Holy Supper—but assert that this takes place spiritually by faith. Under this plausible terminology they really retain the former cross opinion that in the Holy Supper nothing but bread and wine are present and received with the mouth. To them the word 'spiritual' means no more than the presence of Christ's Spirit, or the power of Christ's absent body, or his merit. They deny that the body of Christ is present in any manner or way, since in their opinion it is confined to the highest heaven above, whither we should ascend with the thoughts of our faith and there, but not in the bread and wine of the Holy Supper, seek the body and blood of Christ.*

We believe, teach and confess that in the Holy Supper the body and blood of Christ are truly and essentially present and are truly distributed and received with the bread and wine ...

We believe, teach and confess that with the bread and wine the body and blood of Christ are received not only spiritually by faith, but also orally— however, not in a Capernaitic [cannibalistic] manner, but because of the sacramental union in a supernatural and heavenly way ... Whoever eats this bread eats the body of Christ.

EPITOME, ARTICLE 7

Why were the Lutherans so concerned to reject the spiritual feeding on Christ taught by the 'subtle sacramentarians'? While the *Formula* affirms that Christ's body and blood are present 'in, with and under' the bread and wine, a crudely physical understanding of this is excluded: 'We herewith condemn without any qualification the Capernaitic eating of the body of Christ as though one rent Christ's flesh with one's teeth and digested it like other food.' In its place is affirmed 'a true, though supernatural, eating of Christ's body'. The

Formula rejects the 'subtle sacramentarians' because it is concerned to maintain the *objectivity* of the sacrament—'whoever eats this bread eats the body of Christ'. To say that we feed on Christ only spiritually and by faith would appear to make the sacrament superfluous.

Philip Jakob Spener
FOUNDER OF PIETISM

Spener was born in Alsace in 1635. He received a godly upbringing and went on to become a pastor. He was senior pastor at Frankfurt from 1666 and while there he became the 'patriarch' or chief founder of pietism. He left Frankfurt in 1686 to become court chaplain at Dresden and moved on from there in 1691 to be a pastor at Berlin. He died in 1705.

By the mid-seventeenth century, all was not well with Lutheranism. All citizens were baptized as infants and were therefore believed to be regenerate or 'born again'. All citizens in the Lutheran states were Christians. But while everyone might belong to the church and be instructed in Lutheran doctrine, there was a shortage of living Christian faith. It was this deficiency which pietism sought to rectify. Spener set out his goals in a manifesto for pietist reform, his *Holy Desires*, published in 1675.

The pietists stressed the importance of a living personal faith in Jesus Christ. It is not enough just to be a baptized church member, just to assent to Lutheran doctrine. We need to be born again, to be converted. (Spener did not deny the Lutheran doctrine that infants are born again in baptism, but he held that this grace is normally lost.) True Christianity is not just doctrine to be believed, it is an experience of the Holy Spirit in conversion and new life.

This stress on a living, personal faith did not lead Spener to regard sound doctrine as unimportant, but it did put it in its place. Better a Calvinist (or even a Roman Catholic!) with a living faith in Jesus Christ, than a strictly orthodox Lutheran without such faith. Pietism was a protest against the preoccupation of that time with the minor details of Lutheran orthodoxy. The reform of doctrine had led to an obsession with the minutiae of orthodoxy while the great need was for a reform of life.

Spener stressed the importance of Bible study. It was not sufficient merely to use the Bible to prove Lutheran doctrine and to score points in debate against the enemies of Lutheranism. We need the Holy Spirit to speak to our hearts through the Scriptures and to apply them to us personally. The Bible needs to be read and preached in a devotional way, leading to a changed lifestyle.

Spener lamented the number of unregenerate pastors whose lives did not exemplify what they taught. He urged that theological training should not be preoccupied with teaching the intricacies of Lutheran orthodoxy. Theological training should aim at changing the lives of the students and preparing them to preach practically from the Bible and to care for others pastorally.

Spener introduced an early form of home Bible study group to further these aims. These brought together clergy and laity. Spener believed strongly in *Luther's doctrine of the priesthood of all believers and the need for *all* Christians to exercise a spiritual ministry. Spener's most important convert was A. H. Francke (1663–1727), the other great leader of the early pietist movement. Francke was active mainly at Halle, where a new university was founded on pietist lines.

The influence of pietism has been immense. It has remained a force within the Lutheran churches, especially in certain areas, such as Württemberg in southern Germany, and Norway. Spener's godson, Count Zinzendorf (1700–60), played a leading role in the Moravian church, the influence of which spread throughout the world. The *Wesleys were deeply influenced by the Moravians, and through them the whole evangelical movement. Evangelicalism is to the Anglo-Saxon world what pietism is to Lutheranism. Pietists, Moravians and Evangelicals have all played a leading role in the missionary movement.

Today 'pietist' has become almost entirely a derogatory word. The popular image of the pietist is of someone who is excessively preoccupied with his own personal salvation, who sees salvation in terms of withdrawal from the world and inner peace of mind. His aim is to save individuals, but he has no concern for society at large; he is so concerned about the world to come that he has little time for the needs of this world. It is true that pietism has sometimes degenerated into this caricature, but this was not true of the original pietists. The pietist and evangelical traditions, when they have been healthy and vigorous, have balanced the individual and the corporate, the this-worldly and the other-worldly.

Thirdly, we must accustom the people to believe that mere knowledge is by no means sufficient for true Christianity— which is much more a matter of behaviour. In particular, our dear Saviour often designated love as the true hallmark of his disciples—John 13:34–35; 15:12; 1 John 3:10,18; 4:7,8,11,12,13, 21. Similarly, the beloved John in his old age (according to Jerome in his commentary on Galatians 3:6) was in the habit of saying little else to his disciples other than 'Little children, love one another'. Eventually they became so fed up with always hearing the same thing that they asked him why he constantly repeated it. He replied, 'Because it is the Lord's command and if it comes to pass, that suffices.' Certainly, for one who believes and through faith is blessed, his whole life and fulfilment of God's commands consists in love.

HOLY DESIRES

THE REFORMED
TRADITION

Ulrich Zwingli
THE SWISS REFORMATION

Ulrich Zwingli is the founder of Swiss Protestantism and the first of the Reformed theologians. He was born on New Year's Day 1484, fifty-two days after *Luther, at Wildhaus, some forty miles from Zurich. He arrived at a Protestant position at about the same time as Luther, largely independently of him. Their backgrounds were different— Luther was taught the 'modern way' by the disciples of *Gabriel Biel, while Zwingli was trained in the 'old way' of *Thomas Aquinas. Zwingli was also strongly influenced by the Humanism of *Erasmus, unlike Luther. As a result of these educational differences, Luther and Zwingli approached theology differently. In particular, Zwingli felt that no doctrine should be *contrary* to reason, while Luther allowed considerably less role for reason in theology. This difference was seen especially in their respective attitudes towards the presence of Jesus Christ in the Lord's Supper.

In 1506 Zwingli was appointed parish priest at Glarus. While there he began to attack the mercenary trade. At this time Swiss soldiers were in great demand as mercenaries—it was a lucrative source of income, much like Swiss banking today. Zwingli came to see the practice as immoral and began to preach against it. This did not go down well at Glarus, so in 1516 Zwingli moved to become parish priest at Einsiedeln—then, as now, a popular centre of devotion to the Virgin Mary. While at Glarus and Einsiedeln, Zwingli read widely and it was during this time that the foundations of his Reformed beliefs were laid. In particular, he came to realize the supreme and final role of Scripture. In 1518

Zwingli became parish priest at the Grossmünster (Great Cathedral) at Zürich. There he began to preach systematically through whole books of the Bible. This practice was common in the early church, but in Zwingli's time it came as a radical innovation.

At Zürich Zwingli gradually introduced reform, at first with the approval of the Roman Catholic authorities. As late as 1523 he received a warm letter from the pope! In 1522 he produced the first of his many Reformation writings, which helped to spread his ideas widely through Switzerland. The Reformation in Zürich was largely complete by 1525, when the mass was abolished, to be replaced by a simple communion service. Other Swiss cantons also decided for the reform and Zwingli's goal of a united evangelical Switzerland looked possible. To this end he formed an alliance of evangelical cantons, but the Roman Catholic cantons felt threatened and formed a rival alliance. The outcome was war, in 1529. After a lull, fighting broke out again in 1531 and Zwingli was himself killed on the battlefield, at Kappel.

One of Zwingli's first writings was his *The Clarity and Certainty of God's Word*, published in 1522. Here Zwingli propounded the fundamental Protestant principle of the final authority of Scripture. God's word is certain. When God speaks, it comes to pass—'God said, "Let there be light," and there was light' (Genesis 1:3). God's Word is also clear. But this does not mean that it cannot be misunderstood. If we come to the Bible with our own opinions and interpretation and seek to force it into that mould, we will not hear its message. But when God speaks to his children, his word brings its own clarity with it. Then we can understand it without any human instruction—not because of our own understanding but because the Holy Spirit illuminates us and enables us to see God's word in its own light. We must avoid the error of subjecting the word of God to an infallible human interpreter—such as the pope or a council. In practice that means that the Bible is twisted to support preconceived ideas. Certainty comes not from human learning nor from church authority but from humbly listening to God himself. This was Zwingli's own experience:

When I was younger, I gave myself overmuch to human teaching, like others of my day, and when... I undertook to devote myself entirely to the Scriptures I was always prevented by philosophy and theology. But eventually I came to the point where, led by the word and Spirit of God, I saw the need to set aside all these things and to learn the doctrine of God direct from his own word. Then I began to ask God for light and the Scriptures became far clearer to me—even though I read nothing else— than if I had studied many commentators and expositors.
THE CLARITY AND CERTAINTY OF GOD'S WORD

Zwingli discovered in practice that sincerely seeking to hear God's word did not necessarily end all disagreement. He found himself engaged in controversy with two other reform groups over the nature of the sacraments. First, there were those at Zürich who wanted a more radical reform. They were not satisfied with a Reformed state church but wanted a voluntary church of committed Christians, to be entered by adult baptism. At first Zwingli and these radicals had much in common, but by 1525 matters had come to a head and the Zürich city council, with Zwingli's approval, acted against them. In the same year, Zwingli wrote his *Baptism, Rebaptism and the Baptism of Infants*. In it he defended infant baptism, on the basis that it is the sign of the covenant and the covenant embraces the whole family and not just the individual. But while he maintained the practice of infant

baptism, Zwingli (unlike Luther) broke with the Catholic belief that baptism bestows (even on infants) new birth and the forgiveness of sins. He came to see baptism as primarily an outward sign of our faith.

The second controversy was with Luther, over the presence of Jesus Christ in the Lord's Supper. Luther rejected the Roman doctrine of transubstantiation, but continued to believe in the real presence of Christ's body and blood 'in, with and under' the bread and the wine. Zwingli was won away from this belief in 1524 by the Dutchman Cornelius Hoen. From then on he rejected the doctrine of real presence and maintained that the bread and the wine are merely symbols of Christ's body and blood. Through the Holy Spirit, Jesus Christ is present at the communion service—but his body and blood, his humanity, is confined to heaven, at the right hand side of the Father. The Lord's Supper is a thanksgiving memorial in which we look back to the work of Jesus Christ on the cross. It is also a fellowship meal in which the body of Christ is present—in the form of the congregation. Zwingli maintained this stand to the end of his life. In a *Confession of Faith*, written in 1530, he set out his mature teaching:

I believe that in the holy eucharist (that is, the supper of thanksgiving) the true body of Christ is present by the contemplation of faith. In other words, those who thank the Lord for the kindness conferred on us in his Son acknowledge that he assumed true flesh and in it truly suffered and truly washed away our sins by his own blood. Thus everything done by Christ becomes present to them by the contemplation of faith. But that the body of Christ, that is his natural body in essence and reality, is either present in the Supper or eaten with our mouth and teeth, as is asserted by the papists and by some who long for the flesh pots of Egypt [Lutherans], we not only deny but firmly maintain to be an error opposed to God's word... The natural body of Christ is not eaten with our mouth as he himself showed when

*he said to the Jews who were disputing
about the corporeal eating of his flesh,
'The flesh counts for nothing' [John
6:63] ... The words 'This is my body'
should be received not literally, but
figuratively, just as the words 'This is
the passover' [Exodus 12:11].*

CONFESSION OF FAITH

Zwingli here reiterates the arguments that
he had used against Luther at the Marburg
Colloquy the previous year. Zwingli argued
powerfully against a physical presence of
Christ's body in the Lord's Supper, but he
did not altogether escape the danger of
reducing it to a mere memorial. His
contribution was primarily the negative
work of criticizing the old. It was left to
others, especially *Bucer and *Calvin, to
build a positive doctrine of the Supper on
that foundation.

Zwingli met an early death on the
battlefield. There was no time for his thought
to mature or for him to present a solid
exposition of Reformed theology. This task
was left to Calvin, with the result that
Reformed Protestantism is known as
Calvinism, not Zwinglianism. But if the
building was left to others and if Zwingli was
to a large extent forgotten, the fact remains
that it was he who laid the foundations of
Swiss Protestantism and Reformed theology.

Martin Bucer
THE FATHER OF CALVINISM

Martin Bucer was born in 1491 at
Schlettstadt in Alsace. At the age of fifteen
he became a Dominican friar. Like *Zwingli,
he was trained in the 'old way' of *Thomas
Aquinas and also came under the influence
of *Erasmus' Humanism. In 1518 he
attended the General Chapter of the
Augustine friars at Heidelberg. *Luther was
speaking and Bucer became an instant
convert. A few years later, in 1523, he settled
in Strassburg. The Reformation had already
been introduced there by Matthew Zell and a
number of Reformers were to live there for a
shorter or longer period—*John Calvin,

Wolfgang Capito, Kaspar Hedio, Peter
Martyr, Jakob and John Sturm. But it was
Bucer who became the leading Reformer of
Strassburg.

Strassburg became a major centre of the
Reformation. In many ways it set an
example for others to follow. Its educational
reforms, pioneered by John Sturm especially,
with the support of Bucer, were copied all
round Europe. Bucer was also concerned for
pastoral care as well as reform of doctrine.
His *True Pastoral Care* is one of the most
important sixteenth-century works on that
subject. Bucer also saw the need for
discipline in the church and sought to
introduce it at Strassburg. In 1546 he
proposed the introduction of small groups
within the congregation, for spiritual
edification. This may well have inspired
*Spener in the following century. But in 1546
Strassburg was forced to surrender to the
emperor's army and had to accept the
Interim settlement of religion that he
imposed. Bucer refused to compromise in
this way and accepted an invitation to
become Regius professor of divinity at
Cambridge. He died there in 1551. After the
collapse of the Interim settlement,
Strassburg became militantly Lutheran, and
Bucer was no longer honoured there.

Bucer left no organized group behind
him and until recently he has been largely
neglected. But in fact his influence has been
considerable, in two directions. While at
Cambridge he was able to influence the
course of the English Reformation,
especially through *Thomas Cranmer.
Bucer's hand can be seen in the two prayer
books of Edward VI's reign (1549 and 1552).
He wrote a book on *The Kingdom of Christ*
as a blueprint for a Christian England. The
death of Edward in 1553 prevented its
implementation, but it remained influential,
especially on the later Puritan movement.
Bucer's greatest influence has been through
John Calvin, who spent the years 1538 to
1541 at Strassburg. During this time Bucer
was able to influence his thinking in a
number of key areas. He has been called,
with pardonable exaggeration, the father of
Calvinism.

Much of Bucer's efforts were directed in the cause of church unity. Like Erasmus he disliked division and strife, and like *Melanchthon he was often felt to be too conciliatory and was therefore mistrusted. His initiatives were not always prudent and they sometimes backfired. As one modern writer has put it, his approach often amounted to 'an olive branch from a catapult'. The recipients were sometimes left smarting.

Bucer was enthusiastic in the search for reconciliation between Protestants and Roman Catholics. From 1539 to 1541 there was a series of colloquys aimed at uniting the two parties in Germany. The last, at Regensburg, came nearest to success, agreement being reached on the doctrine of justification by faith. But Luther for one felt that Bucer had given too much and said that 'Bucer stinks because of Regensburg'. (To be fair, it should be noted that both Melanchthon and Calvin had gone along with the agreement.) Bucer also sought to win over the Anabaptists. All over Europe they were savagely persecuted, but in Strassburg they were treated kindly. Bucer debated with them and many were won over to his way. But this was not a purely one-way process. Bucer listened as well as argued and was willing to learn. His concern for church discipline sprang at least partly from his debates with the Anabaptists.

Bucer sought reconciliation with Roman Catholics and Anabaptists. He also sought to heal the rift within the Protestant camp. The dispute over Christ's presence in the Lord's Supper had split the Reformers into two opposing camps—the Lutherans and the Swiss. When Bucer was first confronted with the case for seeing the bread and the wine as mere symbols, he sought to defend the doctrine of Christ's real presence. Eventually, however, he concluded that this was not possible from the Bible alone and so he moved into the Swiss camp. But in 1528, after the controversy was well under way, he came to the conclusion that the Swiss had misunderstood Luther, that Luther did not in fact teach a *local* presence of Christ's body and blood in the bread and wine. He then

decided that the two parties could be drawn together and sought a mediating position between them.

He combined elements of both Zwingli's and Luther's positions. With Zwingli, he held that 'the bread and the wine... in themselves are completely unchanged but merely become symbols through the words and ordinance of the Lord'. With Luther, he held that in the eucharist we receive 'the very body and blood of the Lord, so that by their means we may increasingly and more perfectly share in the imparting of regeneration' and 'more perfect communion, or the greater perfecting in us of communion, in the body and blood of the Lord' (*Confession on the Eucharist 52* (1550)). In other words, Bucer held to a *real feeding* on Christ's body and blood but without their *real presence* in the bread and wine. This middle position was not acceptable to Luther. At the Marburg Colloquy in 1529 he said to Bucer, 'I cannot regard you as my disciple... It is quite obvious that we do not have the same spirit'.

The year 1530 saw the reading of the *Augsburg Confession* to the emperor Charles V. Bucer and others produced a rival *Confession of the Four Cities* (Strassburg, Konstanz, Memmingen and Lindau) which states:

> To all those who sincerely have given their names among his disciples and receive this Supper according to his institution, [Christ] deigns to give his true body and true blood to be truly eaten and drunk for the food and drink of souls, for their nourishment unto life eternal.

CONFESSION 18

The confession also rejects the idea that 'nothing save mere bread and mere wine is administered in our Suppers'.

In 1536 Bucer met with the Lutherans at Wittenberg to discuss this matter further. He signed a *Wittenberg Concord*, drawn up by Melanchthon, which appeared to teach a clearly Lutheran position. But to Luther's disgust, Bucer later gave this his own private, and somewhat perverse, interpretation, emptying many of the statements of their natural meaning. Bucer's own attempts to establish a firm 'centre party' between the Lutherans and the Zwinglians met with only limited success. His most solid achievement was the recruitment of Calvin to the cause.

This is how we can faithfully serve the Lord: we should in an orderly manner elect and install ministers from every level of society. The aim is to have those who are trusted and loved by all, who are also gifted and zealous for this ministry and for true pastoral care... That way the five tasks of pastoral care will be performed: to seek and to find all the lost; to bring back those that are scattered; to heal the wounded; to strengthen the sickly; to protect the healthy and to put them to pasture.
TRUE PASTORAL CARE, SUMMARY

John Calvin
SCHOLAR OF GENEVA

John Calvin was born in 1509 at Noyon, in northern France. He studied at Paris, Orleans and Bruges universities and became an admirer of *Erasmus and Humanism. He himself produced in 1532 a work of Humanist scholarship (a commentary on the Roman philosopher Seneca's *Clemency*), which failed to make the impact for which he had hoped. At about this time Calvin was converted:

Since I was too obstinately devoted to the superstitions of popery to be easily extricated from so profound an abyss of mire, God by a sudden conversion subdued and brought my mind to a teachable frame, which was more hardened in such matters than might have been expected from one at my early period of life.

He immediately devoted himself to theological study. In 1533 he was associated with a mildly Protestant speech given by the new rector of Paris university, Nicholas Cop. Calvin had to leave town in a hurry. The following year a number of 'placards' attacking the Roman mass were posted round Paris—one on the door of the royal bedchamber, if the report is to be believed. The king, Francis I, was furious and launched a vigorous onslaught on the evangelicals. Calvin left France and settled in Basel, to study and to write. By the summer of 1535 he had finished the first edition of his *Institutes*. But his peaceful life of scholarship was to be short. In 1536 he was on his way to Strassburg when a local war forced him to make a detour through Geneva—the most fateful traffic diversion in European history, as has been said. Geneva had just accepted the Reformation, partly for political reasons. Calvin planned to spend only one night there, but Farel, the leader of the Genevan Reformers, came to urge him to stay.

After having learned that my heart was set upon devoting myself to private studies, for which I wished to keep myself free from other pursuits, and finding that he gained nothing by entreaties, he [Farel] proceeded to utter an imprecation that God would curse my retirement and the tranquillity of the studies which I sought, if I should withdraw and refuse to give assistance, when the necessity was so urgent. By this imprecation I was so stricken with terror that I desisted from the journey which I had undertaken.

The city council noted the employment of 'that Frenchman'. Calvin ministered in Geneva from 1536 to 1538. But at this stage he was still impetuous and immature. A row over the issue of church government led to his exile and he withdrew to Basel, to resume his studies. But again this was not to be. *Martin Bucer urged him to come to Strassburg to minister to the small congregation of French refugees. Calvin resisted until Bucer took a leaf out of Farel's book and threatened him with the example of Jonah. Calvin reluctantly gave way. Apart from poverty, his years at Strassburg were not unpleasant. He enjoyed his contact with Bucer and the other Reformers and profited greatly from it. He was able to take part in the colloquys between Protestants and Roman Catholics in the years 1539 to 1541, becoming well acquainted with *Melanchthon in the process. He also acquired a wife—the widow of a convert from Anabaptism. But while Calvin was at Strassburg, the church at Geneva was going from bad to worse. Eventually, in 1540, the magistrates in desperation asked him to return. He was appalled, having earlier stated of the prospect of a return to Geneva that 'I would prefer a hundred other deaths to that cross, on which I should have to die a thousand times a day'. Eventually however, 'a solemn and conscientious regard to my duty prevailed with me to consent to return to the flock from which I had been torn—but with what grief, tears, great anxiety and distress I did this, the Lord is my best witness'.

Calvin returned to Geneva in 1541. His fears were amply justified. There was to be a long and bitter struggle in which Calvin fought for the spiritual independence of the Genevan church and for the imposition of a rigorous discipline. The rules which he sought to impose (including regulation of dress and prohibition of dancing) were mostly traditional medieval laws. The novelty lay in his determination actually to enforce them—and that on the *whole* of Genevan society, not exempting the ruling classes. For many years Calvin had to face intense opposition from the magistrates, but eventually his opponents were discredited and there was a pro-Calvin city council. In the final years of his life he was highly respected, though his wishes were not always obeyed. He died in 1564.

Calvin has not had a good press. He himself wrote in 1559 that 'never was a man more assailed, stung and torn by calumny' than he was. These words were to be more prophetic than he could have realized. He is blamed for the doctrine of predestination— so clearly taught by *Augustine, by most medieval theologians and by all the Reformers. It is true that Calvin heightened it somewhat, but no more than had some medieval theologians, such as *Bradwardine. He is vilified for his part in the execution of the heretic Servetus (for denying the doctrine of the Trinity)— although his contemporaries applauded him almost to a man and although many of those considered saintly today (such as Thomas More) persecuted heretics more fiercely than did Calvin. Calvin must be judged against the background of his times. He is accused of being the 'dictator of Geneva'—while even at the height of his power his authority was primarily moral rather than legal and he had to seek the approval of the city council before publishing his books. Of course he was not perfect. He himself acknowledged that he suffered from a bad temper. He was intolerant, assuming too readily that opposition to *his* teaching was opposition to *God*'s word—a fault shared with many others then and now. To some extent Calvin's ill-repute is the fault of his disciples who often upset the careful balance of his theology by making the doctrine of predestination central and foundational whereas Calvin was careful to keep it in its place.

Calvin transformed Geneva. The Scots Reformer *John Knox declared it to be 'the most perfect school of Christ that ever was in the earth since the days of the apostles. In other places I confess Christ to be truly preached. But manners and religion to be so sincerely reformed, I have not yet seen in any other place.' This was the result of Calvin's rigorous discipline. For those who disliked it, Calvin suggested that 'they should build a city where they can live as they want, since they don't want to live here under the yoke of Christ'. It was also the result of a massive influx into the tiny city of French and other refugees, drawn mostly by their admiration of Calvin. Calvin's primary concern was for his homeland (France) and many who came to Geneva returned to pastor the growing number of French Protestant churches. Calvin founded an academy to train them, the precursor of the modern university of Geneva drawing upon the educational pattern that he had seen in Strassburg.

Calvin claimed, with some justice, that 'I have a natural love of brevity'. Yet he was one of the most prolific writers in the history of the church. His output would have been remarkable for a full-time scholar—yet Calvin fitted it into a schedule that would have exhausted two lesser men. Apart from his many responsibilities at Geneva, he was the most important leader of the international network of Reformed churches. His letters fill many large volumes and a list of their recipients would read like a *Who's Who* of Reformation Europe.

Calvin wrote many polemical treatises. Several of these were directed against Anabaptism. More important were his attacks on Roman Catholicism. In 1539, after Calvin had been exiled from Geneva, Cardinal Sadolet wrote to the Genevans urging them to return to the Roman fold. The letter was forwarded to Calvin who wrote a *Reply to Sadolet* (in one day!) which is one of his best works. He also published the *Acts* of the early sessions of the *Council of Trent— with an *Antidote*. Calvin was capable of satire as biting as any of Erasmus, as can be seen from his *Admonition* in which it is shown how advantageous for Christendom would be an inventory of the bodies and relics of saints.

Again, let us consider how many fragments [of the cross] are scattered up and down over the whole globe. A mere enumeration of those of which I have a catalogue would certainly fill a goodly volume. There is no town, however small, which has not some morsel of it, and this not only in the principal cathedral church of the district, but also in parish churches. There is no abbey so poor as not to have a specimen. In some places, larger fragments exist, as at Paris in the Holy Chapel, at Poitiers and at Rome, where a crucifix of tolerable size is said to be made entirely out of it. In short, if all the pieces which could be found were collected into a heap, they would form a good shipload, though the gospel testifies that a single individual was able to carry it. What effrontery then thus to fill the whole world with fragments which it would take more than three hundred men to carry!... Not content with imposing on the rude and ignorant, by displaying a piece of common wood as the wood of the cross, they have declared it every way worthy of adoration. This doctrine is altogether devilish.

TREATISE ON RELICS

Calvin also found himself forced against his will to write against Lutherans. Two Lutheran pastors, Westphal and Hesshusius, attacked his doctrine of the Lord's Supper and Calvin responded. Eventually he abandoned the controversy, which grieved him because he saw himself as a disciple of *Luther. Not all of Calvin's treatises were polemical. One of the finest is a *Short Treatise on the Lord's Supper,* which sets out his teaching in a conciliatory fashion, as the middle way between *Zwingli and Luther.

Calvin preached regularly throughout his time at Geneva. From 1549 his sermons were recorded in shorthand. A number were published in the sixteenth century, but the majority remained in the Genevan library in shorthand form. Incredibly, these were sold off by weight in 1805 and three quarters of them are lost. Those which survive are now being published.

Calvin wrote commentaries on many of the books of the Bible—Genesis to Joshua, Psalms, all of the prophets except Ezekiel 21–48 and all of the New Testament except 2 and 3 John and Revelation. These commentaries were often based on earlier sermons or lectures. Calvin's commentaries are among the very few written before the last century which are still of value for understanding the meaning of the text (as opposed to those which might be read today for edification rather than for the light that they shed on the text of the Bible). He is the only writer ever to belong without question both to the first rank of theologians and to the first rank of commentators.

Calvin is best known for his *Instruction in the Christian Religion* (commonly called the *Institutes*). This work went through four major editions in Calvin's lifetime. The first edition was of pocketbook length and appeared in 1536. There were six chapters, the first four of which followed the pattern of Luther's catechisms. At the last minute Calvin added a lengthy dedication to King Francis I, who was harrying the French evangelicals and branding them as Anabaptists. Calvin presented his work to the king as an apology or defence of evangelical doctrine. The second edition, which appeared in 1539, was three times the length of the first. The next, in 1543, was not much longer, but reflected the influence of Bucer and the stay at Strassburg. Finally, the definitive edition was published in 1559, about five times the length of the first. Calvin stated that 'I never felt satisfied until the work was arranged in the order in which it now appears. Alongside these Latin editions there were French translations, mostly by Calvin himself. The *Institutes* was not simply a theological treatise—it was a 'sum of piety' (1536 title page) for the edification of the people of France. The French editions are important for the history of the developing French language as no work of such weight had previously appeared in French.

What was the purpose of the *Institutes*? Calvin himself explained this at the beginning of the 1539 edition. Believing in brevity, he did not wish to enter into long theological discussions in his commentaries. These topics are therefore covered in the *Institutes*, which is to be seen as a companion to the commentaries and as a preparation for the study of the Bible itself. In studying Calvin, this pattern should be followed. When reading the commentaries, one can turn to the *Institutes* for theological guidance and when reading the *Institutes* one can turn to the commentaries (or sermons) for a fuller explanation of the scriptural passages cited.

Our wisdom, in so far as it ought to be deemed true and solid wisdom, consists almost entirely of two parts—the knowledge of God and of ourselves. But as these are connected together by many ties, it is not easy to determine which of the two precedes and gives birth to the other. For, in the first place, no man can survey himself without forthwith turning his thought towards the God in whom he lives and moves ... The miserable ruin into which the revolt of the first man has plunged us compels us to turn our eyes upwards ... We are urged by our own evil things to consider the good things of God—and indeed we cannot aspire to him in earnest until we have begun to be displeased with ourselves ... On the other hand, it is evident that man never attains to a true self-knowledge until he has previously contemplated the face of God and come down after such contemplation to look into himself. For (such is our innate pride) we always seem to ourselves just and upright and wise and holy until we are convinced, by clear evidence, of our injustice, vileness, folly and impurity. Convinced, however, we are not if we look to ourselves only, and not to the Lord also. For he is the only standard by the application of which this conviction can be produced ... Since nothing appears within us or around us which is not tainted with very great impurity, so long as we keep our mind within the confines of human pollution, anything which is in some small degree less defiled delights us as if it were most pure.

INSTITUTES 1:1:1–2

It is of importance to call to mind what was formerly taught: First, that since God by his law prescribes what we ought to do, failure in any one respect subjects us to the dreadful judgement of eternal death, which it denounces. Secondly, because it is not only difficult, but altogether beyond our strength and ability, to fulfil the demands of the law, if we look to ourselves and consider what is due to our merits, no ground of hope remains, but we lie forsaken of God under eternal death. Thirdly, that there is only one method of deliverance which can rescue us from this miserable calamity—namely that when Christ the Redeemer appears, by whose hand our heavenly Father, out of his infinite goodness and mercy, has been pleased to succour us, if we with true faith embrace this mercy and with firm hope rest in it.

INSTITUTES 3: 2: 1

When we see the visible sign we must consider what it represents, and by whom it has been given to us. The bread is given us to figure the body of Jesus Christ, with command to eat it—and it is given to us by God, who is certain and immutable truth. If God cannot deceive or lie, it follows that it accomplishes all which it signifies. We must then truly receive in the Supper the body and blood of Jesus Christ, since the Lord there represents to us the communion of both. Were it otherwise, what could be meant by saying, that we eat the bread and drink the wine as a sign that his body is our meat and his blood our drink? If he gave us only bread and wine, leaving the spiritual reality behind, would it not be under false colours that this ordinance had been instituted? ... We all then confess with one mouth, that on receiving the sacrament in faith, according to the ordinance of the Lord, we are truly made partakers of the proper substance of the body and blood of Jesus Christ. How that is done, some may deduce better and explain more clearly than others. Be this as it may, on the one hand, in order to exclude all carnal fancies [i.e. the Lutheran view], we must raise our hearts upward to heaven, not thinking that our Lord Jesus is so debased as to be enclosed under some corruptible elements [i.e. 'in, with and under' the bread and wine]. On the other hand, so as not to impair the efficacy of this holy ordinance, we must

hold that it is made effectual by the secret and miraculous power of God and that the Spirit of God is the bond of participation [in Christ's body and blood]—this being the reason why [the sacrament] is called spiritual.

SHORT TREATISE ON THE LORD'S SUPPER 16, 60

Heidelberg Catechism (1563)

In 1559 the Palatinate, one of the German states, acquired a new ruler, the elector Frederick III. He wished to advance the Reformed faith there. To this end, he commissioned a catechism, for use in the churches and the schools. This was written in 1562 by a number of theologians from Heidelberg university, principally Zacharias Ursinus and Kaspar Olevianus, both still in their twenties. The following year it was approved by the synod of Heidelberg and published. That same year it was also translated into Latin and other languages. It is one of the most popular of the Reformation catechisms and has been widely distributed. It has been said to combine the intimacy of *Luther, the charity of *Melanchthon and the fire of *Calvin.

The text comprises 129 questions and answers. These are divided into 52 Sundays, so that the catechism can be fitted into a year's programme. The whole is divided into three parts: Man's Misery, Man's redemption and Thankfulness.

Q.1: What is your only comfort in life and in death?

That I, with body and soul, both in life and in death, am not my own but belong to my faithful Saviour Jesus Christ. He, with his precious blood, has fully satisfied for all my sins and redeemed me from all the power of the devil ... By his Holy Spirit he assures me of eternal life and makes me willing from the heart and ready henceforth to live for him.

Q.21: *What is true faith?*

It is not only a certain knowledge by which I hold for truth all that God has revealed to us in his word—but also a heartfelt trust, which the Holy Spirit works in me by the Gospel, that not only to others but also to me forgiveness of sins, eternal righteousness and blessedness are given by God, out of sheer grace, for the sake of Christ's merit alone.

Q.56: *What do you believe concerning the forgiveness of sins?*

That God, for the sake of Christ's satisfaction [on the cross], will no more remember my sins, nor the sinful nature with which I have to struggle all my life long. Instead, he graciously bestows on me the righteousness of Christ, that I may never more come into condemnation.

Q.76: *What does it mean to eat the crucified body and drink the shed blood of Christ?*

It means not only to embrace with a believing heart the entire passion and death of Christ, thereby obtaining forgiveness of sins and eternal life, but in addition to be more and more united to his blessed body by the Holy Spirit ... so that although he is in heaven and we are on earth, we are nonetheless flesh of his flesh and bone of his bone and live and are ruled for ever by one Spirit, as are the members of our body by one soul.

Q.78: *Do the bread and wine [in the Lord's Supper] become the real body and blood of Christ?*

No. But as in baptism the water is not changed into the blood of Christ nor becomes the washing away of sins itself, being only the divine token and assurance of it—so also, in the Lord's Supper, the holy bread does not become the body of Christ itself, although according to the nature and usage of sacraments it is called the body of Christ.

Q.79: *Why then does Christ call the bread his body and the cup his blood or the new testament in his blood? Why does St Paul call them the communion of the body and blood of Christ?*

Christ does not speak in this way without great cause. It is his aim not only to teach us thereby that, just as bread and wine sustain this temporal life, so also his crucified body and shed blood are the true food and drink of our souls for eternal life—but also much more to assure us by this visible sign and pledge that we partake as really of his true body and blood, through the working of the Holy Spirit, as we receive with our bodily mouths these holy tokens in remembrance of him. He also wishes to assure us that all his sufferings and obedience are as certainly our own as if we had ourselves in person suffered everything and given satisfaction [for sin].

Jakob Arminius
QUESTIONING PREDESTINATION

Jakob Hermandszoon (who took the Latin name Arminius) was born before 1560 at Oudewater in Holland. After a tragic youth, in which he suffered a number of bereavements, he went to Leiden and Geneva universities, among others. At Geneva he studied under Theodore Beza, *Calvin's successor, who gave him a warm testimonial when he left. He returned to Amsterdam in 1587 and the following year was ordained pastor there. In 1589 Arminius was called upon to defend the Calvinistic doctrine of predestination against the attacks of Dirk Coornhert. But on weighing up the rival arguments, Arminius found himself siding with Coornhert and prudently kept silent. In the early 1590s, while lecturing on Romans, Arminius questioned the Calvinist interpretation of chapters 7 and 9. This led to controversy and to questions about his orthodoxy, which were to continue until his death. In 1602 there was an outbreak of plague and Arminius was diligent in ministering to his flock, despite the risks involved. Several professors at Leiden died and Arminius was nominated to fill one of the vacant posts. His appointment was vigorously opposed by Francis Gomarus, the senior theological professor at Leiden and a strict Calvinist. Eventually Arminius was cleared of charges against him and took up his appointment in 1603. But Gomarus was not satisfied and the controversy continued until Arminius' death in 1609.

Arminius was reticent about expounding his views openly—probably for fear of the consequences. Very little of his work was published until after his death. But his views on predestination are clearly set out in his *Declaration of Sentiments* (1608). There are four 'decrees' of God. First, he decreed to appoint Jesus Christ as the mediator to win salvation for man. *Secondly*, he decreed to accept and save all who would repent and believe in Jesus Christ and to reject impenitent unbelievers. *Thirdly*, God decreed to provide the means necessary for man to repent and believe. *Finally*, God decreed the salvation of certain specific individuals—because he foresaw that they would believe and persevere to the end. In this way Arminius rejected the Augustinian/Calvinist idea of unconditional election—that God chooses or elects people for salvation regardless of any foreseen merit in them. But it does not follow that Arminius had a high view of man's natural capacities.

In his lapsed and sinful state, man is not capable, of and by himself, either to think or to will or to do that which is really good. But it is necessary for him to be regenerated and renewed in his intellect, affections or will and in all his powers, by God in Christ through the Holy Spirit, that he may be qualified rightly to understand, esteem, consider, will and perform whatever is truly good.
DECLARATION OF SENTIMENTS

It follows that even the regenerate or born-again Christian 'can neither conceive, will nor do any good at all, nor resist any evil temptation, without [God's] preventing [preceding] and exciting, following and cooperative grace'. Arminius was careful to stress to the full our dependence upon God's grace. But he differed from the Augustinian position at one vital point. We are dependent upon God's grace, but this grace is given in such a way that man is left to decide whether or not he will accept it. God's grace makes our salvation *possible*, not *inevitable*. Thus the ultimate choice regarding salvation is made by man himself. God's election and predestination of individuals are based not upon his sovereign choice but upon his foreknowledge of *our* choice. While for *Augustine and Calvin it is ultimately true that we choose God because he has chosen us, for Arminius the reverse is true. This question still divides people into 'Arminians' and 'Calvinists'.

Arminius' death by no means ended the controversy. He left behind him many followers and in 1610 forty-six Arminian pastors met at Gouda and produced a *Remonstrance*. There were five points:

● God chose to save through Jesus Christ all those who through the grace of the Holy Spirit would believe on him and persevere to the end.

● Jesus Christ, by his death on the cross, obtained forgiveness of sins for all, but only believers partake of it.

● Fallen man will of his own free-will think nothing that is truly good. He needs to be born again by God, in Christ, through the Holy Spirit in order to do that which is truly good.

● We can do no good without God's grace preceding, awakening, following and co-operating with us. But this grace is not irresistible.

● True believers are enabled by grace to persevere to the end and be saved. But whether it is possible through sloth or negligence to lose this grace is uncertain. [Arminius himself was agnostic upon this point. Arminians have usually tended to assert that it *is* possible to fall from grace and lose one's salvation, this being more consistent with the desire to give man the ultimate choice about his salvation.]
Because of the *Remonstrance*, the

Arminians came to be called Remonstrants. The controversy raged fiercely until the *Synod of Dort answered the five points of the *Remonstrance*.

Synod of Dort (1618–19)

The controversy over the teaching of *Arminius became linked with rival Dutch political factions. There was even the danger of civil war. After a struggle the anti-Remonstrant party won and called a synod, which met at Dordrecht (Dort) from 1618 to 1619. This was not merely a national synod—delegations were present from England, the Reformed German states, Switzerland and Geneva (not yet part of Switzerland). The French Reformed Church was prevented by the king from sending a delegation, but approved the decisions of the synod afterwards.

The *Remonstrance* was unanimously rejected and the synod drew up a response, the 'canons' of Dort. The five points of the *Remonstrance* are answered under five headings—of which the third and the fourth are combined, as the third point of the *Remonstrance* was considered orthodox. The canons were signed by all the members of the synod.

Election is the unchangeable purpose of God, whereby before the foundation of the world he has out of mere grace, according to the sovereign good pleasure of his own will, chosen from the whole human race (which had fallen through their own fault from their primitive state of rectitude into sin and destruction) a certain number of persons to redemption in Christ. From eternity he appointed Christ to be the mediator and head of the elect and the foundation of salvation.
CANON 1:7

This was the sovereign counsel and most gracious will and purpose of God the Father: that the quickening and saving efficacy of the most precious

death of his Son should extend to all the elect for bestowing upon them alone the gift of justifying faith, thereby to bring them infallibly to salvation. That is, it was the will of God that Christ by the blood of the cross ... should effectually redeem ... all those and those only who were from eternity chosen to salvation.
CANON 2:8

All men are conceived in sin and by nature children of wrath, incapable of saving good, prone to evil, dead in sin and in bondage to it. Without the regenerating grace of the Holy Spirit they are neither able nor willing to return to God, to reform the depravity of their nature, nor to dispose themselves to reformation.
CANON 3/4:3

When God accomplishes his good pleasure in the elect or works true conversion in them, he does not merely cause the gospel to be preached externally to them and powerfully illuminate their minds by the Holy Spirit ... By the efficacy of the same regenerating Spirit he pervades the inmost recesses of the man; he opens the closed and softens the hardened heart; he circumcises that which was uncircumcised and infuses new qualities into the will, which though previously dead he quickens; from being evil, disobedient and refractory he renders it good, obedient and pliable; he actuates and strengthens it so that, like a good tree, it may bring forth the fruits of good actions.
CANON 3/4:11

By reason of the remains of indwelling sin and the temptation of sin and the world, those who are converted could not persevere in a state of grace if left to their own strength. But God is faithful and having conferred grace, mercifully confirms and powerfully preserves them in it even to the end.
CANON 5:3

The points covered in the above extracts *later* came to be seen as the 'five points of Calvinism', summed up in the mnemonic TULIP.

T = Total depravity. This is an unhappy expression which creates the impression that all people are as depraved as they could be. Apart from being manifestly untrue, such a doctrine is expressly denied by the canons of Dort. The phrase 'total depravity' should be understood in the sense that every part of man is affected by the fall and that he can make no move towards God without his grace.

U = Unconditional election. We choose God because he first chose us. This is the fundamental point at issue between Arminius and the Augustinian/Calvinist tradition.

L = Limited atonement. While the death of Jesus Christ is more than sufficient to expiate all the sins of all people, God's intention in giving him was not merely to make *possible* the salvation of all, but actually and infallibly to save the elect alone. This doctrine was expounded at length by *John Owen. It is foreign to *Calvin himself and has never commanded the assent of all Calvinists. It is not held by any school of thought other than the Reformed.

I = Irresistible grace. God's grace works in the elect in such a way as to guarantee that they will respond to it. The effect of this grace is not to destroy the will but to evoke a willing response. The sinner finds it irresistible in the same way that a young man might find a girl's charms 'irresistible'.

P = Perseverance of the saints. Those who are truly converted will certainly be saved—*not* regardless of how they live but because God will preserve them from finally turning away from him.

Jonathan Edwards
REVIVALIST PHILOSOPHER

Jonathan Edwards was born in 1703 at East Windsor, Connecticut. In 1716 he went to Yale university as a student and later became a tutor there. While he was religious from his youth, he had in the early 1720s a conversion experience which brought home to him in a deeper way the sovereignty and the grace of God. In 1727 he became minister of the Congregational Church at Northampton in Massachusetts, in succession to his grandfather, Solomon Stoddard. During Edward's time at Northampton there was revival in the parish—in 1734/35 arising from his own preaching, and from 1740 arising out of the ministry of George Whitefield in New England. But Edwards' relationship with his congregation was not wholly satisfactory. He sought to tighten the requirements for membership, which had been relaxed by his grandfather, and as a result was dismissed by the congregation in 1750. The following year he went to Stockbridge as a missionary to the Indians and while there wrote a number of his greatest works. In 1757 he was invited to be president of the College of New Jersey (now Princeton University) and reluctantly accepted. On his arrival in 1758 he was inoculated against smallpox, because of an epidemic, but died soon after from the side-effects.

Jonathan Edwards was both a defender and a critic of the revivals of his time. His notorious sermon on *Sinners in the Hands of an Angry God*, in which he laid especial stress on God's wrath, was one of those which sparked off revival.

The God that holds you over the pit of hell, much as one holds a spider or some loathsome insect over the fire, abhors you and is dreadfully provoked. His wrath towards you burns like fire; he looks upon you as worthy of nothing else, but to be cast into the fire; he is of purer eyes than to bear to have you in his sight; you are ten thousand times more abominable in his eyes than the most hateful venomous serpent is in ours. You have offended him infinitely more than ever a stubborn rebel did his prince—and yet it is nothing but his hand that holds you from falling into the fire every moment.

In 1737 he wrote *A Faithful Narrative* in which he describes the effects of the earlier revival. But as time went by he discovered that not all of the conversions during the revival were genuine—some of those who professed conversion soon lapsed into their old godless ways. This led Edwards to write his *Religious Affections* in 1746, in which he examined the nature of true religion. Against the rationalist opponents of the revivals, he maintains that true religion lies not in the mind but in the 'affections' (the heart, emotions, will). But against the uncritical supporters of the revivals, he points out that not all religious affections are an evidence of God's grace. They can be fervent, lead to an outward change of life, lead to confidence before God and to moving testimonies—yet without there being a true change of heart. Edwards' book has much to say to the issues raised by the modern 'charismatic movement'. He wholeheartedly approves of a felt and experienced 'heart religion', but warns powerfully about the dangers of being misled by a superficial emotionalism.

As in worldly things worldly affections are very much the spring of men's motion and action; so in religious matters the spring of their actions is very much religious affections. He that has doctrinal knowledge and speculation only, without affection, never is engaged in the business of religion. Nothing is more manifest in fact, than that the things of religion take hold of men's souls no further than they affect them... I am bold to assert that there never was any considerable change wrought in the mind or conversation of any person, by anything of a religious nature that ever he read, heard or saw, who had not his affections moved... In a word, there never was anything considerable brought to pass in the heart or life of any man living, by the things of religion, that had not his heart deeply affected by those things.
RELIGIOUS AFFECTIONS 1: 2

Jonathan Edwards was a determined opponent of *Arminianism. At the end of his life he wrote *The Christian Doctrine of Original Sin Defended*. But his best-known work is his *Freedom of the Will*, published in 1754. Edwards accepts the freedom of the will in a very limited sense—we are free to act as we choose. But what we choose is determined by the strongest motives that confront us, the greatest apparent good. Fallen man is morally impotent—what he lacks is not the *ability* to do good but the *will* or desire.

Edwards has been called the greatest American philosopher, largely on the basis of this work. He was the father of New England Theology—a leading exponent of which was his son Jonathan Edwards Junior (1745–1801). In due course it gave birth to New Haven Theology, as seen in *Charles Finney.

THE ANABAPTISTS

Schleitheim Confession (1527)

The magisterial Reformers reformed the church's doctrine, but there was much that they left unchanged. In particular, they shared with medieval Catholicism the ideal of a Christian state in which all citizens are baptized members of a single church with a uniform creed—which inevitably implies the coercion of dissenters. This ideal was challenged by some for whom the Protestant Reformation was not radical enough—the Anabaptists. The two ideals came into open conflict in Zürich. In the early years of the reform, *Zwingli worked hand in hand with a group of radicals—Conrad Grebel, Felix Manz and others. They maintained a common front until 1523. But the issues of the state church and infant baptism divided them. It seems that Zwingli himself opposed infant baptism for a time—but drew back when he realized that it is essential if a state church is to be maintained. The radicals' opposition to infant baptism hardened and in 1525, after a public disputation with Zwingli, they began to (re)baptize believers. The town council responded by ordering the exile of all those rebaptized, and in the following year the death penalty was introduced for rebaptizing. In January 1527 Felix Manz was executed by drowning.

Infant baptism was the obvious point of disagreement but the issues were more fundamental. The Anabaptists rejected the state church, to which all were forced to belong. For them, Christian faith was free and voluntary, not to be coerced. The church is a voluntary association of committed disciples. The Reformers recognized that not all citizens were true Christians, but they saw the elect as an unknown number within the state church—we cannot know for sure who they are. The Anabaptists disagreed.

They felt that the church should consist *only* of true believers, of committed disciples. The true church is not the unknown number of the elect within the all-embracing state church—it is a visible group of disciples who have separated themselves from the world (which includes the state church). Its purity is to be maintained by excluding unrepentant sinners. All church members are committed Christians and are to be actively involved in spreading the faith. The Anabaptist ideal of the church was rejected in the sixteenth century. But the rise of a secular society and the decline of nominal Christianity has led to a sharper contrast in modern Western society between committed Christians and non-Christians. Today all churches are forced by circumstances to accept at least part of the Anabaptist concept of the church.

The early Anabaptist leaders had little opportunity to write. Most of them survived only for a few years, on the run. The most important and authoritative statement of early Anabaptist faith is found in the *Schleitheim Confession*. A number of Anabaptist leaders met in February 1527 at Schleitheim, not far from Schaffhausen. They produced seven articles of faith. The main author appears to have been Michael Sattler, a former prior who spent some time at both Zurich and Strassburg (where he discussed with *Bucer and Capito). In May 1527 he was apprehended by the Roman Catholic authorities and burnt at Rottenburg, near Tübingen. His wife was drowned a few days later.

The seven articles are not a comprehensive statement of faith, but cover the main points of difference between the Anabaptists and the Reformers, as well as points where the Anabaptists had previously disagreed among themselves.

● Baptism is not for infants, but for those who have already consciously decided to be Christians.

*Baptism shall be given to all those who
have learned repentance and
amendment of life, and who believe truly
that their sins are taken away by Christ,
and to all those who walk in the
resurrection of Jesus Christ, and wish to
be buried with him in death, so that they
may be resurrected with him, and to all
those who with this significance request
it [baptism] of us and demand it for
themselves. This excludes all infant
baptism, the highest and chief
abomination of the pope. In this you
have the foundation and the testimony
of the apostles (Matthew 28, Mark 16,
Acts 2,8,16,19).*
ARTICLE 1

● Baptized believers who fall into sin
and refuse correction are to be banned from
fellowship.
● The breaking of bread is a fellowship
meal in remembrance of Jesus Christ and is
only for baptized disciples.
● Believers are to be separate from
this wicked world—which includes the
Roman and Protestant state churches as well
as military service. Pastors are to be chosen
from men of good repute in the world. They
are to be supported by their flock.
● The [magistrate's] sword is ordained
by God to be used by worldly magistrates to
punish the wicked. In the church, the only
weapon to be used is excommunication.
Jesus Christ forbids the use of violence so the
Christian cannot accept the office of
magistrate.
● It is wrong for Christians to swear
oaths.

Menno Simons
ANABAPTIST LEADER

Menno Simons was born in Friesland, North
Holland, in 1496/97. In 1524 he became a
priest, but before long he began to doubt the
doctrine of transubstantiation. He then
turned to the Bible (for the first time.) and
came to the conclusion that the Roman
teaching was false—but stayed in his post.

Some time later he heard of the martyrdom
of an Anabaptist nearby. 'It sounded very
strange to me to hear of a second baptism. I
examined the Scriptures diligently and
pondered them earnestly, but could find no
report of infant baptism.' He then turned to
the early Fathers and Reformers, but found
no coherent scriptural defence of infant
baptism. He concluded that 'we were
deceived in regard to infant baptism'—but
did nothing about it. So far he had had no
direct contact with Anabaptists.

In 1534 the city of Münster was taken
over by some of the wilder revolutionary
Anabaptists. They saw it as the New
Jerusalem prophesied in Revelation.
Polygamy was introduced—on the basis of
the Old Testament. Roman Catholics and
Protestants united to besiege the city, which
fell in 1535. There was a bloodbath. The
affair of Münster served to discredit the
Anabaptist cause for some time. But,
ironically, Münster marked the end of
revolutionary Anabaptism. From now on it
was the pacifist evangelical Anabaptism
which predominated—and inherited the
reputation of Münster.

Menno saw the effects of Münster and the
persecution of the scattered and leaderless
Anabaptist brethren. His conscience smote
him for his hypocritical life of outward
conformity to Rome. He began openly to
preach what he believed and after nine
months, in 1536, he left home to become a
wandering Anabaptist preacher. For eighteen
years he travelled constantly—nowhere was
safe for him. But in 1554 he was able to settle
on the estate of a sympathetic nobleman in
Holstein, North Germany. Here he was able to
write and to publish his works in peace, until
his death in 1561.

Menno became the leader of the
Anabaptist movement in Holland and North-
West Germany. He organized independent
congregations with their own leaders. In due
course his followers came to be known as
Mennonites. The movement grew in
(relatively) tolerant Holland. Over the
centuries, other Anabaptist groups have also
come to be called Mennonites. In the
eighteenth century the Mennonites spread to

Russia, at the invitation of Catherine the Great. Later, persecution in Russia caused migration to North America, especially in 1873–82 and 1923–30. Today there are some 700,000 Mennonites worldwide, of whom about a half are in the United States and Canada.

Menno held to the evangelical Anabaptist position, as set out in the *Schleitheim Confession*. He opposed the revolutionary Anabaptists, holding to a firmly pacifist position, as do most Mennonites today. He also opposed the 'spiritualist' Anabaptists, who relied on the 'inner light' for special private revelations. Menno sought to base his teaching on the Bible alone. Like the Reformers, he held that Scripture alone is the supreme and final norm for all doctrine. But he did not follow the Reformers in the deep respect that they retained for the writings of the early church Fathers (while insisting that they must be tested by Scripture).

Menno illustrates the danger of neglecting tradition when one interprets the Bible. He held that Jesus Christ 'did not become flesh *of* Mary, but *in* Mary'. In other words, while affirming that Jesus was truly human, he did not believe that his humanity was taken from Mary—who was only his 'host mother'. This position had already been rejected as a heresy in the second century, and Menno illustrates the adage that those who neglect history are condemned to repeat it. (To be fair, it must be remembered that the early Anabaptist leaders were wanted men, without the opportunity for leisurely study.) The Mennonite churches have not followed Menno at this point.

Menno Simons was one of the very few Anabaptist leaders to exercise a lengthy ministry (twenty-five years), to write extensively (his *Complete Works* contains more than a thousand large pages) and to leave behind him an organized movement. The Mennonites today have much in common with the Baptists, but they are noted for their stress on radical discipleship, including pacifism.

We have not a single command in the Scriptures that infants are to be baptized, or that the apostles practised it, therefore we confess with good sense that infant baptism is nothing but human invention and notion, a perversion of the ordinances of Christ, a manifold abomination standing in the holy place where it ought not to stand.
FOUNDATION OF CHRISTIAN DOCTRINE 1:E

Good brethren, because holy Christian baptism is a washing of regeneration, according to the doctrine of Paul [Titus 3:5], therefore none can be washed therewith to the pleasure and will of God save those who are regenerated through the word of God. For we are not regenerated because we are baptized, as may be perceived in the infants who have been baptized—but we are baptized because we are regenerated by faith in God's word. For regeneration is not the result of baptism, but baptism the result of regeneration. This may not be controverted by any man on the basis of Scriptures. Therefore all the learned ones must be shamed before this passage of Paul, let them be ever so learned, who so shamefully teach and make the simple to believe that infants are regenerated in baptism. Beloved reader, such teaching and belief is verily nothing but fraud and deceit. For if the infants were regenerated as the learned ones say, then their whole course would be humility, long-suffering, mercy, pure and chaste love, true faith, certain knowledge, sure hope, obedience to God, spiritual joy, inward peace and an unblameable life—for these are the true and natural fruits of the new heavenly birth. But what fruits are found in infants, every reader may judge from everyday experience.
CHRISTIAN BAPTISM 3

THE BRITISH
REFORMATION

William Tyndale
THE BIBLE INTO ENGLISH

William Tyndale was born in the 1490s on the Welsh border. He was educated at Magdalen Hall, Oxford and later at Cambridge. He then became tutor to the family of Sir John Walsh at Little Sodbury, north of Bath. While living in this household, Tyndale experienced at first hand the ignorance of the local clergy. To one cleric he is reported to have declared that 'if God spare my life, ere many years pass, I will cause a boy that driveth the plough shall know more of the Scriptures than thou dost', echoing *Erasmus' preface to his Greek New Testament. This task became Tyndale's life-work.

The only English translation of the Bible at this time was the *Wyclif Bible*, which was distributed by the Lollards, the followers of *Wyclif. This was available only in manuscript form and was inaccurate, having been translated from the Latin Vulgate. For fear of the Lollards, the church had banned the English Bible since 1408. Tyndale's aim was to make a new, accurate translation from the original Hebrew and Greek. He hoped to win the patronage of Cuthbert Tunstall, the scholarly bishop of London who was a friend of Erasmus. But the bishops were more concerned to prevent the spread of *Luther's ideas to England than to promote the study of the Bible, and Tunstall refused to support Tyndale. In due course Tyndale obtained financial support from a number of London merchants.

England was clearly no safe place to be translating the Bible so Tyndale left for Germany in 1524, never to return. By early 1525 the New Testament was ready for the press. It was being printed at Cologne when the authorities were alerted and raided the press. Tyndale managed to escape in time, taking with him some of the printed leaves. He went to Worms, where the first complete English New Testament was printed in 1526. There were a number of later revised editions. In 1530, Tyndale's translation of the Pentateuch (Genesis to Deuteronomy) was published at Antwerp, where he had now settled.

I beseeche you therfore brethren by the
mercifulness of God, that ye make youre
bodyes a quicke sacrifise, holy and
acceptable unto God which is youre
resonable servynge off God. And fassion
note youre selves lyke unto this worlde.
But be ye chaunged [in youre shape] by
the renuynge of youre wittes that ye
maye fele what thynge that good, that
acceptable, and perfaicte will of god is.
TYNDALE'S NEW TESTAMENT, 1526 (ROMANS 12:1–2)

Tyndale's New Testament was smuggled into England. At the end of 1526, Tunstall preached against it and had copies ceremonially burnt at St Paul's Cross. The following year, archbishop Warham of Canterbury bought up a considerable number of copies—effectively financing a further printing! Tyndale's translation has had an immense influence and has rightly earned him the title of 'the father of the English Bible'. It could almost be said that every English New Testament until this century was merely a revision of Tyndale's. Some 90 per cent of his words passed into the King James Version and about 75 per cent into the Revised Standard Version.

Tyndale also wrote a number of other works, of which the best known are his *Parable of Wicked Mammon* (a treatise on justification by faith alone, drawing heavily on Luther, merely translating him in places), and *The Obedience of a Christian Man* (on the duty of obeying civil authority, except where loyalty to God is concerned). Thomas More vigorously attacked 'the captain of English heretics' and Tyndale replied.

Tyndale planned to translate the entire Old Testament. But in 1535 he was betrayed by a fellow-Englishman at Antwerp and arrested. The following year he was strangled and then burnt at Brussels. It is reported that his final words were: 'Lord, open the king of England's eyes'. Whether or not this prayer was answered, Henry VIII, encouraged by *Cranmer, permitted the publication of English translations of the Bible from 1535, all drawing heavily on Tyndale. These helped to prepare the ground for the introduction of Protestant ideas in the reign of Edward VI.

Faith is, then, a lively and stedfast trust in the favour of God, wherewith we commit ourselves altogether unto God. And that trust is so surely grounded and sticks so fast in our hearts, that a man would not once doubt of it, although he should die a thousand times therefor. And such trust, wrought by the Holy Ghost through faith, makes a man glad, lusty, cheerful and true-hearted unto God and unto all creatures.

A PROLOGUE UPON THE EPISTLE OF ST PAUL TO THE ROMANS (1526)

Thomas Cranmer
THE LANGUAGE OF WORSHIP

Thomas Cranmer was born in 1489, in Nottinghamshire. He studied at Jesus College, Cambridge and became a fellow in 1511. In the early 1520s he was among a group of young scholars who met in the White Horse Inn at Cambridge to discuss *Erasmus' Greek New Testament. It was the 'king's matter' which propelled Cranmer into public life. Henry VIII desperately needed a male heir for the stability of the realm. England had only recently emerged from the period of turmoil known as the Wars of the Roses. It was essential that the succession be

unquestioned. The queen, Catherine, had produced only one surviving child—Mary. To complicate matters, Catherine had been married to Henry's older brother Arthur before his early death—which meant that her marriage to Henry was contrary to Leviticus 20:21. Henry wanted an annulment of the marriage on these grounds—seeing the lack of a male heir as God's judgement on an unlawful union. (Leviticus 20:21 actually mentions childlessness.) Normally there would have been no problems, but the pope was being controlled by the emperor Charles V—who happened to be Catherine's nephew, and so opposed to the annulment. In 1529 Cranmer put forward the bright idea of consulting the universities for their judgement. Henry heard of this and sent Cranmer on a tour of the European universities.

At this time the 'Reformation Parliament' (1529–36) put through a series of laws gradually severing all links between the English Church and Rome. This culminated in the *Act of Supremacy* in 1534 which declared the sovereign to be 'the only Supreme Head in earth of the Church of England'. In the meantime, the archbishop of Canterbury had died in 1532 and Henry had appointed a reluctant Cranmer to replace him. Cranmer fitted the post admirably, for two reasons: he believed sincerely in the authority of the 'godly prince' over the church (i.e. it was not merely a tactical position), and his views moved gradually in the direction of Protestantism, at about the right speed for the royal will. But this belief was to bring Cranmer to the greatest crisis of his life, at the end.

During the later years of Henry's reign there was a constant power struggle between the conservative Catholic faction and those desiring Protestant reform. At first Cranmer gained some notable victories—the publication of an English Bible (drawing heavily on *Tyndale's translation) and its installation in every parish church; the publication in 1536 of *Ten Articles* which leaned gently in a Lutheran direction. But in 1539 there was a Catholic reaction with the publication of *Six Articles* of an anti-Protestant nature, which Cranmer opposed. The following year, his ally Thomas Cromwell fell from favour and was beheaded. Cranmer's enemies tried to topple him too, but Henry, who respected him, always protected him.

When Edward VI succeeded Henry in 1547, the time was ripe for real reform with Cranmer at the forefront. In 1549 the first English *Boke of the Common Prayer* was published. This was a Protestant work, but carefully written so as not to cause unnecessary offence to traditional Catholics. The Holy Communion 'commonly called the masse' still looked very much like the old mass to the uninitiated. The Catholic party exploited this fact to interpret it in a traditional sense. Because of this and in the light of suggestions from Peter Martyr and *Bucer (who had become professors at Oxford and Cambridge at Cranmer's invitation), a revised prayer book was introduced in 1552. In some ways there were few changes, but the ambiguities of 1549 were gone and the result was an unequivocally Protestant work. As a leading scholar of Catholic sympathies has put it, this prayer book 'is *not* a disordered attempt at a catholic rite, but the only effective attempt ever made to give liturgical expression to the doctrine of "justification by faith alone" '. There are few differences between the 1552 prayer book and the 1662 version, which reigned supreme in Anglicanism for three hundred years. One item which Elizabeth I removed in 1559, in order not to antagonize her Roman Catholic subjects more than necessary, was the inclusion in the Litany of: 'From the tyranny of the Bishop of Rome and al hys detestable enormities... Good Lorde, delyver us'!

The reign of Edward also saw doctrinal reform. In 1547 a *Book of Homilies* was published, many of them being written by Cranmer. These were evangelical sermons to be read in parishes where there was no qualified preacher. In 1553 Cranmer and Ridley (bishop of London) produced *Forty-two Articles*, which were later modified to become the *Thirty-nine Articles*.

Edward died young in 1553 and was succeeded by Mary, a zealous Roman Catholic. She set about dismantling the Edwardian Protestant settlement. At first she moved slowly and with moderation, but in 1555 the burning of Protestant heretics began. A number of bishops were burnt, including Latimer and Ridley in October 1555. Latimer encouraged Ridley with the words: 'Be of good comfort master Ridley and play the man. We shall this day light such a candle by God's grace in England as (I trust) never shall be put out'. Latimer died quickly but Ridley died a slow and agonizing death. One of the witnesses was Cranmer. The government worked hard to persuade him to recant his Protestant beliefs. In particular, they exploited his belief in the sovereign's authority over the church—his sovereign was now ordering him to revert to Roman Catholicism. Under extreme psychological pressure Cranmer gave way and recanted. But then Mary made a great mistake—she ordered that Cranmer should be burnt despite his recantation. It was arranged that Cranmer would publicly renounce Protestantism at his execution—but instead he renounced his recantation and reaffirmed his Protestant convictions in full. He was rushed to the stake, where he held his right hand (which had signed the recantation) in the flames until it was burnt.

When Mary came to the throne, Protestantism was not particularly popular. But by an unwise and unpopular alliance with Spain, and by the executions, Mary burnt Protestantism into the English consciousness, earning the title 'Bloody Mary'. The courageous martyrdoms of Cranmer, Latimer, Ridley and some two hundred others won the hearts of the people for Protestantism in a way that the legislation of Edward's reign could never have achieved.

Almightie God, the father of oure Lorde Jesus Christ, whiche desireth not the death of a synner, but rather that he maye turne from his wickednes & lyve: & hath geven power & commanndement to hys ministers, to declare and pronounce to his people beinge

*penitente, the absolucion and remission
of theyr synnes: he pardoneth and
absolveth all them which truely repent,
and unfeynedly beleve his holy gospell.
—wherefore we beeseche him to graunte
us true repentaunce and his holye
spirite, that those thinges may please
him, which we doe at this present, &
that the rest of oure lyfe hereafter, maye
be pure & holye: so that at the laste we
maye come to hys eternall ioye, through
Jesus Christ our Lorde. Amen.*

THE BOKE OF COMMON PRAYER (1552):
MORNING PRAYER

*Take and eate this, in remembraunce
that Christe died for thee, and feede on
him in thy hearte by faythe, wyth
thankesgevinge.*

*Drinke thys in remembraunce that
Christes bloude was shed for thee, & be
thankeful.*

*O Lord and heavenly father, we thy
humble servauntes, entierly desyre thy
fatherly goodnes, mercifullye to accepte
thys oure Sacrifice of prayse and
thankesgevyng: most humbly beseching
thee to graunt that by the merites &
death of thi sonne Jesus Christ, and
through faith in his bloud, we and al thy
whole church, may obtayne remission of
our sinnes, & al other benefites of his
Passion. And here we offre and present
unto thee, O lord, our selves, our soules
and bodies, to be a reasonable, holy and
lively Sacrifice unto thee, humbly
besechyng thee, that al we whiche be
partakers of this holye Communion,
maye be fulfilled wyth thy grace &
heavenly benediccion. And althoughe we
be unworthy, throughe our manifold
sinnes, to offre unto thee ani sacrifice:
yet we beseche the to accepte this our
bounden duetie and service, not
wheighing our merites, but pardoning
our offences, through Jesus Christ our
Lord: by whome and with whome, in the
unitie of the holy gost, al honour and
glori be unto thee O father almightye,
worlde wythout ende. Amen.*

THE BOKE OF COMMON PRAYER (1552): COMMUNION

John Knox
THUNDERING SCOT

John Knox was born around 1513 at
Haddington, not far from Edinburgh. He was
educated at St Andrews university and was
subsequently ordained. At the age of about
thirty he was won over to Protestantism. He
was deeply impressed by his contemporary
George Wishart, who preached the gospel
fearlessly and paid for it by being burnt at
the stake at St Andrews in 1546. For the next
thirteen years Knox travelled widely. He
spent nineteen months as a French galley
slave, after taking part in an abortive revolt
at St Andrews. He was in England during
the latter part of the reign of Edward VI and
took part in the final stages of preparing
*Cranmer's 1552 Book of Common Prayer.

When Mary became queen in 1553 he fled
to continental Europe. For a time he was
pastor of the English exile congregation at
Frankfurt, where he became embroiled in
controversy. Knox and others had gone
beyond the *Book of Common Prayer*,
introducing a more thoroughly Reformed
pattern of worship. But the more
conservative exiles in other European cities
were displeased and sent Richard Cox and
others to put Knox right. They remonstrated
with him, saying that 'they would have the
face of an *English* church'. Knox replied,
'The Lord grant it to have the face of Christ's
church'. This conflict was the precursor of
the Puritan controversies during the reign of
Elizabeth I, with some wanting to preserve
the *Book of Common Prayer* and others
wanting a fuller Reformation in line with the
1461 Reformed churches in continental
Europe. Cox managed to have Knox expelled
from Frankfurt (by drawing attention to his
radical political views) and Knox went to
Geneva. He was an ardent admirer of
*Calvin's Geneva. While there he wrote his
infamous *First Blast of the Trumpet against
the Monstrous Regiment [Reign] of Women*
(1558). This attack on female rulers was
aimed at Mary Tudor, queen of England.
In 1558 Elizabeth came to the English
throne and she did not take kindly to Knox's
work.

In 1559 Knox returned to Scotland, where he helped to reform the church. With others he drafted the *Book of Discipline* (1561) and the *Book of Common Order* (1564). He was also the most important of the 'Six Johns' (six Scots reformers named John) who in four days in August 1560 drew up the *Scots Confession*. This confession of faith was ratified by the Scots Parliament and became the confession of the Scots Reformed Kirk until in 1647 the *Westminster Confession* was adopted.

Knox's second blast against the monstrous regiment of women was his sustained opposition to Mary Stuart (Mary Queen of Scots) until her flight to England in 1568. He pushed through the Scottish reformation despite her resistance. His major work was his *History of the Reformation of Religion within the Realm of Scotland*, which did not appear in full until 1644. Knox died in 1572.

Even after we are reborn, if we say that we have no sin, we deceive ourselves and the truth of God is not in us. It is therefore essential for us to lay hold on Christ Jesus, in his righteousness and his atonement, since he is the end and consummation of the Law and since it is by him that we are set at liberty so that the curse of God may not fall upon us, even though we do not fulfil the Law in all points. For as God the Father beholds us in the body of his Son Christ Jesus, he accepts our imperfect obedience as if it were perfect, and covers our works, which are defiled with many stains, with the righteousness of his Son.
SCOTS CONFESSION 15

The notes, signs and assured tokens whereby the spotless bride of Christ is known from the horrible harlot, the false Kirk, we state, are neither antiquity, usurped title, lineal succession, appointed place, nor the numbers of men approving an error ... The notes of the true Kirk, therefore, we believe, confess and avow to be: first, the true preaching of the Word of God, in which

God has revealed himself to us, as the writings of the prophets and apostles declare; secondly, the right administration of the sacraments of Christ Jesus, with which must be associated the Word and promise of God to seal and confirm them in our hearts; and lastly, ecclesiastical discipline uprightly ministered, as God's Word prescribes, whereby vice is repressed and virtue nourished.
SCOTS CONFESSION 18

Thirty-nine Articles

The *Thirty-nine Articles* of the Church of England form its principal confession of faith. They are found in the *Book of Common Prayer*. They began their life in 1553, during the reign of Edward VI, when *Cranmer and Ridley drew up *Forty-two Articles*. In 1563, after the restoration of Protestantism by Elizabeth I, archbishop Matthew Parker revised them, producing the *Thirty-nine Articles*. The Latin text was approved by the Convocation (of the clergy) that year. In 1571 an English translation was approved and published. There were minor alterations in the text until the definitive form was reached in 1604. The present preface dates from 1628.

Despite attempts to prove the contrary, of which the boldest was by *Newman, the articles clearly teach a moderate form of Calvinism. If they present a *via media* or middle path it is the same one that all the Reformers sought—a middle way between the errors of Roman Catholicism and Anabaptism. Until the last century all the clergy were required to give assent to the articles, as were those wishing to take degrees at Oxford and Cambridge. Since 1865 a looser form of assent has been required of the clergy alone.

Holy Scripture containeth all things necessary to salvation: so that whatsoever is not read therein, nor may be proved thereby, is not to be required of any man, that it should be believed as

*an article of the faith, or be thought
requisite or necessary to salvation.*
ARTICLE 6

*The condition of man after the fall of
Adam is such, that he cannot turn and
prepare himself, by his own natural
strength and good works, to faith and
calling upon God. Wherefore we have no
power to do good works pleasant and
acceptable to God, without the grace of
God by Christ preventing [preceding] us,
that we may have a good will, and
working with us when we have that good
will.*
ARTICLE 10

*We are accounted righteous before God,
only for the merit of our Lord and
Saviour Jesus Christ by faith, and not
for our own works or deservings.*
ARTICLE 11

*Predestination to life is the everlasting
purpose of God, whereby (before the
foundations of the world were laid) he
hath constantly decreed by his counsel
secret to us, to deliver from curse and
damnation those whom he hath chosen
in Christ out of mankind, and to bring
them by Christ to everlasting salvation,
as vessels made to honour.*
ARTICLE 17

*The church hath power to decree rites or
ceremonies, and authority in
controversies of faith. And yet it is not
lawful for the church to ordain any
thing that is contrary to God's word
written, neither may it so expound one
place of Scripture that it be repugnant
to another.*
ARTICLE 20

*It is a thing plainly repugnant to the
word of God, and the custom of the
primitive church, to have publick prayer
in the church, or to minister the
sacraments in a tongue not
understood of the people.*
ARTICLE 24

*There are two sacraments ordained of
Christ our Lord in the gospel, that is to
say, baptism and the Supper of the
Lord.*
ARTICLE 25

*Baptism is not only a sign of profession,
and mark of difference, whereby
Christian men are discerned from
others that be not christened, but it is
also a sign of regeneration or new birth
whereby, as by an instrument, they that
receive baptism rightly are grafted into
the church; the promises of the
forgiveness of sin and of our adoption
to be the sons of God by the Holy Ghost
are visibly signed and sealed; faith is
confirmed and grace increased by virtue
of prayer unto God. The baptism of
young children is in any wise to be
retained in the church, as most
agreeable with the institution of Christ.*
ARTICLE 27

*The body of Christ is given, taken and
eaten in the [Lord's] Supper, only after
an heavenly and spiritual manner. And
the mean whereby the body of Christ is
received and eaten in the Supper is
faith.*
ARTICLE 28

Richard Hooker
ESTABLISHMENT MAN

When Mary died, in 1558, Elizabeth I came
to the throne. The following year there was a
settlement of religion which was essentially
a compromise. Elizabeth herself wanted a
more conservative reform, one in which a
number of 'catholic' elements would remain.
But she had a problem. The leading Roman
Catholic clergy from Mary's reign were not
prepared to accept any more flirtations with
Protestantism. On the other hand, most of
the leading Protestants had been abroad
during the reign of Mary. They had been to
places like Zürich and Geneva and most of
them had come to desire a more radical
reform than that of the 1552 *Book of*

Common Prayer, at the end of Edward's reign. In the end the 1559 Elizabethan Settlement approximated very closely to that of 1552. For Elizabeth, this was the upper limit—no more reform would be allowed (nor was it). But for most of her new bishops, this was the bottom line, a tolerable level of reform. They accepted it for fear that refusal would open the door to Roman (or even Lutheran) 'wolves'. One of the leading bishops, John Jewel, who defended the Elizabethan Settlement against Rome, called it 'this golden, or rather, leaden mediocrity'. He assumed that more reform would come in due course—those who resisted it were 'Crying that the half is better than the whole'.

But not all of the leading Protestants were prepared to accept the Elizabethan Settlement. There were some, especially those who had spent Mary's reign in Geneva, who agitated for further reform and sometimes went so far as to refuse to conform. They had learned at Geneva that it was not necessary for the church to be subservient to the state. They came to be known as Puritans. They were members of the Church of England who desired to see it more thoroughly reformed—there was no question of leaving it or allowing more than one church in the land. Towards the end of Elizabeth's reign a new attitude began to appear within the Church of England. Some of its new leaders regarded the Elizabethan Settlement not merely as an acceptable form of Protestantism but as an especially desirable form. The chief apologist for this new attitude was Richard Hooker. While Jewel was the chief apologist for the Elizabethan Settlement against Rome, Hooker became its chief apologist against Puritanism.

Richard Hooker was born in 1553/54 near Exeter. He went to Exeter grammar school. Jewel, who had been in Zürich with his uncle, took him under his wing and arranged a place for him at Corpus Christi College, Oxford, where in due course he became a fellow. In 1585 he was appointed master of the Temple, in London, through the patronage of the archbishop of York, whose son he was tutoring. The Puritan Walter Travers was already reader at the Temple, but had been passed over for promotion to master because of his Puritan convictions. Travers continued preaching in the afternoons and Hooker preached in the mornings—with the result that 'the forenoon sermon spake Canterbury and the afternoon Geneva'. Hooker stepped down in 1591 and took a living in Wiltshire—although he probably never ministered there. Ending absenteeism among the clergy was one of the Puritan reforms which Hooker opposed. He died in 1600.

Hooker was a man of one work—*The Laws of Ecclesiastical Polity*. This comprises eight books, of which only the first five were published in his lifetime. It was not until 1661/62 that all eight books were published, and it is widely believed that the last three books have been 'doctored' in one way or another.

The Reformation began as, among other things, a protest against the influence of Aristotle on theology. But in the latter half of the sixteenth century Aristotle came to dominate Protestant theology. Hooker was an ardent admirer of Aristotle and drew upon *Thomas Aquinas, another devotee of Aristotle.

Hooker had no qualms about the role of the sovereign in the church. This was questioned by both the Roman Catholics (in the name of papal authority) and the Puritans (in the interests of scriptural authority and links with the international Reformed movement). Hooker's slogan was 'by the goodness of Almighty God and his servant Elizabeth, we are.'

The Puritans opposed many of the traditional Catholic practices retained by the Church of England—such as the use of the wedding ring and the wearing of surplices by the clergy. They held that the Bible is a complete guide to all church life and that no ceremonies should be added which are not found in Scripture. Hooker inclined more to the Lutheran view that no ceremonies should be allowed which are *contrary* to Scripture. He denied that the Bible gives us one complete blueprint for church life. He argued that church laws can be defended on other than scriptural grounds—by reason or from tradition.

Human laws are measures in respect of men, whose actions they must direct. Howbeit such measures they are, as have also their higher rules to be measured by—which rules are two: the law of God and the law of nature. So that laws human must be made according to the general laws of nature, and without contradiction unto any positive law in Scripture.
ECCLESIASTICAL POLITY 3:9:2

Neither may we in this case lightly esteem what has been allowed as fit in the judgement of antiquity, and by the long continued practice of the whole church—from which unnecessarily to swerve, experience has never yet found it safe ... That which is new, if it promise not much, fears condemnation before trial—till trial, no man acquits or trusts it, what good soever it pretend and promise. So that in this kind there are few things known to be good, till such time as they grow to be ancient.
ECCLESIASTICAL POLITY 5:7:1,3

Hooker was above all an establishment man, concerned to defend the status quo. It is debatable to what extent he supported the Elizabethan Settlement simply because it *was* the settlement. One thing Hooker would never have been is a *Reformer*. His formal doctrinal positions differ little from the Calvinism of Jewel, but the spirit of the two men is markedly different.

William Perkins
PURITAN MODERATE

William Perkins was born in Warwickshire in 1558. In 1577 he went to Christ's College, Cambridge, where he became a Fellow in 1584. Some time early in the 1580s he was converted from a loose life to serious godliness. He represents the moderate wing

of Elizabethan Puritanism. In 1587 he was summoned before the Vice-Chancellor of the university to answer charges relating to one of his sermons. His answers revealed that he was uneasy about certain aspects of the Prayer Book (such as kneeling to receive communion), but that his belief in submission to lawful authority was strong enough to overcome these qualms. The 1580s saw an attempt by some Puritans to set up a shadow Presbyterian organization (with ministers and 'lay elders' gathered together into presbyteries) alongside the existing system of government by bishops. Perkins may well have sympathized with Presbyterianism, but he took care not to reveal any opinions on the matter—except that he strongly opposed any *separation* from the established church.

At this time the government was clamping down on Puritan non-conformity. Perkins felt that there were matters of greater importance than disputes over liturgy or church government. He shared the Puritan concern for deeper reform—but sought this through a deepening of personal spirituality and pastoral care, rather than through further legislation. Perkins' policy became widespread among the Puritans as they faced their inability to change the Elizabethan Settlement. By devoting themselves to pastoral care and spirituality they made a deep mark on the nation—with lasting spiritual and political consequences for England, the New World and elsewhere.

From 1584 Perkins became lecturer (preacher) at Great St Andrew's church in Cambridge, where he remained until his death in 1602. From this position he exercised a considerable influence over generations of undergraduates and thus set his mark on the Puritan movement of the seventeenth century, both in England and among the New England settlers. His extensive writings were no less influential. He wrote against Rome—as in his *Reformed Catholic*. 'By a Reformed Catholic I understand anyone that holds the same necessary heads of religion with the Roman Church, yet so as he pares off and rejects all errors in doctrine whereby the said religion is corrupted.' Perkins wrote theological works, especially on the doctrine of predestination. In 1595/96 there was a controversy over predestination at Cambridge, where the views of *Arminius had been anticipated. Archbishop Whitgift, a staunch anti-Puritan, approved nine Lambeth Articles which set out a strongly Calvinist doctrine of predestination. Perkins also wrote in defence of the doctrine, anticipating the teachings of the *Synod of Dort.

Perkins is best known as a practical writer. He introduced the art of casuistry (applying general ethical principles to specific cases of conscience) to Protestantism. Following the lead of *Bucer, he stressed the importance of Christian *experience*. The concept of conversion became more prominent than it had been with the Reformers. With Perkins there begins an interest in the 'order of salvation'—the normal order of events in conversion and sanctification. Perkins' stress on conversion was to be influential on both pietism (as with *Spener) and Evangelicalism (as with the *Wesleys). The stress on personal experience led to the question of assurance—how can I know if I have a true saving experience of Jesus Christ? Many of the Puritans failed to heed *Calvin's warning here: 'if you look to yourself, damnation is certain'. Instead, they urged people to seek assurance by looking within themselves for the evidences of conversion. But as one hymn writer put it, 'they who fain would serve thee best, are conscious most of wrong within', and the inevitable outcome was that many struggled long and hard to find assurance. While *Luther and Calvin had seen assurance of salvation as part of saving faith, the Puritans tended to separate them and to make assurance an experience subsequent to conversion.

A man that does but begin to be converted is even at that instant the very child of God, though inwardly he be more carnal than spiritual ... The first material beginnings of the conversion of a sinner, or the smallest measure of renewing grace, have the promises of this life and the life to come ... A constant and earnest desire to be reconciled to God, to believe and to repent, if it be in a touched heart is accepted by God as reconciliation, faith, repentance itself ...To see and feel in ourselves the lack of any grace pertaining to salvation, and to be grieved therefore, is the grace itself ... He that has begun to subject himself to Christ and his word, though as yet he be ignorant in most points of religion, yet if he have a care to increase in knowledge and to practise that which he knows, he is accepted of God as a true believer ... The foresaid beginnings of grace are counterfeit unless they increase.

A GRAIN OF MUSTARD SEED OR THE LEAST MEASURE OF GRACE THAT IS OR CAN BE EFFECTUAL TO SALVATION (THE SIX CONCLUSIONS WHICH ARE EXPOUNDED THROUGHOUT THE WORK)

Westminster Confession

When Elizabeth died in 1603 she was succeeded by James I, previously king of Presbyterian Scotland. During his reign there was a shift in the attitudes of the bishops. While in the Elizabethan period episcopacy (government of the church by bishops) was defended on the grounds that it was desirable or at least tolerable, under James many began to argue that it was the one divinely ordained form of church government. (In doing so they were responding to similar claims made for Presbyterianism in the latter part of the sixteenth century.) While under Elizabeth both the bishops and their Puritan critics shared a common Calvinist theology, many of the new bishops rejected it. They denied the doctrine of predestination and were therefore called Arminians, though their theology was very different from that of *Arminius. They desired more ritual in church worship and saw regular participation in the sacraments as the way to salvation. So while under Elizabeth the Puritans differed from the establishment over questions of church government and ceremony, in the seventeenth century there was a much more serious theological divide. This worsened under James' son Charles I, who succeeded him in 1625. Charles strongly favoured the 'high church' party and promoted them to positions of leadership. When someone, wishing to know more of their beliefs, asked what the Arminians held, the reply was 'all the best bishoprics and deaneries in England'!

William Laud became archbishop of Canterbury in 1633 and sought to impose high church ways. Those who resisted were punished severely—many had their ears cut off. But in 1637, Charles and Laud made the mistake of seeking to impose the *Book of Common Prayer* on Presbyterian Scotland. This provoked opposition which led in due course to the Civil War between Charles and Parliament. The result was the victory of Parliament and the execution of Laud and, eventually, Charles himself. The Puritans by now would not accept anything less than radical change. Episcopacy was to be abolished 'root and branch'.

At first the initiative lay with the Presbyterians. The Scots wanted the Church of England to become like the Church of Scotland. To this end, Parliament convened the Westminster Assembly, which met in more than a thousand sessions from 1643 to 1649—and irregularly thereafter. The membership was overwhelmingly Presbyterian—many of those who were not Presbyterian left. The aim was to legislate for one common Presbyterian establishment of religion for the British Isles. To this end the assembly produced a *Directory for the Publick Worship of God*, designed to replace the *Book of Common Prayer*. They produced the *Shorter and Larger Catechisms*, which have acquired a status comparable to *Luther's two catechisms. But their greatest achievement was the *Westminster Confession*, a statement of seventeenth-century Reformed belief comparable in length and status to the Lutheran *Augsburg Confession*. The *Westminster Confession*

was intended to replace the *Thirty-nine Articles*. it is a considerably longer document, and the moderate Calvinism of the Articles gave way to a much stricter Calvinism. In addition, the Confession reflects seventeenth-century British Calvinism, which differs in a number of ways from the teaching of *Calvin himself. Three examples show this clearly:

● In the seventeenth century, 'covenant theology' became very popular within Calvinism. This meant taking the idea of the covenant as an organizing principle in theology. In particular, it involved the contrast between a 'covenant of works' between God and Adam before the fall and a 'covenant of grace' between God and the church. None of this is to be found in Calvin.

The first covenant made with man was a covenant of works, wherein life was promised to Adam, and in him to his posterity, upon condition of perfect and personal obedience. Man by his fall having made himself incapable of life by that covenant, the Lord was pleased to make a second, commonly called the Covenant of Grace: whereby he freely offereth unto sinners life and salvation by Jesus Christ, requiring of them faith in him, that they may be saved; and promising to give unto all those that are ordained unto life his Holy Spirit, to make them willing and able to believe.
WESTMINSTER CONFESSION 7:2–3

● The Confession teaches 'limited atonement'—that the intention of the cross is the salvation of the elect alone. Jesus Christ purchased salvation 'for all those whom the Father hath given unto him' (8:5). This teaching accords with the *Synod of Dort, but is foreign to Calvin.

● For both Luther and Calvin saving faith *includes* assurance of salvation. But in seventeenth-century British Calvinism it became more normal to regard personal assurance as *possible* for all believers, but as something *distinct* from saving faith. This means that it is possible and may become normal for those with saving faith to lack assurance. This is the position of the Confession. It has led in some Calvinist churches to a situation where assurance of salvation is rare and is even frowned upon—a complete reversal of Calvin's own position.

Assurance [of salvation] doth not so belong to the essence of faith, but that a true believer may wait long, and conflict with many difficulties, before he be partaker of it: yet, being enabled by the Spirit to know the things which are freely given him of God, he may, without extraordinary revelation, in the right use of ordinary means, attain thereunto.
WESTMINSTER CONFESSION 18:3

The catholick or universal church, which is invisible, consists of the whole number of the elect that have been, are, or shall be gathered into one, under Christ the head thereof; and is the spouse, the body, the fulness of him that filleth all in all. The visible church, which is also catholick or universal under the gospel (not confined to one nation, as before under the law) consists of all those throughout the world that profess the true religion, together with their children; and is the kingdom of the Lord Jesus Christ, the house and family of God, out of which there is no ordinary possibility of salvation.
WESTMINSTER CONFESSION 25:1–2

Q.1: What is the chief end of man?

A: Man's chief end is to glorify God and to enjoy him forever.

Q.33: What is justification?

A: Justification is an act of God's free grace, wherein he pardoneth all our sins, and accepteth us as righteous in his sight, only for the righteousness of Christ imputed to us, and received by faith alone.

Q.34: What is adoption?

A: Adoption is an act of God's free grace, whereby we are received into the number, and have a right to all the privileges of the sons of God.

Q.35: What is sanctification?

A: Sanctification is the work of God's free grace, whereby we are renewed in the whole man after the image of God, and are enabled more and more to die unto sin, and live unto righteousness.
SHORTER CATECHISM

The *Westminster Confession* was not adopted by the Church of England, but it was widely accepted by the English-speaking Reformed churches. The Church of Scotland adopted it in 1647, in the place of the earlier *Scots Confession* drawn up by *John Knox and others.

John Owen
CROMWELL'S ARBITER

With the Westminster Assembly, the victory of Presbyterianism appeared assured. But the Presbyterians turned out to be no more tolerant than the Arminians before them and their popularity waned. As John Milton put it, 'new presbyter is but old priest writ large'. Presbyterianism was imposed by Parliament, but the authority of Parliament was dependent on the army, which had defeated the king. The army was dominated by Independents, who believed in the autonomy of the local church. They held that each local congregation should be free to order its own affairs. Oliver Cromwell, the brilliant leader of the army, was an Independent, and when he became Lord Protector it was this position that he favoured.

Although Cromwell was not a tolerant man by twentieth-century standards, by the standards of his day he was enlightened and generous. Until his time, all but a few extreme separatists had wanted one uniform state church to which all would conform—they differed only concerning which uniform this state church would wear. Cromwell changed this. He appointed a board of 'Triers', composed of thirty-eight members. These included Presbyterians, Independents and Baptists, clergy and laity. It was their duty to judge the fitness of candidates for service in a parish. The aim was that every parish should have a godly evangelical minister—be he Presbyterian, Independent or Baptist. Furthermore, there was toleration of churches outside of the parish system. While some positions were not tolerated— such as Roman Catholicism or the denial of the Trinity—there was far more toleration than had previously existed. This system continued until the restoration of the monarchy in 1660, on the return of Charles II, when the episcopal system was restored and dissent was outlawed.

One of the brains behind Cromwell's system was John Owen. He was born in 1616 near Oxford and went to Queen's College, Oxford. But he left in 1637 because of the religious changes introduced by Laud. In the 1640s he served as minister of two Essex churches. At first his sympathies were Presbyterian, but he moved to an Independent position. He won Cromwell's favour in 1651 and was appointed Dean of Christ Church, Oxford. The following year he became Vice-Chancellor of the university. In 1660, with the restoration of the monarchy, he was expelled from Christ Church. He left Oxford and continued to preach and to write until his death in 1683.

Owen was the greatest of the seventeenth-century Independents. He was one of the authors of a set of *Humble Proposals*, presented to Parliament in 1652. In 1654 these became the basis for Cromwell's settlement and Owen was one of the thirty-eight 'Triers' who administered it. Owen also took a leading role at the Savoy Assembly, which met at the Savoy Palace in London in 1658. This was a Congregationalist or Independent gathering and produced the *Savoy Declaration of Faith* which, unlike the *Westminster Confession*, has never been widely used.

Owen is also known as the greatest exponent of the doctrine of 'limited atonement'. His *Death of Death in the Death of Christ* (1647) is the classic defence of the doctrine. Those who hold to universal atonement (Jesus Christ died for the sins of all men) are accused of teaching an ineffectual atonement. The cross merely makes it *possible* for all to be saved—it does not guarantee or actually *achieve* the salvation of anyone. The doctrine of limited atonement, by contrast, makes the salvation of the elect (and them alone) not merely possible but certain.

There are two major weaknesses in this much-used argument. First, the doctrine of predestination is being used as a controlling principle, to determine other doctrines (in this instance, the doctrine of the cross). *Calvin himself never exalted the doctrine of predestination to such a central and dominating position—he took care to put it in its rightful place. Second, the cross is being considered in isolation. Calvin's position would be that the salvation of the elect is made certain and not merely possible, not by the cross seen in isolation but by the combined work of Father, Son and Holy Spirit. It is the work of the Holy Spirit, leading us to faith in Jesus Christ, which makes our salvation not merely possible but certain.

[To those who state] 'God bestows faith on some, not on others', I reply: Did [Jesus Christ] purchase this distinguishing grace [the gift of faith] for those who receive it, in a manner not true of those who do not receive it? If that is so, then Christ did not die equally for all—for he died that some might have faith, but not others.

Indeed, in comparison he cannot be said to die at all for those others. For he did not die in order that they might have faith—and he knew that all the rest [of his work] would be unprofitable and fruitless without faith. But suppose, on the other hand, that [saving faith] is not purchased for [the elect] by Christ. Then have those that are saved no more for which to thank Christ than those that are damned—which is strange and

*contrary to Revelation 1:5,6: 'Unto him
that loved us and washed us from our
sins in his own blood ... '.*
DEATH OF DEATH IN THE DEATH OF CHRIST 3:2

Second London Confession (1677)

The period of the Commonwealth, under
Oliver Cromwell, saw the rise of the
Independents, the greatest of whom was
*John Owen, as a serious force. The
toleration offered by Cromwell's settlement
also helped the rise of other groups, such as
the Baptists. Their greatest representative in
the seventeenth century was *John Bunyan.
The Baptists shared with the
Congregationalists the belief in the
autonomy of the local congregation. They
also saw the church as a voluntary gathering
of believers, as did many of the
Congregationalists. But they went further in
rejecting the baptism of infants. Baptism
was only for those who had made a personal
confession of saving faith.

In 1644 seven Baptist congregations in
London published a confession of faith, the
first London Confession. In 1677 another
confession appeared, being a Baptist
revision of the *Westminster Confession.*
Because this was a time of persecution for
dissenters, the authors did not add their
names to it. But in 1689 the situation had
changed and the second London Confession
was recommended by the representatives of
more than a hundred Baptist congregations.
It has become the most authoritative of the
Baptist confessions. In America it was
adopted by the Baptist Association meeting
at Philadelphia in 1742—thus becoming
known as the *Philadelphia Confession.*

In many ways the Baptists resemble the
Anabaptists of the sixteenth century—in
their rejection of infant baptism and of the
state church. But there are other matters in
which they differ from the Anabaptists—in
allowing Christians to become magistrates
and to swear oaths, and in accepting war.

The majority of seventeenth-century
English Baptist groups had emerged from
Puritanism and their theology is best
understood as a Baptist modification of
Reformed theology.

*The members of these [local] churches
are saints by calling, visibly manifesting
and evidencing (in and by their
profession and walking) their obedience
unto that call of Christ; and do willingly
consent to walk together, according to
the appointment of Christ; giving up
themselves to the Lord, and one to
another, by the will of God, in professed
subjection to the ordinances of the
Gospel. To each of these churches thus
gathered, according to his mind
declared in his word, he hath given all
that power and authority, which is in
any way needful for their carrying on
that order in worship and discipline,
which he hath instituted for them to
observe; with commands and rules for
the due and right exerting, and
executing of that power.*
SECOND LONDON CONFESSION 26: 6–7

*Baptism is an ordinance of the New
Testament, ordained by Jesus Christ, to
be unto the party baptized a sign of his
fellowship with him in his death and
resurrection; of his being engrafted into
him; of remission of sins; and of his
giving up into God, through Jesus
Christ, to live and walk in newness of
life. Those who do actually profess
repentance towards God, faith in and
obedience to our Lord Jesus Christ are
the only proper subjects of this
ordinance.*
SECOND LONDON CONFESSION 29:1–2

John Bunyan
GOD'S PILGRIM

John Bunyan was born in 1628 at Elstow
(near Bedford), the son of a poor brazier or
tinker. He served with the Parliamentary
army from 1644 to 1646/47. In 1649 he

married the daughter of godly parents and through her began to seek after God. But it was only after several years of deep inner turmoil (described in his spiritual autobiography *Grace Abounding to the Chief of Sinners*) that he eventually came to find peace with God. He was greatly helped by John Gifford, the Independent pastor of St John's Church in Bedford. In 1653 Bunyan became a member of this congregation and before long he began to preach. He was outstanding as a preacher—*John Owen, one of the most learned men of the time, on being asked by Charles II why he listened to an uneducated tinker, replied: 'Could I possess the tinker's abilities for preaching, please your majesty, I would gladly relinquish all my learning.'

In 1660 the monarchy was restored, with the return of Charles II, and this meant persecution for those who would not conform to the new Anglican settlement. Bunyan was imprisoned that year for preaching and remained in jail almost continuously until 1672, because he would not undertake to cease preaching. He was also briefly imprisoned in 1677. It was while in prison that he wrote his best-known works, *Grace Abounding* and *Pilgrim's Progress*. He died in 1688, as the persecution of the dissenters was coming to an end.

Pilgrim's Progress is Bunyan's great masterpiece. It was published in 1678 and sold for eighteen pence. It has since been translated into about 100 different languages and has been printed countless times. In *Grace Abounding* Bunyan described his own experience in very personal terms. The pattern of his conversion would be of direct relevance to only a few. But in *Pilgrim's Progress* the experiences of Pilgrim are the experiences of every Christian as he walks through this life. Bunyan describes the trials and the temptations, the joys and the comforts of the Christian life in a way that has appealed to many far removed from his particular Calvinist, Baptist tradition. *Pilgrim's Progress* has also inspired a number of other works. Of particular interest is a short story by the nineteenth-century American writer

Nathaniel Hawthorne, called *The Celestial Railway*, which effectively relates Bunyan's tale to our modern age, with our more liberal values.

As I walked through the wilderness of this world, I lighted on a certain place, where there was a den. And I laid me down in that place to sleep and as I slept I dreamed a dream. I dreamed, and behold I saw a man clothed with rags, standing in a certain place, with his face from his own house, a book in his hand and a great burden upon his back. I looked and saw him open the book and read therein. And as he read, he wept and trembled, and not being able longer to contain, he brake out with a lamentable cry, saying, 'What shall I do?'...

[Christian] ran thus till he came at a place somewhat ascending; and upon that place stood a cross and a little below in the bottom, a sepulchre. So I saw in my dream, that just as Christian came up with the cross, his burden loosed from off his shoulders and fell from off his back, and began to tumble and so continued to do till it came to the mouth of the sepulchre, where it fell in and I saw it no more.

[The citizens of Vanity Fair] therefore brought [Faithful] out to do with him according to their law. And first they scourged him, then they buffeted him, then they lanced his flesh with knives; after that they stoned him with stones, then pricked him with their swords; and last of all they burned him to ashes at the stake. Thus came Faithful to his end. Now I saw that there stood behind the multitude a chariot and a couple of horses, waiting for Faithful who (so soon as his adversaries had dispatched him) was taken up into it, and straightway was carried up through the clouds, with sound of trumpet, the nearest way to the Celestial Gate.
PILGRIM'S PROGRESS

John & Charles Wesley
THE EVANGELICAL AWAKENING

John Wesley was born in 1703, his father being rector of Epworth, in Lincolnshire. When he was only five, the rectory burnt to the ground one night. John was trapped upstairs and was rescued at the last minute from an upper window. This led his mother to view him as 'a brand plucked from the fire' (Zechariah 3:2), preserved for a special task. He studied at Christ Church, Oxford, and in 1725 he was ordained. He returned to Oxford, to be a Fellow of Lincoln College, and while there became one of the founders of the Holy Club. This was for those who were serious about the practice of their religion. In 1735 Wesley went as a missionary to Georgia, but failed dismally. His inadequacies were exposed the very day after his arrival, by a Moravian pastor. (The Moravians were pietists, in the tradition of *Spener.)

He said, 'My brother, I must first ask you one or two questions. Have you the witness within yourself? Does the Spirit of God bear witness with your Spirit, that you are a child of God?' I was surprised and knew not what to answer. He observed it, and asked, 'Do you know Jesus Christ?' I paused and said, 'I know he is the Saviour of the world.' 'True', replied he, 'but do you know that he has saved you?' I answered, 'I hope he has died to save me.' He only added, 'Do you know yourself?' I said, 'I do.' But I fear they were vain words.
JOURNAL, 7 FEBRUARY 1736

By the time of his return to England in 1738 Wesley was even more aware of his spiritual need. 'I went to America to convert the Indians—but oh! who shall convert me!' But deliverance was at hand. Wesley received further help from the Moravians, especially one Peter Böhler, and matters came to a head later that year.

In the evening I went very unwillingly to a society in Aldersgate Street, where one was reading Luther's preface to the Epistle to the Romans. About a quarter before nine, while he was describing the change which God works in the heart through faith in Christ, I felt my heart strangely warmed. I felt I did trust in Christ, Christ alone, for salvation. And an assurance was given me that he had taken away my sins, even mine, and saved me from the law of sin and death.
JOURNAL, 24 MAY 1738

Traditionally, this is seen as Wesley's conversion. It seems probable that he had already been a committed Christian for some years. The new element was the assurance of salvation. (Interestingly, John's father, who himself came from a Puritan, nonconformist family, had told him on his deathbed that the strongest proof of Christianity is the inward witness of the Holy Spirit.) To many in the Church of England it seemed presumptuous to claim any such *assurance*. But Wesley came to see it as 'the very foundation of Christianity' and 'the main doctrine of the Methodists'.

John Wesley was not the only one to undergo such a conversion. His younger brother Charles (1707–88) preceded him by three days as did George Whitefield by several years. They began to preach the message of salvation by faith in Jesus Christ. But such teaching was not welcome in the pulpits of the Church of England. This was a time of considerable moral and religious decline in England. Unbelief was becoming fashionable and many of the clergy preached little more than a barren moralism. The preaching of the Wesleys and the other Evangelicals, or 'Methodists' as they came to be called, came as a clarion call to return to the gospel, the good news of salvation in Jesus Christ. As pulpits closed to them, first Whitefield and then Wesley began, in 1739, to preach in the open air. Circumstances had pushed them into the most effective way of reaching the mass of the populace, many of whom were not touched by the churches.

Evangelical preachers went about preaching in the market places and wherever they could gather an audience. John Wesley himself travelled some 5,000 miles a year every year, on horseback, at a time when the major roads resembled the country dirt tracks of today. (Not for nothing has he been called 'God's horseman'.) He would stop several times a day and preach to whoever would listen. 'I look upon all the world as my parish. Thus far I mean, that in whatever part of it I am, judge it meet, right and my bounden duty to declare, unto all that are willing to hear, the glad tidings of salvation.' Sometimes, especially in the early years, he would meet with a hostile reception, including stoning. But he persevered and was still preaching in the open air at the age of eighty-seven, shortly before his death. There are few areas in England where Wesley did not preach.

Wesley and the other Evangelical preachers had to face opposition, from the clergy and from all levels of society. But at the same time, many responded. Through their preaching Britain experienced the Evangelical Revival and many were brought into a living personal knowledge of Jesus Christ. As a result of the revival, Evangelicalism became a major factor in Anglo-Saxon Protestantism—and for much of the time since then, the dominant factor. The Wesleys gathered their converts into societies, which existed alongside the local parish churches. But the hostility of the Church of England led to their separation from the established church, to form the Methodist Church. Not that the Church of England itself was untouched. As a result of the revival, the Evangelicals became in due course the major group in the Church of England, a position that they retained until the latter part of the nineteenth century. The traditional free churches (the Presbyterians, Congregationalists and Baptists), which had declined in numbers and vitality, were also revived and grew rapidly.

The revival dramatically influenced the church in England. But its effects were not merely ecclesiastical. Through the revival the lower classes were touched by the gospel in a way that had not previously occurred. Indeed, all levels of society were affected and the moral tone of the nation changed

significantly. It has been said that without the revival Britain would probably have faced a revolution like the French Revolution. In the nineteenth century the 'non-conformist conscience' was a powerful factor in politics. The roots of the trades union movement and the Labour Party go back into Evangelicalism. The social and political life of the nation was profoundly affected in many ways.

The Evangelicals had a faith to preach. They also had a faith to sing about. Charles Wesley was probably the greatest English hymn-writer ever. The basic tenets of the Evangelical message can be summarized from his hymns.

● The centrality of Jesus Christ.

Jesus! the name that charms our fears,
That bids our sorrows cease;
'Tis music in the sinner's ears,
'Tis life and health and peace.

Jesus! the name high over all,
In hell or earth or sky;
Angels and men before it fall,
And devils fear and fly.

Jesus! the name to sinners dear,
The name to sinners given;
It scatters all their guilty fears,
It turns their hell to heaven.

● The cross of Jesus Christ.

He breaks the power of cancelled sin,
He sets the prisoner free;
His blood can make the foulest clean,
His blood availed for me.

See all your sins on Jesus laid;
The Lamb of God was slain,
His soul was once an offering made
For every soul of man.

And can it be that I should gain
An interest in the Saviour's blood?
Died he for me, who caused his pain?
For me, who him to death pursued?
Amazing love! how can it be
That thou, my God, shouldst die for me?

He left his Father's throne above,
So free, so infinite his grace;
Emptied himself of all but love,
And bled for Adam's helpless race;
'Tis mercy all, immense and free;
For, O my God, it found out me.

● The experience of conversion.

Long my imprisoned Spirit lay
Fast bound in sin and nature's night;
Thine eye diffused a quickening ray,
I woke, the dungeon flamed with light;
My chains fell off, my heart was free;
I rose, went forth and followed Thee.

Jesus the prisoner's fetters breaks,
And bruises Satan's head;
Power into strengthless souls he speaks.
And life into the dead.

Hear him, ye deaf, his praise, ye dumb,
Your loosened tongues employ;
Ye blind, behold your Saviour come;
And leap, ye lame, for joy!

● Assurance of salvation.

No condemnation now I dread.
Jesus and all in him is mine!
Alive in him, my living head,
And clothed in righteousness divine,
Bold I approach the eternal throne,
And claim the crown, through Christ
my own.

● Holiness of life.

O thou who camest from above
The pure celestial fire to impart,
Kindle a flame of sacred love
On the mean altar of my heart.

There let it for thy glory burn
With inextinguishable blaze,
And trembling to its source return
In humble love and fervent praise.

Jesus confirm my heart's desire
To work and speak and think for thee;
Still let me guard the holy fire,
And still stir up thy gift in me.

Ready for all thy perfect will,
My acts of faith and love repeat,
Till death thy endless mercies seal,
And make the sacrifice complete.

● Sharing the good news.

O that the world might taste and see
The riches of his grace;
The arms of love that compass me
Would all mankind embrace.

His only righteousness I show,
His saving truth proclaim;
'Tis all my business here below
To cry: 'Behold the Lamb!'

Happy if with my latest breath
I may but gasp his name;
Preach him to all and cry in death:
'Behold, behold the Lamb!'

THE ROMAN CATHOLIC
RESPONSE

Ignatius Loyola
SOCIETY OF JESUS

Iñigo López was born in the early 1490s into a noble family at Loyola, just south of the Pyrenees. He embarked upon a military career, caring little for the things of God. But he was brought to a halt at the siege of Pamplona in 1521, when his leg was mangled by a cannon ball. Ignatius was laid up for a considerable period and turned to read a *Life of Christ* and the lives of the saints. This led to his conversion and resolve to become a soldier of Jesus Christ. When his leg was better he made a pilgrimage to the monastery of Montserrat, near Barcelona, where he made his general confession and exchanged clothes with a beggar. He then spent a year of solitude and prayer at Manresa. During this time he underwent deep spiritual experiences and drew up the first draft of his *Spiritual Exercises*. *Thomas à Kempis' *Imitation of Christ* influenced him deeply at this stage. After visiting Rome and Jerusalem he returned to study in Spain (1524–28) and at Paris (1528–35).

In 1534 Ignatius founded the Society of Jesus. He and six companions took vows of poverty and celibacy. In 1537 they went to Rome and offered their services to the pope. They won support from some of the leading figures at Rome and in 1540 Pope Paul III sanctioned the Society of Jesus. Ignatius became the first General of the Jesuits and organized the order. He drew up its *Constitutions* from 1547 to 1550 and made further improvements until his death in 1556. The Jesuits had three major aims: to reform the church from within (by education especially); to fight heresy (especially Protestantism); to preach the gospel to the pagan world. In addition to the three normal vows of poverty, celibacy and obedience, the Jesuits added a fourth: going without delay wherever the pope might order for the salvation of souls. The Jesuits included some of the greatest figures of the Catholic Reformation, such as the missionary Francis Xavier and the theologian *Robert Bellarmine.

Ignatius' greatest work is his *Spiritual Exercises*, one of the major spiritual classics. This was completed during his time at Paris. The *Spiritual Exercises* is not a book to be read for spiritual edification but a guide for people who are leading other Christians in spiritual growth. They have been described as a summary in dehydrated form of Ignatius' own experience from his conversion on his sick bed to his time in Paris. The aim is to take the disciple systematically through the process of Ignatius' conversion in order to produce the same effect. The goal is to discover God's will for one's life, and to dedicate oneself completely to the service of Jesus Christ— ideally as a Jesuit. The exercises are designed to last four weeks, though each 'week' may be shorter or longer than seven days.

● The emphasis of week one is on the purgation of sin. The disciple is to examine his conscience and confess his faults. He is to meditate on the realities of sin and hell. The disciple is to be thankful that he has been spared this fate until now and is to resolve to forsake sin.

The fifth exercise is a meditation on Hell ... The first point will be to see with the eyes of the imagination these great fires, and the souls [of the lost] as it were in bodies of fire. The second will be to hear with the ears of the imagination the wailings, the howlings, the cries, the

*blasphemies against Christ our Lord
and against all the saints. The third will
be to smell the smoke, the sulphur, the
filth and the putrid matter. The fourth
will be to taste with the taste of the
imagination bitter things, such as tears,
sadness and the worm of conscience.
The fifth will be to feel with the touch of
the imagination how the fires touch and
burn the soul.*

SPIRITUAL EXERCISES WEEK 1

● The emphasis of week two is on the
kingdom of Jesus Christ. The disciple
meditates on the main events of Jesus' life
from his birth to his entry into Jerusalem on
Palm Sunday. The aim of the week is for the
disciple to resolve to serve under the
standard of Jesus Christ, rather than that of
the devil. At this stage there may come the
resolve to turn one's back on the world and
embrace the 'religious' life, especially as a
Jesuit.

● In the third week the disciple
meditates on the passion of Jesus Christ.

● In the fourth week the disciple
meditates on the risen Jesus Christ.

The *Spiritual Exercises* include eighteen
Rules for Thinking with the Church. These
show how the Jesuit was to subordinate his
thinking totally to the Roman Catholic
Church.

*In order to know rightly what we ought
to hold in the church militant, the
following rules are to be observed.*

*1. Laying aside all private
judgement, we ought to keep our minds
prepared and ready to obey in all things
the true spouse of Christ our Lord,
which is our holy mother, the
hierarchical church ...*

*13. To make quite sure of our
orthodoxy, if the hierarchical church
pronounces to be black that which
appears to be white, we ought to hold it
to be black. For we believe that between
Christ our Lord the bridegroom and the
church his bride there is one and the
same Spirit, which governs and directs
us to the salvation of our souls; and that*

*our holy mother the church is guided
and ruled by the same Spirit and Lord
that gave the Ten Commandments.*

SPIRITUAL EXERCISES

The Jesuits have been immensely influential
in the Roman Catholic Church. This
influence has served to fan opposition, as
from *Pascal, for instance. The order was
suppressed by the pope in 1773, but was
restored again in 1814. It remains very
powerful to the present day.

Council of Trent (1545–63)

From 1539 to 1541 there were a number of
colloquies in Germany at which leading
Protestant and Roman Catholic theologians
sought to reach an understanding. On the
Roman Catholic side these involved some of
the leading Catholic Humanists—disciples
of *Erasmus who were sympathetic to the
Protestant doctrine of justification by faith,
but did not wish to see the division of the
Western Church. Cardinal Contarini, who
played a leading role at the colloquy of
Regensburg, had himself had a conversion
experience which in many ways paralleled
*Luther's. But while agreement was reached
at Regensburg over justification by faith,
when it came to transubstantiation and
papal authority there was no room for
compromise.

The failure of the attempts to conciliate
the Protestants opened the door to the
Roman hardliners. In the early years of the
Reformation the popes had strongly resisted
the idea of a council. But in the 1530s Pope
Paul III made several abortive attempts to
call one. Finally in 1542, after the failure of
Regensburg, he called the Council of Trent.
The choice of venue was subtle—within the
territories of the German Emperor, yet near
enough to Rome to ensure papal control of
the council.

The Council of Trent met in three phases:
1545–47, 1551–52, 1562–63. It is the

nineteenth of the general or ecumenical councils recognized by the Roman Catholic Church. But while it was called ecumenical or world-wide, more than two-thirds of the bishops who attended were Italian. Thus the council was not representative of even the Roman Catholic world and it was certainly not free of papal control.

The work of the council was twofold—the definition of Roman Catholic doctrine in opposition to Protestantism and the introduction of disciplinary reforms within the Roman Catholic Church. There were definitions of doctrine over a wide range of areas—Scripture and tradition; original sin; justification; the sacraments; purgatory; relics and images; indulgences. The council produced more definition and legislation than the previous eighteen general councils put together. In 1564, the year after the close of the council, Pope Pius IV confirmed all the decrees of the council. He also published in that year a *Profession of Tridentine Faith*, also known as the *Creed of Pius IV*. This summarizes many of the anti-Protestant decisions of the council. Protestant converts to Rome were required to give assent to it.

Trent was attacked by leading Protestant theologians. One of the first responses came from *Calvin, who in 1547 published *The Acts of the Synod of Trent with an Antidote*. He was so sure of his case that he published the text of Trent in full before attacking it! A fuller and more considered response came from the Lutheran theologian Martin Chemnitz who from 1565 to 1573 published an *Investigation of the Council of Trent* in which he answered the council at great length.

The first major decree of the council concerned the question of Scripture and traditions:

Our Lord Jesus Christ, the Son of God, first promulgated [the gospel] with his own mouth and then commanded it to be preached by his apostles to every creature as the source both of every saving truth and of rules of conduct. [The council] perceives that this truth and discipline are contained in the

written books and in unwritten traditions—those unwritten traditions, that is, which were either received by the apostles from the mouth of Christ himself or were received from the apostles themselves (having been dictated by the Holy Spirit) and have come down even to us, having been transmitted as it were hand by hand. [The council], following the examples of the orthodox fathers, receives and venerates, with equal affection of piety and reverence, all the books of both Old and New Testaments (since one God is author of both) and the said traditions, whether pertaining to faith or to discipline, as having been dictated either by Christ's own word of mouth or by the Holy Spirit and having been preserved by an unbroken succession in the Catholic Church.

DECREE CONCERNING THE CANONICAL SCRIPTURES (1546)

This decree came in due course to be misunderstood. As Latin words subtly changed their meaning, it was thought to concern the issue of unwritten doctrinal traditions. But in fact the traditions in mind at Trent were ceremonies and practices, such as infant baptism or Sunday worship. There was a considerable debate about the meaning of this decree in the Roman Catholic Church during the period of the *Second Vatican Council, when the same topic was discussed.

The *Decree Concerning Justification* (1547) was one of the most important produced by the council:

[Adults] are disposed to justification as follows: Being quickened and aided by God's grace, they conceive faith by hearing and are freely moved towards God, believing those things to be true which have been divinely revealed and promised—and in particular believing that the ungodly are justified by God through his grace, through the redemption that is in Christ Jesus. Understanding themselves to be sinners,

*they are profitably alarmed through fear
of God's justice and are raised to hope
by turning themselves to consider his
mercy and they trust that God will be
propitious to them, for Christ's sake.
They then begin to love him as the
source of all righteousness and are for
that reason moved against sins by a
certain hatred and detestation—that is,
by that penitence which must be
performed before baptism. Finally, they
resolve to receive baptism, begin a new
life and keep God's commands.*

DECREE CONCERNING JUSTIFICATION, CHAPTER 6

This decree was intended to define the
doctrine of justification in an anti-Protestant
direction. And yet in recent years the Roman
Catholic theologian *Hans Küng has argued,
in his doctoral thesis *Justification*, that there
is no irreconcilable difference between the
Protestant and Roman Catholic
understandings of justification. What is
more, his thesis has met with widespread
approval. The main thrust of the decree is
about the justification of the adult convert.
Taking into account the different meanings
given to key words such as 'justification' and
'faith' by the two sides, their positions are
not that starkly opposed. But moving on to
other questions covered in the decree—the
effects of sin committed after baptism, the
meriting of eternal life at the last
judgement—the difference becomes
pronounced. It needs to be remembered that
the justification of the adult convert is a
largely theoretical issue—the majority of
Roman Catholics are baptized as infants. For
them, the reality which they face is sin
committed after baptism. If they repent and
confess their sin to a priest, the *eternal*
punishment due to sin (hell) is remitted,
according to Trent. But there still remains a
temporal punishment which must be paid by
the sinner himself. This he can do through
fasting, good works, penances, indulgences,
etc. If he dies 'insolvent', without having
paid off this debt, he goes to purgatory,
where he suffers the pains of hell until the
debt is paid. So the reality of the Christian
life, according to Trent, is one of salvation

by merit—although this merit is obtained
only with the help of God's grace.

Trent became not just *a* but *the* council of
the Roman Catholic Church. It became the
normative statement of anti-Protestant
Counter-Reformation Roman Catholicism.
Earlier councils were read in the light of
Trent and interpreted in accord with it. In
this way, Trent dominated the Roman
Catholic Church for some 400 years, the
period of 'Tridentine Catholicism'. This was
brought fo a close by the Second Vatican
Council, which produced even more
documents than Trent and which breathed a
very different spirit. Trent has now become
just one of the councils of the past.

Teresa of Avila
GOD'S GADABOUT

Teresa de Cepeda y Ahumada was born in
1515 at Avila, into an old Spanish family. In
1528 her mother died. At about this time her
childhood piety began to evaporate and she
developed an interest in books of chivalry
and began to think of marriage. But in 1531
her father entrusted her to an Augustinian
convent for her education and while there
she felt a call to the monastic life. Her father
was reluctant, so in 1535 she ran away from
home and joined the Carmelite monastery of
the Incarnation at Avila. But entering a
religious order did not solve all her spiritual
problems. She had difficulties with her
spiritual life and with prayer until, in 1554,
she had a deeper experience of conversion.
First, she was deeply moved by the sight of a
statue of Jesus Christ after he had been
scourged. 'I felt so keenly aware of how
poorly I thanked him for those wounds that,
it seems to me, my heart broke. Beseeching
him to strengthen me once and for all that I
might not offend him, I threw myself down
before him with the greatest outpouring of
heart.' This led her to place all her trust in
God. At that time she also read *Augustine's
Confessions, and was encouraged by the
examples there of God's grace. 'By
considering the love [God] bore me, I
regained my courage, for I never lost

confidence in his mercy—in myself I lost it many times.'

After this deeper conversion, Teresa progressed rapidly in the life of prayer. But there were problems. At first her confessors believed that her unusual experiences came not from God but from the devil. One of her confessors asked her to write an account of her spiritual experiences, which she did in her *Life*. The first draft was completed in 1562. A few years later Teresa revised it and extended it to include the period to 1565.

At about the same time, Teresa wrote *The Way of Perfection*, on the life of prayer. The first draft was completed by 1566 and it was revised soon afterwards for the benefit of the censors. Teresa comments on the Lord's Prayer and also writes in defence of 'mental prayer'. At this time many Spanish theologians were saying that ordinary folk should confine themselves to merely vocal prayer (reciting prayers without using the mind). Against them, Teresa stresses the importance of praying with the mind—but without despising vocal prayer. She rejects the idea that 'you are speaking with God while you are reciting the Our Father and at the same time in fact thinking of the world.'

Teresa's third great work is her *Interior Castle*. This was written in the space of a few months in 1577. It is Teresa's greatest book on prayer, where her mature teaching is set out systematically. The castle is a picture of the human soul in which there are seven dwelling places. God himself dwells in the seventh or innermost place. The purpose of the life of prayer is to progress through these seven dwelling places to God himself.

The way into the castle is through the gate of prayer. This leads to the *first* dwelling place—for those who have some desire for good and who pray occasionally, but who are still wrapped up in the world. These need to know themselves better and to see the ugliness of sin. The *second* dwelling place is for those who are willing to struggle against sin and to persevere in the life of prayer. This leads to the *third* dwelling place, for those who seek to avoid all sin (including 'venial' or lesser sins), but who are still held back by the love of wealth,

honour and health. The first three dwelling places can be reached by our own efforts, aided by God's grace.

The four remaining dwelling places are entered through passive or supernatural prayer—a gift of God. It comes directly from him and not through our own efforts. If the earlier stages of prayer can be compared to the labour of channelling water through irrigation canals, passive prayer can be compared to a spring of water surging up from the ground where it is needed. The last four dwelling places are the places of infused recollection, prayer of union with God, spiritual betrothal with him and finally spiritual marriage in the innermost dwelling place. Teresa herself reached the final stage in 1572.

Teresa's book is a classic exposition of the stages of mystical prayer. It is unfortunate that Spanish translation of the Bible were forbidden so there is little biblical content in Teresa's work. Indeed, because of the obsessive caution of the Inquisition, many other spiritual writings were denied to her. This grieved her, but 'the Lord said to me: "Don't be sad, for I shall give you a living book."' It is the living book of her experience that is the strength of Teresa's works.

Let's strive to make more progress in self-knowledge. In my opinion we shall never completely know ourselves if we don't strive to know God. By gazing at his grandeur, we get in touch with our own lowliness: by looking at his purity, we shall see our own filth; by pondering his humility, we shall see how far we are from being humble.
INTERIOR CASTLE 1:2:9

Teresa was not merely a contemplative. She also fought to reform her order. By this time the Carmelites had relaxed some of their early strictness. Teresa wished to found a house where the primitive Rule of 1209 could be observed strictly. After facing much opposition, she was able to do this in 1562, founding St Joseph's at Avila. From 1567 she set about founding other such houses throughout Spain and the new order came to be known as the Discalced (or 'unshod') Carmelites. She encountered much opposition from the official 'Calced' Carmelites and from the suspicious church authorities—the papal nuncio in Spain called her a 'restless gadabout'! But she won an important ally in the person of John of the Cross (1542–91), who became the joint-founder of the Discalced Carmelites. He was also one of the greatest mystical writers, being known especially for his *Ascent of Mount Carmel* and *The Dark Night of the Soul*.

Robert Bellarmine
OPPOSING PROTESTANTISM

Roberto Francesco Romolo Bellarmino was born in Tuscany, the nephew of the future Pope Marcellus II, in 1542. In 1560 he joined the Jesuits and in 1569 he was sent to Louvain, to help to stem the onslaught of Protestantism. He became the first Jesuit professor of theology at Louvain University, in 1570. But after six years he was recalled to Rome, to become professor of controversial theology at the Roman College. In 1599 he was made a cardinal. He served for a time as archbishop of Capua (from 1602 to 1605), but was recalled to Rome for a wider ministry. He died in 1621.

Bellarmine devoted himself to the controversy with Protestantism. He never met Protestant leaders personally, but he took care to represent their positions fairly. He was prepared to acknowledge strengths as well as weaknesses in their theology. His aim was to answer Protestantism by reasoned argument, rather than abuse or naked appeal to authority. He devoted himself to the study of the Bible, the early church Fathers and church history to equip himself for his task. He was a formidable opponent and chairs of theology were founded in some Protestant universities for the purpose of refuting him. His greatest work was a three-volume *Disputations on Controversies about the Christian Faith against the Heretics of this Time* (1586–93).

This was generally reckoned to be one of the best statements of Roman Catholic theology, as defined at the *Council of Trent.

Tenthly, Bernard can be cited [as teaching justification by faith alone] and often is. In his 22nd Sermon on the Song of Solomon he speaks thus: 'Let him who out of remorse for his sins hungers and thirsts for righteousness, believe in you, the one who justifies the ungodly, and he will have peace with you, being justified by faith alone'... Bernard is speaking of a living faith, joined with charity. Such a faith hungers and thirsts for righteousness and feels remorse for sins—not from fear of punishment but from love of righteousness. Therefore it is just as if Bernard had said: 'Whoever turns away from sin with his whole heart and desires to make amends to the Lord by works of penance—such a one is reconciled to the Lord through living faith and fervent charity, even before he undertakes the works'... Therefore the testimonies of the ancient Fathers sometimes show that faith alone justifies, but never in the sense that our adversaries understand it.

JUSTIFICATION 1:25

Bellarmine's views on the papacy caused him some trouble. He opposed those who held that the pope has *no* power in temporal, as opposed to spiritual, matters. But he also denied that the pope has any *direct* temporal power. Rulers receive their authority from God. The pope has only an *indirect* temporal jurisdiction—if a ruler prejudices the eternal salvation of his subjects, the pope may intervene (even to the extent of deposing the ruler and releasing the subjects from their obligation to obey him). This might appear to grant the pope considerable power, but it was not good enough for Pope Sixtus V. In 1590 he put the first volume of Bellarmine's *Controversies* (where his direct temporal power was denied) on the Index of Forbidden Books.

Bellarmine was an important figure at

Rome. He was one of the commission that produced the 1592 revision of the Latin Vulgate translation of the Bible. He was also involved in the early stages of the affair of Galileo, who was condemned for teaching that the earth rotates about the sun. The Inquisition declared in 1616 that it is the earth, not the sun, that is at the centre of the universe and that the sun moves round the earth, not vice versa. Bellarmine was entrusted with the task of communicating this to Galileo. For a time Galileo kept quiet and it was not until the 1630s that he was in serious trouble with the Inquisition.

Blaise Pascal
THE HEART HAS ITS REASONS

Blaise Pascal was born in 1623 at Clermont-Ferrand, in France. When he was only three his mother died and he and his two sisters were educated by their father. He was a brilliant pupil, especially in the area of maths. He designed and produced the first calculator, he paved the way for the invention of the barometer and he pioneered the theory of probability.

In 1646 Pascal came across the Jansenists. Jansenism was a seventeenth-century movement within the Roman Catholic Church which aroused deep controversy, especially in France. Cornelius Jansen was the Roman Catholic Bishop of Ypres. He was concerned that the Roman Catholic Church was becoming morally lax and was drifting away from *Augustine's teaching on grace. He himself studied Augustine's works intensely and wrote a massive exposition of his teaching, entitled *Augustinus*, whose publication he prudently delayed until after his death in 1640. This met with immediate opposition from the Jesuits, the party most opposed to Augustinianism. They induced the pope in 1653 to condemn five propositions, allegedly drawn from the *Augustinus*. But this did not end the controversy. The Jansenists responded by accepting that the condemned propositions were heretical, but denying that Jansen had taught them. During Pascal's lifetime there was a bitter struggle between the Jesuits and the Jansenists, with the latter fighting for their survival.

Through the Jansenists, the Pascal family were converted to a more serious religious commitment. Blaise continued with his scientific pursuits. In 1651 his father died, and one of his sisters became a nun at Port Royal, the centre of Jansenism. Blaise was opposed to this at the time, but in 1654 he underwent a second and definitive conversion. He recorded this in his *Memorial*, which he carried with him to his death.

'God of Abraham, God of Isaac, God of Jacob', not of the philosophers and scholars. Certitude, certitude, feeling, joy, peace. God of Jesus Christ.'

After his conversion, Pascal's links with Port Royal were strengthened. The year 1655 was a time of crisis for Jansenism. Antoine Arnauld, the leader of the movement, was on trial before the Sorbornne for his views. Pascal came to his defence with a series of anonymous *Provincial Letters*. These are among the greatest satirical works ever, aimed at the Jesuits. The anonymous author presents himself as a puzzled bystander writing about events at Paris to a country friend. Pascal argues that the Jansenist doctrine of grace is not that of *Calvin, as was charged, but that of Augustine and the Dominican theologians. He also ridiculed the Jesuit doctrine of 'probabilism', whereby they were able to allow low moral standards. The doctrine simply stated that where there was a difference of opinion among moral theologians, the confessor is obliged to follow that opinion which most favours the sinner. Thus if one reputable authority (e.g. a Jesuit) held something not to be sin, the confessor was forbidden to impose a stricter view on the penitent, even if all other writers were united in condemning it as sin. This doctrine was originally designed to protect the penitent from over-harsh confessors who might on their own authority refuse absolution. But the Jesuits were using it to reduce to a bare minimum the definition of sin—because any action defended by any one authority, however outrageously, could no longer be treated as a sin.

'To be sure, Father,' I said. 'there is a lot of profit to be derived from your [Jesuit] doctors. Why, when two people do the same thing, the one who does not know their doctrine is sinning, and the one who does know it is not! So it at once instructs and justifies. God's law made transgressors, according to St Paul—and this one makes almost everyone innocent. I beg you, Father, to tell me all about it. I will not leave you until you have told me the chief principles established by your casuists.'
PROVINCIAL LETTERS 6

Pascal's greatest work is his *Pensées (Thoughts)*. These are fragments, often written on scraps of paper. They were intended as material for an *Apology for the Christian Religion*, addressed to sceptics and rationalists—the first modern attempt at Christian apologetic. But Pascal's health began to break in 1658 and he died in 1662, at an early age. One of his best-known arguments is that of the wager. Is there a God or not? Is there such a thing as eternal life? Reason cannot conclusively decide, but we must nonetheless choose how to live. What are the stakes? We wager with our single short earthly lives. If we win, the gain is an eternity of happiness. Even if we lose (because there is no God), all that we lose in this life is vice, while we still gain a virtuous character. For the prudent gambler there is only one sensible choice. The sceptic ought at least to examine the claims of Christianity seriously.

Pascal allowed only a limited role for philosophy and reason:

Reason's last step is the recognition that there are an infinite number of things which are beyond it. It is merely feeble if it does not go as far as to realise that.
PENSÉES 188

The heart has its reasons of which reason knows nothing.
PENSÉES 423

Pascal's aim was not to lead people to a philosophical grasp of God but to point them to God as revealed in Jesus Christ.

It is not only impossible but useless to know God without Christ.
PENSÉES 191

Knowing God without knowing our own wretchedness makes for pride.
    Knowing our wretchedness without knowing God makes for despair.
    Knowing Jesus Christ strikes the balance because he shows us both God and our own wretchedness.
PENSÉES 192

PART 5

Christian Thought in the Modern World

1800 ONWARDS

The Reformation gave birth to the three major confessions in the Western Church—Roman Catholicism (as defined at the *Council of Trent), Lutheranism (as defined in the *Augsburg Confession* and the *Formula of Concord*) and Calvinism (as defined in the *Heidelberg Catechism* and the *Westminster Confession*). During most of the period from 1500 to 1800, theological debate took place mainly *within* these confessions. This was the period of confessional theology. But that has changed in the last two centuries.

During the medieval centuries and until about 1700, the truth of Christianity was largely unquestioned within Christendom. The medievals may have struggled with how to relate faith and reason. The Reformation debates concerned what is true Christianity. But whether Christianity is true was all but unquestioned. The eighteenth century saw the emergence of a significant movement, Deism, which advocated a simplified and 'pure' religion based on reason, as an alternative to the superstitions of Christian revelation. Deism was a *rival* religion, even if this may sometimes have been thinly disguised by the pretext of returning to primitive Christianity or to the essence of Christianity. Deism challenged the church from *outside* and by the end of the eighteenth century the theology of the churches remained predominantly orthodox. But during the nineteenth and twentieth centuries this picture has significantly altered.

In the modern world, the Christian faith has had to face a wide range of challenges:

☐ *Rationalism.* In the seventeenth century on a small scale and in the eighteenth century on a much larger scale, people began to attack Christianity in the name of reason. With Deism this took the form of a rival concept of God and religion; before long it was to become an attack on God and religion. In the nineteenth century atheism and agnosticism (a word coined by T.H. Huxley in 1870) became common for the first time in the Christian West. Confidence in the power of reason has waxed and waned in the modern world, but the attack on revelation has continued unabated. This has come at a time when all traditional authorities are being questioned—not just Christian authorities.

☐ *Science.* Modern science emerged in the seventeenth century, in soil watered by Christianity. While the actual findings of science have had very little bearing on the truth or otherwise of Christianity, modern science has affected Christianity in other ways. The scientific method implies the testing of all claims and the refusal to accept any authority as beyond criticism. This method has been immensely successful in science and that has encouraged similar scepticism towards authority in other areas where it might not be so applicable. Also, modern science has given birth to technology, which has transformed our lives. It has helped to undermine man's sense of dependence upon God. As Bertrand Russell aptly put it, a fisherman in a sailing boat is more likely to pray than one in a motor boat. The benefits of technology also make it easier to live for this world alone and to forget about the next.

☐ *Historical Criticism.* In the nineteenth century, historical criticism emerged. This was a new and more rigorous approach to history, practised by a new breed of professional historians. The critical historian thinks no longer in terms of *authorities*, which would rarely be questioned, but of *sources*, which must be questioned and tested. This approach has been applied to Christian history with devastating effect. The biblical records were analysed, often by people whose beliefs were far from orthodox. The Bible came to be seen less as an authority to be accepted and more as a source to be criticized. In the same way, the records of the life of Jesus Christ were examined and attempts were made to present a radically new picture of him. The history of Christian doctrine was also studied systematically and the ways in which it has changed over the ages came to light.

☐ *Secularization.* As the Christian faith has ceased to command universal acceptance, society has turned to other ideological bases. For much of the world that has meant adopting a new secular 'religion', Marxism-Leninism. In the West, society is based on secular, non-religious assumptions. Religion is increasingly seen as a private affair for the individual, a matter for personal preference, like choosing to join a tennis club. This process has been encouraged by the emergence of a more pluralist society, where a variety of different religions are practised.

All of these changes have profoundly challenged Christian theology. Underlying them is the rejection of authority. Until the last century Christianity was all but universally seen in Christendom as a 'given', as a revelation from God which must be accepted by faith. Theological debates between and within different confessional traditions concerned the *identity* of that revelation. But since the last century the very idea of a revelation has been radically questioned—not just by unbelievers, but by theologians within the mainstream churches. It is true that the questioning of authority in the modern period has had some value in theology. There has been a healthy questioning of ill-founded assumptions. But the trouble is that while scepticism towards established authorities is the lifeblood of science, say, it is more like the kiss of death for theology. Any religion bearing more than a passing resemblance to Christianity must be based on some authority. If Christianity is about God revealing himself in Jesus Christ and rescuing man from his plight, there must be some submission before a given authoritative revelation. But to *what* must this submission be made (if at all) and on *what* terms? It is these questions which have divided Christian theologians in the modern era. The significant differences between theologians today lie less *between* different confessions and cut more *across* all confessions. This is becoming true even where the Protestant/Roman Catholic divide is concerned. Increasingly, groups of Protestants and Roman Catholics are finding that what unites them (e.g. charismatic experience, liberalism, *Liberation Theology) is at least as significant as that which unites them to their fellow Protestants or Roman Catholics.

THE LIBERALS

Liberalism is a thorough-going adaptation of Christian theology to the modern world. Liberals are prepared to sacrifice many elements of traditional Christian orthodoxy in their search for contemporary relevance.

Friedrich Schleiermacher
ROMANTIC RELIGION

Friedrich Daniel Ernst Schleiermacher was born in 1768 at Breslau in Silesia (now in Poland), the son of a Reformed army chaplain. He received a pietist upbringing in the tradition of *Spener and entered a pietist theological seminary. But this traditional theology was unacceptable to him so he left to complete his theological training at the University of Halle. After his ordination, most of his ministry was exercised in Berlin. In addition to pastoring a Reformed church, he helped to found Berlin University and became a professor of theology there. His pastoral work included preparing Bismarck, the great Prussian statesman, for confirmation. He died in 1834.

*Karl Barth aptly stated that Schleiermacher founded not just a school of thought but an era. He is the founder not just of the liberal school of theology but of the whole of modern theology. His views are set out in two major works:

● *Religion: Speeches to its Cultured Despisers* (1799) may be seen as the debut of liberal theology. (Theologically, the 'nineteenth century' extends from 1799 to the First World War.) In these speeches Schleiermacher attempted to defend religion against scepticism—but the concept of religion which he defended was radically new.

● *The Christian Faith* was a major work of systematic theology. It first appeared in 1821–22, with a revised edition in 1830–31.

Schleiermacher's *Speeches on Religion* discuss the nature of religion. His pietist upbringing had taught him that religion is more than merely theology and ethics, knowledge and action, knowing and doing the right thing. 'Piety cannot be an instinct craving for a mess of metaphysical and ethical crumbs.' Religion belongs to a third realm—that of feeling. 'True religion is sense and taste for the infinite.' It is important to be clear what Schleiermacher is saying. He goes beyond the traditional pietist claim that religion involves *more* than knowledge and action. Instead he sees it as something *distinct* from knowledge and action.

In order to make quite clear to you what is the original and characteristic possession of religion, it resigns at once all claims on anything that belongs either to science or morality... Ideas and principles are all foreign to religion... If ideas and principles are to be anything, they must belong to knowledge which is a different department of life from religion.
SPEECH 2

It does not follow that religion is *unrelated* to knowledge and action. 'I do not mean that one could exist without the other—that, for example, a man might have religion and be pious and at the same time be immoral.' On the contrary, religion is in fact the true foundation for both knowledge and action.

To wish to have true science or true practice without religion, or to imagine it is possessed, is obstinate, arrogant delusion and culpable error ... What can man accomplish that is worth speaking of, either in life or in art, that does not arise in his own self from the influence of this sense for the infinite?
SPEECH 2

For Schleiermacher, religion is separate from theology, but this does not mean that the latter has no place. Doctrines and dogmas are not religion: 'they are not necessary for religion itself, scarcely even for communicating religion.' But theology cannot be avoided and it is a proper concern when we come to *reflect* upon religion. While religion is not itself knowledge, there is such a thing as knowledge *about* religion—theology. Those who object to religion because of the narrow-minded obscurantism of some theologians have missed the point that theology and religion are two different things.

Schleiermacher's approach was radically new. He took the pietist insight about the need for a felt and experienced religion to the extreme that religion is nothing but feeling and experience. Belief, in the sense of accepting doctrines, is foreign to religion: 'So far is it from being the highest in religion, as is asserted, that it must be rejected by all who would force their way into the sanctuary of religion.' This means a new conception of Christianity. Until Schleiermacher, Christian theology was seen as the account of God's revelation—found in Scripture, tradition, nature or some combination of these. Schleiermacher made it the study of religion, of man's religious experience. He gives the word revelation a radically new sense. It becomes the religious experience of each individual. 'Every intuition and every original feeling proceeds from revelation ... If nothing original has yet

been generated in you, when it does come it will be a revelation for you also.'

Schleiermacher opens the door to a 'Christianity' which no longer accepts the teaching of the Bible as normative, which is no longer tied to an external norm. By sharply dividing religion and theology he rescued religion from the rational attacks of the sceptics—but in such a way that he appears to have rescued the form at the cost of the content.

In *The Christian Faith* Schleiermacher works out his new approach in terms of systematic theology. The position of the *Speeches on Religion* is moderated, but the essential stance remains unaltered. The essence of piety is neither knowing nor doing, but 'the consciousness of being absolutely dependent or, which is the same thing, of being in relation with God.' 'Christian doctrines are accounts of the Christian religious affections set forth in speech.' Statements about God's attributes, for instance, are not about God himself but about the way in which our feeling of absolute dependence is to be related to him. The Bible is treated as a record of man's religious experience rather than a revelation from God or a record of God's acts in history.

Schleiermacher's criterion for theology is conformity not to the doctrine of the New Testament, but to the experience recorded in the New Testament. The question which he asks of all doctrine is: what significance does this have for Christian experience? This is commendable as a positive goal but is mistaken as a negative criterion. While it is desirable to relate doctrine to experience, to tailor doctrine to fit experience is dangerous—because *we* concept of Christian experience may be defective and because we are liable to prune doctrines because we cannot see their value for experience. It is more important that experience should be tested by the norm of Scripture than that doctrine should be pruned in the light of experience.

Schleiermacher applied his method to the person and work of Jesus Christ. He demanded that there be a parity between these two doctrines. We should ascribe to the person of Jesus Christ no more dignity than is demanded by his activity (work). Otherwise there is an incongruity—as if we should require someone to be a prince in order to polish the palace floors. On the other hand, we cannot attribute to Jesus Christ any activity which is out of proportion to his dignity, since it would no longer truly be *his* activity. The desire to relate together the person and the work of Jesus Christ is commendable—but again it becomes dangerous when it is taken as a negative criterion by which to prune biblical doctrine. A low view of the work of Jesus Christ will result in a low view of his person.

Schleiermacher's concept of the work of Jesus Christ is too low—because of his inadequate view of man's sinfulness (he has very little to say about guilt before God, for instance). Jesus Christ did not come to atone for sin but came to be our teacher, to set us an example. His work is essentially to arouse in us the consciousness of God. In order for him to accomplish this activity, the only deity that he requires is a perfect consciousness of God. While the consciousness of God in us is obscured and powerless, in him, it was perfect at every moment. This makes it 'a continual living presence and with a real existence of God in him'. He differs from other men only by his 'essential sinlessness and absolute perfection'. This difference from us gives him all that we need for our salvation. Likewise, his humanity, differing from ours only in its perfection, makes it available to us. The work of Jesus Christ, as perceived by Schleiermacher, makes his resurrection, ascension into heaven and second coming superfluous. Belief in these doctrines 'is no independent element in the original faith in Christ, of such a kind that we could not accept him as redeemer or recognise the being of God in him, if we did not know that he had risen from the dead and ascended to heaven, or if he had not promised that he would return for judgement.' They are unnecessary for Christian doctrine, to be believed or not according to our estimate of the reliability of Scripture.

The combination of an inadequate view of man's sinfulness, leading to a defective view of the work of Jesus Christ, leading in turn to a low view of his person, recurs throughout liberal theology. Richard Niebuhr described liberal theology as follows: 'A God without wrath brought men without sin into a kingdom without judgement through the ministration of a Christ without a cross.' This liberal optimism received a hard knock in the First World War, which gave birth to the Neo-Orthodox reaction of Barth and others.

Albrecht Ritschl
JESUS THE PERFECT MAN

Albrecht Benjamin Ritschl was born at Berlin in 1822, the son of a Lutheran pastor who later became a bishop. He became a professor of theology, first at Tübingen, from 1852 to 1864, and then at Göttingen until his death in 1889. He wrote two major works: *The Christian Doctrine of Justification and Reconciliation* (three volumes, 1870–74) and a three-volume *History of Pietism* (1880–86), a movement of which he disapproved. He followed in the liberal tradition pioneered by *Schleiermacher, but modified the latter's thought in a number of vital areas. He was the most influential of the nineteenth-century liberals and the Ritschlian school was very strong in the latter part of the century and the beginning of the next.

Like Schleiermacher, Ritschl based his theology on Christian experience. But he found Schleiermacher's approach, with its stress on feelings and the emotions, too subjective and 'mystical'. His solution was to turn to history, as the cure for both subjectivism and rationalism. Theology is to be based on God's revelation in Jesus Christ, recorded in the New Testament. Ritschl's opposition to individualism and subjectivism also emerges in his stress on the communal side of Christianity. Ritschl stresses that Christian salvation is experienced only in the fellowship of the church. This is not because the church stands between the individual and God as a legally appointed mediator, but because Christianity can be experienced only within a living community. You can no more be a Christian in solitary isolation than play a game of football on your own.

One cannot arrive at and maintain individual conviction of faith in isolation from the already existing community of faith ... The blessings which accrue to the individual are only imparted to him in common with all the others with whom he is bound up, through the same salvation, in the unity of the church ... The individual can therefore appropriate the forgiveness of sins by faith only when he unites in his faith at once trust in God and Christ, and the intention to connect himself with the community of believers.

THE CHRISTIAN DOCTRINE OF JUSTIFICATION AND RECONCILIATION VOLUME 3, CHAPTER 2

Ritschl became infamous for his claim that theological statements are value judgements rather than theoretical judgements which can logically be proved. He did not mean that theological statements are purely personal and subjective—like an individual's preference for one colour scheme rather than another. He wished to emphasize that theological statements are not open to a detached, morally neutral assessment. He believed that the early church Fathers had corrupted Christianity by importing Greek philosophy into it—thus turning the God of the Bible into the absolute of the philosophers, and the Jesus of the Gospels into the eternal Word of Greek Platonism. It was left to Ritschl's disciple *Harnack to trace the course of this corruption in detail.

For Ritschl the starting-point for theology is not speculation about God as he is 'in himself', but his action for us in giving us the forgiveness of sins through Jesus Christ. Ritschl took the concepts of sin and salvation more seriously than Schleiermacher—but still not seriously enough. He denied the doctrine of original sin and insisted that it is possible to lead a life without sin. There is no wrath of God

against sin and the reconciliation brought by Jesus Christ is essentially a change in *our* attitude to God, not vice versa. Correspondingly, Ritschl has a low view of the person of Jesus Christ. Like Schleiermacher, Ritschl can speak of Jesus' deity, but by this he means his perfect humanity. He was God in the sense that he had a perfect knowledge of God and was united to him in moral obedience. Because Christians experience God's love in Jesus Christ they can ascribe to him the *value* of God. But essentially the difference between him and us is one of degree rather than kind. Ritschl was unwilling to speak of Jesus Christ as pre-existent (existing before his birth of Mary) and he conceived of his continuing activity today largely in terms of his posthumous influence.

Ritschl was deeply concerned about ethics and his whole thought has a moralistic tinge to it. The kingdom of God is an important concept for him. He interprets it largely in terms of the moral unification of the human race through love. His weak doctrine of sin did not prevent him from accepting the then fashionable idea that the human race was steadily evolving towards perfection—a faith which was rudely shaken by the First World War, but which is by no means dead even after the Second World War. His teaching on the kingdom of God stimulated the rise of the 'Social Gospel' movement, led especially by the American theologian Walter Rauschenbusch (1861–1918). This movement saw the central task of the church as the transformation of society, to bring it into conformity with God's kingdom.

Adolf von Harnack
WHAT IS CHRISTIANITY?

Adolf Harnack was born at Dorpat (modern Estonia) in 1851, the son of a German theological professor. He followed in his father's footsteps, becoming a professor at Leipzig (1876), Giessen (1879), Marburg (1886) and finally Berlin (1888–1921). He fell out of favour with the church authorities for his liberal views and attempts were made to block his appointment to Berlin. But he met with favour from the state, and in 1914 Kaiser Wilhelm II ennobled him, making him Adolf *von* Harnack.

Harnack was above all a historian of dogma. His major work was a three-volume *History of Dogma* (1886–89). In this he extended to the time of *Luther and beyond, but concentrated especially on the early church. Harnack was the greatest expert on the early church Fathers in his generation. He believed, with *Ritschl, that the gospel had been corrupted by the alien influence of Greek philosophy. He sought to trace the history of this process of 'hellenization'. The simple religion of Jesus was changed, especially by the apostle Paul, into the religion about Jesus, which in turn was transformed into the dogma of the incarnation of God the Son.

Harnack summarized his beliefs in a series of popular lectures, given in the winter of 1899/1900. One of the audience took them down in shorthand and they were immediately published under the title of (literally translated) *The Essence of Christianity*. They were soon translated into English with the title *What is Christianity?* Harnack seeks to answer this question not as an apologist, nor as a philosopher, but as a historian. His source materials are Jesus and his gospel—but not simply that. It is necessary also to consider the outworking of his teaching over the ages—just as one cannot understand a tree by simply studying the roots, without the trunk. This faces us with the problem of the changing form of the Christian message over the ages.

There are only two possibilities here: either the gospel is in all respects identical with its earliest form (in which case it came with its time and has departed with it); or else it contains something which, under differing historical forms, is of permanent validity. The latter is the true view.
WHAT IS CHRISTIANITY? LECTURE 1

We must distinguish between the kernel of the gospel which is contained in the changing husk of outward forms. Those who refuse this distinction and will not acknowledge growth or decay, but claim that 'everything is of equal value and alike permanent' are mistaken. They are refuted by the facts of history (as set out in the *History of Dogma*).

Harnack examines the teaching of Jesus. He considers it under three headings:

Firstly, the kingdom of God and its coming. Secondly, God the Father and the infinite value of the human soul. Thirdly, the higher righteousness and the commandment of love.
WHAT IS CHRISTIANITY? LECTURE 3

But when all is said and done, these three coalesce, 'for ultimately the kingdom is nothing but the treasure which the soul possesses in the eternal and merciful God'.

Harnack then traces the progress of this gospel throughout Christian history. It is a sad tale with the pollution of the gospel by Greek philosophy, the stifling of the freedom of the gospel by ecclesiastical legalism, the fossilization of the living message into changeless dogma. But none of this can destroy the gospel. Throughout history it has remained alive, even in the least promising surroundings.

If we were right in saying that the gospel is the knowledge and recognition of God as the Father, the certainty of redemption, humility and joy in God, energy and brotherly love; if it is essential to this religion that the founder must not be forgotten over his message, nor the message over the founder, history shows us that the gospel has, in point of fact, remained in force, struggling again and again to the surface.
WHAT IS CHRISTIANITY? LECTURE 16

Harnack's essence of Christianity was based on his conception of the person and teaching of Jesus Christ. In the nineteenth century the methods of historical criticism were applied to the person of Jesus. A series of scholars offered reconstructions of the 'Jesus of history', usually ending with a non-miraculous figure who preached not about himself but the simple liberal message of the brotherhood of man and the fatherhood of God—today sometimes summarized irreverently as 'bomfog'. These accounts claimed to be scientific and objective—but in fact the authors were filtering out those features of the gospel accounts (such as the supernatural) which they found unpalatable. As one Roman Catholic critic of Harnack put it, 'The Christ that Harnack sees, looking back through nineteen centuries of Catholic darkness, is only the reflection of a Liberal Protestant face, seen at the bottom of a deep well.' Albert Schweitzer in his doctoral thesis described *The Quest of the Historical Jesus* (1906). He also criticized the arbitrary nature of the exercise. The liberal portrait of Jesus, he claimed, was 'a figure designed by rationalism, endowed with life by liberalism, and clothed by modern theology in a historical garb.' Schweitzer drew attention especially to the apocalyptic elements in Jesus' teaching and expectations, which had been largely overlooked in the nineteenth century. He succeeded not just in describing but also in terminating the nineteenth century 'quest'—although in recent years there have been moves to return to it, albeit in a different manner.

Harnack's views also fell out of favour theologically. He was the last of the great nineteenth-century liberals. After the First World War his former student *Karl Barth and others launched the Neo-Orthodox movement, which reversed many of the liberal positions. In 1920 Harnack and Barth both addressed a student conference. Harnack's reaction to Barth's address was dramatic: 'Not one word, not one sentence could I have said or thought. I saw the sincerity of Barth's speech, but its theology frightened me.' This led to a famous exchange of correspondence between the two in 1923, in which there was no real meeting of minds. Liberalism was long out of vogue, but today it is re-emerging. A recent popular work, *The Myth of God Incarnate,* is an attempt to rehabilitate the old liberal view of Jesus Christ.

THE EVANGELICALS

Evangelicals have, to a greater or lesser extent, sought to adapt to the modern world. But they have insisted that this process should not lead to the distortion of the biblical gospel.

Charles Finney
PROMOTING REVIVAL

Charles Grandison Finney was born in 1792 at Warren in Connecticut. He studied law and became a barrister. In 1821 he was converted to Jesus Christ from a position of scepticism, through studying the Bible for himself. Soon after, he felt the call to leave the practice of law for the preaching of the gospel. When a client asked him to appear in court on his behalf Finney replied, 'I have a retainer from the Lord Jesus Christ to plead his cause and I cannot plead yours'. He began to preach and in 1824 was ordained into the Presbyterian ministry. He then began to conduct 'revivals' in the eastern states. His methods, which were unconventional, came to be known as the 'new measures'. These included the holding of inquiry meetings for those seeking salvation.

While the prevailing *Calvinism encouraged people to wait passively for God to convert them, Finney portrayed conversion as an act of the human will well within our reach. This emphasis on human responsibility is also found in his teaching on revivals. Traditionally a revival had been seen as a sovereign act of God, for which we can pray but which God gives only when it pleases him. Finney stressed the importance of preparation for revival. Revivals can be promoted—in fact he appeared to imply that they will inevitably follow when certain conditions are fulfilled. This teaching is found in his *Lectures on Revivals of Religion*,

published in 1835. These have been extremely influential and helped to change the character of American evangelism. Finney saw his stress on human responsibility and initiative as a counterbalance to the prevailing teaching that we can only be passive before the sovereign grace of God—Calvinist 'cannotism', as it has been called. Unfortunately his own teaching has often been taken to the opposite extreme—indeed it is debatable that were he to return to the United States today he would preach strongly on the need to depend on the grace of God.

In 1835 Finney became a professor of theology at Oberlin College in Ohio and from 1851 to 1866 he was its president. He stood in the tradition of New England Theology. The orthodox Calvinism of *Jonathan Edwards, especially his teaching on the atonement, was modified by his son Jonathan Edwards Junior (1745–1801). His thought was developed further by Nathaniel Taylor (1786–1858) whose views came to be known as New School Calvinism or the New Haven Theology. Finney's theology, expounded especially in his *Lectures on Systematic Theology* (1846–47) stands in this tradition. He remained an active evangelist and pastor (in the Congregationalist Church from 1835) all his life. He was also concerned for social reform and was a vigorous opponent of slavery. He died in 1875.

Finney stressed the freedom and power of the human will. This follows from his theory of moral government. God rules the physical universe through the laws of nature, which are inevitable. The stone thrown in the air has no choice—it *must* come down. But God is also the moral governor of the universe, through his moral laws. These are not inevitable—we do have a choice. God's moral law tells us to love one another but this law, unlike the law of gravity, we are free to obey or disobey. God tells us what is right and threatens us with sanctions, but the choice is ours. This choice is free—it is decided by the will which is undetermined by a sinful 'nature' or by any other factor.

This stress on the will as free and undetermined leads Finney to deny the doctrine of original sin. Children are not born with a sinful nature moulding their wills. But why then do *all* sin? Finney acknowledges that sin is a certainty, though not a necessity. His explanation is that we are all born with physical depravity—with a bias towards self-gratification. This, combined with the fact of temptation, makes it certain that when we reach the age of moral accountability we will voluntarily choose to sin. Finney attempts to escape the doctrine of original sin, but his doctrine of physical depravity, plus the way in which he combines the certainty of sin with its voluntary character, means that he has smuggled most of *Augustine's doctrine of original sin in through the back door without declaring it. A recent interpreter has accused him of 'semantic somersaults in redefining total depravity and original sin in psychological rather than biological categories.'

The weakest point in Finney's system is his insistence that the will is totally unconditioned and random. He was right to insist that our choices are free in the sense of being voluntary and spontaneous. He was right to point to the problems inherent in the idea that we are controlled by a sinful 'nature'—language not found in the New Testament. But his own position does not do justice to the concept of moral character. Moral character for Finney is moral choice and action, not something which *influences* the will. For Finney, the ultimate explanation of why a person performs a kind deed is that he *chose* to, not that he is a kind

person. Morality is seen as a series of independent moral decisions, not the cultivation of a moral character. Thus the evangelist's aim is to bring about an instantaneous decision of the will rather than a radical change of character which in one sense is a life-long process. Finney's theology encourages a concept of evangelism as producing isolated decisions rather than radical changes of heart.

Because for Finney morality is simply moral acts of will, at any one moment we are choosing one of two supreme ends—selfishness or love. This doctrine of the 'simplicity of moral action' means that there is no middle ground, no possibility other than total love or total sinfulness.

Obedience to moral law cannot be partial, in the sense that a moral agent can partly obey and partly disobey at the same time ... The only sense in which obedience to moral law can be partial is that obedience may be intermittent. That is, the subject may sometimes obey, and at other times disobey. He may at one time be selfish, or will his own gratification, because it is his own, and without regard to the well-being of God and his neighbour, and at another time will the highest well-being of God and the universe, as an end, and his own good only in proportion to its relative value. These are opposite choices, or ultimate intentions. The one is holy; the other is sinful. One is obedience, entire obedience, to the law of God; the other is disobedience, entire disobedience, to that law. These, for aught we can see, may succeed each other an indefinite number of times, but coexist they plainly cannot.
LECTURES ON SYSTEMATIC THEOLOGY 15:1

Peter Forsyth
THE CENTRALITY OF THE CROSS

Peter Taylor Forsyth was born at Aberdeen in 1848, the son of a postman. Having studied classics at Aberdeen University he

went to Gottingen to study theology under
*Ritschl. After further training in Hackney
College, a theological college which became
New College, London, he entered the
Congregationalist ministry and served as
pastor of five different churches. At first he
stood in the liberal tradition, but during his
last pastorate he underwent an Evangelical
conversion.

*It also pleased God by the revelation of
his holiness and grace, which the great
theologians taught me to find in the
Bible, to bring home to me my sin in a
way that submerged all the school
questions in weight, urgency and
poignancy. I was turned from a
Christian to a believer, from a lover of
love to an object of grace.*

POSITIVE PREACHING AND MODERN MIND,
CHAPTER 7

In 1901 he became principal of Hackney
College—a post which he held until his
death in 1921. P.T. Forsyth was in many
ways a man born out of due time. He
anticipated in a striking manner many of the
positions taken by the Neo-Orthodox school.
*Karl Barth, on hearing a quotation from
Forsyth, responded: 'If Forsyth had not said
what he said *when* he said it, I would have
said he was quoting me.'

P.T. Forsyth turned from liberalism to an
Evangelical faith. But he did not return to
the old orthodoxy. His theology was
thoroughly based on the Bible, but he fully
accepted the methods and results of biblical
criticism—which questioned the reliability
of the Bible in places and disputed the
authorship of some biblical books. Forsyth's
position was what was then called 'believing
criticism'—a combination of biblical
criticism and acceptance of the doctrines of
the gospel. For Forsyth, God's supreme
revelation is in Jesus Christ, and especially
in the cross. The apostles preached about
this and their preaching is found in the New
Testament. So authority in Christian
theology lies in the gospel, which is recorded
in the Bible, rather than in the Bible itself as
a book. The Bible is authoritative as the

supreme witness to Jesus Christ.

P.T. Forsyth's conversion was to the
Evangelical gospel. Like the New Testament
itself, he saw the cross as the centre of the
Christian faith. Liberalism taught the love of
God but denied his holy wrath against sin—
thus ending with a sentimental concept of
love (a weakness apparent in much theology
today). Forsyth rediscovered God's holiness
and his wrath against sin. 'The love of God is
not more real than the wrath of God. For he
can be really angry only with those he loves.'
All men are by nature in rebellion against
God and alienated from him. But on the cross
God in Christ reconciles us to himself.

*The sacrifice of Christ was a penal
sacrifice. In what sense is that so?...
There is a penalty and curse for sin; and
Christ consented to enter that region.
Christ entered voluntarily into the pain
and horror which is sin's penalty from
God. Christ, by the deep intimacy of his
sympathy with men, entered deeply into
the blight and judgement which was
entailed by man's sin, and which must
be entailed by man's sin if God is a holy
and therefore a judging God... You can
therefore say that although Christ was
not punished by God, he bore God's
penalty upon sin.*

THE WORK OF CHRIST, CHAPTER 5

Forsyth is also known for his interpretation
of the incarnation of Jesus Christ. In the
nineteenth century there was a widespread
feeling that the traditional doctrine of the
incarnation did not do sufficient justice to
the humanity of Jesus Christ. The definition
of the *Council of Chalcedon affirmed his full
humanity—but it was smothered by his full
deity. To say that Jesus Christ experienced
human weakness while at the same time
having divine omnipotence appears to be a
contradiction in terms. In Germany there
arose a theory of *kenosis* to explain this.
Jesus Christ emptied (Greek *ekenose*) himself
(Philippians 2:7). In the incarnation God the
Son emptied himself of his deity—or of at
least some divine attributes, such as
omnipotence, omniscience and

omnipresence. This theory was popular for a time, but provoked devastating criticism. God cannot simply shrug off some of his attributes. Forsyth, together with other British theologians of his generation, sought to modify the theory to meet the criticisms.

He argued that the human weariness of Jesus, as recorded in the Gospels (his tiredness, his ignorance, etc.) leaves us with only two options—he either concealed his deity or emptied himself. The former is morally unacceptable as it reduces the incarnation to a charade. The latter is correct. But Forsyth admits that God cannot lose his attributes. Instead they can become latent or potential. In the incarnation Jesus Christ voluntarily limited himself—he reduced or retracted his divine attributes so as to make them potential rather than actual. This is the *kenosis* or self-emptying. There is also a reverse process of *plerosis* or self-fulfilment. In his earthly life Jesus regained the divine attributes by a gradual moral reconquest. Such a view Forsyth does not see as limiting God's omnipotence—on the contrary, God's omnipotence means that he can do all that is demanded by love. His self-limitation in the incarnation is his greatest ever exercise of moral freedom. 'The Godhead that freely made man was never so free as in becoming man.

I am aware of the kind of objection raised to the kenotic theory. Many difficulties arise readily in one's own mind. It is a choice of difficulties. On the one hand living faith finds it difficult to believe that the Christ who created it was not God. And on the other thought finds it hard to realise how God should become Christ. But it is something gained to note that the chief difficulties arise on the latter head, in connexion with the way in which the fact comes to pass rather than with the fact itself. That is, they are scientific and not religious. When we are not so much questioning the fact as discussing the manner of it—not the what *but the* how—*it is a matter of theological science not of religious faith. And the*

science of it can wait, but the religion of it cannot.

THE PERSON AND PLACE OF JESUS CHRIST, CHAPTER 11

Benjamin Warfield
THE INFALLIBLE BIBLE

Benjamin Breckenridge Warfield was born in 1851 near Lexington, Kentucky. After studying at Princeton and Leipzig he taught at a theological seminary in Pittsburgh from 1878 to 1887. He then became professor of didactic and polemical theology at Princeton Theological Seminary, where he remained until his death in 1921. Shortly after his marriage at the age of twenty-five, he and his wife were caught in a severe thunderstorm and her state of mind was permanently affected. Warfield devoted himself to caring for her until her death in 1915. As a result he hardly ever left Princeton.

B.B. Warfield is one of the great representatives of the 'Princeton school'. Princeton Theological Seminary was founded in 1811 and in 1820 Charles Hodge (1797–1878) began to teach there. Hodge held to the 'Old School' Calvinism in opposition to the 'New School' Calvinism of *Finney and others. His best-known work is his three-volume *Systematic Theology* (1871–73). His son A.A. Hodge succeeded him as professor and was in turn succeeded by B.B. Warfield. The Princeton theologians held strictly to one particular stream of Reformed theology and maintained the infallibility of the Bible against the critics. They were immensely learned and ably defended the traditional evangelical Reformed position, but suffered from the weakness of excessive rigidity. As a recent writer has put it, 'they fired heavy theological artillery at every idea that moved and were almost indecently astute at distinguishing biblical and Reformed truth from all error'. In the early years of the twentieth century there was no shortage of error to oppose. In 1929 the seminary began to move in a liberal direction and John Gresham Machen (1881–1937), the greatest representative of the school, helped to found a new Westminster Theological Seminary to continue the old tradition—which it has done to the present day.

B.B. Warfield is best known for his exposition of the doctrine of Scripture. He was the ablest defender in his time of the traditional belief that the Bible is the inspired and infallible word of God. He shows how clear is the teaching of Jesus Christ and the New Testament writers on this matter. They regarded the (Old Testament) scriptures as the oracles of God. For them 'Scripture says' is equivalent to 'God says'. The Bible is 'breathed out by God' (2 Timothy 3:16). He is its author. This belief is based not (as is sometimes alleged) on one or two isolated proof texts but on a mass of biblical evidence, which Warfield cites.

The effort to explain away the Bible's witness to its plenary inspiration reminds one of a man standing safely in his laboratory and elaborately expounding... how every stone in an avalanche has a defined pathway and may easily be dodged by one of some presence of mind. We may fancy such an elaborate trifler's triumph as he would analyse the avalanche into its constituent stones and demonstrate of stone after stone its pathway is definite, limited and may easily be avoided. But avalanches, unfortunately, do not come upon us stone by stone, one at a time, courteously leaving us opportunity to withdraw from the pathway of each in turn—but all at once, in a roaring mass of destruction. Just so, we may explain away a text or two which teach plenary inspiration, to our own closet satisfaction, dealing with them each without reference to its relation to the others—but these texts of ours, again, unfortunately do not come upon us in this artificial isolation. Neither are they few in number. There are scores, hundreds of them—and they come bursting upon us in one solid mass. Explain them away? We should have to explain away the whole New Testament. What a pity it is that we cannot see and feel the avalanche of texts beneath which we lie hopelessly buried as clearly as we may see and feel an avalanche of stones!
THE INSPIRATION OF THE BIBLE

If God is the author of the Bible, does this mean that he dictated it—that the human authors were no more than secretaries or even typewriters? Some conservative Evangelicals have at times come close to saying this, but Warfield is certainly not guilty of it. If the Bible is God's word, it is also man's word. To deny either is wrong. God rules the affairs of men through his providence and he draws us to himself by his grace—but in neither instance does the work of God mean that we are inactive. So also the Bible is fully God's word and also fully the words of its human authors. This can be seen from their distinctive styles and from other characteristics of the individual authors.

How can both God and man be the author of the Bible? The trouble is, says Warfield, that too many see these two as in opposition to one another, so that the one takes over where the other ceases. This is wrong.

The Scriptures... are conceived by the writers of the New Testament as through and through God's book, in every part expressive of his mind, given through men after a fashion which does no violence to their nature as men, and constitutes the book also men's book as well as God's, in every part expressive of the mind of its human authors.
THE BIBLICAL IDEA OF INSPIRATION

The human writers wrote freely—but they were prepared for their task by God and he revealed himself to them to the extent that was necessary for their task. 'If God wished to give his people a series of letters like Paul's, he prepared a Paul to write them— and the Paul he brought to the task was a Paul who spontaneously would write just such letters.' The result is that the writers wrote precisely what God wanted—so that one can talk of 'verbal inspiration', or the inspiration of the very words of the text (this in opposition to the idea that God merely put ideas into the minds of the writers and left them to get on with the task of writing them down as best they could). Because the writers wrote precisely what God wanted, the message of the Bible is his message and the Bible can be called his word. It follows therefore that what the Bible teaches is true.

In the early years of the twentieth century, liberalism made deep inroads into Evangelical churches and organizations. In the United States there was a concerted attempt to reverse the tide. From 1910 to 1915 twelve small books, entitled *The Fundamentals*, were sent free of charge to every theological student and Christian worker in the USA. These set out to defend not the distinctive beliefs of any one denomination but the basic truths of Protestant Christianity—such as the deity of Jesus Christ; his atonement, resurrection and second coming; the inspiration and authority of the Bible. The outcome was a full-scale controversy. This did not prevent the liberals from taking over most of the mainstream Protestant denominations, but it did lead to the formation of a solid conservative Evangelical coalition to maintain the Evangelical position. The coalition drew together Evangelicals from a variety of confessional backgrounds— Lutheran, Reformed, Anabaptist, etc. They were united on the basic doctrines of the Evangelical faith.

The rallying point was the inspiration and infallibility of Scripture—which served as a touchstone for orthodoxy as it was a doctrine which united the movement against liberalism and which could fairly be held to undergird the other elements of orthodox Protestantism. At first, conservative Evangelicalism was pushed into a backwater of church life. But it has grown dramatically over the years, while in the USA and elsewhere the mainstream liberal churches have declined almost as dramatically. Since the 1974 *Lausanne Congress, the conservative Evangelical movement is reckoned as a third force in world Christianity, to be reckoned with alongside Roman Catholicism and the *World Council of Churches.

Conservative Evangelicals have been united by their doctrine of Scripture—but this does not mean that they have all held the same doctrine. Warfield's position represents the middle ground. In the United States especially, there is the 'fundamentalist' movement which is not so careful to acknowledge the human side of the Bible and which is wedded to the 'dispensationalist' interpretation, popularized by the famous *Scofield Bible*. Fundamentalism has tended to be anti-intellectual and hostile to culture. On the other side of Warfield stand those who wish to maintain the inspiration and authority of Scripture, who wish it to be the final norm for faith and who would not feel free to criticize its theology—but who do not feel that this need exclude factual errors in the Bible in the areas of history or geography, say. This position was taken by Warfield's Scottish contemporary James Orr (1844–1913) and some other leading British Evangelicals of his generation. The contributors to *The Fundamentals* came from all three of these schools—including Warfield and Orr themselves. Orr's approach declined in popularity among conservative Evangelicals, but has reappeared in recent years—its most distinguished advocate being *G.C. Berkouwer.

Gerrit Berkouwer
THE HUMANITY OF THE BIBLE

Gerrit Cornelius Berkouwer was born in Holland in 1903. After studying at the Free University in Amsterdam he became a pastor in the Gereformeerde Kerk, the breakaway Reformed church in Holland. In 1945 he returned to the Free University as professor of dogmatics, where he remained until his retirement.

G.C. Berkouwer is a prolific author. Instead of writing a systematic theology, he embarked upon a series of fourteen dogmatic studies. In these he takes a topic, such as *Faith and Justification* or *Sin*, and discusses it, interacting with current debate. He has also written a number of works on *Karl Barth, the most important being *The Triumph of Grace in the Theology of Karl Barth* (1954). Berkouwer has been influenced by Barth over the years, but he remains critical of some aspects of his theology. He wrote a major work on *The Conflict with Rome* in 1948. On the basis of his writings, Berkouwer was invited to the *Second Vatican Council as an official observer—which led to his *The Second Vatican Council and the New Catholicism* (1964).

G.C. Berkouwer stresses that the aim of the theologian is not to produce a logically coherent system for its own sake. Theology must always relate to the Bible and to the needs of the pulpit:

Theology is relative to the word of God. This relativity is decisive for the method and significance of theology. It means that theology is occupied in continuous attentive and obedient listening to the word of God. And since listening, unlike remembering, is always a thing of the present moment, theological questions must have relevance and timeliness. Theology is not a complex system constructed for their own entertainment by scholars in the quiet retreat of ivory towers. It must have significance for the unquiet times; but it can achieve its proper relevance only in obedient attentiveness, not to the times first of all, but to the word.

FAITH AND JUSTIFICATION, CHAPTER 1

Most controversial of Berkouwer's writings is his *Holy Scripture*, the Dutch original of which appeared in two volumes (1966). In his early years Berkouwer followed *B.B. Warfield in his doctrine of Scripture. But in the years following his appointment as professor he moved to a less conservative position, which he expounds in his book.

Berkouwer recognizes that the Bible is 'God-breathed' (2 Timothy 3:16) and this 'points to the mystery of its being filled with

truth and trustworthiness'. Berkouwer does not want to deny that the Bible is God's word. But he lays greater stress on the humanity of Scripture than does Warfield. The divine origin of the Bible does not exclude the human element. 'God's word has not come to us as a stupendous miracle that shies away from every link with the human in order thus to be truly divine. Rather, when God speaks, human voices ring in our ears.'

It is important that we acknowledge the humanity of Scripture, says Berkouwer. There are many fundamentalists who lay all their stress on the divine origin of the Bible but neglect and all but deny its human character. They think that they are thus honouring God's word, but their neglect of its human aspect leads them to misinterpret it and in fact to abuse God's word. It is only as we recognize the human character of the Bible, interpreting each passage in its historical setting, that we will interpret it correctly. Thus, ironically, those who speak the most about the authority of the Bible (because of their stress on its divine origin) have often mishandled it and twisted its message (because of their neglect of its human, historical character).

Berkouwer's stress on the humanity of Scripture does not prevent him from speaking of the 'identity' between the human words and God's speaking. But the implications of the Bible's human character must be taken seriously. The biblical authors do not appear to know more than their contemporaries about science. They wrote at particular times and expressed themselves in the ways of the time. There is no such thing as a 'timeless' message—not even in the Bible. But does this not affect the Bible's truthfulness? The reliability of the Bible must, says Berkouwer, be seen in terms of its purpose, as described in 2 Timothy 3: 16–17: 'useful for teaching the truth, rebuking error, correcting faults, and giving instruction for right living, so that the person who serves God may be fully qualified and equipped to do every kind of good deed.'

Berkouwer's teaching on the Bible is found in summary form in *A Unanimous*

Testimony of Faith, a confession of faith written by Berkouwer and Herman Ridderbos for the General Synod of the Reformed Churches in the Netherlands, and received by the synod in 1974. God has revealed himself in the 'history of Israel and has also given us 'through the service of man, the witness of this revelation in the Holy Scriptures... in an undeceivable and unshakeable foundation for the church'. He gave his Spirit to the biblical writers so that 'by their word he might communicate, interpret his word in a clear, reliable and authoritative way and commit it to writing for the church of all ages'. These writings 'bear traces of their humanness in various ways and we can understand the Scriptures only by due consideration of them'. These ways include their languages, the literary forms used and the circumstances of the times in which they were written. The inspiration of the Holy Spirit does not remove all human limitations. Here we must consider the purpose for which Scripture is given—'not in order to give infallible divine information concerning all kinds of arbitrary matters, but to make us understand how God wants us to know him rightly and to fear him'. This means that we can welcome scholarly study of the Bible. But the humanity of Scripture does not mean that it is not God's word for us. The scriptures speak to us in such a way that they are recognized to be God's word. Furthermore, Jesus Christ himself accepted them as God's word. The church has no other ground or guideline for her faith than Scripture. 'We cannot truly confess our faith in any other way than in reverent subjection to this word, and to this word alone.'

In the last ten years or so there has been an intense controversy among American Evangelicals over the reliability of Scripture. A significant minority urges that we distinguish between what the Bible *teaches* and what it *touches*. The Bible teaches only about matters of belief and practice, theology and ethics. The Bible only 'touches' on matters of science, geography, etc. and in these areas it is not necessarily correct. Thus the Bible is infallible in its teaching on

theology and ethics. Against this view there has been a strong insistence upon the 'inerrancy' of Scripture—that the Bible is true even when it speaks of science or geography. This position has sometimes been stated in an extreme and immoderate form. A careful, balanced statement of it is found in the *Chicago Statement on Biblical Inerrancy*, produced in 1978 by 284 Evangelical scholars and pastors. Inspiration, 'though not conferring omniscience, guaranteed true and trustworthy utterance on all matters of which the biblical authors were moved to speak and write.' Scripture 'is true and reliable in all the matters it addresses,' so that 'Scripture in its entirety is inerrant, being free from all falsehood, fraud or deceit.'

While the Bible itself warns against intruding into other people's controversies (Proverbs 26:17), such an important question cannot be allowed to pass without comment.

● Words like 'infallibility' and 'inerrancy' do not resolve the issue, as those who use them immediately have to qualify them to avoid misunderstanding. Ultimately they simply mean that the Bible is *true*— which might be a more helpful term to use. What is needed is not more slogans (like 'inerrancy') but a sober account of what we mean when we say that the Bible is true.

● Too often questions of reliability and questions of interpretation are confused. To maintain for example that Genesis 1 is true does not of itself tell us how literally or otherwise it is to be taken. Granted that it was not written as a scientific treatise, how was it meant to be taken?

● Talk of inerrancy must not lead us to ascribe greater accuracy to the text than the authors meant. To take an obvious example, *strict* inerrancy would mean that Jesus fed a crowd of 5,000 men exactly, to the nearest man (Mark 6:44). Yet such an interpretation is rejected by Matthew 14:21: '*about* five thousand men'.

It is wrong arbitrarily to forbid the Bible to teach about geography or history. It is right to affirm that the Bible is true. Yet such an affirmation must not be used to impose a degree of accuracy that was never intended, to short-cut questions of interpretation or to deny that the form in which the biblical message comes to us is that of particular cultures of the past.

Helmut Thielicke
PREACHING TO MODERN PEOPLE

Helmut Thielicke was born at Barmen in 1908. Having studied theology at a number of German universities he became, in 1936, a professor at Heidelberg University. But in 1940 he was dismissed because of his outspoken criticism of Nazi policy. After a brief spell in the army, he served as a Lutheran pastor. In 1945 he returned to academic life, becoming professor of systematic theology at Tübingen University. In 1954 he moved to Hamburg University to become professor of systematic theology and dean of the newly-founded theology faculty. In addition to his academic work, Thielicke remained a regular and popular preacher. In his preaching, as in his theology, he always sought to relate the gospel to the modern world. His publications include many volumes of sermons. His two major works are a multi-volume *Theological Ethics*, written in the years from 1955, and a three-volume systematic theology entitled *The Evangelical Faith* (1968–78). He died in 1985.

Thielicke's concern in his *Theological Ethics* is to speak to modern man. So much modern preaching moves in an otherworldly sphere which does not impinge upon our secular existence. Thielicke sympathizes with the concerns of *Bonhoeffer and *Bultmann to address modern man—though not necessarily with their conclusions. He warns about the two dangers to be avoided. On the one hand there are those who are so determined to reinterpret the gospel for modern man that they are 'practically drowning in hermeneutical reflection'. On the other hand, there are those 'who shy away from the heresies that could result and who often go on preaching with an artificially preserved naïveté as if we were still living in the sixteenth century.'

Preaching and ethical discussion today must relate to secular man. Thielicke wishes to 'rescue Christian dogmas from the sphere of the otherworldly and bring the church out of the ghetto and back to earth, to the place where man actually lives in his secularity and where he "may" live with his faith.' He is concerned about the schizophrenic Christian who lives in two worlds—who attends Sunday worship but who finds that it does not relate to the realities of secular life from Monday to Friday.

Thielicke protests against the attitude which regards ethics as merely the practical epilogue to dogmatics. Ethics is more than the practical outworking of faith. If dogmatics can be seen as 'faith reflecting on its object', ethics is 'faith inquiring as to the conduct faith posits for man towards himself, his neighbour, the world and its orders.' Practical obedience is not a supplementary addition to faith. Either faith is real—in which case it is translated into obedience—or it is unreal and merely a lie (1 John 2:4).

Thielicke's theological ethics are Evangelical ethics. They are not about how to act in order to be justified, but about how the justified man will act. Thielicke's concern is to 'formulate an evangelical ethic for which the fact of justification is decisive'. But while Thielicke's starting point is traditional, he seeks to penetrate into areas too often neglected by traditional ethics. It is not enough simply to treat the individual in their relationship to God, their family and their immediate neighbours. Ethics must also consider our political, social and economic lives—areas where most of us encounter the real problems of conscience. Another commonly neglected problem concerns the conflict between rival ethical claims. It is not enough simply to expound principles without considering the situations where these principles clash—which is where the difficult ethical situations arise.

The theme of applying Christian truth to the modern world receives even fuller treatment in *The Evangelical Faith*. The first of the three volumes is explicitly devoted to *The Relation of Theology to Modern Thought*

Forms. Theology is the attempt to address the Christian faith to the contemporary world. As this world changes from generation to generation, so must the form of address. It is therefore quite mistaken to think of theology as timeless and unchanging—'no form of preaching nor theological system can contain timeless validity and simply be accepted by later generations.' To put it simply, theology must scratch where it itches.

It is over the business of relating to contemporary thought that theologians are most divided today. But it is important to discern what is the real issue and it is this that Thielicke analyses carefully. The issue is not *whether* to relate theology to the modern world. All theologians of any distinction are doing that. The controversy concerns how to do it. Often theologians are called 'conservative' or 'modern' according to their approach. Thielicke recognizes that there exists such a divide, but finds neither term satisfactory to describe the issues at stake—both because they can degenerate into mere slogans and because they do not point to the heart of the matter. So-called conservatives do not deny the need to be 'modern' and are not concerned simply to conserve the past. Thielicke prefers to divide theologies into two basic types: Cartesian and non-Cartesian.

The 'Cartesian' approach (so-called after the philosopher Descartes) is concerned primarily with the world, with the modern recipients of the Christian message. This concern is not wrong in itself—indeed *all* vital theology is concerned with its audience. But with Cartesian theology it becomes the starting point—and in such a way that it controls the whole process. Cartesian theology begins with a view of man as 'come of age'. Christian theology is then built on a secular analysis of man and trimmed to fit it. This approach leads to the erosion of Christian doctrine and a preoccupation with methods of interpreting the faith for today. Thielicke quotes an apt saying of *Karl Rahner: 'They are continually sharpening knives and no longer have anything to cut.' Thielicke sees the Cartesian approach in

*Schleiermacher, *Bultmann and *Tillich. He finds this approach tragic in that the method inevitably forces the theologian to edit the gospel and only some of its contents 'can slip through the net of the prior conditions'. This is not the desire of the theologian and there arises a discrepancy between his personal faith and what he can express intellectually.

The other approach is 'non-Cartesian'. It is often called conservative, but this term can be misleading. The non-Cartesian approach is not simply a desire to preserve the past. There are some who simply regurgitate the theology of previous centuries and try to conceal this by using modern techniques of communication, 'which simply deck out the corpse in such a way as to suggest that it is still alive'. This approach is wrong:

A past which is conserved traditionalistically is an alteration rather than a preservation of the past. The fidelity of unchanged repetition is a sham fidelity. To repeat Luther's sayings about government unaltered in a democratic age instead of adjusting them to the new situation is to be false to Luther.

EVANGELICAL FAITH, VOLUME 1, 6:2

Non-Cartesian theology seeks to be contemporary, to address modern man. This means that, as with Cartesian theology, the contemporary world-view is taken seriously. If we love our neighbour and desire to reach him with the gospel we will not be satisfied until we *understand* him. We will not simply attribute his rejection of or indifference to the gospel to his own hardness. We must be prepared to ask if it is *our* fault, if we really belong to our own age. But while non-Cartesian theology takes the contemporary world-view seriously, it refuses to make it *normative*. It is not the starting-point for theology. The gospel must be actualized—addressed to the actual situation of modern man. But this must not happen by a process of accommodation—by pruning the gospel to make it fit a modern world-view. We must recognize that ultimately natural man cannot receive the gospel—the Holy Spirit must apply it. It is the recognition of this point, without using it as an excuse to avoid constructing a contemporary and relevant theology, that is the mark of a vital non-Cartesian theology.

THE NEW ORTHODOXY

After the First World War there was a reaction
against Liberalism, in the direction of orthodoxy.
This had much in common with Evangelicalism, but
was a Neo-Orthodoxy, not a return to the old
orthodoxy.

Karl Barth
LET GOD BE GOD

Karl Barth was born at Basel in 1886, the
eldest son of a Reformed pastor. After
studying theology at the universities of
Bern, Berlin, Tübingen and Marburg he
became a Reformed minister in Switzerland.
While pastoring the church at Safenwil, near
Aarau, he wrote a commentary on *The
Epistle to the Romans*, which was published
in 1919. This 'landed like a bombshell in the
playground of the theologians', as a Roman
Catholic has put it. Barth became the leader
of the Neo-Orthodox reaction to nineteenth-
century liberalism. He became a professor of
theology at Göttingen, Münster and Bonn
Universities. With the rise of Adolf Hitler he
became a leading figure in the Confessing
Church and the prime author of the 1934
Barmen Declaration. The following year he
was dismissed by Hitler and was returned to
Switzerland, where he became professor of
theology at Basel until his retirement in
1962. He died in 1968.

Barth was trained by many of the
leading liberal theologians of the early
twentieth century. But during the First
World War he came to question their
teaching. The horrors of the war itself
challenged liberal optimism about human
progress and perfectibility. Barth was
particularly shaken by the fact that almost
all of his former teachers had in August 1914
signed a proclamation in support of the
Kaiser's war policy. 'For me at least,

nineteenth-century theology no longer held
any future.' Positively, Barth was influenced
by his friends Christoph Blumhardt and
Eduard Thurneysen, by reading
*Kierkegaard and Dostoevsky—and
especially by studying the Bible itself. He
came to see the bankruptcy of liberalism,
which exalted man at the expense of God,
which studied man's religion rather than
God's revelation. 'The ship was threatening
to run aground; the moment was at hand to
turn the rudder an angle of exactly 180
degrees.' This Barth did in his *The Epistle to
the Romans*. Here he emphasized the deity of
God, God as the 'wholly other', the 'infinite
qualitative distinction' between God and
man. You don't say 'God' by saying 'man' in
a loud voice. Theology is the study not of
human philosophy or religious experience
but of God's word. Barth was taken aback by
the response to his book.

*As I look back upon my course, I seem to
myself as one who, ascending the dark
staircase of a church tower and trying to
steady himself, reached for the
bannister, but got hold of the bell rope
instead. To his horror, he had then to
listen to what the great bell had sounded
over him and not over him alone.*
CHRISTIAN DOGMATICS, FOREWORD

In 1927 Barth published the first of a
projected series of volumes on *Christian
Dogmatics*. But it was criticized for being
based on existentialist philosophy. As a

result Barth decided to start again and in 1932 the first volume of his *Church Dogmatics* appeared. During his lifetime he published no less than twelve fat volumes of the *Church Dogmatics*—totalling roughly 6 million words. (Parts of an incomplete thirteenth volume were published by him and others.) The *Church Dogmatics* is without parallel in its length and thoroughness. Even *Thomas Aquinas' *Sum of Theology* is dwarfed! Pope Pius XII (who made the 'infallible' definition of Mary's assumption in his *Munificentissimus Deus*) described Barth as 'the greatest theologian since St Thomas Aquinas', a remarkable tribute. It is interesting that although Barth was deeply critical of Roman Catholicism, his writings have attracted attentive study and positive assessment from many Roman Catholic scholars—such as *Hans Küng. Barth himself commented that 'the most comprehensive expositions, the most penetrating analyses, and even the most interesting evaluations of the *Church Dogmatics* and of the rest of my work have thus far [1958] come from the Catholic camp'—with one or two exceptions such as *Berkouwer.

Barth's theology is a theology of the word. It is the word of God, God's revelation, that is the subject matter of theology. Barth laid a heavy stress on God's revelation, on the Bible, and saw himself as returning to many of the insights of the Reformers, especially *Calvin. But he was not simply returning to the traditional understanding of the Bible—his was a *Neo*-Orthodoxy rather than a return to the old orthodoxy. For Barth, God's word is seen in dynamic rather than static terms. It is to be thought of not as doctrine or words or statements but as an *event*, something which happens. God's word is the event of God speaking to man in Jesus Christ; it is God's personal revelation of himself to us. The old orthodoxy erred, according to Barth, by making of God's word a static object (such as the Bible) which man can analyse and dissect—like a dead body. But God's word confronts us not as an *object* which we can control, but as a *subject* which controls and acts upon us. The scientist

cannot create a flash of lightning nor keep one in his laboratory for the purposes of study—he can simply observe it when it happens. In the same way, Jack the Ripper was not an object the police could study and control—they could only experience him as an active subject to whom they reacted. So also, God's word is something that happens to us—the event of God speaking to us through Jesus Christ. It is not a static manual of information (like a railway timetable), but a dynamic event demanding a response (like a proposal of marriage).

God's *revealed word* is the event of God speaking to man and revealing himself through Jesus Christ. But how can we know about this? The Bible, God's *written word*, is the witness to the event of God's revelation—as an artist might 'capture' a flash of lightning on his canvas. The Old Testament points forward to Jesus Christ in expectation; the New Testament looks back to him in recollection. Their function, like that of John the Baptist, is to point to Jesus Christ—'Behold the Lamb of God'. (From the days of Barth's first pastorate, Grünewald's portrait of John the Baptist pointing to the crucified Jesus Christ hung over his desk.) The church today, through the *proclaimed word* (in preaching, theology, sacrament), also bears witness to the revealed word. This proclamation is to be based on the written word, the Bible—the church has no right to preach anything else.

The written word of Scripture and the proclaimed word are not themselves revelation, but they are fallible human words pointing to God's revelation. As human words they are limited and weak, but they *become* God's word when he chooses to speak through them. God has spoken to man through Jesus Christ. The Bible bears witness to this. The church proclaims this biblical witness. As the Bible is read and proclaimed today so God speaks again, through the written and proclaimed word. Thus, when God so chooses, the written and proclaimed word actually becomes that to which they bear witness—God speaking personally to us in Jesus Christ. Thus the Bible is God's word in that it attests past revelation and promises future revelation. These three forms of God's word—revealed, written and proclaimed—are inseparable. There is only one word, in a threefold form—an analogy to the doctrine of the Trinity.

Because for Barth God's word is an event, something that happens, he cannot simply call the Bible God's word. The Bible is the word of God only in the sense that it witnesses to the past event of God speaking and that God again speaks through it today. Barth is often criticized for denying that the Bible *is* God's word. But once 'word of God' has been defined as ' the event speaking to us', it is simply impossible to equate the Bible with God's word. A book cannot strictly be called an event—any more than an elephant could be called a punctuation mark. But to say that it all follows from Barth's definition of 'God's word' is not to deny that there is a real point of difference. Barth makes a valuable protest against the excessively static conception of God's word which simply equates it with a book—but himself leans too far the other way. Consider again the example of a proposal of marriage, sent to a girl through the post. In one sense the proposal is an event. When she opens the letter, it *becomes* a proposal of marriage. If the letter never reached her there would in one sense never have been a proposal of marriage. But in another, real sense the letter *is* a proposal of marriage irrespective of whether she ever receives it and it remains a proposal of marriage long after both parties are dead. So also, God's word can be understood *both* as the event of God speaking to us *and* as the content of that speech found in the Bible.

For Barth, theology is to be based on God's word alone—not on human philosophy. (This is why he abandoned the first volume of his *Christian Dogmatics*—because it was not sufficiently clear at this point.) Barth was opposed to all natural theology—theology based on creation or on human reason, independently of the Christian revelation. Thomas Aquinas developed a two-tier system in which reason establishes God's existence and some of his attributes while revelation builds certain specifically Christian doctrines upon this foundation. The Reformers abandoned this approach and based their theology simply on the biblical revelation. In the eighteenth century the Deists built a rival religion based *purely* on nature and reason. In reaction to this, the defenders of orthodoxy adopted a position similar to Thomas'—accepting the validity of natural theology, but denying its adequacy or completeness. Liberalism also started with the agenda of the secular world and built its theology on that foundation—with disastrous results.

Barth's remedy is to abolish all natural theology and to insist upon God's word as the *sole* basis for theology—thus making an explicit principle out of the largely unformulated approach adopted by the Reformers. This principle provided a firm ideological basis from which to oppose the incursion of Nazi ideals into the church and came to expression in the *Barmen Declaration*. But just at that time, while the fight against Nazism was at its height, Barth's friend and ally Emil Brunner broke ranks with a work entitled *Nature and Grace*. He argues that there are two revelations of God—in creation as well as in Jesus Christ. While the former may not suffice for the construction of a natural theology, it does provide a 'point of contact' for the gospel. For instance, our conscience makes us aware of sin and the gospel is addressed to this awareness. He claimed, with considerable justice, that his less extreme position was closer to the Reformers than was Barth's. Barth responded swiftly and vehemently in a work entitled *Nein!* (*No!*) in which he savages Brunner. (The violence must be excused by the urgency of the situation in Germany.) For Barth there is only one revelation of God—in Jesus Christ. Without the gospel there can be no real concept of sin. The gospel comes to us not as an aeroplane seeking a suitable landing strip in our existing consciousness, but as a bomb which clears its own space to land.

Who was right? Barth feared that Brunner was opening the door to a new liberalism in which man's natural understanding of God would control and distort God's revelation. He feared that Brunner (out of the conflict, in Zürich) was opening the door to Nazi influence in the church. He also feared another threat. The philosopher Ludwig Feuerbach, in his *The Essence of Christianity* (1841) claimed that all theology (talk about God) is really anthropology (talk about man). To state that God is loving and wise, say, is to assert the supreme value of *human* love and wisdom. Cultures attribute to God those qualities which they find praiseworthy. Religion is man's primitive and indirect form of self-knowledge—which is now superseded by philosophy.

Feuerbach's ideas were immensely influential—on Marx who saw this as the explanation of religion; on Freud who saw God as the projection into heaven of a father figure. *Schleiermacher and the liberal tradition, basing theology on human religious experience, were particularly vulnerable to these charges—as is *Bultmann more recently. Barth's whole theology can be seen as a sustained response to Feuerbach, an attempt to show that God is *not* made in man's image. To understand God, we should not start with an abstract idea of the meaning of the word 'God' and then relate this idea to the Christian God. This was the way of Thomas Aquinas who started with natural theology; the way of most traditional systematic theologies which start with the doctrine of God *before* considering his self-revelation. Instead we should start with God as revealed in Jesus Christ.

God is not an abstract category by which even the Christian understanding of the word has to be measured, but he who is called God [in the Bible] is the one God, the single God, the sole God.
THE CHRISTIAN UNDERSTANDING OF REVELATION

Barth's rejection of all natural knowledge of God means that the Christian God is totally unknown outside of Jesus Christ, that he comes to the unbeliever as a complete stranger. Barth has been criticized for taking too seriously the atheist understanding of man as godless. Even atheistic man has a 'God-shaped blank'. While Barth was right to warn of the dangers of allowing a pre-Christian understanding to *control* Christian doctrine, he goes too far in making Christian doctrine a totally alien message. Towards the end of his life, Barth slightly modified his position. He contrasted Jesus Christ, the one word of God and the one light of life, with other 'true words' and 'lesser lights' through which he speaks. These include the non-Christian world and the physical creation. But Barth still insists that these are not independent of the one revelation of God in Jesus Christ.

God's one word to man is in Jesus Christ. All of God's dealings with man are in and through Jesus Christ. This principle negatively excludes natural theology. But positively it is also a guiding principle for all Christian theology. All doctrines are to be interpreted Christologically. This leads to what is sometimes called 'Christomonism' or, less kindly, 'creeping Christology'. Barth preferred the term 'Christological concentration'. This principle leads to a radical revision of certain traditional doctrines. It is wrong to suppose that God sees some people as 'in Christ' and others as 'in Adam' or 'outside of Christ'. God looks upon *all* men in Jesus Christ, as forgiven—even though they may themselves refuse to recognize this. It is illegitimate to seek to show people their sinfulness by preaching the law (e.g. the Ten Commandments) to them. The doctrine of sin cannot be understood independently of Jesus Christ. Those who do not know him have no true knowledge of sin. Again, sin must be seen as our reaction to God's grace, not vice versa. It is wrong to suppose that the incarnation of Jesus Christ took place *because* man sinned. Barth offers a brilliant new insight into traditional doctrines in the light of his Christological principle. But while it is a stimulating exercise to seek to view all Christian doctrines Christologically, to turn this into a rigid controlling principle leads to a distortion of the biblical picture in places.

Barth remained consistent in his basic positions. But he mellowed a little with the years and revised some judgements. His initial hostility towards nineteenth-century liberalism was later qualified. He came to see the nineteenth-century theologians (even Schleiermacher) as great men who struggled in a difficult age and from whom we can learn. This does not mean that he ceased to be aware of their errors, but rather that he began to see their greatness. In the early years of the Neo-Orthodox movement, Barth and others had stressed the deity of God—to the extent of being in danger of the opposite error to Schleiermacher, that of making 'God great for a change at the cost of *man*'. Later, in a lecture on *The Humanity of God* (1956) Barth acknowledged that they had been too one-sided, because of the pressing need of the time. Now there needed to be another change of direction, in distinction from but not in opposition to the earlier emphasis on God's deity. Alongside and included in the deity of God is his humanity—in Jesus Christ. 'In Jesus Christ there is no isolation of man from God or of God from man.' As he put it elsewhere, in 1948, 'the message of God's grace came to seem more urgent than the message of God's law, wrath, accusation and judgement.' Another interesting change in Barth's position is his rejection in later years of the doctrine of infant baptism. In the fragments that he published of the unfinished thirteenth volume of the *Church Dogmatics* he comes out clearly against the practice, which he had earlier defended.

Barth remained all his life a humble believer. In a funeral tribute to Barth, Hans Küng recalled how at the conclusion of a discussion he had conceded that Barth had good faith. Barth's response is interesting:

So you allow me good faith. I have never conceded myself good faith. And when once the day comes when I have to appear before my Lord, then I will not come with my deeds, with the volumes of my Dogmatics *in the basket upon my back. All the angels there would have to laugh. But then I shall also not say, 'I have always meant well; I had good faith'. No, then I will only say one thing: 'Lord, be merciful to me a poor sinner!'*

Gustaf Aulén

Gustaf Aulén was born in 1879. He was, together with Anders Nygren and Gustav Wingren, one of the leading Swedish theologians of this century. Aulén and Nygren shared many ideas in common with the Neo-Orthodoxy of *Barth and others, though they had their own distinctive approach.

From 1913 to 1933 Aulén was professor of theology at the University of Lund. He then served as bishop of Strängnäs from 1933 to his retirement in 1952, when he returned to Lund, until his death in 1977. He played a leading role in the ecumenical movement, being vice-president of the 1937 Edinburgh Faith and Order Conference. He also played an important part in the first general assembly of the *World Council of Churches at Amsterdam in 1948. During the war he took a firm stance against Nazism. He also wrote church music.

Aulén wrote a number of books including a systematic theology entitled *The Faith of the Christian Church* (1923). But he is best known for a course of lectures which he gave in 1930, published in an abridged English translation under the title *Christus Victor*. Aulén's aim in this work was to correct the traditional account of the history of the idea of the atonement, as expounded by *Ritschl, *Harnack and many others. Ritschl saw the history as a conflict between two opposing doctrines: the objective doctrine, as formulated by *Anselm and the subjective doctrine as formulated by *Abelard. According to the *objective* doctrine Christ died in order to satisfy God's justice, in order to make us acceptable to God. It is God who needs to be reconciled to us. According to the *subjective* doctrine Christ came and died in order to change us, rather than to change God's attitude to us. It is we who need to be reconciled to God.

According to Ritschl's interpretation, the early church had no thought-out doctrine of the atonement. Aulén disagreed. He saw in the early church the *classic* or dramatic idea of the atonement. This is a doctrine of the atonement in the full and proper sense, not just a confused way of thinking. It is a doctrine which is quite distinct from the other two and, according to Aulén, superior to them. It interprets the atonement as 'a divine conflict and victory' over the evil powers of the world. Unlike the other two approaches, 'it represents the work of atonement or reconciliation as from first to last a work of God himself'. This view Aulén discerned in the teaching of the early church, especially focussing on *Irenaeus. He also claimed that it is the dominant idea in the New Testament itself. The Lutheran Aulén also saw it re-emerging 'more vigorously and profoundly expressed than ever before', in *Luther.

Why had this approach been neglected by the histories of doctrine? Aulén gives various reasons, including the fact that it had not been formulated in the precise manner of the other two. 'The "mythological" language of the early church about Christ's redemptive work, and the realistic, often undeniably grotesque imagery, in which the victory of Christ over the devil, or the deception of the devil, was depicted in lurid colours' was an obstacle. The trouble lay in a failure to 'penetrate behind the outward form to the underlying idea'. Here Aulén is alluding to the 'motif-research' of his contemporary Nygren. This approach sought to go beyond the forms and expressions in which doctrine is clothed, to reach the underlying motif.

Aulén's work proved to be immensely fruitful in stimulating further discussion of the doctrine of the atonement. But the way in which he stated his case has serious flaws. His interpretation of the objective doctrine, as taught by Anselm, is not altogether fair. More importantly, he falls to a large extent into the same trap as Ritschl, tending to regard the three doctrines as rivals, as alternative views. Thus he held that Luther taught the classic doctrine, not the objective or subjective doctrine. But it has proved more fruitful to interpret these three views as complementary, not contradictory. Many of the early Fathers view Christ as the one who has put us right with God by his death (objective view), whose love for us awakens our love for God (subjective view) and who

has won the victory over the powers of evil (classic view).

Aulén has stimulated historians to discern different views of the work of Christ in earlier writers. The 'objective' and 'subjective' views are reasonably clear, but the 'classic' view has been understood in different ways. Many interpreters would divide Aulén's classic view into two: Christ's victory over Satan and his work as the Second Adam bringing immortality and incorruption. These two cannot be totally distinguished from one another—but nor can the other views. When all is said and done the four views are four perspectives on the same reality, not four totally separate and distinct theories. They are four different aspects of the work of the one Christ, which is a unified whole.

Barmen Declaration (1934)

In the early 1930s, Adolf Hitler and the Nazi party came to power in Germany. Their rise led to the emergence within German Protestantism of a group called the 'German Christians'. The German Christians sought to blend Nazism or German nationalism and Christianity. They wanted the church to provide a religious sanction for Nazism. In 1933 they won a massive victory in the church elections. They then introduced, among other things, the notorious 'Aryan paragraph'—forbidding the church to employ people who were racially impure ('non-Aryans'—e. g. Jews) or married to such.

The German Christians were opposed by Pastor Martin Niemöller, who founded a 'Pastors' Emergency League' in 1933. This became the 'Confessing Church'—so called because they opposed Hitler and the German Christians by confessing Jesus Christ as the one Lord of the church, who must determine its belief. The Confessing Church set up a shadow church government, in opposition to the German Christians.

The leading ideological opposition to the German Christians came from *Karl Barth. Already, before the birth of Nazism, he had identified the supreme error of modern Protestantism as natural theology—the attempt to ground Christian theology on any basis other than God's word. When the 'other basis' was an obscure philosophy, this could appear to be an abstract and unimportant theological debate. But when it became Nazism, the issue immediately became burningly relevant and practical. Barth spoke out consistently against the German Christians—not on merely political grounds but on the fundamental theological ground that natural theology is wrong. The German Christians had the effect of thrusting Barth's theological agenda to the fore and of gaining for him a wider and ultimately more sympathetic audience than he might otherwise have expected.

The first Confessing Synod of the German Evangelical Church met at Barmen in May, 1934. It accepted a *Declaration*, drawn up largely by Barth (and based on a previous declaration composed by Barth and adopted earlier that year by the German Reformed churches). The *Barmen Declaration* consists of six articles:

● The first article rejects the idea of any divine revelation alongside God's word in Jesus Christ. 'Jesus Christ, as he is testified to us in the Holy Scripture, is the one word of God, whom we are to hear, whom we are to trust and obey in life and in death.'

● The second article rejects the idea that there are areas of life not under the lordship of Jesus Christ—such as politics.

● The third article rejects the idea that 'the church can turn over the form of her message and ordinances at will or according to some dominant ideological and political convictions'.

● The fourth article rejects the idea that the church should follow the Nazi state in adopting the 'Führer principle'—by setting up powerful church rulers apart from the regular pastoral ministry, contrary to Matthew 20:25–26.

● The fifth article rejects the idea that the state should try to usurp the functions of the church (by becoming 'the single and total order of human life') or that the church should expand its duties into the affairs of the state and so 'become itself an organ of the state'.

● The sixth article rejects the idea that the mission of the church can be subjected to worldly goals.

Finally, the Confessing Synod declared these truths to be 'the not-to-be-circumvented theological foundation of the German Evangelical Church'.

The *Barmen Declaration* failed to unite the Confessing Church since many Lutherans found its strong Barthian tone unacceptable. The Confessing Church provided a sustained, but largely ineffectual, opposition to Nazi policies within the church. The *Barmen Declaration* has been influential as a theological statement, outside of its original setting.

Dietrich Bonhoeffer
THE COST OF DISCIPLESHIP

Dietrich Bonhoeffer was born in 1906 at Breslau, then in Germany but now in Poland. His father was a professor of psychiatry and an agnostic, as were all Bonhoeffer's brothers. Bonhoeffer studied theology at Tübingen and Berlin and went on to become a Lutheran pastor. After pastoring the German congregation at Barcelona and spending a year at the Union Theological Seminary in New York (where he met *Reinhold Niebuhr) he became a lecturer at Berlin University in 1931. But the rise to power of Adolf Hitler in 1933 disrupted his career. Two days after Hitler became Chancellor, Bonhoeffer opposed the Nazi *Führerprinzip* (leadership principle) in a radio address—which was cut off before the end. That autumn he left for London to pastor the German congregation there. He was wholeheartedly behind the Confessing Church and the *Barmen Declaration*.

In 1935 he returned from London and helped to run a small theological seminary for the Confessing Church, until this was closed by the authorities in 1937. Increasing restrictions were imposed on Bonhoeffer himself—he was forbidden to lecture at Berlin, to preach, and finally in 1941 to write or publish. In 1939 he joined the German resistance movement and it was arranged for him to work for the German Counter-Intelligence. He became deeply involved in a plot to assassinate Hitler and overthrow the Nazi state. But in April 1943, shortly after becoming engaged to be married, he was arrested by the Gestapo, though the authorities were not yet aware of the extent of his involvement with the resistance. In September 1944, incriminating evidence was discovered and Bonhoeffer's fate was sealed. On 8 April 1945, he received a summary court martial and the following morning was hanged together with Admiral Canaris and others who had plotted against Hitler. His last words on being taken away for his trial were, 'This is the end—for me the beginning of life'.

The best-known of Bonhoeffer's pre-war works is his *Cost of Discipleship* (1937). In it he distinguishes between cheap and costly grace.

Cheap grace is the preaching of forgiveness without requiring repentance, baptism without church discipline, communion without confession, absolution without personal confession. Cheap grace is grace without discipleship, grace without the cross, grace without Jesus Christ, living and incarnate.

COST OF DISCIPLESHIP CHAPTER 1

Cheap grace starts with the fact that even the best Christians remain sinners and uses this to *justify* living a life of sin. Any attempt to lead a serious life of discipleship is branded as legalism or 'enthusiasm'.

[Costly] grace is costly because it calls us to follow, and it is grace because it calls us to follow Jesus Christ. It is costly because it costs a man his life, and it is grace because it gives a man the only true life. It is costly because it condemns sin, and grace because it justifies the sinner. Above all, it is costly because it cost God the life of his Son.

COST OF DISCIPLESHIP, CHAPTER 1

But is Bonhoeffer not rejecting the teaching of the Reformation? Is not 'cheap grace' to be identified with *Luther's 'justification by faith alone'? No. Cheap grace is a perversion of the Reformation doctrine. For Luther, justification by faith alone is the word of consolation to the disciple, to the one who is striving to follow Jesus Christ. 'So far from dispensing him from discipleship, this grace only made him a more earnest disciple.' But later generations left out the obligation of discipleship. 'Costly grace was turned into cheap grace without discipleship.' This is to pervert the doctrine. 'Those who try to use this grace as a dispensation from following Christ are simply deceiving themselves.'

All hangs on how the doctrine of grace is *used.*

If grace is God's answer, the gift of Christian life, then we cannot for a moment dispense with following Christ. But if grace is the data for my Christian life, it means that I set out to live the Christian life in the world with all my sins justified beforehand. I can go and sin as much as I like, and rely on this grace to forgive me, for after all the world is justified in principle by grace. I can therefore cling to my bourgeois secular existence, and remain as I was before, but with the added assurance that the grace of God will cover me.

COST OF DISCIPLESHIP, CHAPTER 1

The word of forgiveness is addressed to 'those who from the bottom of their hearts make a daily renunciation of sin and of every barrier which hinders them from following Christ, but who nevertheless are troubled by their daily faithlessness and sin.' It is not an encouragement to live a sinful life on the ground that all will be forgiven anyway.

During his imprisonment Bonhoeffer wrote to his friends and it is for these *Letters and Papers from Prison* that he is most famous. In his final year he wrote enigmatically about 'religionless Christianity'. His untimely death had the double effect of preventing him from explaining and developing his ideas while bestowing on them the aura of his martyrdom. His prison teaching can either be interpreted in line with his earlier writings or, as has happened in some brands of 'secular Christianity' since the 1960s, be taken as a radically new departure. The verdict of *Helmut Thielicke is judicious: Bonhoeffer 'has simply left the slogans behind as thorns in our soul to keep us salutarily disturbed'.

Bonhoeffer, brought up in a secular family and engaged in a very secular employment and in activities (the plot) which would not have been sanctioned by the church, was made forcefully aware of the modern secular world. He was concerned about how to confront secular religionless man. Since about the time of the thirteenth century, humankind has moved steadily towards independence from God. God has been progressively excluded from science, art and even ethics. Education and politics have been freed from church control. As the philosopher Kant put it, humanity and the world have 'come of age'. Increasingly man runs his affairs without reference to God. He may make a mess of them—as in the Second World War—but this does not induce him to return to the authority of God. A young adult may make a mess of his life, but he cannot return to become again a little child under his parents. Bonhoeffer was radical in seeing this process not as the history of man's progressive apostasy from God but as a right and proper development.

God would have us know that we must live as men who manage our lives without him ... Before God and with God we live without God. God lets himself be pushed out of the world onto the cross.
LETTERS AND PAPERS FROM PRISON, 16 JULY 1944

The new situation caused Bonhoeffer to question 'what Christianity really is, or indeed who Christ really is, for us today'. For nineteen centuries Christianity has assumed the fact of religion and presented itself as the true religion. But how do we speak to a secular non-religious world? Do we confine our appeal to the dwindling circles of the religious? Do we attempt to catch modern people when they are weak—when they have been bereaved or are facing some other crisis—and bring them back to religion? Bonhoeffer considered such attempts ignoble and unchristian. We need to question the assumption that people need to be religious in order to become Christian. Such a requirement may be compared to the demand that Gentile converts be circumcised and become Jews—which Paul vigorously resisted.

Bonhoeffer's proposal is a 'religionless Christianity'—that we should see Jesus Christ as 'lord of the religionless'. *Bultmann sought to eliminate myth from the gospel. On the one hand, Bonhoeffer charges him with falling into the liberal error of purging out 'mythological' elements and reducing Christianity to its 'essence'. But on the other hand, he charges Bultmann with not being radical enough. The problem for modern man is not just 'myth', but religion itself. Modern man has as much problem with the concept of God as with the concept of miracle. The Christian today must learn to speak of God in a secular way and to live his Christianity in a secular way. The believer 'must live a "secular" life, and thereby share in God's sufferings'. 'It is not the religious act that makes the Christian, but participation in the sufferings of God in the secular life.'

What on earth does Bonhoeffer mean? How can there be a religionless Christianity? In opposing religion Bonhoeffer was following *Barth (who greatly influenced him), who distinguished between man's search for God in religion (which leads to idolatry) and God's reaching out to man in his revelation. Bonhoeffer takes up Barth's negative approach to the concept of religion and broadens its scope. In advocating a 'religionless Christianity' Bonhoeffer wishes to see Christianity purged of certain facets of bourgeois religiosity:

● *Metaphysics*. Religion has taken God's transcendence philosophically and made him abstract and remote. Salvation then comes to be seen as escape to another world—with the result that this world is devalued and neglected.

● *Individualism*. Related to metaphysics is individualism—preoccupation with one's own individual piety. Bonhoeffer recognized the need for an individual, personal faith, but 'religion' emphasizes this to the detriment of the church and the world.

● *Partiality*. Religion confines Christianity to one area of life—an ever-dwindling area as the process of secularization proceeds. The result is that Christians live increasingly in a ghetto, remote from the concerns of the secular world.

The 'religious' version of Christianity leads to a church composed of individuals preoccupied with personal salvation. Their religion leads them to withdraw from secular society and its concerns and to devote their energies to 'religious' activities. The 'world' is seen primarily as a source of potential recruits—an alien realm to be entered with the aim of rescuing others and withdrawing them also into the religious realm. While such a picture contains an element of caricature, it undoubtedly approximates to the truth closely enough to cause concern.

Bonhoeffer wanted to bring God and the church back into the secular world. God is to be seen at the *centre* of life—not just at its boundaries. God is transcendent, but this does not mean that he is infinitely remote. 'God is beyond in the midst of our life.' This is why the Christian must learn to live his Christianity and speak of God in a secular way. The church is not to be preoccupied with its own religious concerns, but to serve the world. It is to follow the pattern of Jesus, 'the man for others'. There must be a secular interpretation of Christianity and the church.

How should this be taken? Bonhoeffer himself continued to talk of God and he envisaged that the 'new style' Christian would continue to maintain a life of prayer, at least in private. His last reported statement expresses confidence in life after death and his final act at the foot of the gallows was to pray. We do not know how Bonhoeffer would have developed his thought had he lived and there is little profit in speculating about it. Our task is to be challenged by his strictures and to seek to respond to them in our own situation today.

Reinhold Niebuhr
CHRISTIANITY'S SOCIAL RELEVANCE

Reinhold Niebuhr was born in 1892 at Wright City, Missouri. His father was a German immigrant and a Lutheran pastor. Niebuhr was himself ordained in 1915 and for thirteen years pastored the Bethel Evangelical Church of Detroit. In 1928 he became professor of applied Christianity at Union Theological Seminary in New York, where he remained until his retirement in 1960. He died in 1971. His younger brother, H. Richard Niebuhr, was also a distinguished theologian and is known especially for his *Christ and Culture* (1951).

In his years in the pastoral ministry Niebuhr was deeply concerned about social ethics. He exercised a prophetic ministry in Detroit, seeing and drawing attention to the injustices of capitalism. He sought to ' "debunk" the moral pretensions of Henry Ford, whose five-dollar-a-day wage gave him a world-wide reputation for generosity'. In 1927 Ford brought out a new car, which was enthusiastically received. But Niebuhr drew attention to the human cost in terms of hardship to the Ford employees. Many of them had been laid off for a year with no source of income. This and other experiences taught him 'the irrelevance of the mild moralistic idealism, which I had identified with the Christian faith, to the power realities of our modern technical society'. He rejected the liberal optimism of his youth, based on a belief in the inherent goodness of man and the inevitability of human progress. Instead he became one of the most perceptive exponents in this century of the Christian doctrine of original sin, especially in its social and historical manifestations.

It is the absurd notion of modern liberalism, both Christian and secular, that the Christian estimate of man's sinfulness is determined by the biblical account of the fall of Adam, and that it can be dismissed by anyone who does not find this primitive account credible. Actually, the estimate is supported by overwhelming evidence taken both from a sober observation of human behaviour and from introspective analysis.

INTELLECTUAL AUTOBIOGRAPHY

During his years in the pastoral ministry, Niebuhr kept a diary. Extracts from this he published in 1929 as *Leaves from the Notebook of a Tamed Cynic*. In one entry he noted how a particular church had finally found a new pastor after raising the salary to $15,000, no mean sum in 1924.

I don't know whether that was the factor which finally solved their problem, but at any rate they have the man they want. I suppose it is not easy to get a combination of Aristotle and Demosthenes, and on the current market, that ought to be worth $15,000. Nevertheless there must be some limit to this matter of oversized salaries.

There ought to be some questioning too about the growing tendencies of churches to build their congregations around pulpit eloquence. What kind of fundamental ethical question can a man be eloquent about when he draws that much cash, particularly since a Croesus or two usually has to supply an undue proportion of it? I don't know anything about the prophet of the Lord who accepted this call, but I venture to prophesy that no sinner in that pagan city will quake in his boots in anticipation of his coming.

The idea of a professional good man is difficult enough for all of us who are professionally engaged as teachers of the moral ideal. Of course, 'a man must

live' and it is promised that if we seek first the kingdom and its righteousness 'all these things shall be added unto us'. But I doubt whether Jesus had a $15,000 salary in mind. If the things that are added become too numerous they distract your attention terribly. To try to keep your eye on the main purpose may only result in making you squint-eyed. I hope the new prophet won't begin his pastorate with a sermon on the text 'I count all things but loss'.

LEAVES FROM THE NOTEBOOK OF A TAMED CYNIC, 1924

Niebuhr was one of America's leading political philosophers. His views progressed throughout his life. He began by accepting the optimism of the liberal approach, believing that science and a better education would inevitably eradicate the evils of society. His Detroit experiences convinced him of the error of this approach and he came to accept some of the Marxist critique of liberalism—but without ever accepting Marxism uncritically. He later became more critical of Marxism, commenting that 'the deepest tragedy of our age… is that the alternative to capitalism has turned out to be worse than the disease which it was meant to cure.'

Niebuhr criticized liberalism in his first major work, *Moral Man and Immoral Society* (1932). He shows how the evils of society are caused as much by groups as by the selfishness of individuals. Furthermore, 'the collective self-regard of class, race and nation is more stubborn and persistent than the egoism of individuals.' This is why society cannot be changed merely by changing individuals, educationally or ethically. We must recognize that politics is ultimately a power struggle between rival groups.

Relations between groups must therefore always be predominantly political rather than ethical—that is, they will be determined by the proportion of power which each group possesses at least as much as by any

rational and moral appraisal of the
comparative needs and claims of each
group.

MORAL MAN AND IMMORAL SOCIETY,
INTRODUCTION

Justice will be best maintained in society by
ensuring a fair distribution of power
between the different groups, preventing
any one from dominating the others. 'An
uneasy balance of power would seem to be
the highest goal to which society could
aspire.'

Niebuhr's greatest work is his two-
volume *Nature and Destiny of Man* (1941–
43), based on a series of lectures delivered at
Edinburgh in 1939. In this work his political
and social insights into the nature of man are
developed theologically.

THE EXISTENTIALISTS

One major strand in twentieth-century philosophy is existentialism. Some Christian theologians have sought to reinterpret Christianity in predominantly existentialist terms.

Søren Kierkegaard
THE INFINITE GULF

Søren Aabye Kierkegaard was born in 1813 at Copenhagen, the youngest son of elderly parents. After a secluded and unhappy childhood he went to university, where he led a life of self-indulgence. But he was unable to shake off the melancholy which plagued him all his life. After a long period of study he graduated in theology in 1840, but never proceeded to ordination. He became engaged, but broke it off and never married. He devoted himself to a life of thought and writing until his early death in 1855.

Kierkegaard's writings arose out of his tragic and lonely life. He has rightly been compared to prophets like Jeremiah who out of their deep personal experience saw the errors of their contemporaries and yet failed to convince them. He opposed the currently dominant philosophy of Hegel (which had deeply influenced him). He attacked the superficiality of the nominal Christianity practised in the Lutheran state church, drily commenting that 'Christianity has been abolished by expansion'. Kierkegaard died with few friends or supporters. Yet he has become one of the greatest philosophical influences upon the twentieth century. Many of his ideas profoundly influenced the young *Karl Barth. He is seen as the father of both Christian and secular existentialism.

Fundamental to Kierkegaard's thought is the infinite gulf between God and man. Contemporary Danish Lutheranism saw an easy continuity between man and God, man's moral strivings and God's holiness. This Kierkegaard vigorously rejected. There is an infinite qualitative gulf between time and eternity, between the finite and the infinite, between man and God. God is 'the absolutely Unknown'. There is also a chasm between the sinfulness of man and the holiness of God. Kierkegaard rightly perceived that without a sense of sin there will be no true Christianity. 'Take away the alarmed conscience and you may close the churches and turn them into dancing-halls.' This prophetic word speaks as powerfully to our present situation where many apparently lively forms of Christianity are shallow and rootless because they lack this sense of sin. This aspect of Kierkegaard deeply influenced Karl Barth and the Neo-Orthodox movement. In 1921 Barth wrote that 'if I have a system, it is limited to a recognition of what Kierkegaard called the "infinite qualitative distinction" between time and eternity.'

The infinite gulf between God and man can be bridged only by God himself. This he has done—in the incarnation of Jesus Christ. But this does not move Kierkegaard to favour the contemporary 'quest for the historical Jesus' and the belief that it is important to reconstruct the historical personality of Jesus. God revealed himself in Jesus Christ, but this is a *veiled* revelation. In Jesus Christ, God appears *incognito*. God was made manifest in Jesus Christ, but this was not apparent to the casual observer. It is only to the eye of faith that God is seen in Jesus Christ. There was no special advantage in having been a contemporary of Jesus without this faith. Jesus' *real* contemporaries are those who have faith in him—it is they and they only who truly encounter him. It follows that merely historical knowledge of Jesus is of little value.

If the contemporary generation had left nothing behind them but these words: 'We have believed that in such and such a year the God appeared among us in the humble figure of a servant, that he lived and taught in our community and finally died', it would be more than enough. The contemporary generation would have done all that was necessary; for this little advertisement, this nota bene *on a page of universal history, would be sufficient to afford an occasion for a successor, and the most voluminous account can in all eternity do nothing more.*

PHILOSOPHICAL FRAGMENTS, CHAPTER 5

Here again, Kierkegaard influenced the early Barth, who adopted the ideas of veiled revelation and the divine incognito. His ideas have also proved congenial to those like *Bultmann who are extremely sceptical about our ability to know about the historical figure of Jesus. Kierkegaard himself accepted the gospel accounts at their face value and did not question their historicity. But the principle enunciated above has been used to make a theological virtue of extreme scepticism about the historicity of the Gospel accounts.

Kierkegaard rejected the idea that truth is merely objective and can be reached by detached rational enquiry. Truth, says Kierkegaard, lies in subjectivity. This approach is seen in his *Journal* for 1835.

The thing is to understand myself, to see what God really wishes me to do; the thing is to find a truth which is true for me, to find the idea for which I can live and die. What would be the use of discovering so-called objective truth, ... what good would it do me to be able to

explain the meaning of Christianity if it had no deeper significance for me and for my life;—what good would it do me if truth stood before me, cold and naked, not caring whether I recognised her or not, and producing in me a shudder of fear rather than a trusting devotion?

Faith is not rational. It is the acceptance of the absurd, of paradox. Kierkegaard is a follower of *Tertullian's 'It is credible because it is absurd'. Faith is a personal decision, an act of affirmation, a leap into the dark. The believer is not to be compared to the chemist, calmly, objectively and rationally analysing a chemical substance. Faith involves risk, personal involvement. It is not the end-product of a mathematical proof. It is through personal commitment that we come to know God, not vice versa. It is said that 'love is blind; marriage is an eye-opener'—and this is true, even if the eye-opening need not involve the disillusionment implied by the cynic. It is *only* in the context of a committed relationship that the deeper knowledge comes. So also, faith is a step of commitment involving risk.

Kierkegaard's personality and his method of writing led him to make extreme statements. He himself described his work as 'just a bit of cinnamon'. He was offering not a rounded system but a spicy corrective. He was like the sailor who leans far over in one direction to prevent his boat from overbalancing in the other direction. If his writings are taken in this spirit—as provocative, prophetic spice rather than as staple diet—they are rewarding. But if his ideas are taken too seriously they quickly lead to error in a number of ways:

● The stress on the infinite gulf between God and man is a helpful corrective. But we must never lose sight of the fact that man is made in God's image and that this image is not totally obliterated. In Kierkegaard, as in some of the less cautious pronouncements of Neo-Orthodox theologians, there is a tendency to portray man as sinful *because* he is created and finite. This is wrong.

● Kierkegaard rightly stressed that mere historical knowledge of Jesus Christ does not equal faith. The Reformers made the same point. But it does not follow that historical knowledge is useless. It is a strange response to Jesus' claim that 'he who has seen me has seen the Father' (John 14:9), to profess a near total lack of interest in the historical figure of Jesus.

● It is true that faith involves personal involvement, that there is an element of risk. But faith must not be portrayed merely as a blind leap into the dark, as an arbitrary act in defiance of reason. Marriage is an act of trusting personal commitment and a step into the unknown, but it is not (for those with any sense!) an irrational leap into the dark. It is a step into the unknown, made on the basis of that which is already known. Faith is neither totally rational nor totally irrational.

Rudolf Bultmann
GOSPEL WITHOUT MYTH

Rudolf Bultmann was born in 1884 at Wiefelstede, near Oldenburg in (West) Germany. He studied theology at the Universities of Tübingen, Berlin and Marburg. He then began to lecture at Marburg, Breslau and Giessen Universities. But the majority of his academic career was spent as professor of New Testament at Marburg from 1921 until his retirement in 1951. He remained an honorary professor at Marburg until his death in 1976.

Bultmann was a New Testament scholar, rather than a theologian. In fact he was probably the greatest New Testament scholar of the twentieth century—certainly the most influential. His earliest major work was a *History of the Synoptic Tradition* (1921). In this he brings to the study of the Gospels the form-critical approach, of which he was one of the pioneers. He analysed the Gospel narratives into different types or forms. By this means he sought to trace their development in the earlier oral tradition, and their function in the early church and thus to assess their historicity. Bultmann concluded that most of the recorded sayings of Jesus have their origin not in Jesus himself but in the life of the early Christian communities. He became exceedingly sceptical regarding the possibility of knowing more than the barest outline of the life of Jesus.

Nineteenth-century liberalism confidently reconstructed a portrait of the 'Jesus of history', Jesus as he really was who turned out to be a good liberal Protestant. Albert Schweitzer, in his *The Quest of the Historical Jesus* (1906), chronicled and exposed this process. Bultmann's own upbringing was in the liberal tradition, but like *Barth he reacted against it—though not as radically as did Barth. Both men agreed in rejecting the liberal search for the historical Jesus. Barth used the rising tide of scepticism about the possibility of reconstructing a historical portrait of Jesus to urge that we should return to the Christ of the New Testament message—thus 'gathering apologetic figs from sceptical thistles', as *Harnack put it.

Bultmann also opposed the liberal quest, for three reasons. First, Bultmann's sceptical approach to the Gospels made it *impossible* to reconstruct a historical portrait of Jesus. Only a minimal knowledge of the historical Jesus is possible—certainly not enough to write a Life. Secondly, knowledge of the historical Jesus is *unnecessary*. The gospel requires no firmer historical basis than that Jesus lived and died, claims Bultmann, echoing *Kierkegaard. Thirdly, interest in the historical Jesus is actually *illegitimate*! Bultmann takes Paul's statement that we no longer know Jesus Christ 'after the flesh' (i.e. in a carnal, or worldly manner) to mean that Paul was no longer interested in the *historical* Jesus. He also claimed that the Reformation principle is justification by faith alone and not by history. (In fact the Reformation principle is more accurately summarized as justification by (the historical) Jesus Christ alone, received through faith alone. While the Reformers stressed that saving faith is *more* than merely belief in the historical events of the Gospels, they never imagined that it could be *less* than this.)

Barth and Bultmann both rejected the liberal quest for the Jesus of history, but they then parted company. Barth put in its place a (largely orthodox) dogmatic theology—which he sought to cut loose from historical critical studies, to the dismay of his former teacher, Harnack. Bultmann replaced the liberal quest with an extreme form of historical scepticism about Jesus—which remained dominant in Germany for a long period until in the 1950s some of his disciples began a 'new quest for the historical Jesus'—which is far removed from the liberal variety. Bultmann rejected liberalism to replace it (eventually) with an existentialist version of Christianity. He himself perceived that while, like Barth, he had turned to a theology of the word of God, his own rejection of liberalism was less radical than Barth's. 'I have endeavoured throughout my entire work to carry farther the tradition of historical-critical research as it was practised in "liberal" theology and to make our recent theological knowledge the more fruitful as a result.' But while Bultmann's *method* differs from that of liberalism, his conclusions have often been as unorthodox if not more so. Bultmann is best known for his programme of *demythologizing*. While Barth stressed the word of God, Bultmann tackled an issue largely neglected by Barth—hermeneutics, or the science of interpretation. How do we bridge the gulf between the first century and the twentieth century? How is the New Testament message to be applied to our generation? Bultmann attempted to answer this question in an essay on *New Testament and Mythology* (1941)—one of the most significant theological works of the century.

For Bultmann, the interpreter's problem lies in the 'mythical' world-view of the New Testament. By this he means the 'three-storey' universe (heaven above and hell below) and the belief in the supernatural—angels, demons, miracles. This world-view is *presupposed* by the New Testament writers. But it is obsolete today. 'Modern man' cannot accept the New Testament message because he cannot accept the mythical world-view.

It is impossible to use electric light and the wireless and to avail ourselves of modern medical and surgical discoveries and at the same time to believe in the New Testament world of spirits and miracles.
NEW TESTAMENT AND MYTHOLOGY

It is impossible today to accept the mythical world-view—and it is also unnecessary. There is nothing specifically Christian about such a world-view. It is simply the world-view of a pre-scientific age.

How should we react to this? It is impossible, says Bultmann, to redeem the situation by selecting which elements to believe and which to discard. The mythical world-view hangs together as a whole.

Bultmann's solution is to *demythologize*. This involves not the elimination of the mythical statements of the New Testament, but their interpretation. Bultmann criticizes liberals such as Harnack for eliminating the mythology and thus reducing the gospel to 'a few basic principles of religion and ethics'. Bultmann rejects this method. His aim is to interpret the New Testament mythology, and in particular to give it an *existentialist* interpretation. He considers this justified by the nature of myth itself.

The real purpose of myth is not to present an objective picture of the world as it is, but to express man's understanding of himself in the world in which he lives. Myth should be interpreted not cosmologically, but anthropologically, or better still, existentially.
NEW TESTAMENT AND MYTHOLOGY

Such an existentialist interpretation bypasses the obstacle of the obsolete world-view and presents modern man with the *real* scandal of the gospel.

Bultmann's existentialist interpretation reduces the New Testament message to a close approximation to the teaching of the secular existentialist philosopher Martin Heidegger (died 1976), a colleague of Bultmann at Marburg from 1922 to 1928.

Bultmann himself acknowledges this, but retorts that philosophy is saying the same thing as the New Testament and saying it independently. Bultmann's demythologized gospel becomes a message about man and his need to act authentically in the face of dread and anxiety. Faith is 'to open ourselves freely to the future', it is 'obedient self-commitment and inward detachment from the world'. Apparently objective mythical statements have become existential statements about man. Bultmann himself admits to substituting anthropology for theology, to interpreting statements about God as statements about human life. 'It is therefore clear that if a man will speak of God, he must evidently *speak of himself*.'

Bultmann has had to face many criticisms. While he disavows the liberal way of reducing the content of the Christian faith, the end product is no more hospitable to traditional doctrines than was liberalism. Such familiar doctrines as the incarnation, atonement, resurrection and second coming of Jesus Christ are all branded as mythical and are dissolved in an existentialist interpretation. The resurrection, for instance, is 'utterly inconceivable' as a historical event. The real Easter event is the miracle of faith in the message of the cross. Such 'interpretation' leaves very little of the *Apostles' Creed* intact.

It has rightly been observed that what Bultmann eliminates from the New Testament is not just myth but *history*. What he teaches is justification by (personal existential) faith alone and not by history (the saving events recorded in the Gospels). The Jesus Christ whom we encounter today is the Christ of preaching, not the Jesus of history. As one interpreter has put it, 'God's great drama has become an "existentialist private performance."'

Bultmann has rightly drawn our attention to the issue of interpretation. The gulf between our modern world-view and the biblical world-view(s) is crucial. But two different issues are being blurred. First, there is the question of the shape, size and age of the universe. Here it can be acknowledged that all educated modern

people hold a (scientific) view of the universe different from that held by the biblical writers. But this is not a major problem as the biblical message is not about such matters.

Secondly, there is the modern belief that the universe is a closed physical mechanism of cause and effect and that nothing happens which cannot be explained in such terms. Related to this is the denial of the supernatural and of the possibility of God intervening in this world. These questions clearly *do* impinge directly upon much of the New Testament message. But here one can no longer generalize about 'modern man'. Many educated people from all walks of life still believe in the supernatural God's intervention in this world in sending his Son and by raising him from the dead—doctrines derided by Bultmann. Outside organized religion, there is much evidence (such as interest in the occult) that the 'official' dogma of a closed physical universe does not satisfy ordinary people.

Bultmann fails to distinguish between the findings of *science* concerning the structure of the universe and a particular *philosophical* stance, which excludes the supernatural. He states that the only criticisms of the New Testament world-view which are valid are those which arise *necessarily* out of the modern situation—not those arising from optional philosophical positions. By this criterion he should have accepted the validity of the scientific understanding of the structure of the universe, not of philosophical rejection of the supernatural.

Bultmann translates Christianity into terms of existentialist philosophy. But how does this differ from what *Augustine did with Neo-Platonism or *Thomas Aquinas with Aristotelianism? Augustine and Thomas clearly acknowledged the primacy and authority of the Christian revelation. They both parted company with their philosophy where they saw that it conflicted with Scripture—e.g. over the goodness of creation or the eternity of the universe. Bultmann, by contrast, does not accord Scripture such a normative role and is not as critical of existentialism as were these others of their philosophies. Bultmann has been criticized for taking the modern world-view as normative and not allowing Scripture or the Christian message to contradict it. He himself replied to the charge and it is fitting to allow him the last word, even if one is not convinced by it.

It is of course true that demythologizing takes the modern world-view as a criterion. To demythologize is to reject not Scripture or the Christian message as a whole, but the world-view of Scripture, which is the world-view of a past epoch, which all too often is retained in Christian dogmatics and in the preaching of the church. To demythologize is to deny that the message of Scripture and of the church is bound to an ancient world-view which is obsolete.

JESUS CHRIST AND MYTHOLOGY, CHAPTER 3

Paul Tillich
SHAKING THE FOUNDATIONS

Paul Tillich was born in 1886 in the province of Brandenburg in (present-day East) Germany, the son of a Lutheran pastor. He studied theology at the Universities of Berlin, Tübingen, Halle and Breslau. During the First World War he served as an army chaplain. From 1919 he taught theology and philosophy in the Universities of Berlin, Marburg, Dresden, Leipzig and Frankfurt. But in 1933 he was dismissed by the Nazis because of his socialist commitments. He went to the USA and (thanks to *Reinhold Niebuhr) became professor of philosophical theology at the Union Theological Seminary in New York until his retirement in 1955. He then taught at Harvard and Chicago Universities until his death in 1965.

Tillich's greatest work was a three-volume *Systematic Theology* (1951–63). In it he sets out his theological approach.

A theological system is supposed to satisfy two basic needs: the statement of the truth of the Christian message and the interpretation of this truth for every new generation. Theology moves back and forth between two poles, the eternal truth of its foundation and the temporal situation in which the eternal truth must be received.

SYSTEMATIC THEOLOGY 1:3

He opposed orthodoxy, which he accused of confusing eternal truths with a particular temporary expression of them. Orthodoxy takes a theology which was addressed to the past and addresses it to today's situation, which it no longer fits. He also opposed the 'kerygmatic theology' of *Barth and others. This theology avoids the mistake of simply *identifying* the unchangeable message of the gospel with the Bible or with traditional orthodoxy, but it overemphasizes the eternal truth at the expense of the temporal situation.

The result is that 'the message must be thrown at those in the situation—thrown like a stone'. He said that the imbalance of kerygmatic theology needed to be corrected by 'apologetic theology'. 'Apologetics' was a dirty word to Barth and his followers, and Tillich sought to rehabilitate it.

Apologetic theology must heed the warning of the Neo-Orthodox—it must beware of allowing the Christian content to be swallowed up by the contemporary situation. But despite this danger, the task of apologetic must be attempted; the situation must be taken seriously.

Apologetic theology 'answers the questions implied in the "situation" in the power of the eternal message and with the means provided by the situation whose questions it answers.'

Apologetic theology seeks a method which will relate the eternal message and the contemporary situation without smothering one or the other. Tillich has such a method—his 'method of correlation', a way of adapting the Christian message to the modern mind without losing its distinctive character. His method is first to take seriously the questions posed by the modern situation (as much kerygmatic theology fails to do) and then to provide answers which are based on the eternal message (and not simply derived from the contemporary situation).

The great majority of theologians would accept the validity of this method—the need to address the eternal message to the contemporary situation. But many of them would feel that Tillich did not succeed in his aim. They would claim that he fell into the trap which he himself describes—that of sacrificing elements of the eternal truth to the situation. His exposition of the Christian faith is predominantly philosophical—biblical passages are few and far between in his *Systematic Theology*. God is presented as 'that which concerns us ultimately' or 'the ground of our being'. God is not *a* Being (who may or may not exist), but Being-itself. In fact it is as atheistic to affirm God's existence as to deny it! God can be described as personal, but he is not a person. Tillich's view of God is well-expressed in a sermon on *The Depth of Existence*.

The name of this infinite and inexhaustible depth and ground of all being is God. That depth is what the word God means. And if that word has not much meaning for you, translate it, and speak of the depths of your life, of the source of your being, of your ultimate concern, of what you take seriously without any reservation. Perhaps, in order to do so, you must forget everything traditional that you have learned about God, perhaps even that word itself. For if you know that God means depth, you know much about him. You cannot then call yourself an atheist or unbeliever.

It is only the person who in complete seriousness can say that life is shallow who is an atheist.

Tillich's influence has waned since his death. But his approach to the doctrine of God is still followed by many. John Robinson, in his *Honest to God* (1963), was the most influential popularizer of his views. More recently Don Cupitt has written a blistering attack on the traditional Christian doctrine of God, entitled *Taking Leave of God* (1980), in which he advocates a 'Christian-Buddhist' concept of God similar to that of Tillich. There are many today within the churches who continue to speak of God but who admit that as regards the traditional Christian conception of God as a Being who exists, they are atheists.

RECENT DEVELOPMENTS

Many Protestant theologians today stand in the Liberal, Evangelical, Neo-Orthodox or Existential traditions. Others have adopted different approaches. Process Theology offers a new doctrine of God. Moltmann and Pannenberg are two contemporary theologians who have developed their own individual theologies.

Process Theology
THE EVOLVING GOD

After the First World War, Process Philosophy was developed by A.N. Whitehead (died 1947) and Charles Hartshorne. This philosophy, which includes a view of God, has been adopted by theologians, giving rise to Process Theology. Its best-known exponents are J.B. Cobb, S.M. Ogden and W.N. Pittenger. It is very influential, especially in the USA. A Roman Catholic version is found in the writings of *Teilhard de Chardin.

*Greek philosophy thought of being and permanence as primary, becoming and change as secondary and relatively unreal. This means that God is thought to be unchanging and therefore free from emotions and suffering, remote from the realm of becoming and change. Salvation is the process of escaping from the realm of becoming and thus being impassible (immune from suffering) like God. God inhabits a changeless eternity. He is outside time, which is a secondary and temporary phenomenon. The implications of this philosophical theory can be illustrated by considering our view of ourselves. Am 'I' an . individual who lives for some seventy years through a variety of circumstances and experiences? If so, what is the 'I', since I change dramatically through the seventy

years? Process Philosophy maintains that the primary, most real thing is not 'I' as an entity or individual who happens to pass through time, but the series of experiences which make up the process of my life. The idea of 'I' as an individual who travels through time is not an illusion, but it is an abstraction. The primary reality is the *process* of my life—the concept of 'I' as an individual is a secondary abstraction. For Process Philosophy is process, becoming, change that is primary and ultimate—a complete reversal of the Greek view. Process Philosophy fits well into the modern world, where reality is seen in evolutionary terms— as dynamic and unfolding rather than static and 'given'.

The Greek approach leads to a picture of God as eternal in the sense of being outside time, as unchanging and static, as the cause of all things who is not affected by them (the 'Unmoved Mover'). But this contrasts with the God of the Bible who acts and relates to us in time, who is dynamically involved in the world, and who is affected by his people to the extent of grieving over them. Traditional philosophical theology accepts the Greek view of God and seeks to reconcile the biblical picture to it. *Anselm does this very frankly. How, he asks, can God be both compassionate [as the Bible teaches] and passionless [as philosophy teaches]? The answer is that God is compassionate in terms of our experience, while not compassionate in terms of his own being.

For when you behold us in our wretchedness, we experience the effects of compassion, but you do not experience the feeling. Therefore you are both compassionate (because you save the wretched and spare sinners) and not compassionate (because you are not affected by sympathy for wretchedness).

ANSELM, PROSLOGION 8

This is not a biblical paradox. It is simply the irreconcilable conflict between the (biblical) view of God as compassionate and the (Greek) view of God as impassible.

Process Theology rejects classical theism, replacing it with a 'dipolar' concept of God. This is based on a distinction between 'abstract existence' and 'concrete actuality'. World decathlon hero Daley Thompson has an 'abstract existence' as a brilliant athlete, while this is seen in a varied 'concrete actuality' as be manifests his brilliance by jumping, running, throwing, etc. Process Theology is prepared to accept Greek ideas of God as eternal, unchanging and the cause of all things—but only with reference to his abstract existence. God is eternal in the sense that he always has been and always will be. But he travels *with us* along time. At this moment, 1982 is past and 2082 is future for God. He is unchanging in that his love remains constant, but not in the sense of being static and inactive. He is the cause of all things in that they have their existence from him and are dependent upon him. But he is not unaffected by his creation. He gives the universe a real though limited freedom so that we can become cause and he become effect. If I reject him, I grieve him. Thus we have a 'dipolar' view of God—as cause *and* effect.

The process view of God is often called 'panentheism' or 'neoclassical theism'. God is not unaffected by the world (classical theism) nor identified with it (pantheism), but he both affects and is affected by it. All that happens takes place *in* God—the world

is God's body. The relation between God and the world can be compared to that between mind and body. God and the world move together through time.

Process Theology makes an eloquent biblical protest against classical theism and sees itself as a return to a more biblical view of God. Most of the points made against classical theism are valid and today the irreconcilable difference between the Greek philosophical and biblical views of God are widely recognized. But unfortunately, Process Theology falls into the same error as classical theism, allowing its philosophical starting point to distort its understanding of God. Two examples show this clearly:

● Process Theology denies that God knows the future, on the grounds that it does not yet exist. God is omniscient—but this means that he knows all that exists and can be known, not that he knows that which does not yet exist. Everyone would agree that an omniscient God does not know the name of Henry VIII's seventh wife (who never existed). Similarly, his ignorance of the future (which does not yet exist) does not undermine his omniscience. But the Bible portrays God as one who *does* know the future. Behind this lies the issue of God's relation to time. If classical theism makes the mistake of seeing God as *outside* time, Process Theology makes the opposite mistake of making him the prisoner of time—controlled by it just as we are, travelling with us along time. If we are to take seriously God's immanence and transcendence, we must see him as both active in time and yet transcending our time. God can be compared not to a police car travelling with us along the road, nor to a satellite remotely observing us from space, but to a helicopter which can both travel along the road and yet rise above it.

● Process Theology reacts against the classical theist view that creation cannot affect God, to the extent of making God dependent upon the universe. It is often held that God *needs* the universe and that the universe is eternal. But the Bible portrays God as the one who freely brought the universe into existence out of nothing. While

JÜRGEN MOLTMANN | 221 |

the biblical view is of a God who reacts with the world and is affected by it (as Process Theology maintains), he is also a God who is independent of the world, and not dependent upon it as the mind/body analogy suggests.

Process Theology is a fresh, new approach which sheds light on the biblical doctrine of God. But once Process Philosophy is allowed to *control* our concept of God and to censor the biblical account, Process Theology begins to distort the biblical doctrine just as the Greek philosophical view has done.

For [Process Theology], since all existence... is a 'becoming' and a 'belonging'—a process which is societal in character—God himself as the chief exemplification of such categories is taken to be the supreme instance of becoming and of belonging. The former is a way of insisting that he is not to be envisaged as so much above temporal succession that history is irrelevant to him... The latter (belonging) is true of God precisely because he is so related to the world that there is between him and that world a 'give-and-take'... He is influenced by what happens.

W. N. PITTENGER, PICTURING GOD, CHAPTER 4

Jürgen Moltmann
THE CRUCIFIED GOD

Jürgen Moltmann was born in 1926 at Hamburg. From 1945 to 1948 he was a prisoner of war in Belgium and Britain. It was during this time that he came to Christian faith, thus becoming 'the first black sheep in my enlightened Hamburg family'. In 1952, after studying theology, he became a pastor. He was made professor at the church seminary at Wuppertal in 1958, and in 1967 he became professor of systematic theology at Tübingen University, where he remains to this day.

Moltmann is a prolific writer. His major works fall into two groups. The aim of the first three was 'to look at theology as a whole from one particular standpoint'. These

volumes contain some brilliant and fresh insights into the Christian faith, but they also suffer from the inevitable one-sidedness that comes from concentrating on a single perspective. Thereafter he embarked on a new series of 'systematic contributions to theology', under the overall title of 'Messianic Theology'. These are systematic in that there is a progression through various doctrines, with a thorough discussion of each one in turn. But the aim is to produce 'contributions', written from one particular theologian's perspective, not a fully rounded dogmatic system. In other words, Moltmann is not attempting to reduplicate *Barth's *Church Dogmatics*. Three works have so far appeared in this series and a further two are projected.

Moltmann's first major work was his *Theology of Hope* (1964) in which the Christian faith is viewed from the perspective of future hope in general and the resurrection of Christ in particular. This book established him as one of the major theologians of the generation following Barth and *Bultmann. For some time biblical studies have recognized the vital role played by eschatology (the doctrine of the end) in the New Testament—not just as a belief about certain events at the end of time but as a factor which moulds *all* Christian theology. Moltmann is one of the first dogmatic theologians to attempt seriously to expound theology in this light. He complains that relegating the doctrine of the last things to the 'last day' makes of them a mere appendix to theology, a last chapter of a systematic theology which is unrelated to the rest. Moltmann seeks to restore eschatology to the centre of theology.

From first to last, and not merely in the epilogue, Christianity is eschatology, is hope, forward looking and forward moving, and therefore also revolutionising and transforming the present. The eschatological is not one element of Christianity, but it is the medium of Christian faith as such, the key in which everything in it is set, the glow that suffuses everything here in the

dawn of an expected new day ... The
eschatological outlook is characteristic
of all Christian proclamation, of every
Christian existence and of the whole
church.
THEOLOGY OF HOPE, INTRODUCTION

The eschatological perspective means that
revelation is interpreted as *promise*, as the
ground for future hope. This is the basis for
mission—which is seen as the
transformation of the world in anticipation
of the promised new creation. The church is
'like an arrow sent out into the world to point
to the future'. The goal of Christian mission
is not merely an individual, personal,
'spiritual' salvation. It is also the realization
of the hope of justice, the socializing of
humanity and peace for all creation. This
'other side' of reconciliation with God has
been neglected in the Christian church, says
Moltmann. The church is to work for social
change *now*—on the basis of *future* hope.
The New Testament sees the expectation of
God's salvation in the future not as an
excuse for inactivity now, but as the
encouragement that 'in the Lord your labour
is not in vain' (1 Corinthians 15:58). Social
action is grounded in Christian hope. This
theology of hope has been very influential,
both in the *World Council of Churches and
in *Liberation Theology.

In *The Crucified God* (1972) Moltmann
expounds the doctrine of God from the
perspective of the cross. This means an end
to ideas of God as impassible and remote
from the world. The Christian God is a
suffering God of love. Moltmann accepts
that God is unchangeable and impassible in
one sense: unlike his creatures, he cannot be
forced to change or suffer by something
external to himself. But this does not exclude
two other possibilities. God is free to change
himself. More significantly, he is free to
allow himself to be changed by others; to
allow others to make him suffer. This does
not prejudice God's sovereignty. God's
suffering is not a suffering imposed from
outside, caused by weakness, but the
suffering of love, an active suffering. God
voluntarily opens himself to the possibility

of being affected by his creatures. This is an
accepted suffering, a free suffering of love,
as opposed to an unwilling suffering.
Without such suffering we cannot speak of a
God of love. Moltmann movingly links this
concept of a suffering God with Jewish
experience, using an extract from a book by
Elie Wiesel, a survivor of the holocaust.

The SS hanged two Jewish men and a
youth in front of the whole camp. The
men died quickly, but the death throes of
the youth lasted for half an hour.
'Where is God? Where is he?' someone
asked behind me. As the youth still hung
in torment in the noose after a long
time, I heard the man call again, 'Where
is God now?' And I heard a voice in
myself answer: 'Where is he? He is here.
He is hanging there on the gallows ...'
THE CRUCIFIED GOD, CHAPTER 6:9

'Any other answer would be blasphemy,'
concludes Moltmann. 'There cannot be any
other Christian answer to the question of this
torment.'

In *The Church in the Power of the Spirit*
(1975) Moltmann considers the doctrine of
the church from the perspective of Pentecost
and the doctrine of the Holy Spirit. The
church is to be open—'open for God, open for
men and open for the future of both God and
men'. This demands renewal in the church as
it faces a rapidly changing world. But 'what
is required today is not adroit adaptation to
changed social conditions, but the inner
renewal of the church by the spirit of Christ,
the power of the coming kingdom.' This
book is rightly seen as the least profound of
his major works.

The narrow focus of the first three books,
each looking at theology as a whole from one
particular viewpoint, is both their strength
and their weakness. The latter is largely
corrected in the following volumes, which
build on the insights of the earlier series,
integrating them into a more balanced
overall perspective. The first of these is *The*
Trinity and the Kingdom of God (1980),
where Moltmann develops some of the
themes of *The Crucified God* especially. The

doctrine of God's passibility is spelt out in greater detail. In *The Crucified God* Moltmann had sought to base the doctrine of the Trinity upon the event of the cross, and Jesus' cry of dereliction in particular. In *The Trinity and the Kingdom of God* this is broadened out and the doctrine of the Trinity is developed out of the whole 'history of the Son', from his incarnation to his parousia at the End.

Moltmann breaks with the Western tradition which starts with God's unity and then proceeds to ask about his Trinity. His way is to start with the 'trinitarian history of God', with a dynamic portrayal of the acts of all three persons in the creation and redemption of the world. This leads him to a 'social doctrine of the Trinity', in which the threeness is taken seriously. He found inspiration while writing the book from a famous fifteenth-century Russian icon which portrays the Trinity as three people in an intimate harmony. He claims that stress on the unity of God has led to authoritarian and repressive regimes in church and society. By contrast, Moltmann uses his social doctrine of the Trinity to develop a 'trinitarian doctrine of the kingdom', drawing upon the ideas of *Joachim of Fiore, and thus a 'trinitarian doctrine of freedom'. The doctrine of the Trinity is not an exercise in abstract theology, but serves as a foundation for the liberating mission of the church in society today.

God in Creation (1985) sets out an 'ecological doctrine of creation'. In each of the earlier volumes Moltmann was concerned to spell out the political outworkings of his theology; in this and the next volume that is focussed especially into a concern for ecology. The present crisis demands, he claims, a stress on God's immanence, in contrast to the emphasis on God's transcendence which has predominated in the past. So Moltmann focusses on the role of the Holy Spirit, whom he sees as God indwelling creation. He also asks not just what it means for the universe that it has been created by God, but also what it means for God to be creator. In this book, as in others, Moltmann interacts with Jewish theology, which influences his thought at a number of key points.

The Way of Jesus Christ (1989) is a fresh and wide-ranging new approach to the person of Christ, again with an eye to ecological concerns. Moltmann seeks to develop a new approach for the 'postmodern world', focussing especially on contemporary problems such as poverty, the nuclear threat and the ecological crisis. He seeks to build on the positive features of earlier approaches to the person of Christ, but also to address the current situation. As in all of his books since *Theology of Hope*, this includes an emphasis on future hope. Moltmann also, as the title suggests, devotes attention not just to right belief about Jesus, but to 'christopraxis', to the ethical teaching of Jesus. This is seen in his application of the Sermon on the Mount not just to private life, but also to the public and political arena.

Wolfhart Pannenberg
FAITH ROOTED IN HISTORY

Wolfhart Pannenberg was born in 1928 in Stettin in Germany—now Szczecin in Poland. After the war he studied at Berlin and Göttingen Universities. During these years he moved beyond secularism to Christian faith. In 1950 he went to Basel to study theology under *Karl Barth. The following year he moved to Heidelberg. There he was one of a group of research students who subsequently came to be known as the 'Pannenberg circle'. Their discussions bore fruit in a joint publication entitled *Revelation as History* (1961). The group continued to meet regularly until 1969, when differences over the historicity of the resurrection undermined their common approach. Pannenberg became a lecturer in theology at Heidelberg in 1955. In 1958 he moved to become professor of systematic theology at a church seminary at Wuppertal—where he was for a time a colleague of *Moltmann. He then became professor of systematic theology at Mainz University in 1961 and in 1968 he moved to the same post at Munich University, where he remains.

While Pannenberg was deeply influenced by Barth, he has reacted against him at some points. In particular, he opposes the attempt of Barth, *Bultmann and others to divorce theology from historical criticism. He rejects the twentieth-century tendency to ignore the 'Jesus of history' (the picture of Jesus given by historical criticism) and to base theology exclusively on the 'Christ of faith' (Jesus as proclaimed by the early church). Pannenberg insists that theology must be based on history and must be open to investigation by other disciplines. To claim that an event such as the resurrection of Jesus Christ is accessible only to 'faith' is to withdraw the gospel from the market place of human knowledge, to make theology an esoteric study for those in the know.

Pannenberg offers a radically new concept of revelation, which he expounds in seven dogmatic theses in *Revelation as History*. Against the Neo-Orthodox and existentialist approaches, which divorced revelation from history, Pannenberg locates God's revelation in the events of history—especially in the person of Jesus Christ and supremely in his resurrection. Barth vehemently opposed any attempt to demonstrate the historicity of the resurrection and saw its truth as accessible only to those with faith. Pannenberg argues that this turns theology into a private theory of the believer, divorced from the rest of human knowledge. The Christian faith becomes 'truth for the in-group'. He insists that the truth-claims of Christianity, and the historicity of the resurrection in particular, are open to verification. He claims that the evidence points clearly to Jesus' resurrection from the dead. To come to believe in Jesus' resurrection is simply to acknowledge the truth that lies before our eyes. Accepting its truth 'is a natural consequence of the facts'. If it is hidden from most people it is not because their reason needs to be supplemented by some other means of knowing. Rather, 'they must use their reason in order to see correctly'. Faith is not something that is brought to the event of the resurrection in order to be able to see it—faith is itself

kindled by the event. Does this not render faith superfluous? No. Historical criticism yields probabilities, not certainties. We cannot *prove* that ancient historians did not invent a fictitious person called Julius Caesar in order to play a prank on posterity. Such a hypothesis is extremely unlikely—but it cannot be disproved. Historical criticism, based on the evidence, shows the probability of the resurrection. Faith goes beyond (but not against) knowledge by giving us certainty. In the same way, rational argument can demonstrate the extreme likelihood of my wife's fidelity, but my trust in her goes beyond a merely probable opinion to become a sure confidence. While such faith may go beyond the evidence, it is based securely on evidence which is accessible to all.

For Pannenberg, revelation is found in history—not just a special portion of history known as 'salvation history' but *all* of history, *universal* history. This means that God's revelation is not complete until the end of history. But we are not left in the dark. 'In the fate of Jesus, the end of history is experienced in advance as an anticipation.' In fact with the resurrection of Jesus, the end of history has already occurred—because 'the end of the world will be on a cosmic scale what has already happened in Jesus'. This means that no further revelation of God can be expected. He does continue to disclose himself in history after the time of Jesus, 'but not in any fundamentally new way, but rather as the one who has already been revealed in the fate of Jesus'.

Pannenberg offers a valuable corrective to the major trends of twentieth-century theology. His stress on the resurrection as an objective, verifiable event brings theology back into contact with history. But it must not be forgotten that faith is more than rational evaluation of evidence. There is a immoral and spiritual dimension to our reaction to Jesus Christ. 'This is the judgement, that the light has come into the world, and men loved darkness rather than light, because their deeds were evil' (John 3:19). This is why 'no one can say "Jesus is Lord" except by the Holy Spirit' (1 Corinthians 12:3).

Pannenberg has written many major works over the years. But his best known and probably greatest work is his *Jesus—God and Man*, which appeared in 1964. Here he argues that there are two different ways of approaching Christology, the doctrine of Jesus Christ. One is 'Christology from above'—which starts with the divine Son of God and then asks how and in what way he became man. The other is 'Christology from below'—which starts with the man Jesus of Nazareth and then asks how and in what way he was God. Pannenberg discounts the former approach. Christology from above presupposes Jesus' deity—while the most important task for Christology today is precisely to demonstrate his deity. Christology from above leads to a reduced interest in the historical Jesus—attention being focussed instead on discussing how the 'two natures' of deity and humanity can be united in one person. Pannenberg's way is to start 'from below', from the historical Jesus, and from there to arrive at his deity. It is the resurrection which demonstrates his deity. 'If Jesus, having been raised from the dead, is ascended to God and if thereby the end of the world has begun, then God is ultimately revealed in Jesus.' The resurrection shows Jesus' unity with the Father. It is the vindication by God of all his earlier claims— which would otherwise have remained empty assertions. The incarnation, God becoming man, is thus seen as the conclusion, not the starting-point, of Christology.

In his revelational unity with God, which constitutes Jesus' own divinity, Jesus at the same time still remains distinct from God as his Father. The beginning of the doctrine of the Trinity lies in this.
JESUS—GOD AND MAN, CHAPTER 4

Feminist Theology

The twentieth century began with demands for women to have the vote. At the end of the century this has led on to much more radical demands for greater justice and equality. This quest has had major implications both for the church and for Christian theology. The most obvious and visible manifestation is the issue of women's ordination. But the challenge to theology is no less radical, with questions about the portrayal of God as Father and the concept of a male Saviour. There is also concern about the way in which traditional Christianity has been overwhelmingly patriarchal, based on male rule with women having a clearly subordinate role. The view of some of the church Fathers that it is only the male that fully possesses the image of God is a good example of this. Feminist theology, like *Liberation Theology, is a broad term covering a wide range of approaches. Space permits a brief mention of just four of these.

There are some whose feminist concerns have led them to reject the Christian faith. Most noteworthy among these is the (former) Roman Catholic Mary Daly. Her *The Church and the Second Sex* (1968) was an important early contribution to feminist theology. But by the time of her *Beyond God the Father* (1973) she had parted company with the Christian faith. She is sceptical of those who think that the Bible can be disentangled from the patriarchal tradition. 'It might be interesting to speculate on the probable length of a "depatriarchalized Bible". Perhaps there would be enough salvageable material to comprise an interesting pamphlet.'

One who has sought to trace alternative non-patriarchal strands in the Christian tradition is another Roman Catholic, Rosemary Radford Ruether, perhaps the most prolific of the feminist theologians. In an essay on 'The Liberation of Christology from Patriarchy' she argues that the ministry of Jesus proclaimed good news for despised people, including women. The first witnesses to the resurrection were women. Jesus' approach overturned established hierarchies. But the church had to relate to the patriarchal, hierarchical society of its time. This led to two different approaches. One of these continued stress on equality, seeing it as an anticipation of the age to come and therefore linking it with the practice of celibacy. The other approach adopted the patriarchal and hierarchical framework of society at large. The first approach gave birth to groups which in due course came to be seen as heretical. It also gave birth to the monastic movement, which was accommodated within the mainstream church—but in subjection to the patriarchal hierarchy. Protestantism eliminated the first approach and thus strengthened the patriarchal emphasis. But the 'eschatological counter-culture' reappeared in the guise of various sects. Ruether urges that we need to overcome the common presupposition that underlies *both* approaches: that patriarchy is the original order of nature. We need instead to think of an original order that was egalitarian and see the patriarchal state as a distortion of nature. Redemption is then seen to include the restoration of the original, authentic, egalitarian nature.

Elisabeth Schüssler Fiorenza's *In Memory of Her* (1983), the title echoing Mark 14:9, is another work which has had a major influence. She stresses the need to see the role that women played in early Christian history, a role that is often overlooked by male biblical exegesis. 'Both Christian feminist theology and biblical interpretation are in process of rediscovering that the Christian gospel cannot be proclaimed if the women disciples and what they have done are not remembered.' The book has two goals: 'to reconstruct early Christian history as women's history in order not only to restore women's stories to early Christian history but also to reclaim this history as the history of women and men.'

Finally, there is the evangelical movement of feminist theology, which seeks to incorporate feminist concerns within a framework of submission to biblical authority and loyalty to evangelical beliefs. Elaine Storkey would be a leading British representative of this approach. In her *What's Right with Feminism* (1985) she urges a biblically-based Christian feminism as a 'third way' between on the one hand a Christian anti-feminism and on the other hand a feminism which parts company with biblical teaching.

Christian feminists are not therefore wanting any power struggle with men. That would be entirely foreign to their agenda. Nor are they wanting to construct an all-female reality which washes its hands of any involvement with the other sex. But they are not happy simply to slip into a slot marked 'woman' and live their lives according to a set of prescribed cultural and essentially non-biblical values. The message they bring is a message of liberation, and it is for men also.

WHAT'S RIGHT WITH FEMINISM

THE ROMAN CATHOLICS

Until recently the Roman Catholic Church has been predominantly negative towards the modern world. But since Pope John XXIII the key word has been 'modernization', bringing the Roman Catholic Church into the twentieth century.

John Henry Newman
THE DEVELOPMENT OF DOCTRINE

John Henry Newman was born in 1801 into an Evangelical family. When he was fifteen he was deeply influenced by various Calvinist writings and underwent an Evangelical conversion: 'I fell under the influences of a definite Creed, and received into my intellect impressions of dogma which, through God's mercy, have never been effaced or obscured.' He studied at Oxford and in 1822 became a Fellow of Oriel College. Here his Evangelical convictions were undermined. First, he experienced a drift towards liberalism. Then he received a strong impulse in a different direction, from John Keble. Keble pointed him to the early church Fathers and this influenced his thinking in a 'catholic' direction.

In 1833 Keble preached his famous sermon on National Apostasy and this is traditionally seen as the launching of the Oxford Movement. Ironically, in the light of later developments, the occasion for the launch was the threat to the Church of England posed by the Catholic Emancipation Act of 1829 (giving Roman Catholics great political freedom) and the plan to weaken the Church of England in (Roman Catholic) Ireland. The positive principles of the movement include the following beliefs: episcopacy as the divinely-appointed means of church government, and the doctrine of apostolic succession (bishops who stand in an unbroken line from the apostles succeed to their authority); the right of the church to govern herself without state interference; the importance of the sacraments—including the doctrine of baptismal regeneration (new birth through baptism), the real presence (of Christ's body and blood in the eucharist) and the eucharist as a sacrifice offered to God. In many ways the Oxford Movement was a reaffirmation of traditional high church views. But its founders introduced a radically new element by turning to the early church in *opposition* to the Protestant Reformation. Some of them were violently hostile to the Reformers. (Their opponents in Oxford hit upon the brilliant idea of erecting a memorial to the martyr bishops *Cranmer, Latimer and Ridley by public subscription—thus forcing leaders of the Oxford Movement to declare their hands openly.)

The movement's views were expounded in a series of *Tracts for the Times*, begun in 1833—with the result that its adherents were called 'Tractarians'. The anti-Protestant tone caused much offence. Newman at this stage, in common with others, saw the Church of England as the middle way between Protestantism and Roman Catholicism. He still retained the traditional belief that the pope was the Antichrist. The early church he saw as the golden age, to which they were returning in pursuit of a pure catholic faith, not tainted by medieval Rome. The catholic faith was to be discerned by the principle enunciated by Vincent of Lerins (early fifth century): 'we hold to that which has been believed everywhere, always and by everyone [within the Catholic Church]'. In 1841 Newman wrote *Tract Ninety*. In this he argued that the *Thirty-nine Articles* were compatible with the teaching of the *Council of Trent. While the articles were *ambitious* of a Protestant interpretation, they were *patient* of Catholic interpretation. This tract aroused a storm of protest, which led to the termination of the series. One leading figure observed that he would no longer trust Newman with his silver.

Newman was disappointed at this time by the actions of the bishops. They were making decisions which seemed to indicate that despite the claims of the Tractarians the Church of England was after all a Protestant church. Newman lost his faith in the Church of England and gradually withdrew from involvement in it, leaving Oxford for a monastic retreat at Littlemore nearby. Intuitively he had come to see that it was Rome after all which was the true Catholic Church. But while his heart was won, his head knew that in many ways Rome differed from the early church. How could his head be reconciled to his heart? Gradually he came to see the answer in the concept of the *development* of doctrine. He set this out in his famous *Essay on the Development of Christian Doctrine*, written while an Anglican as a defence of his conversion to Rome. The *Essay* was published unaltered after his conversion in 1845, with a postscript submitting it to the judgement of the church.

Newman began by establishing that 'whatever be historical Christianity, it is not Protestantism. If ever there were a safe truth, it is this.' And Protestants know it. They prefer to forget the Middle Ages—and they are none too happy with the early church either. (Newman's point is reflected by the manner in which many Protestants speak of 'historic Christianity', when they really mean 'Protestantism since the sixteenth century'.) But Newman has to admit, as a good historian, that the Roman Catholic Church is not identical to the early church. There is, though, an essential identity between the early Catholic Church and the modern Roman Catholic Church.

Did St Athanasius or St Ambrose come suddenly to life, it cannot be doubted what communion they would mistake for their own. All surely will agree that these fathers, with whatever differences of opinion, whatever protests, if we will, would find themselves more at home with such men as St Bernard or St Ignatius Loyola, or with the lonely priest in his lodgings, or the holy sisterhood of mercy, or the unlettered crowd before the altar, than with the rulers or the members of any other religious community.

ESSAY ON THE DEVELOPMENT OF CHRISTIAN DOCTRINE, 3:1

Having ascertained that the Roman Catholic Church is the closest approximation to the early church, Newman needs to explain the changes. He does not accept the traditional claim that the Roman Catholic Church is 'always the same', never changing. He does not overcome history by dogmatic assertions of changelessness, as in the papal bull *Ineffabilis Deus*. Instead he acknowledges change and seeks to explain it.

Changes came because doctrine *develops*. Such growth or development of doctrine is inevitable: the church grows in understanding over the ages; the unsystematic doctrine of the Bible needs to be ordered and arranged; there is the need to react to false teaching; new ages pose new questions which demand new answers. Change and development are inevitable. But not all change or development is healthy— there are cancerous growths. How can development be tested?

Newman gives seven tests of a faithful development of doctrine. These include a continuity of basic principle throughout the development, a logical sequence from one doctrine to another and the test of time. He uses all of these tests to defend Roman Catholic developments in doctrine. But he did not imagine that these tests were sufficient on their own—that the private individual or scholar could use them to discern for himself true and false developments. The church needs an infallible arbiter to discern between the true and the false. Without such a guide, the church is caught on the horns of a dilemma. Either she retains an organizational unity at the expense of unity of doctrine (leading to a broad comprehensive church like the present Church of England), or she maintains unity of doctrine at the expense of organizational unity (with small dogmatic sectarian churches each claiming purity of doctrine). The infallible guide enables one to combine organizational unity with doctrinal unity. But where is such an infallible guide to be found? There is only one serious contender, claims Newman. Only the Roman Catholic Church combines both prominence and permanence. Roman doctrine has a consistency which its opponents 'feel to be superhuman, though they will not allow it to be divine'—i.e. many see it as satanic.

Newman presents a very powerful case and it is not surprising that many of his fellow Tractarians found it persuasive. (Strangely, it was the former Evangelicals among the Tractarians—such as Henry Manning and the Wilberforces—who followed Newman to Rome; those from a high church background do not appear to have felt the force of his argument.) But there are a number of weaknesses. First, it is one thing to explain *how* doctrines have developed (which Newman does ably). It is another thing to *justify* these developments. Newman shows, for instance, how the idea that we need to offer God 'satisfaction' for sins committed after baptism (found in *Tertullian and *Cyprian) leads on naturally to the Roman ideas of penance, merits, indulgences, purgatory and masses for the dead. The development is there—but is it the emergence of truth or rather a progressive corruption following from an early mistake about the forgiveness of post-baptismal sin? Secondly, Newman dismisses the Eastern Orthodox churches without adequately considering their claims. He refers to 'the infallible *western* church'. But if there is to be an infallible guide, why should it be the Western rather than the Eastern Catholic Church? In many ways the Eastern Orthodox concept of authority can claim to be older than the later papal system.

Newman makes a good *prima facie* case for the infallible church. He gives good reasons why it should be desirable. But there are also good reasons against it. Once the church becomes the infallible interpreter of Scripture, the latter has lost its real authority. Once the church has spoken on a subject, the Bible is no longer allowed to contradict her. Christians read the Old Testament through the eyes of the New Testament. One clear word in the New Testament declaring all foods clean (Mark 7:19) is sufficient to abrogate all the Old Testament food laws. The acceptance of the New Testament leaves the Old Testament with only a *relative* authority—because the New Testament tells us how to read it in a Christian way. Newman himself accepts that the relation of the church's teaching to the Bible can fairly be compared to that of the New Testament to the Old. But while it is God's unique revelation in his Son Jesus Christ which justifies us in according such a status to the New Testament, what is the new factor which enables the church likewise to relativize the New Testament? The pope is not to Jesus Christ what the latter is to Judaism.

Also, an examination of some of the irreformable dogmas promulgated by the infallible church—such as the Virgin Mary's immaculate conception and assumption (defined in *Ineffabilis Deus* and *Munificentissimus Deus*)—suggests that the price to be paid for doctrinal uniformity is too high. Such dogmas show the need for all doctrine to be tested by the Bible—even at the expense of opening the doors to a variety of interpretations.

Newman's ideas met with a frosty reception in the ultra-dogmatic nineteenth-century Roman Catholic Church. It was his fellow ex-Evangelical, Henry Manning, who became Cardinal Archbishop of Westminster (although Newman was eventually made a cardinal in 1879). Manning was of a different temper to

Newman. 'The appeal to history is heresy and treason', he maintained. But Newman's day was to come. If the *First Vatican Council, which defined papal infallibility, was Manning's council, the *Second Vatican Council, which acknowledged development in doctrine, may be called Newman's council. It has even been claimed, with tongue in cheek, that in the long run it was the Roman Catholic Church which was converted to Newman, not vice versa.

Ineffabilis Deus (1854)

At the beginning of the medieval period the idea began to creep in that the Virgin Mary had lived without sin. *Augustine at least allows for the possibility that she may not have sinned. By the seventh century the idea of the sinlessness of Mary became generally accepted. But *when* was she delivered from sin? *Anselm held that she was born with original sin. *Bernard of Clairvaux, *Bonaventure and *Thomas Aquinas held that she was conceived with original sin but cleansed of all sin before her birth. It was *Duns Scotus who argued that Mary was conceived immaculately, i.e. that she was preserved from sin in her very conception, not just after it. He held this on the ground that it is more perfect to preserve someone from original sin than to liberate them from it. Jesus Christ, as the perfect redeemer, must have redeemed someone in the most perfect way possible—and who could be more fitting than his mother?

The doctrine of Mary's immaculate conception became a bone of contention between the Franciscans (Duns Scotus's order) and the Dominicans (Thomas Aquinas' order). So fierce was the controversy that in 1483 Pope Sixtus IV declared that the church had not yet decided on the matter and that neither side was heretical. Similarly, the *Council of Trent simply excludes the Virgin Mary from its decree on original sin. But eventually the doctrine of immaculate conception became generally accepted within the Roman Catholic Church. In 1854 it was solemnly defined as a dogma by Pope Pius IX, in the bull *Ineffabilis Deus* (named, as is customary, from the opening words of the bull).

We declare, pronounce and define that the most blessed Virgin Mary, at the first instant of her conception was preserved immaculate from all stain of original sin, by the singular grace and privilege of the omnipotent God, in virtue of the merits of Jesus Christ, the saviour of mankind, and that this doctrine was revealed by God and therefore must be believed firmly and constantly by all the faithful.

This pronouncement has implications beyond the doctrine of Mary. First, what is the *oasis* for the dogma? It is not Scripture, which does not teach the sinlessness of Mary, let alone her immaculate conception. It might appear to be tradition since the bull affirms that 'this doctrine has always existed in the church as a doctrine that has been received from our ancestors and that has been stamped with the character of revealed doctrine.' The church, the bull declares, never changes, diminishes or adds to her doctrine. This looks like an appeal to the testimony of unchanging tradition, but in fact it is the reverse. History shows that the major figures in the tradition (e.g. Augustine and Thomas Aquinas) not only did not hold the doctrine but expressly denied it. The bull represents not the fruit of tradition but the triumph of dogma over tradition. What then is the basis for the dogma? It is the consensus on the subject in the contemporary church. Pius had in 1849 invited the opinions of the bishops and the bull describes the strong affirmative response that he had received. Trent's exclusion of Mary from its decree on original sin is cited as evidence that Scripture and tradition do not *oppose* the doctrine. But the positive proof offered is the contemporary consensus in the church.

Secondly, if the bull reflects an increasing reliance on the contemporary consensus of the church, in defiance of

Scripture and tradition, it also represents a step forward for papal authority. The 1854 definition was in many ways a trial run for the doctrine of papal infallibility, defined at the *First Vatican Council in 1870. The next Marian dogma was her Assumption into heavenly glory, defined in the 1950 apostolic constitution *Munificentissimus Deus*.

First Vatican Council (1869–70)

In the centuries following the Reformation there were two rival views of authority in the Roman Catholic Church. The minority view, known as 'Gallicanism' since it was mainly found in France, saw the pope as a constitutional monarch. Following *William of Ockham and the conciliar movement of the fourteenth and fifteenth centuries, the Gallicans affirmed the authority of the general council over the pope. They held that the pope's judgement is not irreformable until it receives the consent of the church. These positions found classic statement in *Four Articles* promulgated at Paris in 1682. But by the nineteenth century the Gallican cause was in decline.

The majority view was that the pope was the absolute monarch in the church and that general councils derive their validity from him. It came to be known as 'Ultramontanism' (beyond the mountains (Alps) in Rome). In the nineteenth century the Ultramontane party was strong and agitated hard for the definition of papal infallibility. Pope Pius IX (pope from 1846 to 1878) held strongly to this view. In 1868 he called the First Vatican Council, which met from 1869 to 1870.

The council met at a time when the papal states, the area of central Italy traditionally ruled by the pope, were threatened by the new Italian state. They were being defended by a French army. But the outbreak of war between France and Prussia in 1870 forced the French army to withdraw. The Italian army took Rome and the pope suspended the council indefinitely. During the eight months of its activity the council produced two dogmatic constitutions. The first, *The Catholic Faith*, covered God as creator, revelation, faith and the relation of faith to reason. Far more important was the second, *The Church of Christ*, which defined papal infallibility.

By the time of the council, the majority of Roman Catholic bishops believed in papal infallibility. But such a term needs clarification. *When* is the pope infallible? The Englishman W. G. Ward, a convert from Anglicanism, took the extreme position that the pope's 'every doctrinal pronouncement is infallibly directed by the Holy Ghost'. While such views were held by a minority, the majority held to a much more modest concept of infallibility. In what *areas* is the pope infallible? Is he infallible on matters of history for instance? Finally, is the pope infallible in isolation from the church and the bishops? These questions were debated at the council.

A significant minority of the bishops did not want to see papal infallibility defined, for a variety of reasons. Some did not believe it. Some were afraid of extreme views, such as that of Ward. Others felt the definition to be *inopportune* even if true—and were therefore called 'Inopportunists'. They were concerned about the harmful effects of the definition upon relations with the Eastern Orthodox and Protestant churches—fears which were amply justified. *John Henry Newman (not at the council) had just such fears. In a private letter to his bishop he noted that while a council ought to strengthen the church, this one was set to cause fear and dismay by a 'luxury of devotion' (the definition).

When we are all at rest and have no doubts ... suddenly there is thunder in the clear sky, and we are told to prepare for something we know not what, to try our faith we know not how. No impending danger is to be averted, but a great difficulty is to be created. Is this the proper work for an ecumenical council?

The Ultramontanes controlled the council. Cardinal Manning (the former Evangelical) and others packed the deputation concerned with drafting the doctrinal definitions, to ensure that none of the minority opposed to the definition of infallibility should be included. In fact one of the twenty-four chosen by them and elected to the deputation had at the last minute changed his views and now opposed the definition of infallibility!

The crucial votes came in July 1870. At the penultimate vote on the text of the definition three-quarters of the bishops voted in favour. A deputation from the minority opposition went to see the pope and begged for a more moderate statement—but to no avail. Those still opposed to the definition decided that at the final session they could vote neither for it (because no one would believe them) nor against it (because of the scandal it would cause). They accordingly wrote to the pope reaffirming their opposition to the definition. They informed him that they were leaving the council in order not to have to vote against him—and to return to their dioceses 'grieving that in the existing sad condition of things, we shall find the peace and tranquillity of consciences disturbed'. At the final vote, with the minority absent, the decree was adopted by 533 votes to 2 against.

Faithfully adhering to the tradition received from the beginning of the Christian faith, for the glory of God our saviour, the exaltation of the Catholic religion and the salvation of Christian people, with the approval of the sacred council, we [i.e. Pius IX] teach and define that it is a divinely revealed dogma that: The Roman pontiff, when he speaks ex cathedra (that is, when in discharge of the office of pastor and doctor of all Christians and by virtue of his supreme apostolic authority, he defines a doctrine regarding faith or morals to be held by the universal church) by the divine assistance promised to him in blessed Peter, is possessed of that infallibility with which the divine redeemer willed that his church should be endowed for defining doctrine regarding faith or morals. Therefore such definitions of the Roman pontiff are irreformable of themselves, and not from the consent of the church.

But if anyone (which may God avert) presume to contradict this our definition, let him be anathema.
THE CHURCH OF CHRIST, CHAPTER 4

There are several points to be noted. First, it is only solemn 'ex cathedra' pronouncements that are infallible. Secondly, the infallibility extends only to the area of theology and ethics. Thirdly, the pope's infallibility is immediate, from God. The decree does not require him to consult or listen to the church and his infallibility is not dependent on the approval of the bishops or the church. Fourthly, there is a claim to be following tradition from the beginning, but this should not be taken too seriously. The objections to the definition were precisely on the grounds that it was contrary to earlier tradition. Pius's attitude is caught in his response to one of the bishops at the council: 'Tradition? *I* am the tradition.'

All of the bishops in due course accepted the definition, some only after months of turmoil. As some of the French opponents had observed before the council, while Roman Catholics might differ about the infallibility of either the pope or a council in *isolation* from the other, there is no room for doubt where they are united. 'A conciliar decision clothed with the pontifical assent, or a pontifical utterance corroborated by the consent of the bishops—infallibility is there, or it is nowhere.' To accept the definition was the only logical step for a Roman Catholic. But not all of them did. One of the leading opponents of infallibility, the great German church historian Ignaz von Döllinger, refused to submit and was excommunicated. The 'Old Catholic Church' was formed by those who could not accept the new definition.

Only one infallible definition has been made since 1870: the definition in the 1950 *Munificentissimus Deus* of Mary's assumption into heaven. Many believed that Vatican I would be the last Roman Catholic council, no more being needed now that the pope had acquired an absolute authority. But in 1961 Pope John XXIII called the *Second Vatican Council. At this council steps were taken to redress to some extent the imbalance of the earlier council by stressing the role of the bishops.

The doctrine of papal infallibility is of course not accepted by Eastern Orthodox or Protestants. Far from leading to a torrent of converts to Rome, as Manning and others had confidently prophesied, the definition widened the gulf between Rome and the other churches. Today it is questioned even within the Roman Catholic Church. *Hans Küng has written forcefully against it. A recent study has argued that the First Vatican Council is invalid because of the lack of freedom at the council—but this contention has not met with much support.

Munificentissimus Deus (1950)

The idea that the Virgin Mary was assumed or taken up into heaven (like Enoch and Elijah in the Old Testament) is first found in some fourth-century writings. Gradually it gained support and by the end of the eighth century, it was generally held in the East, thanks especially to *John of Damascus. It took longer to become widely believed in the West. In more recent times, from the seventeenth century, there has been pressure for its definition as a dogma. This was done in 1950 by Pope Pius XII in his apostolic constitution *Munificentissimus Deus*. It should be noted that the definition does not specify whether or not Mary died before her assumption—whether she escaped death or was raised from it. The majority of, but not all, Roman Catholic theologians believe that she actually died.

Since [Jesus Christ] was able to do [Mary] so great an honour as to keep her safe from the corruption of the tomb, we must believe that he actually did so ... The majestic mother of God ... finally achieved, as the supreme crown of her privileges, that she should be preserved immune from the corruption of the tomb and, like her Son before her, having conquered death should be carried up, in body and soul, to the celestial glory of heaven, there to reign as Queen at the right hand of her Son, the immortal king of the ages.

The doctrine of the assumption is not merely about an (allegedly) historical episode in Mary's life. It is the foundation of a number of other beliefs about her—notably that she is Queen of Heaven and that she is the Mediatrix, who mediates between us and God. The role of Mary has been progressively heightened in Roman Catholicism in recent centuries, although there was resistance to the idea of further definition at the *Second Vatican Council. In 1891, Pope Leo XIII stated in an encyclical that 'nothing is bestowed on us except through Mary, as God himself wills. Therefore as no one can draw near to the supreme Father except through the Son, so also one can scarcely draw near to the Son except through his mother.'

As with the doctrine of the immaculate conception, defined in the 1854 bull *Ineffabilis Deus*, there are wider implications. The dogma has no support from Scripture, nor from the earliest tradition—though these are claimed to provide its 'ultimate foundation'. The apostolic constitution emphasizes rather the 'theological suitability' of the doctrine and the consensus in the *contemporary* Roman Catholic Church. As with the immaculate conception, this definition demonstrates the church's ability to proclaim dogmas on the basis of her own authority, without the support of Scripture or early tradition.

This dogma, as the other Marian doctrines, is related to the understanding of Jesus Christ. The debates of the fourth and fifth centuries led to the clear affirmation of the deity of Jesus Christ. His full humanity was in theory equally affirmed (e.g. at the *Council of Chalcedon), but in practice it has tended to be swamped by his deity. He was no longer looked upon as one who really experienced temptation like us, yet without sinning (as in Hebrews 2:17–18; 4:14–16). Popular piety felt the need for someone in heaven who could really understand and sympathize with human frailty and weakness. It is because the full humanity of Jesus Christ has often been neglected that many of the excessive doctrines about Mary have arisen.

Pierre Teilhard de Chardin
EVOLUTIONARY MYSTIC

Marie-Joseph-Pierre Teilhard de Chardin was born in rural France in 1881. He went to a Jesuit school and proceeded to join the order. He became a professional palaeontologist (student of extinct species), and this led to an interest in the origins of man. He was involved in the discovery of Peking Man in 1929.

In addition to his distinguished scientific work, Teilhard was interested in the relation of Christianity to evolutionary thought. Darwin's theory of evolution, expounded in his 1859 *The Origin of Species* and his 1871 *The Descent of Man*, left Christian theologians with three basic options. First, they could refuse to accept it—an option taken by a minority then as now. Secondly, they could seek to accommodate ' evolutionary science with traditional Christian theology. This remains the choice of the majority, retaining a greater or lesser measure of orthodoxy. Thirdly, they could seek to reinterpret Christian theology in evolutionary terms. Teilhard's is one of the best known of such radical reinterpretations. It bears a striking resemblance to Protestant *Process Theology.

Teilhard's theological views did not meet with favour from his Jesuit superiors. He was consistently refused permission to publish his theological and philosophical

works, and submitted obediently. He was also forbidden to accept a professorship at the Collège de France, a great honour. But on his death in 1955, his friends were able to start publishing his works. The lest known are *The Phenomenon of Man, Le Milieu Divin* and *The Future of Man*, which appeared in French from 1955 to 1959. At the time of the *Second Vatican Council, when there was a new openness to modern thought, Teilhard became very popular within the Roman Catholic world, but his popularity has since waned. His thought has also been received positively by some non-Christian thinkers. The agnostic Sir Julian Huxley contributed a warm introduction to the English translation of *The Phenomenon of Man*:

Though many scientists may, as I do, find it impossible to follow him, all the way in his gallant attempt to reconcile the supernatural elements in Christianity with the facts and implications of evolution, this in no way detracts from the positive value of his naturalistic general approach.
THE PHENOMENON OF MAN, INTRODUCTION

Teilhard sees evolution as a universal law of existence, and views Christianity accordingly. This leads to a striking reinterpretation of many fundamental Christian themes:

● Creation is seen as the process of evolution. Sin is reinterpreted as the inevitable imperfection that accompanies the evolutionary process. Evolution and perfection are as incompatible as the idea of a square circle. Evil is to be seen as the by-product of the process of evolution. As Huxley rightly observed, 'The theologian [may perhaps consider] that his treatment of the problems of sin and suffering was inadequate or at least unorthodox.'

● Teilhard did not reject the traditional view of the historical Jesus as the incarnate Son of God. But his stress lay more on the 'cosmic Christ'. The 'total Christ' or Christ's mystical body is evolving within the setting of human evolution. Redemption is to be seen as this evolutionary process.

● Human history is evolving to its climax, when all will be consummated in Christ. This Teilhard calls the 'Omega point'.

● All of this implies a new concept of God, as in Process Theology. God is to be seen not as immutably transcending the world but as active and involved in the process of evolution—and indeed inseparable from it.

Teilhard makes a valiant attempt at relating Christianity and evolutionary thought. His aim may be compared to that of *Augustine in relating Christianity and Neo-Platonism or to that of *Thomas Aquinas with Aristotle. But Teilhard gives too much to evolutionary thought and the Christian element is not sufficiently preserved. He himself saw his thought as tentative and designed to open up new horizons rather than to settle all questions. Perhaps he can best be compared to *Origen, another great pioneer and speculative thinker, whose ideas were not acceptable as they stood.

Jesus on the cross is both the symbol and the reality of the immense labour of the centuries which has, little by little, raised up the created spirit and brought it back to the depths of the divine milieu. *He represents (and in a true sense, he is) creation as, upheld by God, it re-ascends the slopes of being, sometimes clinging to things for support, sometimes tearing itself from them in order to pass beyond them, and always compensating, by physical suffering, for the setbacks caused by its moral downfalls.*
LE MILIEU DIVIN

And then will be the end. Like a vast tide the Being will have dominated the trembling of all beings. The extraordinary adventure of the world will have ended in the bosom of a tranquil ocean, of which however each drop will still be conscious of being itself. The dream of every mystic will have found its fill and proper fulfilment. God will be all in all.
THE FUTURE OF MAN, CONCLUSION

Second Vatican Council (1962–65)

The definition of papal infallibility by the *First Vatican Council did not end all controversy within the Roman Catholic Church. Under Pius' successor, Leo XIII (1878–1903), there was a movement of 'Catholic Modernism'. This was the Roman Catholic equivalent of Protestant liberalism, the leading figures being Alfred Loisy and George Tyrrell. They accepted the most sceptical conclusions of biblical criticism. They rejected the idea of any infallible doctrine or dogma—whether from Bible, church or pope. On the other hand, they defended the Roman Catholic Church against the attacks of *Harnack and others, but on liberal grounds, as an institution with a constantly evolving religion. Leo's successor, Pius X, condemned the movement, excommunicated its leaders and required the clergy to take an anti-modernist oath.

This led to a clamp-down on free thought and on biblical studies within the Roman Catholic Church. There were slight relaxations after the Second World War, but little change. Then in 1958 a new pope was elected—John XXIII. As an old man of nearly 77 he was seen as a 'caretaker pope', unlikely to do more than preserve the status quo. But his pontificate marks the turning point of modern Roman Catholicism. He stressed the church's need of 'aggiornamento'—being brought up to date. The church needs to catch up with the modern world. While dogma does not change, its form of expression can and must. Protestants are to be seen as 'separated brethren' rather than wicked heretics. In 1961 Pope John called the Second Vatican Council.

The council met from 1962 to 1965. John XXIII had taken the lid off the pot. When the bishops came together they discovered to their surprise that the progressives were in the majority. The council brought into the open profound changes in attitude that had been taking place under the surface since the First Vatican Council. The extensive documents of Vatican II breathe a spirit quite different from that of the earlier council. They are pastoral rather than dogmatic; the tone is conciliatory rather than confrontational—regarding other Christians, other religions and the modern world. Religious persecution, which plays such a major role in the history of the Roman Catholic Church, is rejected and there is a willingness to acknowledge that the church has made mistakes. The two most important documents are the dogmatic constitutions on *The Church* and *Divine Revelation*.

The Church seeks to redress the imbalance of the First Vatican Council, which laid all its stress on the absolute sovereignty of the pope. (This was partly because the council had been forced to close prematurely.) If Vatican I stressed the pope's role as the successor of Peter, Vatican II portrays the order of bishops as 'the successor to the college of the apostles in teaching authority and pastoral rule'. The college of bishops has supreme and full power over the universal church, but only 'together with its head, the Roman pontiff, and never without this head'. It is the pope who has full, supreme and universal power over the church and who can exercise this freely.

At the council there was a division between those who wanted to accelerate further development of the doctrine of Mary and those who wanted to see the brakes applied. The parties divided over the issue of whether or not to have a separate document on Mary, thus magnifying her status. By a narrow majority (1,114 to 1,074) the council voted against. Mary is discussed in the final chapter of *The Church*. This makes the point that she is to be seen as part of the church, not as separate from it. All the traditional doctrines about Mary are reaffirmed, including her immaculate conception and assumption into heaven (defined in *Ineffabilis Deus* and *Munificentissimus Deus*). Some wanted Mary to be defined as 'Co-Redemptrix' (the one who, together with Jesus Christ, redeemed the world). The term was not used but nonetheless Mary's role In

redemption is clearly stated. Her consent was necessary for the incarnation of Jesus Christ and she co-operated actively in the work of human salvation; she gave life to the world—'Death through Eve, life through Mary'; she 'was united with Jesus in suffering as he died upon the cross'; Mary is the Mediatrix, who mediates between us and God. But, it is claimed, all this 'in no way obscures or diminishes the unique mediation of Christ, but rather shows its power'.

Divine Revelation saw an even more pronounced struggle between the conservatives and the progressives, as it went through no less than five drafts. The first draft was ultra-conservative and was decisively rejected by some 60 per cent of the council fathers. Five points in particular were found unacceptable: revelation was seen simply as revealed doctrines; tradition and Scripture as two sources of revelation; tradition as adding to revelation; inspiration as implying 'absolute immunity of the entire sacred Scripture from error'; the task of theology as simply harmonizing Scripture with the church's teaching. Pope John referred the text to a new body for substantial revision. Three years and four drafts later the final document was accepted by 2,344 votes to 6. All five of the objected points had been revised:

● Revelation was now seen as God revealing *himself* (not just doctrines) through deeds and words:

This plan of revelation is realised by deeds and words having an inner unity: the deeds wrought by God in the history of salvation manifest and confirm the teaching and realities signified by the words, while the words proclaim the deeds and clarify the mystery contained in them. By this revelation then, the deepest truth about God and the salvation of man is made clear to us in Christ, who is the Mediator and at the same time the fullness of all revelation.
DIVINE REVELATION 1:2

● The gospel is the one source of all saving truth. It is transmitted to us in two ways—by tradition and by Scripture. Tradition here is an all-embracing term: 'the church, in her teaching, life and worship, perpetuates and hands on to all generations all that she herself is, all that she believes.'

● Care is taken not to state that tradition *adds* to Scripture. This had been believed to be the teaching of the *Council of Trent, but in the years immediately preceding Vatican II a number of Roman Catholic scholars vigorously disputed this interpretation of Trent. The council took care to leave the question open. But it does refer to the development of doctrine, following *Newman: 'For as the centuries succeed one another, the church constantly moves forward toward the fullness of divine truth until the words of God reach their complete fulfillment in her.' This meansthat while the seed of all doctrine is found in Scripture, it is not sufficient on its own to teach Catholic doctrine: 'It is not from sacred Scripture alone that the church draws her certainty about everything which has been revealed.' This was a last-minute addition at the request of Paul VI, pope from 1963 to 1978.

● The concept of the inerrancy of Scripture is qualified:

Therefore, since everything asserted by the inspired authors or sacred writers must be held to be asserted by the Holy Spirit, it follows that the books of Scripture must be acknowledged as teaching firmly, faithfully and without error that truth which God wanted put into the sacred writings for the sake of our salvation.

DIVINE REVELATION 3:11

This is capable of a wide range of interpretations according to what one thinks that God might have wanted in Scripture for our salvation. Does it mean all that as a matter of fact is there? Does it mean theology and ethics only? Does it mean the gospel only? If so, could it be reduced to mean only a truth like 'God is love'?

● The Bible was let loose at Vatican II. The laity must read it for, as *Jerome says,

'ignorance of the Scriptures is ignorance of Christ'. Catholics are to co-operate with Protestants in translating the Bible. 'The study of the sacred page is, as it were, the soul of sacred theology.' This is a far cry from the not-so-ancient claims of Roman Catholic apologists that the church could manage perfectly well without the Bible. Catholic biblical scholarship is warmly encouraged. But it is to be 'under the watchful care of the sacred teaching office of the church' and 'with loyalty to the mind of the church'. The teaching office of the church 'is not above the word of God, but serves it'—yet 'the task of authentically interpreting the word of God ... has been entrusted exclusively to the living teaching office of the church'. Vatican II goes a long way towards encouraging a revival of biblical scholarship, but it is still the infallible church which remains the final norm.

With Vatican II the 400-year period of 'Tridentine Catholicism' came to a close. Fortress Rome has become the pilgrim church. The 'prisoner of the Vatican' has become a jet-setting charismatic star. Dialogue has replaced persecution. Hostility towards Protestantism has become an eagerness to learn. Reform has come in worship and in many other areas. So much has happened so quickly that there is uncertainty and confusion in many areas. Popes Paul VI and John Paul II have at times sought to bolt the stable door—but the horse is nowhere to be found. Time alone will tell which way the Roman Catholic Church will go, but one thing is certain—it will not be back to the period before Vatican II.

Karl Rahner
ANONYMOUS CHRISTIANITY

Karl Rahner was born at Freiburg-im-Breisgau in 1904. He joined the Jesuits and in 1948 he became professor of dogmatic theology at Innsbruck. Since then he has also held chairs at Munich and Münster Universities. He is the author of a multi-volume series of *Theological Investigations*, each comprising a collection of essays topically arranged. He has also written a systematic theology entitled *Foundations of Christian Faith*, the German original of which appeared in 1976. He was arguably the greatest Roman Catholic theologian of his generation, but his approach to theology has now been overtaken by the more radical approaches of Schillebeeckx and *Küng.

Rahner is famous for his theory of 'anonymous Christianity'. The traditional Roman Catholic position, enunciated with brutal clarity by *Cyprian and restated at the *Fourth Lateran Council, is that there is no salvation outside the one visible organized Catholic Church. There is no salvation in any rival 'churches'. This was stated even more precisely by Pope Boniface VIII in his 1302 bull *Unam Sanctam*: 'We declare, state and define that it is altogether necessary to salvation for every human creature to be subject to the Roman pontiff [pope].' These statements are still accepted in the Roman Catholic Church—but 'reinterpreted'. In 1854, Pope Pius IX reaffirmed the traditional doctrine, but with a vital qualification—those who are 'invincibly ignorant' of the true religion (i.e. whose ignorance is not their fault) are excepted. In 1949 there was a further development. Father Feeney, a hard-line Boston priest, insisted on teaching the traditional view. Rome responded that the statement 'outside the church there is no salvation' remains true, but that it was for the magisterium, the church's teaching office, to interpret it, not the private individual. The controversy dragged on and in 1953 Feeney was *excommunicated* as an obstinate rigorist. The *Second Vatican Council was also clear in rejecting the old interpretation:

Those also can attain to everlasting salvation who through no fault of their own do not know the gospel of Christ or his church, yet sincerely seek God and, moved by grace, strive by their deeds to do his will as it is known to them through the dictates of conscience. Nor does divine providence deny the help

necessary for salvation to those who, without blame on their part, have not yet arrived at an explicit knowledge of God, but who strive to live a good life, thanks to his grace.
THE CHURCH 2:16

[Salvation is] not only for Christians, but for all men of good will in whose hearts grace works in an unseen way. For, since Christ died for all men, and since the ultimate vocation of man is in fact one, and divine, we ought to believe that the Holy Spirit in a manner known only to God offers to every man the possibility of being associated with this paschal mystery.
THE CHURCH IN THE MODERN WORLD 1:22

But on the other hand, Vatican II also declared, 'Whoever knows that the Catholic Church was made necessary by God through Jesus Christ but refuses to enter her or to remain in her, could not be saved.'

Karl Rahner's theory seeks to explain these statements. God desires that all should be saved (1 Timothy 2:4), and faith in Jesus Christ is necessary for salvation. This implies that all people have the chance to believe—and this a real historical chance, not a merely abstract or theoretical chance. How can this be true? Because God's grace is at work in *all* men. Until an individual is effectively confronted by the Christian gospel, the grace of God in Jesus Christ can reach him through a non-Christian religion. More than this, God's grace is even at work in the atheist, who can therefore have true Christian faith, hope and love, while yet remaining an atheist. 'Even an atheist ... is not excluded from attaining salvation, provided that he has not acted against his moral conscience as a result of his atheism.' But how can such a person be said to believe in God? Because it is *God* that he is encountering in his conscience, even though he does not realize it. According to Rahner's 'transcendental philosophy', everyone's experience of the transcendent, the 'absolute mystery', is an experience of God.

*The person who accepts a moral
demand from his conscience as
absolutely valid for him and embraces it
as such in a free act of affirmation—no
matter how unreflected—asserts the
absolute being of God, whether he
knows or conceptualizes it or not, as the
very reason why there can be such a
thing as an* absolute moral demand at
all.

THEOLOGICAL INVESTIGATIONS
VOLUME 9, CHAPTER 9

These 'anonymous Christians' are saved not
by their natural morality but because they
have experienced Jesus Christ's grace
without realizing it. We need to distinguish
between explicit faith and a faith that is real
but unarticulated—which has not yet
penetrated from the heart to the head.

*The 'anonymous Christian' in our sense
of the term is the pagan after the
beginning of the Christian mission, who
lives in the state of Christ's grace
through faith, hope and love, yet who
has no explicit knowledge of the fact that
his life is orientated in grace-given
salvation to Jesus Christ... There must
be a Christian theory to account for the
fact that every individual who does not
in any absolute or ultimate sense act
against his own conscience can say and
does say in faith, hope and love, Abba
within his own spirit and is on these
grounds in all truth a brother to
Christians in God's sight.*

THEOLOGICAL INVESTIGATIONS
VOLUME 14, CHAPTER 17

These ideas, as expounded by Rahner and
others, are very influential today, especially
the idea that one can be an anonymous
Christian without any sort of *religious*
commitment. The anonymous Christian is
one who 'accepts himself in a moral
decision', even if that decision is not made 'in
a religious or "theist" manner'. This serves
to justify 'secular Christianity'—the
interpretation of the church's message and
mission in increasingly secular terms, as

seen in recent statements of the *World
Council of Churches and *Liberation
Theology. If the essence of Christian
discipleship can be manifested without any
conscious religious element, the church is
justified in abandoning her religious
concerns in favour of the vital and pressing
social and political concerns of the day.
Perhaps the greatest weakness in Rahner's
theory is the transformation of an
exceptional possibility (that someone who
has not heard the gospel may be in a state of
grace) into the norm—so that the church is
to treat all men as if they were probably
anonymous Christians, while the biblical
approach is to treat them as if they were lost.

Karl Rahner died in 1984.

Hans Küng
CATHOLIC REBEL

Hans Küng was born in 1928 in the Swiss
canton of Lucerne. After studying for the
priesthood at Rome, he went on to Paris to
prepare his doctoral thesis: *Justification: The
Doctrine of Karl Barth and a Catholic
Reflection*, which was published in 1957.
This was one of those rare doctoral theses
which become epoch-making works. Küng
expounds *Barth's doctrine of justification
and then argues that there is no
irreconcilable difference between this and
the teaching of the *Council of Trent.

*It is without any doubt, then, significant
that today there is a fundamental
agreement between Catholic and
Protestant theology, precisely in the
theology of justification—the point at
which Reformation theology took its
departure. Despite all the difficulties,
have we not, after these 400 years,
come decidedly closer to one another
also on the theological level?*

JUSTIFICATION, CHAPTER 33

What is most significant about the book is
the way that it has been received. Barth
himself responded warmly:

If what you have presented ... is actually the teaching of the Roman Catholic Church, then I must certainly admit that my view of justification agrees with the Roman view; if only for the reason that the Roman Catholic teaching would then be most strikingly in accord with mine!

He then goes on to say that it is Küng's fellow Catholics who must decide whether or not he has been fair to Trent. On the whole, they felt that he had. The effect of Küng's book has been a widespread feeling among Roman Catholic theologians that the doctrine of justification by faith alone is acceptable and need not divide the confessions. Since the Roman Catholic Church reinterprets its faith as it goes along, this fact is at least as significant as the theoretical question of whether or not the doctrines are really compatible. A cynic might observe that Küng has attempted the same as *Newman's *Tract Ninety*, in reverse, and succeeded.

In 1962, Pope John appointed Küng an official theological adviser to the *Second Vatican Council. He was active at the council, but was disappointed with some of its results. Already in 1957 the Holy Office (formerly the Inquisition) had opened a file on Küng because of his *Justification*. As he became more critical of traditional doctrinal positions, warnings were issued by the Holy Office—which in the mid-60s became the Congregation for the Doctrine of the Faith. Most of Küng's major works have led to disapproval at Rome—which may well have contributed to their popularity!

In 1970 Hans Küng celebrated the centenary of the definition of papal infallibility at the *First Vatican Council with the publication of his *Infallible? An Enquiry*. In this book he forcefully attacks the doctrine of papal infallibility. He questions its alleged support from the Bible and church tradition. More fundamentally, he questions whether there can be such a thing as an infallible proposition—whether from the pope, the church or the Bible. He urges that the concept of the infallibility of the church be replaced by its indefectibility.

This means that despite her misunderstandings and errors in points of detail, the church is kept in the truth by God. The negative claim that certain statements contain no error is replaced by the positive claim that the truth of the gospel is preserved in the church, amid all the errors. Allied to this, Küng proposes a revised role for the pope. Instead of being an infallible absolute sovereign he should become the true successor of Peter, exercising a primacy of service and pastoral ministry to the whole church, as exemplified by John XXIII. This approach to the church and the papacy is, claims Küng, in line with Scripture and with the tradition of the first millennium or so.

A Petrine ministry in the church makes sense, and every Catholic accepts it. But the pope exists for the church, and not the church for the pope. His primacy is not the primacy of sovereignty, but the primacy of service. The holder of the Petrine office must not set himself up as overlord either of the church or of the gospel, which is what he does today when, after all the negative experiences of the past and the positive experience of the Council, he interprets theology and church policy in the light of an uncritically adopted tradition.
INFALLIBLE? FOREWORD

Infallible? caused an immense stir. Former allies, such as *Karl Rahner, repudiated Küng's stand. It began to be seriously questioned whether Küng could any longer be considered a Roman Catholic theologian. The German bishops' conference spoke against the book. Proceedings rambled on at Rome but led to little more than a rebuke in 1975.

Hans Küng has been a prolific author and has proved himself a master at writing theology for non-theologians and even for non-Christians. His *On Being a Christian* (1974) became a best-seller in Germany—not the usual fate of lengthy (700 pages) theological tomes. Küng succeeded in presenting the Christian faith in a modern way that speaks to the man in the street. But,

as with most of his other major works, there
were rumblings of discontent at Rome. He
also wrote a major work on *Does God Exist?*
(1978).

The election in 1978 of Pope John Paul II
led to a tougher attitude at Rome. At the end
of 1979 the Congregation for the Doctrine of
the Faith, with the pope's approval, declared
that Küng 'can no longer be considered a
Catholic theologian nor function as such in a
teaching role'. He was not excommunicated
and he did not lose his status as a priest, but
he was not to be seen as a Roman Catholic
theologian. This was a shrewd attempt to
undercut his influence without making him a
martyr. The church demanded that he be
removed from his university post as a
professor of *Catholic* theology at
Tübingen—to which the state responded by
setting up a special professorship for him.
The effectiveness of the church's stand can
be questioned in that a good number of
Roman Catholic scholars who do not share
his views have taken his side over the issue
of his treatment. On the other hand, it is hard
to take seriously a religious body that has *no*
control of what is taught in its name—a
problem besetting many other churches
today.

Küng's output has continued unabated.
In a recent work he writes on *Theology for
the Third Millennium* (1988). In this he
considers the approach to theology in the
'postmodern age'. The modern age began in
the seventeenth and eighteenth centuries
with the Enlightenment. A major feature of
this age was the belief in progress, which
was shattered by the First World War. This
was the beginning of 'postmodernity', a
phenomenon that is today increasingly
recognized. Küng would himself prefer to
call this the 'ecumenical' epoch, 'in the sense
of a new global understanding of the various
denominations, religions, and regions'. His
approach to theology includes, therefore, 'a
new departure toward a theology of the
world religions'.

A WORLD-WIDE FAITH

In recent years theology has ceased to be the sole prerogative of white Europeans. Attempts have been made to develop genuinely Asian, African and Latin American theologies.

World Council of Churches

The World Council of Churches was formally constituted in 1948 at Amsterdam by delegates of 147 churches from 44 countries. It arose out of three earlier movements, the stimulus for which came from a World Missionary Conference held at Edinburgh in 1910.

● *Faith and Order* was a movement arising out of the Edinburgh conference, devoted to working towards the reunion of the divided denominations. Conferences were held in 1927 at Lausanne and 1937 at Edinburgh.

● *Life and Work* was another movement, concerned with the relation of the Christian faith to social, political and economic questions. Conferences were held in 1925 at Stockholm and in 1937 at Oxford.

● *The International Missionary Council* arose more directly out of the Edinburgh conference. It was formed in 1921 and in 1961 it integrated formally with the World Council of Churches.

The 1937 conferences of *Life and Work* and *Faith and Order* both approved the formation of a world council of churches and a conference at Utrecht in 1938 drafted its constitution. But the war delayed its formal launch for a further ten years. Apart from the Roman Catholic Church and some (but not all) Evangelical churches, all significant Christian churches now belong to the World Council of Churches. Since 1961 the Roman Catholic Church has sent official observers to the general assemblies.

In addition to the work at the headquarters in Geneva, the World Council of Churches has held world conferences on Faith and Order, World Mission and Evangelism and other such themes. But its major events are the general assemblies, of which seven have taken place to date.

● Amsterdam (1948). It was at the first general assembly that the World Council of Churches was formally constituted. It began as a 'fellowship of churches which accept our Lord Jesus Christ as God and Saviour'.

● Evanston, Illinois (1954), with the theme *Christ—the Hope of the World*. The goals of evangelism were stated to be the bringing of persons to a personal encounter with Jesus Christ as Saviour and Lord, their incorporation into the full life of the church and the transformation of society to conform to God's intention.

● New Delhi (1961), with the theme *Jesus Christ the Light of the World*. It was the first assembly to meet outside the West. The Eastern Orthodox churches joined the World Council of Churches at New Delhi, and the basis of membership was expanded.

The World Council of Churches is a fellowship of churches which confess the Lord Jesus Christ as God and Saviour according to the Scriptures and therefore seek to fulfil together their common calling to the glory of the one God, Father, Son and Holy Spirit.

● Uppsala (1968), with the theme *Behold! I make all things new.* Six study groups met to discuss and amend documents relating to different topics. Most controversial was the document *Renewal in Mission.* Earlier World Council of Churches' documents had been clear about the importance of bringing non-Christians to faith in Jesus Christ, but this was barely mentioned in the draft document. The 'vertical' dimension of mission, reconciliation with God, was virtually abandoned. All the emphasis lay on the 'horizontal' dimension of reconciliation within humanity. The idea of 'anonymous Christianity' (as expounded by *Karl Rahner) was adopted with the result that religious conversion became of secondary importance. This imbalance led the American Evangelical Donald McGavran to ask 'Will Uppsala betray the two billion [unevangelized]?' Visser't Hooft, the retired general secretary of the World Council of Churches, also stressed the need for balance:

A Christianity which has lost its vertical dimension has lost its salt and is not only insipid in itself, but useless for the world. But a Christianity which would use the vertical preoccupation as a means to escape from its responsibility for and in the common life of man is a denial of the incarnation, of God's love for the world manifested in Christ.
THE MANDATE OF THE ECUMENICAL MOVEMENT

As a result of the debate, the final document was clearer about the need for conversion to Jesus Christ—although 'often the turning point does not appear as a religious choice at all' and there are those who 'unknowing, serve the "man for others"'. Mission is defined in the light of contemporary concerns for a fully human life:

There is a burning relevance today in describing the mission of God, in which we participate, as the gift of a new creation which is a radical renewal of the old and the invitation to men to grow up into their full humanity in the

new man, Jesus Christ.
RENEWAL IN MISSION 1:1

This new manhood is a gift, to be received by faith. Such a response affects our relationships with others. 'For there is no turning to God which does not at the same time bring a man face to face with his fellow men in a new way. The new life frees men for community.' This leads to efforts to break down racial, national and religious barriers. The restoration of true manhood in Jesus Christ includes all moves towards greater justice, freedom and dignity. Christians must therefore be more open and humble towards those who share these goals with them.

Uppsala launched a vigorous debate. A group of Germans from *within* the World Council of Churches drew up a *Frankfurt Declaration* in 1970 which opposed many of the trends of Uppsala—salvation as 'humanization', universalism, anonymous Christianity and others. Other Evangelicals were more positive towards Uppsala, though not uncritical. British Evangelical leader John Stott proposed a definition of mission broadened to embrace both evangelism and service. The debate continued at the Bangkok conference of the Commission on World Mission and Evangelism, on the theme *Salvation Today* (1973). Here the trends of Uppsala were taken further. Salvation was defined in predominantly 'horizontal' terms, in a document composed by *Moltmann:

Salvation works in the struggle for economic justice against the exploitation of people by people.
Salvation works in the struggle for human dignity against political oppression of human beings by their fellow men.
Salvation works in the struggle for solidarity against the alienation of person from person.
Salvation works in the struggle of hope against despair in personal life.
SALVATION AND SOCIAL JUSTICE, INTRODUCTION

It was a Roman Catholic observer at the conference who commented: 'I haven't heard anyone speak on justification by faith. I've heard no one speak of everlasting life. What about God's righteous wrath against sin?' Similar criticism came from the Eastern Orthodox and from Evangelicals. The year after Bangkok saw the Evangelical *Lausanne Congress on World Evangelization, which sought to bring the vertical and the horizontal, the personal and the social together into a healthy balance. Since Bangkok there has also been a trend within the World Council of Churches towards a more balanced position.

● Nairobi (1975), with the theme *Jesus Christ Frees and Unites*. At Nairobi the emphasis of Uppsala and Bangkok on the social and horizontal dimension is retained, but is better integrated with the spiritual and vertical dimension. The phrase 'the whole church bringing the whole gospel to the whole person in the whole world' captures the mood of the assembly. The whole gospel includes both reconciliation to God and 'the responsibility to participate in the struggle for justice and human dignity'. Mission is the confession of Jesus Christ by both word and deed.

Christians are called to engage in both evangelism and social action. We are commissioned to proclaim the gospel of Christ to the ends of the earth. Simultaneously, we are commanded to struggle to realize God's will for peace, justice and freedom throughout society.
CONFESSING CHRIST TODAY

Many people have drawn attention to the remarkable degree of common ground that exists between the report *Confessing Christ Today* from Nairobi, the *Lausanne Covenant* and Pope Paul VI's *Evangelization in the Modern World* (1975—based on the Roman Catholic synod of bishops which met at Rome the previous year). There appears to be much agreement between these ecumenical, Evangelical and Roman Catholic statements—though significant areas of disagreement remain.

● Vancouver (1983), with the theme *Jesus Christ—the Life of the World*. This was preceded in 1982 by a document from the Commission on Mission and Evangelism entitled *Mission and Evangelism—An Ecumenical Affirmation*, which further narrows the gap between the World Council of Churches and the Evangelical position as outlined at the Lausanne Congress.

The year 1982 also saw a major conference at Lima in Peru organized by the Faith and Order Commission. This approved a remarkable document called *Baptism, Eucharist and Ministry*, the fruit of many years of patient preparation. It is remarkable in that it is an agreed statement produced by delegates representing almost every confessional tradition—Roman Catholic, Eastern Orthodox, Lutheran, Reformed, Anglican, Baptist, Pentecostal and others. The document does not signify total agreement, but it does represent a significant extent of common ground.

In order to overcome their differences, believer Baptists and those who practise infant baptism should reconsider certain aspects of their practices. The first may seek to express more visibly the fact that children are placed under the protection of God's grace. The latter must guard against the practice of apparently indiscriminate baptism and take more seriously their responsibility for the nurture of baptised children to mature commitment to Christ.
BAPTISM 16

In 1989 there was another significant meeting of the Commission on World Mission and Evangelism at San Antonio in Texas, with the theme *Your Will be Done: Mission in Christ's Way*. At this conference the 1982 *Mission and Evangelism* document was given considerable prominence. The vexed issue of witness to those of other faiths was considered in a report on 'Turning to the Living God'. This took the line that witness and dialogue do not exclude each other. The church should bear witness to Christ 'to people of every religious and non-religious persuasion'. On the other hand, God is 'present in and at work in people of other faiths'. Witness to them therefore presupposes our presence with them, sensitivity to their beliefs, willingness to serve them, affirmation of what God has done and is doing among them and love for them. There is still an unresolved tension in WCC thought between the call to proclaim the gospel to all and the belief that God is at work in a saving way outside of Christ.

● Canberra (1991) with the theme *Come, Holy Spirit—Renew the Whole Creation.* Here there was a focus on the Holy Spirit, but in a way that at times seemed to be cut loose from the person of Christ. One particular ceremony involved Korean shamanistic ideas and the invocation of the spirits of 'earth, air, water and sea creature'. So concerned were the Eastern Orthodox delegates at this and other happenings that they issued a statement expressing concern at the departure from the WCC's basis and from 'biblically based Christian understandings' of various doctrines. They wondered whether the time had come for the Orthodox and other churches to review their relations with the WCC.

The twentieth century has seen remarkable strides towards Christian unity. There has been little to see in the way of church mergers, but there has been a radical change in the attitudes of different churches to one another. Increasingly there is a spirit of co-operation and friendship. Most churches recognize that they do not possess the whole truth and are open to learn from others. Even the Roman Catholic Church has significantly modified its earlier claims to possess the whole truth. Evangelicals are divided in their attitudes to the ecumenical unity movement, but the majority are ready to acknowledge others as fellow Christians from whom they can learn.

The social dimension of the gospel has been the most explosive item on the agenda of the World Council of Churches since 1968. The increased influence of the non-Western churches since that date has helped to keep it at the forefront of debate. All traditions— Roman Catholic and Evangelical as well as ecumenical—have in the last twenty-five years devoted attention to this theme. There have been excesses, as at Uppsala and Bangkok, and some of the more extreme reactions to them'. But the outcome of the debate has been a serious attempt on all sides to develop a fully-rounded concept of mission and salvation and to escape the past mistake of interpreting them in *purely* individual and 'spiritual' terms.

Martin Luther King
DREAM OF JUSTICE

Martin Luther King was born in 1929 at Atlanta, Georgia. His father and his grandfather were both Baptist ministers, and in due course King decided to follow in their footsteps. In 1951, having gained his BA and his BD he went on to Boston University to study for his PhD on the subject of *Paul Tillich. In 1954 he became pastor of Dexter Avenue Baptist Church in Montgomery, Alabama, and before long found himself propelled into the political arena.

On 1 December 1955 Mrs Rosa Parks, a black woman, was arrested under the city of Montgomery's segregation laws because she refused to surrender her bus seat to a white passenger. The outcome was a boycott of the bus system by the black community, led by Martin Luther King. After about a year the authorities gave way and the buses were desegregated.

King decided to exploit the momentum achieved and in 1957 he founded the Southern Christian Leadership Conference to co-ordinate non-violent action for civil rights. King himself became the acknowledged leader of the civil rights movement. He brought to it his forceful personality, his considerable rhetorical gifts and a distinctive strategy. He embraced the method of non-violent direct action, being deeply impressed by the approach of Gandhi. He also laid stress on the need to register black voters and thus to employ the power of the ballot box.

Martin Luther King was jailed twice, in

1960 and in 1963. On the former occasion he was released through the intervention of the presidential candidate, John F. Kennedy. On the latter occasion, in Birmingham, Alabama, he wrote a famous letter from prison in which he stated that, 'we know through painful experience that freedom is never voluntarily given by the oppressor; it must be demanded by the oppressed'.

In August 1963 he led a historic march on Washington. On arrival he addressed a crowd of more than 200,000 by the Lincoln Memorial, delivering his best-known speech:

I have a dream that my four little children will one day live in a nation where they will not be judged by the colour of their skin but by the content of their character.

I have a dream today.

I have a dream that one day the state of Alabama, whose governor's lips are presently dripping with the words of interposition and nullification, will be transformed into a situation where little black boys and black girls will be able to join hands with little white boys and white girls and walk together as sisters and brothers.

I have a dream today.

The peak of King's influence came between 1960 and 1965. He enjoyed the active support of the Kennedy and Johnson administrations. In 1964 Congress passed the Civil Rights Act, enabling the federal government to enforce the desegregation of public accommodations. The following year, after demonstrations in Alabama, a Voting Rights Act was also passed. In 1964 Martin Luther King was awarded the Nobel Peace Prize. But the following year his leadership of the civil rights movement was challenged. Black Power groups questioned the effectiveness of his non-violent methods. In 1968 he was assassinated by a white gunman in Memphis, Tennessee. In a speech given the day before, he seems almost to have anticipated the end:

I've been to the mountain top. And I've looked over, and I've seen the promised land. I may not get there with you, but I want you to know tonight that we as a people will get to the promised land. So I'm happy tonight. I'm not worried about anything. I'm not fearing any man. Mine eyes have seen the glory of the coming of the Lord.

Martin Luther King succeeded in forcing the civil rights issue on to the attention of the nation. By mobilizing blacks and appealing to the consciences of whites he succeeded in bringing about real political change. But, as he himself saw clearly, the demon of racism is not exorcised in one session. In the south his achievements were substantial, but only partial. In the more complex racial situation of the north his success was much smaller. But the real achievements of his method of non-violent direct action have been much greater than those of any other approach, such as violence. In 1983, the United States made his birthday a national holiday, an honour previously accorded only to George Washington.

Kosuke Koyama
GOD IN A TRANQUIL CULTURE

Kosuke Koyama was born at Tokyo in 1929. After taking his first degree at Tokyo he studied further in the USA, gaining his doctorate from Princeton Theological Seminary in 1959. From 1961 to 1969 he was a missionary in Thailand, teaching in a seminary there. From Thailand he moved in 1969 to become dean of the South East Asia Graduate School of Theology at Singapore. In 1974 he left to teach religious studies at the University of Otago in New Zealand. Since 1979 he has taught at the Union Theological Seminary in New York.

Koyama is best known for his *Waterbuffalo Theology* (1974). On his way to preach in country churches he saw the waterbuffaloes in the paddy fields and this reminded him of how his congregation spent their lives. His sermon must start from the situation of that congregation. 'From talking about the human situation I go on to call God into this real human situation.' He decided that he must subordinate great theological thoughts, like those of *Thomas Aquinas and *Karl Barth, to the needs of the farmers. He gave priority to the farmers over Aquinas and Barth—because he was preaching in Thailand, not Italy or Switzerland.

There is a freshness about Koyama's theology, as can be seen from some of his chapter headings: 'Will the monsoon rain make God wet?'; 'Aristotelian pepper and Buddhist salt'; 'The wrath of God in a culture of tranquillity'. In the last of these he considers the problem of preaching God's wrath in Thailand. Like ancient Greek philosophy, Buddhist culture regards impassibility, imperturbability, tranquillity as the highest good. The idea of God's wrath, God being perturbed by our sin, is a scandal in such a culture. Koyama's solution is not to soft-pedal the idea of God's wrath, as some have done. Talk about the love of God becomes distorted and superficial if it is divorced from his wrath. Thai thought sees God as impassible because it puts him beyond time and history, because Thai Buddhist thought neglects history. This way of thinking is encouraged by the relatively regular and benevolent cycle of nature in Thailand—with few catastrophes like earthquakes or tornadoes. The doctrine of God's wrath can be used to challenge Thai thought at this deeper level and thus to proclaim the doctrine of a God involved in history.

In 1979 Koyama published *Three Mile an Hour God*, a further collection of biblical studies related to South East Asia. In the chapter from which the book takes its title, he contrasts the instant efficiency of modern technology with God's way of teaching his people. God took forty years to train them in the wilderness—at walking pace (3 mph). In the classroom we learn theory, but God teaches us through real-life experience. 'Forty years in the wilderness' points to God's basic educational philosophy. The rest of the Old Testament bears this out.

God walks 'slowly' because he is love. If

he is not love he would have gone much faster. Love has its speed. It is an inner speed. It is a spiritual speed. It is a different kind of speed from the technological speed to which we are accustomed ... It goes on in the depth of our life, whether we notice or not, whether we are currently hit by storm or not, at three miles an hour. It is the speed we walk and therefore it is the speed the love of God walks.

THREE MILE AN HOUR GOD, CHAPTER 1

More recently he has written *Mount Fuji and Mount Sinai* (1984). In this 'pilgrimage in theology' he seeks to relate together the historical experience of the Japanese from 1945 and the theology of the cross. He concludes by drawing four implications from the theology of the cross for today. First, we stand for creation, not for destruction. Secondly, we learn that we do not have the last word about the world and our destiny. That belongs to God, not to us. Thirdly, we become aware of the existence of many gods—gods of colour, weapons, etc. These gods offer us quick solutions. Finally, the theology of the cross gives us a criterion to distinguish between the true God and the false gods, between true and false prophets.

John Mbiti
NO IMPORTED CHRISTIANITY

John Mbiti was born in 1931 in Kitui in Kenya and raised in the Africa Inland Church, the church founded by the Africa Inland Mission. He was educated at Makerere University (Uganda), Barrington College (Rhode Island), and Cambridge University, where he gained his PhD in 1963. This was later published under the title *New Testament Theology in an African Background* (1971). He became dissatisfied with the Africa Inland Church, and left it for the Anglican Church, into which he was ordained. Having been a visiting lecturer at Birmingham and Hamburg, he became professor of religious studies and philosophy at Makerere University. In 1972 he became director of the *World Council of Churches' Ecumenical Institute at Céligny in Switzerland. He is now pastor of a Reformed church in Switzerland. Mbiti is the most prolific of modern African theologians and his writings reflect a wide range of interests: biblical studies, pre-Christian African religious traditions and their encounter with the Christian faith, African culture and theology.

Mbiti, like most African theologians, is critical of the missionary movement in Africa. He expresses gratitude to God for those missionaries who brought the gospel from Europe and America to Africa and acknowledges that Africa wants and needs that gospel. But what Africa does not need is 'imported Christianity, because too much of it will only castrate us spiritually or turn us into spiritual cripples.' The missionaries brought a Westernized Christianity and sought to impose it upon Africa—Western-style dress, music and buildings, Western thought-forms, etc. Africans were taught by word and example that 'they first had to become culturally circumcised before they could become Christians'. It has been noted that Africa lacks its apostle Paul—the apostle who insisted that Gentile converts need not be circumcised and thus become Jewish. Mbiti agrees that the early missionaries were 'devout, sincere and dedicated men and women'. But they were not theologians and they lived in a time when the superiority of European culture seemed self-evident. The result was that mission Christianity did not seriously encounter traditional African religions and philosophy. The rapid growth of the 'Independent Churches', towards whom Mbiti is sympathetic but not uncritical, was one outcome of this failure.

If there is to be a genuinely African Christianity, it must relate to pre-Christian African religions. Mbiti's major writings are devoted to the study of these traditional religions: *African Religions and Philosophy* (1969), *Concepts of God in Africa* (1970), and *The Prayers of African Religion* (1975). His most recent book, *Bible and Theology in African Christianity* (1986) is a broad survey

of contemporary African Christianity.

Mbiti has studied African traditional religions not simply as an anthropological exercise but as part of his theological task. The early missionaries had a predominantly negative attitude towards African traditional religions. They saw them as demonic idolatry, to be swept away by the gospel. Mbiti prefers to see them as a *preparation for the gospel*, echoing the attitude of *Clement of Alexandria and others of the early Fathers towards *Greek philosophy. The pre-Christian African was no atheist. 'God the Father of our Lord Jesus Christ is the same God who for thousands of years has been known and worshipped in various ways within the religious life of African peoples.' He 'was not a stranger in Africa prior to the coming of missionaries.'

In his willingness to ascribe a positive role to African traditional religions, Mbiti does not wish to deny the uniqueness and finality of Jesus Christ as the judge of all other religions:

The uniqueness of Christianity is in Jesus Christ. He is the stumbling block of all ideologies and religious systems... He is 'the Man for others' and yet beyond them. It is he, therefore, and only he, who deserves to be the goal and standard for individuals and mankind... I consider traditional religions, Islam and the other religious systems to be preparatory and even essential ground in the search for the Ultimate. But only Christianity has the terrible responsibility of pointing the way to that ultimate identity, Foundation and Source of security.
AFRICAN RELIGIONS AND PHILOSOPHY, CHAPTER 20

Underlying Mbiti's rejection of 'imported Christianity' is his distinction between the gospel and the Christian faith (which are eternal) and Christianity (which is a particular manifestation of them in a specific culture). 'Christianity is the end result of the gospel coming into a given culture whose people respond to the gospel through faith.' What is needed is African Christianity. This is not the translation into African terms of a pre-existent (Western) Christianity and theology, but the emergence from within African culture of a genuinely African Christianity and theology—with genuinely African worship, community life, education, values, etc.

Mbiti says that the gospel comes to each culture as a stranger, a stranger who settles down. The gospel does not throw out culture—instead it settles in the culture and makes its impact on the lives of the people within that culture. African culture should welcome the gospel as an honoured guest. But does this imply that the gospel cannot criticize culture? No. All human culture, however beautiful and great, is tainted by sin. The gospel does not *reject* culture, but it *transforms* it. The gospel exercises merciful judgement upon culture—evaluating it, judging it and transforming it. Furthermore, the gospel transcends culture, taking over where culture reaches its limits (as with questions of life after death). Therefore the Christian is a 'cultural pilgrim and not a settler, moving even with his cultural luggage towards the eschatological goal of the gospel.'

Liberation Theology
CHRISTIANS OF THE REVOLUTION

South America is a continent rich in natural resources, but with the majority of the population trapped in poverty and squalor. Most of the countries are ruled by a wealthy élite who maintain their position at the expense of the majority. In the 1950s and 1960s attempts were made to bring 'development' to Latin America, the problem being seen as 'underdevelopment'. But these efforts did not succeed in improving the lot of the poor majority and many turned to an alternative analysis of the problem. Latin America suffers not just from underdevelopment but from *oppression*. The problem lies in unjust structures—both within the individual countries (oppressive regimes) and between the region and the 'developed' world (oppressive capitalism).

Latin America needs *liberation* rather than development.

This analysis of the situation came into prominence at the Second Latin American Episcopal Conference at Medellín in Colombia (1968). The bishops' final statement asserted that 'in many places in Latin America there is a situation of injustice that must be recognized as institutionalized violence, because the existing structures violate people's basic rights: a situation which calls for far-reaching, daring, urgent and profoundly innovating changes.' The bishops recognized the temptation to resort to revolutionary violence and indeed the fact that in extreme situations it is justified—but they also warned that 'armed revolution generally gives rise to new injustices, throws more elements out of balance and brings on new disasters'.

The Medellín conference endorsed the new analysis of the situation as one of oppression and the need for liberation. This soon gave birth to Liberation Theology—a theology dedicated to the cause of socio-political liberation. It received a stimulus from the *Second Vatican Council and it borrowed ideas from Western theologians, such as *Moltmann, but it claims to be an essentially Latin American theology and is critical of all Western theologies. The themes of Liberation Theology have been in the forefront of debate in the *World Council of Churches since 1968. Liberation Theology has become exceedingly influential in Latin America. It played a significant role in uniting Nicaragua behind the Sandanista movement—thus helping to depose the dictator Somoza in 1979.

There are many able and prolific exponents of Liberation Theology. Camillo Torres was the movement's first major activist and martyr. He was a Colombian priest who joined the left-wing guerilla movement and was killed in a clash with government forces in 1966. He made the famous claim that 'the Catholic who is not a revolutionary is living in mortal sin'. The first major work of Liberation Theology came from the Peruvian priest Gustavo Gutiérrez: *A Theology of Liberation* (1971).

This remains the most substantial and authoritative exposition of Liberation Theology. More recently he has written a work on spirituality from a Liberation Theology perspective, *We Drink from Our Own Wells* (1983) and a response to the question of evil, *On Job, God-Talk and the Suffering of the Innocent* (1986).

The movement's major exegete is the Mexican academic José Porfirio Miranda, who has written *Marx and the Bible* (1971), *Being and the Messiah* (1973—on John) and *Communism in the Bible* (1981). He has also sought to argue that Marx was more of a Christian than is commonly believed, in his *Marx against the Marxists—the Christian Humanism of Karl Marx* (1978). The Uruguayan Jesuit Juan Luis Segundo has brought a pastoral dimension to the movement with his five-volume *A Theology for the Artisans of a New Humanity* (1968–72) and *The Liberation of Theology* (1975). More recently Segundo has also been writing a five-volume series of studies in Christology entitled *Jesus of Nazareth Yesterday and Today* (1982ff).

Of the other Roman Catholic liberation theologians, two in particular are worthy of mention. Leonardo Boff, a Franciscan from Brazil, is a prolific author who was summoned to Rome to account for himself. Jon Sobrino, a Spanish Jesuit working in El Salvador, wrote *Christology at the Crossroads* (1976), which has been very influential. More recently he also has tackled the question of spirituality with his *Spirituality of Liberation* (1985).

Liberation Theology has its statesmen as well as its activists and theologians. Oscar Romero, the Archbishop of San Salvador was martyred in 1980. Archbishop Helder Camara of Recife in Brazil is an outspoken advocate of the poor and the leading churchman behind the movement today. He has graphically defended his involvement as follows: 'I am trying to send men to heaven, not sheep. And certainly not sheep with their stomachs empty and their testicles crushed.' Romero and Camara should be seen as sympathizers rather than as liberation theologians.

Liberation Theology began as a Roman Catholic movement, but it has spilled over into Protestant theology. Perhaps the best-known Protestant exponent is the Argentinian theologian José Míguez Bonino, author of *Doing Theology in a Revolutionary Situation* (1975—also entitled *Revolutionary Theology Comes of Age*), *Christians and Marxists: The Mutual Challenge to Revolution* (1976) and *Toward a Christian Political Ethics* (1983).

One cannot generalize about Liberation Theology as each exponent views it differently. This survey will therefore be based primarily on the teaching of Gutiérrez.

● Liberation Theology makes no claim to be 'universal theology', applicable to all times and situations. It is theology for the current Latin American situation. In fact, liberation theologians reject the idea of a universal theology as a perversion by abstract Greek thought of the practical, biblical way of thinking. Such a theology, based only on allegedly timeless truths, 'can only be static and, in the long run, sterile'.

● Liberation Theology, says Gutiérrez, 'offers us not so much a new theme for reflection as a *new way* to do theology'. (Hence Segundo can speak of 'the liberation *of* theology'.) Traditional theology has been an abstract presentation of the truths of revelation. Ethical thought and practical action were to be deduced from this theological foundation. But the trouble is that for centuries the church (especially in Latin America) 'devoted her attention to formulating truths and meanwhile did almost nothing to better the world'. Liberation Theology has a different approach. It *starts* with the concrete Latin American situation—oppression. The Christian must be committed to act on behalf of the oppressed. It is *then*, from a position of active involvement, that he does his theology. Liberation Theology is 'a critical reflection on Christian praxis in the light of the word'—it is the theologian theorizing about his practical involvement.

The pastoral activity of the church does not flow as a conclusion from theological premises. Theology does not produce pastoral activity—rather it reflects upon it... This is a theology which does not stop with reflecting on the world, but rather tries to be part of the process through which the world is transformed.

THEOLOGY OF LIBERATION, CHAPTER 1

● Liberation Theology starts with the situation, or to be more precise, with a particular analysis of the situation. Liberation Theology builds upon the Marxist analysis of the Latin American situation—in terms of class struggle, the exploitative role of capitalism and the need for revolutionary struggle. This use of Marxism is justified in a variety of ways. It is compared to the use made of philosophy (Plato, Aristotle, etc.) by traditional theology. It is argued that political neutrality is not possible for the church. To profess political neutrality is in fact to support the oppressive *status quo*. For centuries the Roman Catholic Church in Latin America was allied with the governments. This must now cease. The church must be committed to the poor. It's not enough to *talk* about the church of the poor. The church must *be* a poor church.

● Gutiérrez reinterprets the major themes of theology in the light of these concerns. Salvation is reinterpreted in terms of political liberation. It is wrong to divide history into 'sacred' and 'secular'—God is working out his salvation in *all* of human history. The church's role is not to define the *boundaries* of salvation. The idea of anonymous Christianity (taken from the Second Vatican Council and *Karl Rahner) means that all who are open to their neighbour in love actually know God. The church is to be the *sacrament* or sign of salvation—she is to manifest liberation visibly to the world. The question today about salvation is not *quantitative* (who will be saved), but *qualitative* (what is the nature of salvation), claims Gutiérrez.

● In 1984 the Vatican responded to Liberation Theology with an *Instruction on Certain Aspects of the Theology of Liberation.* This document reaffirms the 'preferential option for the poor' and urges Christians to 'become involved in the struggle for justice, freedom and human dignity'. But it also warns against certain dangers. It is wrong so to emphasize earthly and this-worldly liberation that liberation from sin becomes secondary. In particular, the uncritical use of Marxist concepts is dangerous. If the class struggle is seen as the basic fact of history, all Christian doctrines are interpreted in the light of it and seriously distorted. Starting with revolutionary 'praxis' or action rather than belief means that all contrary ideas are discredited in advance as reflecting the class interests of the oppressors. Furthermore, 'a major fact of our time ought to evoke the reflection of all those who would sincerely work for the true liberation of their brothers: millions of our own contemporaries legitimately yearn to recover those basic freedoms of which they were deprived by totalitarian and atheistic regimes which came to power by violent and revolutionary means, precisely in the name of the liberation of the people... The class struggle as a road toward a classless society is a myth which slows reform and aggravates poverty and injustice.'

These criticisms are directed not at all who have a concern for the liberation of the oppressed but at 'certain forms of liberation theology which use, in an insufficiently critical manner, concepts borrowed from various currents of Marxist thought'. The liberation theologians were not slow in responding. Segundo replied the following year with his *Theology and the Church. A Response to Cardinal Ratzinger and a Warning to the Whole Church.* The next year Gutiérrez also replied in part III of his *The Truth Shall Make You Free.* The debate over Liberation Theology is likely to continue for some time to come. It has yet to be seen what effect the collapse of Marxism in Eastern Europe and elsewhere will have upon the movement.

Lausanne Congress (1974)

The International Congress on World Evangelization, which met at Lausanne in July 1974, is arguably the most significant gathering of Evangelicals ever. There were some 3,000 participants from more than 150 nations, to discuss the theme 'Let The Earth Hear His Voice'. *Time Magazine* called it 'possibly the widest-ranging meeting of Christians ever held'. It marks a turning-point in the development of Evangelicalism this century. Its significance for Evangelicals is in many ways comparable to that of the *Second Vatican Council for the Roman Catholic Church.

The mind of the congress is expressed in a *Covenant*. The first draft, produced several months before the congress, was based on the papers of the main speakers. This was then sent to a panel of consultants who produced a second draft. The second draft was revised at the congress itself by a drafting committee (chaired by John Stott). This third draft was submitted to all the participants, who were invited to propose amendments. In the light of these the drafting committee produced the final draft, consisting of fifteen clauses with an introduction and conclusion. The *Covenant* is a wide-ranging confession of faith, the most representative and authoritative statement of Evangelical belief in modern times. But it is not merely a profession of belief. It is a covenant, a solemn personal pledge to pray and to work for evangelization.

The congress was significant in three major ways. First, as with the gatherings of the *World Council of Churches from the late sixties, the Third World came into its own at Lausanne. Half of the participants, speakers and planning committee were from the Third World. Furthermore, some of the most provocative and influential of the papers delivered were from two Latin Americans, Samuel Escobar and Rene Padilla.

Secondly, as happened with Roman Catholicism at the Second Vatican Council, the previous Evangelical attitude of 'triumphalism' was replaced by an attitude of penitence. Lausanne represents the growing importance and influence of Evangelicalism world-wide, but this has been accompanied by a recognition that all has not been healthy in the past and that lessons can be learned from others.

Thirdly, this penitence is manifest especially in the area of Christian social responsibility. While Evangelicals were at the forefront of social concern in the last century, this century has seen a reversal and, in many instances, total withdrawal from the field. Dissatisfaction with this state of affairs came to a head at Lausanne and found expression in the fifth clause of the *Covenant*. This clause did not satisfy everyone, and there was a minority statement (not from the 'conservatives' but from a 'radical discipleship group') who felt that they wanted to go further than the *Covenant*. At the same time, while there was a stress on social responsibility, all the participants were agreed about the vital urgency of the preaching of the gospel to the whole world.

The *Covenant* serves as an excellent summary of Evangelical belief and commitment in the modern world.

● *We, members of the church of Jesus Christ, from more than 150 nations, . . . are deeply stirred by what God is doing in our day, moved to penitence by our failures and challenged by the unfinished task of evangelization. We believe the gospel is God's good news for the whole world, and we are determined by his grace to obey Christ's commission to proclaim it to all mankind and to make disciples of every nation.*
LAUSANNE COVENANT, INTRODUCTION

● *We affirm the divine inspiration, truthfulness and authority of both Old and New Testament Scriptures in their entirety as the only written word of God, without error in all that it affirms, and the only infallible rule of faith and practice. We also affirm the power of God's word to accomplish his purpose of salvation.*
LAUSANNE COVENANT 2

● *We affirm that God is both the creator and the judge of all men. We therefore should share his concern for justice and reconciliation throughout human society and for the liberation of men from every kind of oppression ... Here too we express penitence both for our neglect and for having sometimes regarded evangelism and social concern as mutually exclusive. Although reconciliation with man is not reconciliation with God, nor is social action evangelism, nor is political liberation salvation, nevertheless we affirm that evangelism and socio-political involvement are both parts of our Christian duty. For both are necessary expressions of our doctrines of God and man, our love for our neighbour and our obedience to Jesus Christ. The message of salvation implies also a message of judgement upon every form of alienation, oppression and discrimination, and we should not be afraid to denounce evil and injustice wherever they exist.*

LAUSANNE COVENANT 5

● *More than 2,700 million people, which is more than two-thirds of mankind, have yet to be evangelized. We are ashamed that so many have been neglected. It is a standing rebuke to us and to the whole church ... All of us are shocked by the poverty of millions and disturbed by the injustices which cause it. Those of us who live in affluent circumstances accept our duty to develop a simple life-style in order to contribute more generously to both relief and evangelism.*

LAUSANNE COVENANT 9

● *Culture must always be tested and judged by Scripture. Because man is God's creature, some of his culture is rich in beauty and goodness. Because he has fallen, all of it is tainted with sin and some of it is demonic. The gospel does not presuppose the superiority of any culture to another, but evaluates all cultures according to its own criteria of truth and righteousness, and insists on moral absolutes in every culture. Missions have all too frequently exported with the gospel an alien culture, and churches have sometimes been in bondage to culture rather than to the Scripture.*

LAUSANNE COVENANT 10

● *Therefore, in the light of this our faith and our resolve, we enter into a solemn covenant with God and with each other, to pray, to plan, and to work together for the evangelization of the whole world.*

LAUSANNE COVENANT, CONCLUSION

The relation between the Lausanne Congress and the World Council of Churches assemblies is interesting. One reason for the calling of the congress was Evangelical concern about the World Council of Churches assemblies of 1968 and 1973. These seemed to place so much stress on the social and political dimensions that man's need to be reconciled to God was largely forgotten. But while Lausanne was partly a reaction against trends in the World Council, it was also influenced by some of the same trends—such as the increased role of the Third World and greater prominence given to social involvement.

The impetus of the congress was maintained by the Lausanne Committee for World Evangelization. This has organized a number of consultations in which specific issues raised by the congress have received more thorough treatment from international teams of experts. Three in particular may be mentioned. At Willowbank (Bermuda) in 1978 the issue of gospel and culture was explored. In 1980 a group met at Hoddesdon (England) to discuss the issue of a simple life-style. Perhaps the most important was the 1982 Grand Rapids (Michigan) consultation on evangelism and social responsibility. Lausanne itself had stated the importance of both, without discussing the relationship between them, a subject which aroused considerable controversy in the following years. The participants at Grand Rapids represented the full range of Evangelical opinion on the subject and yet a real and wide measure of agreement was reached, reflected in the report of the consultation, *Evangelism and Social Responsibility*.

In 1980 there was also a consultation on

world evangelization at Pattaya (Thailand), but this was on a much larger scale, with some 650 participants, from 87 countries. The theme was *How Shall They Hear?* with a heavy stress on evangelism and church growth. The participants split into seventeen 'mini-consultations' to produce reports on Christian witness to different groups of people, such as refugees, Chinese, Muslims, large cities. But many of the participants were concerned that the social and political concern of Lausanne was being lost. Over 200 participants signed at short notice a 'statement of concerns' addressed to the Lausanne Committee, requesting that more attention be given to the issue of social responsibility. These concerns were reflected in the final statement of the consultation. This concludes with twelve pledges of commitment to Christ, the third of which is 'to serve the needy and the oppressed, and in the name of Christ to seek for them relief and justice'.

Finally, in 1989 there was a second International Congress on World Evangelization, at Manila in the Philippines, with the theme 'Proclaim Christ Until He Comes'. There were some 3,500 registered delegates, from 173 countries, with a total of more than 4,700 people attending.

A manifesto was produced with the general title of 'Calling the whole church to take the whole gospel to the whole world'. This begins with 21 succinct affirmations:

3. We affirm that the biblical gospel is God's enduring message to our world, and we determine to defend, proclaim and embody it ...

8. We affirm that we must demonstrate God's love visibly by caring for those who are deprived of justice, dignity, food and shelter.

9. We affirm that the proclamation of God's kingdom of justice and peace demands the denunciation of all injustice and oppression, both personal and structural; we will not shrink from this prophetic witness ...

19. We affirm that world evangelization is urgent and that the reaching of unreached peoples is possible. So we resolve during the last decade of the twentieth century to give ourselves to these tasks with fresh determination.

20. We affirm that God is calling the whole church to take the whole gospel to the whole world. So we determine to proclaim it faithfully, urgently and sacrificially until he comes.

It continues with a fuller statement in twelve sections, under the headings of the whole gospel, the whole church and the whole world. This concludes with a call to the whole church to 'proclaim Christ until he comes'.

BIBLIOGRAPHY

Quotations have been taken from the following books:

Bettenson, Henry 1956 *The Early Christian Fathers* London; OUP

Lossky, Vladimir 1973 *The Vision of God* Leighton Buzzard; Faith Press

Meyendorff, John 1974 *Christ in Eastern Christian Thought* New York; St Vladimir's Seminary Press

Meyendorff, John 1974 *A Study of Gregory Palamas and Orthodox Spirituality* New York; St Vladimir's Seminary Press

Meyendorff, John 1974 *St Gregory Palamas* Leighton Buzzard; Faith Press

Pelikan, Jaroslav 1974 *The Spirit of Eastern Christendom* (600–1700) Chicago & London; University of Chicago Press

John of Damascus 1980 *On the Divine Images* New York; St Vladimir's Seminary Press

Lossky, Vladimir 1957 *The Mystical Theology of the Eastern Church* Cambridge & London; James Clarke

Simeon the New Theologian 1980 *The Discourses* London; SPCK

Boethius 1969 *The Consolation of Philosophy* Harmondsworth; Penguin

Leith, John 1973 *Creeds of the Churches* Atlanta; John Knox Press

O'Meara, John 1969 *Eriugena* Cork; Mercier Press

Fairweather, Eugene 1956 *A Scholastic Miscellany: Anselm to Ockham* London; SCM

Luddy, Ailbe 1947 *The Case of Peter Abelard* Dublin; M.H. Gill

Bernard of Clairvaux 1976 *Five Books on Consideration* Kalamazoo; Cistercian Publications

Bernard of Clairvaux 1977 *Treatises III* Kalamazoo; Cistercian Publications

Bernard of Clairvaux 1980 *Treatises II* Kalamazoo; Cistercian Publications

Bernard of Clairvaux 1980 *On the Song of Songs IV* Kalamazoo; Cistercian Publications

Gilson, Etienne 1955 *History of Christian Philosophy in the Middle Ages* London; Sheed & Ward

McGinn, Bernard 1979 *Visions of the End* New York; Columbia

Schroeder, H.J. 1937 *Disciplinary Decrees of the General Councils* St Louis & London; Herder

Bonaventure 1978 *The Soul's Journey into God* London; SPCK

Thomas Aquinas 1947 *Compendium of Theology* St Louis & London; Herder

Thomas Aquinas 1963 *Summa Theologiae* vol. 58 London; Eyre & Spottiswoode

Miegge, G. 1955 *The Virgin Mary* London; Lutterworth

Oberman, Heiko 1957 *Archbishop Thomas Bradwardine* Utrecht; v/h Kemink

De Jaegher, Paul 1935 *An Anthology of Mysticism* London; Burns & Oates

Oberman, Heiko 1967 *Forerunners of the Reformation* London; Lutterworth

Spinka, Matthew 1953 *Advocates of Reform* London; SCM

Thomas à Kempis 1963 *The Imitation of Christ* London & Glasgow; Collins

McSorley, Harry 1969 *Luther: Right or Wrong?* New York; Newman

Erasmus 1968 *Julius Exclusus* Bloomington & London; Indiana University Press

Dolan, John 1964 *The Essential Erasmus* New York; New American Library

Luther, Martin 1957 *Luther's Works* vol. 31 Philadelphia; Muhlenberg Press

Woolf, Bertram Lee 1953 *Reformation Writings of Martin Luther* vol. 1 London; Lutterworth

Pauck, Wilhelm 1969 *Melanchthon and Bucer* London; SCM

Bromiley, Geoffrey 1953 *Zwingli and Bullinger* London; SCM

Melanchthon, Philip 1965 *Loci Communes* 1955 New York; OUP

Tappert, Theodore 1959 *The Book of Concord* Philadelphia; Fortress

Cochrane, Arthur 1966 *Reformed Confessions of the Sixteenth Century* London; SCM

Wenger, John 1945 'The Schleitheim Confession of Faith', *Mennonite Quarterly Review* 19, 1945

Simons, Menno 1956 *Complete Writings* Scottdale; Herald

Duffield, Gervase 1964 *The Work of William Tyndale* Appleford; Sutton Courtenay

Teresa of Avila 1980 *Collected Works* vol. 2 Washington; Institute of Carmelite Studies

Pascal, Blaise 1967 *Provincial Letters* Harmondsworth; Penguin

Pascal, Blaise 1966 *Pensées* Harmondsworth; Penguin

Schleiermacher, Friedrich 1958 *On Religion* New York; Harper & Row

Berkouwer, Gerrit 1954 *Faith and Justification* Grand Rapids; Eerdmans

Thielicke, Helmut 1974 *The Evangelical Faith* vol. 1 Grand Rapids; Eerdmans

Barth, Karl 1969 *How I Changed my Mind* Edinburgh; St Andrew

Barth, Karl 1954 *Against the Stream* London; SCM

Häring, Hermann & Kuschel, Karl-Josef 1979 *Hans Küng. His Work and His Way* Glasgow; Collins

Bonhoeffer, Dietrich 1971 *The Cost of Discipleship* London; SCM

Bonhoeffer, Dietrich 1971 *Letters and Papers from Prison* London; SCM

Niebuhr, Reinhold 1960 *Moral Man and Immoral Society* New York; Charles Scribner's

Niebuhr, Reinhold 1976 *Leaves from the Notebook of a Tamed Cynic* New York; Da Capo

Niebuhr, Reinhold 1956 *Intellectual Autobiography* New York; Macmillan [in C.W. Kegley & R.W. Bretall (eds) *Reinhold Niebuhr*]

Kierkegaard, Søren 1938 *The Journals* London; OUP

Kierkegaard, Søren 1962 *Philosophical Fragments* Princeton; Princeton University Press

Bultmann, Rudolf 1960 *Jesus Christ and Mythology* London; SCM

Bultmann, Rudolf 1960 *New Testament and Mythology* [in Hans Werner Bartsch (ed) 1964 *Kerygma and Myth* vol. 1 London; SPCK]

Tillich, Paul 1949 *The Shaking of the Foundations* London; SCM

Tillich, Paul 1953 *Systematic Theology* vol. 1 London; James Nisbet

Pittenger, Norman 1982 *Picturing God* London; SCM

Moltmann, Jürgen 1967 *Theology of Hope* London; SCM

Moltmann, Jürgen 1974 *The Crucified God* London; SCM

Moltmann, Jürgen 1981 *The Trinity and the Kingdom of God* London; SCM

Pannenberg, Wolfhart 1968 *Jesus God and Man* London; SCM

Storkey, Elaine 1985 *What's Right With Feminism* London; SPCK

Butler, Cuthbert 1962 *The Vatican Council* London; Collins and Harvill

Bettenson, Henry 1963 *Documents of the Christian Church* London; OUP

Teilhard de Chardin, Pierre 1960 *Le Milieu Divin* London; Collins

Teilhard de Chardin, Pierre 1964 *The Future of Man* London; Collins

Teilhard de Chardin, Pierre 1959 *The Phenomenon of Man* London; Collins

Abbott, Walter 1965 *The Documents of Vatican II* London; Geoffrey Chapman

Rahner, Karl 1972 *Theological Investigations* vol. 9 London; Darton Longman & Todd

Rahner, Karl 1976 *Theological Investigations* vol. 14 London; Darton Longman & Todd

Küng, Hans 1964 *Justification* London; Burns & Oates

Küng, Hans 1971 *Infallible?* London; Collins

World Council of Churches 1982 *Baptism, Eucharist and Ministry* Geneva; WCC

McGavran, Donald 1977 *The Conciliar-Evangelical Debate* South Pasadena; William Carey

Bassham, Rodger 1979 *Mission Theology* South Pasadena; William Carey

King, Martin Luther 1969 *Strength to Love* London & Glasgow; Collins

Bennett, L. 1966 *What Manner of Man?* London; George Allen & Unwin

Koyama Kosuke 1979 *Three Mile an Hour God* London; SCM

Mbiti, John 1969 *African Religions and Philosophy* London; Heinemann

Gutiérrez, Gustavo 1974 *A Theology of Liberation* London; SCM

Vatican 1986 'Instruction on Certain Aspects of the Theology of Liberation', *Evangelical Review of Theology* 10

Douglas, J. D. 1975 *Let the Earth Hear His Voice* and *Proclaim Christ Until He Comes* Minneapolis; World Wide Publications